A SCIENCE IN ITS YOUTH

A.ANIKIN

A SCIENCE
IN ITS
YOUTH

(PRE-MARXIAN POLITICAL ECONOMY)

INTERNATIONAL PUBLISHERS
NEW YORK

Translated from the Russian by K.M. Cook

First paperback edition by International Publishers, 1979
English translation © 1975 by Progress Publishers
Printed in the Union of Soviet Socialist Republics

Library of Congress Cataloging in Publication Data

Anikin, Andreĭ Vladimirovich.

A science in its youth.

Translation of IUnost' nauki.
Includes bibliographical references and index.
1. Economists. 2. Economics–History.

I. Title.
HB76.A5413 1979   330'.09   78-31568
ISBN O-7178-0503 4 pbk.

A $\dfrac{10702-396}{014(01)-79}$ без объявл.

0 602 000 000

CONTENTS

INTRODUCTION

There are scores, or rather hundreds, of scholarly works in various languages on the history of economic thought, and it is not the writer's aim to add yet another to the collection. This book has been written in the form of popular essays, making it possible to pinpoint the most salient biographical and scientific details; the emphasis has been placed on questions which are still most topical in the present day.

The book is intended for the general reader, who may not possess any specialised knowledge of political economy. Some people are accustomed to think of political economy as a dry and boring subject. Yet the economic structure of society contains no fewer fascinating problems and secrets than nature.

In recent times it has become particularly common for scholars in the exact and natural sciences to concern themselves with economic questions.

Nor is it accidental that at the beginnings of economic science we find outstanding thinkers who have left an indelible mark on human culture, people with wide-ranging and original minds, great scientific and literary talent.

ECONOMISTS OF THE PAST
AND THE PRESENT TIMES

Economics has always played a most important part in the life of mankind, and this is particularly true today.

Marx said how absurd it was to maintain that the ancients lived on politics and the Middle Ages on Catholicism. Mankind has always "lived on economics", and politics, religion, science and art could exist only on the basis of economics. The fact that economics was undeveloped in the past is the main reason for such views about these periods. Modern economics plays a vital part in the lives of each and every one of us.

The world of today is actually two different worlds, socialist and capitalist, each with its own economy and its own political economy. The developing countries which have freed themselves from colonial rule are also playing an increasingly important role in the world arena. The need to decide which path of development to take is becoming increasingly urgent for these countries. A study of the history of political economy helps one to understand the problems of the modern world, to understand economic science as an integral part of one's own world outlook.

The classics of bourgeois political economy, particularly Adam Smith and David Ricardo, were the first to develop the theory of the economy as a system in which objective laws operate, independently of human will, but are accessible to human understanding. They believed that the economic policy of the state should not go against these laws, but rest upon them.

William Petty, François Quesnay and other scholars laid the foundations for the quantitative analysis of economic processes. They sought to examine these processes as a kind of metabolism and to define its directions and scope. Marx made use of their scientific achievements in his theory of the reproduction of the social product. The balance between consumer commodities and means of production, the proportions of accumulation and consumption, and the relations between the different branches play a most important part in the modern economy and economic studies. The works of these pioneers of economic science gave birth to modern economic statistics, the importance of which cannot be overestimated.

In the first half of the 19th century economic analysis attempted to employ mathematical methods without which it is now -impossible to conceive of the development of many branches of economic science. One of the pioneers in this field was the French economist Antoine Cournot.

The classics of bourgeois political economy and also exponents of petty-bourgeois and utopian socialism analysed many of the contradictions in capitalist economy. The Swiss economist Sismondi was one of the first to try to understand the causes of economic crises, the scourge of bourgeois society. The great utopian socialist Saint-Simon, Fourier, Owen and their followers made a profound criticism of capitalism and compiled plans for the socialist reconstruction of society.

As V. I. Lenin wrote, "the genius of Marx consists precisely in his having furnished answers to questions already raised by the foremost minds of mankind. His doctrine emerged as the direct and immediate *continuation* of the teachings of the greatest representatives of philosophy, political economy and socialism".[1]

Classical bourgeois political economy was one of the sources of Marxism. Yet Marx's teaching was a revolutionary turning-point in political economy. Marx showed that capital is a social relation, which is essentially the exploitation of the hired labour of proletarians. He explained the nature of this exploitation in his theory of surplus value and showed the historical tendency of capitalism: the aggravation of its antagonistic, class contradictions and the ultimate victory of labour over capital. Thus Marx's economic theory contains a dialectical unity: it both rejects the bourgeois conceptions of his predecessors and creatively develops everything positive which they created. The aim of this book is to reveal and explain this unity.

Scientific socialism is based on the economic theories of Marxism-Leninism. The explanation of the origins and roots of these theories is of great importance if they are to be fully understood and creatively developed.

---

[1] V. I. Lenin, *Collected Works*, Vol. 19, p. 23.

MARX AND HIS PREDECESSORS

Philosophy, political economy and scientific communism are the three component parts of Marxism. The philosophy of Marxism is dialectical and historical materialism. The main principle of historical materialism is that the development of society is based on changes in its economic structure. Political economy studies this structure, and reveals the laws of movement of socio-economic formations and the transition from one formation to another. Scientific communism is the theory of socialist revolution, the ways of building the new, communist society and the basic stages and features of this society.

Each of the component parts of Marxism is also a development of the progressive ideas of earlier thinkers, a development of world science. These three component parts correspond to the three sources of Marxism. As V. I. Lenin wrote, "Marx ... continued and consummated the three main ideological currents of the nineteenth century, as represented by the three most advanced countries of mankind: classical German philosophy, classical English political economy, and French socialism combined with French revolutionary doctrines in general."[1]

This famous thesis is revealed in all its depth and concreteness primarily in the works of Marx himself. Marx described in detail, with great analytical profundity, everything he owed to Hegel and Feuerbach, Smith and Ricardo, Saint-Simon and Fourier. Among the qualities which Marx possessed was a remarkable academic conscientiousness. In particular, his knowledge of the economic literature of the eighteenth and first half of the nineteenth centuries was practically comprehensive.

Marx's main scientific work *Capital* is sub-titled "A Critique of Political Economy". The fourth volume of this work, *Theories of Surplus-Value*, is devoted to a critical analysis of all preceding political economy. Here Marx's main method was to single out in each writer the scientific elements which help in some degree or other to solve the principal task of capitalist political economy—to reveal the law of motion of the capitalist mode of production. At the same time he showed the

---

[1] V. I. Lenin, *Collected Works*, Vol. 21, p. 50.

bourgeois limitations and inconsistencies in the views of these political economists of the past.

Marx devoted a considerable amount of space to the criticism of political economy which he called vulgar, because it aims not at true scientific analysis, but at justifying and openly defending the capitalist system. Naturally the main representatives of this trend of bourgeois political economy also occupy a considerable place in the present volume. In criticising the apologetic views of bourgeois economists Marx developed proletarian political economy.

The reader of *Capital* and Marx's other economic works is presented with a whole gallery of scientific personages of the past. Like every other science, political economy was developed not only by the acknowledged masters, but also by the efforts of many, often lesser-known scholars. The classical school of political economy was for a century and a half a very broad trend within which a large number of scholars worked and wrote. Smith, for example, was preceded by whole generations of economists who thoroughly prepared the ground for him. Therefore, while concentrating mainly on the life and ideas of the most eminent figures, the author of the present volume has also striven to reflect to a certain extent the contribution of lesser-known, but frequently important thinkers with the aim of giving a fuller outline of the development of political economy as a science. It is important to explain the circumstances, the social and intellectual "atmosphere", in which these scholars lived and worked.

To confine a history of political economy to the works of Smith, Quesnay and Ricardo would be as wrong as, for example, to maintain that the whole history of mathematics is contained in the activity of Descartes, Newton and Laplace. Histories of 17th century art acknowledge the "minor Dutch painters" as well as the great Rembrandt.

For over a century now bourgeois science and propaganda has been trying to distort the historical role of Marx as a scientist. Here one can clearly distinguish two lines of approach. The first is to ignore Marx and his revolutionary teaching and to represent him as a figure of little scientific importance or as a figure outside the "Western cultural tradition" and, consequently, outside "true" science. Here the link between Marx and his predecessors, particularly the classical bourgeois economists, is belittled, underrated.

In recent decades, however, the second approach has become more typical: to turn Marx into an ordinary (or even extraordinary) Hegelian and Recardian. Marx's proximity to Ricardo and the whole classical school is emphasised strongly and the revolutionary nature of the turning-point in political economy brought about by Marx is glossed over. This was the attitude adopted by J. A. Schumpeter, the author of one of the largest 20th-century bourgeois works on the history of economic thought. Classing Marx as a Ricardian, he states that Marx's economic teaching differs little from Ricardo's and therefore suffers from the same defects. Incidentally, even Schumpeter admits that Marx "transformed these (Ricardo's — A. A.) forms and he arrived in the end at widely different conclusions".[1]

One frequently encounters the belief that Marxism can be reconciled with modern bourgeois sociology and political economy because they all, it is asserted, proceed from the same source. John Strachey, the well-known British Labour theoretician, wrote that he regarded the latter as "a modest step in the indispensable process of re-integrating Marxism with the Western cultural traditions from which it derives, but from which it has widely diverged".[2]

As we know, in recent years there has been a considerable growth of interest in Marx and Marxism among bourgeois economists. It has become fairly common for them to attempt to use individual elements of Marx's teaching. In framing recommendations on economic policy concerning strategic problems (economic growth, accumulation, distribution of national income), where it is necessary to give a realistic assessment of the state of affairs, the more farsighted scholars are frequently attracted by the methods and results of Marxist analysis.

This growth of interest in Marxism can be seen, for example, from R. L. Heilbroner's history of economic thought up to the present day. This book contains an interesting account of the life and activity of Marx. The author notes that Marxist economic analysis remains the gravest, most penetrating examination the capitalist system has ever undergone. "It is

---

[1] Joseph A. Schumpeter, *History of Economic Analysis*, New York, 1955, p. 390.
[2] J. Strachey, *Contemporary Capitalism*, London, 1956, pp. 14-15.

not an examination conducted along moral lines with head-wagging and tongue-clucking.... For all its passion, it is a dispassionate appraisal and it is for this reason that its sombre findings must be soberly considered." [1]

The "radical" political economy that has appeared recently in the West challenges the orthodoxy of traditional doctrines. The representatives of this trend are particularly critical of the main schools for rejecting socio-economic analysis and for their formalism and sterility. They emphasise the effectiveness of the approach which links Marx with Ricardo: the class analysis of the problem of the distribution of incomes in society.

Naturally, these phenomena are to be welcomed. What must be rejected, however, is the idea of a "merger" of Marxist and bourgeois political economy into a single scientific discipline. For Marxists economic theory is the basis for arguing the need for the revolutionary transformation of society, but bourgeois economists, the radicals included, do not draw these conclusions.

Reformism and the related Right-wing opportunism in the communist and working-class movement tend to regard Marxism as a trend rooted solely in the humanist, liberal school of social thought in the 19th century. The fact that Marxism is primarily the revolutionary ideology of the working class and totally unlike any form of liberalism is glossed over. The theoretical side of Marxism is frequently divorced from its revolutionary practice.

Of great importance for spreading Marxist-Leninist doctrine among the masses is the struggle against "Left"-wing revisionism and dogmatism. The latter tend to ignore the theories and views of the predecessors of Marxism. They also play down the scientific analytical side of Marxism, its view of social development as a process which takes place in accordance with objective laws. Voluntarism in economics and adventurism in politics are typical of "Left"-wing revisionism.

Among the "New Left" one finds those who link Marxism with the anarchist ideas of Proudhon and Kropotkin, with whom Marx is alleged to have had a lot in common. It is a well-known fact, however, that for many years Marx and

---

[1] R. L. Heilbroner, *The Worldly Philosophers. The Lives, Times and Ideas of the Great Economic Thinkers*, 3rd edition, New York, 1968, p. 153.

Engels conducted a fierce battle against Proudhon and his teaching. The idea of a "counter-culture" sometimes develops into the rejection of all aspects and elements of bourgeois culture. Marxism-Leninism has demonstrated in theory and practice the absurdity and harm of attempts to construct a new, anti-bourgeois culture out of thin air. The new culture does not reject the old one out of hand, but makes use of its best, progressive elements.

In this connection it should be noted that in the very first years of Soviet power V. I. Lenin constantly drew attention to the need for making use of all the riches of human culture in building communist society.

Marx, Engels and Lenin exposed and criticised bourgeois economic theories aimed at vindicating the capitalist system, revealed their social origins and aims, and their superficial, unscientific view of the laws and processes of economic development. They were particularly uncompromising in their attacks on ideology which threatened to damage the working-class movement and divert it from revolutionary tasks.

At the same time the Marxist classics intended by their criticism to select from bourgeois economic conceptions the rational elements which promote an understanding of objective reality. They stressed, in particular, the need for a study of concrete economic writings by bourgeois scholars.

THREE CENTURIES

Economists' ideas are to a great extent determined by the level of development of their country's society and economy. Therefore in the accounts of their life and activity the reader of this book will also find a brief outline of the economic features of the period and country.

The development of political economy from the 17th to 19th centuries was predetermined by the growth of a new social order, at that time a progressive one, namely, capitalism. People of great talent and forceful personality emerged, great thinkers.

Let us try to conjure up for a moment a gathering of the economists of three centuries. A varied company indeed!

Most of them are English, but there is a fair sprinkling of Frenchmen. This is understandable. England was the leading capitalist country and even in Marx's time political economy was still regarded as a predominantly English science. In France, too, capitalism began to develop earlier than in most other countries; as a result the term "political economy" was first coined in French. The economists of this period include few Americans, but among them is the wise Franklin.

The first economists were usually, to quote Marx, "businessmen and statesmen". They were prompted to reflect upon economic questions by the practical needs of the economy, trade and state administration.

We see Shakespeare's contemporaries long-haired cavaliers in lace and austere soberly dressed merchants of the age of the early capitalist accumulation. These are the royal counsellors — the mercantilists Montchrétien, Thomas Mun.

Another group. Here we have the founders of classical political economy, Petty, Boisguillebert and other forerunners of Adam Smith, in large wigs and long coats with wide turned-back sleeves. They do not engage in political economy professionally for such a profession does not exist as yet. Petty is a physician and unsuccessful politician, Boisguillebert — a judge, Locke — a famous philosopher, Cantillon — a banker. They usually address kings and governments, but are also beginning to write for the enlightened public. And for the first time they are posing the theoretical problems of the new science. Petty stands out in particular. He is not only a brilliant thinker, but also a vivid and original personality.

And here is the dynamic figure of John Law, the great schemer and adventurist, the "inventor" of paper money and the first theoretician and practitioner of inflation. The rise and fall of Law is one of the most vivid pages in the history of France at the beginning of the 18th century.

The huge wigs, such as we see on portraits of Molière or Swift, are replaced by short, powdered ones with two curls on the temples. The calves are clad in white silk stockings. These are the French economists of the mid-18th century, the Physiocrats, friends of the great philosophers of the Enlightenment.

Their acknowledged leader is Francois Quesnay, a physician by profession and economist by vocation. Another eminent scholar is Turgot, one of the most sagacious and progressive statesmen in pre-revolutionary France.

Adam Smith.... His popularity in Russia was so great that Pushkin, depicting a young man from high society in the 1820s in his famous novel in verse *Eugene Onegin*, wrote that

> *From Adam Smith he sought his training*
> *And was no mean economist;*
> *That is, he could present the gist*
> *Of how states prosper and stay healthy*
> *Without the benefit of gold,*
> *The secret being that, all told,*
> *The* basic staples *make them wealthy.*[1]

Smith's biography is somewhat similar to that of Newton: it contains few external events and an inner intellectual life of great intensity.

The name of Smith's followers is legion. In the late 18th and early 19th centuries being engaged in political economy meant being a follower of Smith. The great Scot began to be "put right" (meaning "right" in the political sense, not only in the sense of "correct"). This was done by such people as Say in France and Malthus in England. Political economy began to be taught in the universities, becoming a "must" for educated young men from the privileged classes.

Now the rich financier and self-taught genius David Ricardo appears on the scene. This is the age of Napoleon, so naturally he is without a wig and is wearing a frock coat and long, tight breeches instead of a long coat and knee-length hose. Ricardo was to complete the development of bourgeois classical political economy. But already during his lifetime there were attacks on Ricardo, who had pointed out the conflict between the interests of the two main classes in capitalist society—the bourgeoisie and the workers.

Ricardo's followers fall into several different groups. On the one hand, the socialists tried to use his theories against the bourgeoisie. On the other, vulgar political economy developed in bourgeois science on the remains of Ricardo's teaching. Thus we approach the 1840s which saw the beginning of the activity of Karl Marx and Frederick Engels.

In expressing the ideas of the most progressive section of the

---

[1] A. Pushkin, *Eugene Onegin*, translated by Walter Arndt, New York, 1963, p. 8.

bourgeoisie, the classical economists clashed with the feudal, land-owing aristocracy which was firmly ensconced in England and which dominated in France until the revolution at the end of the 18th century. They clashed with the state which expressed the interests of the aristocracy and with the established church. And they by no means accepted and approved of everything in the capitalist system. Consequently the lives of many economists were fraught with protest, rebellion and struggle. Even the cautious Smith was subjected to attacks by reactionary elements. Among the socialists of the pre-Marxian period we find people of high principles and great civic and personal courage.

This book does not deal with the pioneers of economics in Russia, although in the period under review Russia produced some bold and original thinkers. Suffice it to mention the fine Russian writer and scientist of the Petrine period Ivan Pososhkov, the author of the first essay in Russia devoted especially to economic questions. A great deal of attention was paid to economic questions by Alexander Radishchev, the revolutionary enlightener and author of the famous book *A Journey from Petersburg to Moscow* in which he criticised the landowners and even the monarchy.

Some important economic works were written by the Decembrists, the participants in the first Russian revolutionary movement, who attempted to organise an uprising against the tsar in December 1825. Among these the works of Nikolai Turgenev and Pavel Pestel stand out in particular. The great Russian writer and revolutionary democrat Nikolai Chernyshevsky was an economic thinker of great profundity and a brilliant critic of bourgeois political economy. Marx thought highly of his scientific writings and practical activity.

However Russia in the 18th and early 19th centuries was considerably behind the West European countries in economic development. Serfdom still existed and bourgeois production relations were as yet only in embryonic form. Hence the strikingly individual character of the development of Russian economic thought. At the same time Marx's economic theory fell on fertile soil in Russia and quickly took root. Russian was the first language into which *Capital* was translated. The Kievan professor N. N. Ziber was one of the first to analyse the connection between Marx's teaching and the doctrines of Smith and Ricardo.

May we express the hope that this book will not require from the reader "the endurance of a camel and the patience of a saint" without which, to quote Heilbroner, it is impossible to read through certain serious works on political economy.

And so from the political economy of the slave-owning society—to the political economy of the mid-19th century. On this long journey we shall be making several stops at key points.

CHAPTER I

ORIGINS

When primitive man made the first axe and bow, it was not *economics*. It was only technology, so to say.

But then a group of hunters with several axes and bows killed a deer. The venison was divided between them, in all probability, equally: if some had received more then others, the latter would simply have been unable to survive. The life of the community grew more complex. A craftsman appeared, say, who made good instruments for the hunters but did not actually hunt himself. Meat and fish then had to be divided between the hunters and fishers, leaving a share for the craftsman, etc. At some stage there began exchange of products of labour between and within communities.

All this, although primitive and undeveloped, was *economics*, for it was a matter not only of people's relations to things — a bow, an axe, or meat — but also their relations with one another in society. And not relations in general, but material relations connected with the production and distribution of goods essential for people's lives. Marx called these relations *production relations*.

Economics is the social production, exchange, distribution and consumption of material goods and the sum total of the production relations arising on this basis. In this sense economics is as old as human society. The economy of the primitive community was, of course extremely simple, since the instruments people used were also extremely simple and their labour skills very restricted. In other words, the *productive forces*, which determine a society's production relations, its economy and other aspects of life, were poorly developed.

WHO WAS THE FIRST ECONOMIST

When did man first start wondering why fire burns or thunder peals? Probably many thousands of years ago. And just as to ponder on the phenomena of the economy of primitive society, which was gradually changing into the first class society — slave-owning society. But these reflections were not and could not be a *science* — a system of human knowledge about nature and society. Science did not appear until the age of mature slave-owning society, which was based on far more developed productive forces. People's knowledge of mathematics or medicine in the ancient states of Sumeria, Babylon and Egypt which existed four to five thousand years ago is sometimes quite impressive. The finest surviving specimens of ancient knowledge belong to the ancient Greeks and Romans.

A definite effort to comprehend the facts of economic life began long before the emergence of a special branch of science, *political economy*, in the 17th century. Many of the economic phenomena investigated by this science were already known to the ancient Egyptians or Greeks: exchange, money, price, trade, profit, interest. Above all people began to reflect upon the main feature of the production relations in that age, slavery.

At first economic thought was not separate from other forms of meditation on society, so it is impossible to say exactly when it first appeared. Not surprisingly economic historians start at different points. Some histories begin with the ancient Greeks, others with a study of ancient Egyptian papyri, the stone cuneiform of the Code of Hammurabi and the Hindu *Vedas*.

Many economic observations and interpretations of the economic life of the Hebrew and other people inhabiting Palestine and the neighbouring lands in the second and first millennium before Christ can be found in the Bible.

However, the fact that, for example, the American historian of economics Professor J. F. Bell devotes a large chapter to the

Bible and completely ignores all other sources of the period is to be explained, one must assume, by circumstances quite unrelated to academic research. Namely, that the Bible is the sacred book of Christianity and most American students are acquainted with it from early childhood. So research is adapting itself somewhat to this fact of modern life.

Ancient Greek society, at the stage of the advanced decline of primitive society and the formation of the slave-owning order, is given splendid literary portrayal in Homer's poems. These monuments of human culture are a veritable encyclopaedia of the life and philosophy of the people who inhabited the shores of the Aegean and Ionian seas about three thousand years ago. The most varied economic observations are skilfully woven into the fabric of the exciting tale of the siege of Troy and the wanderings of Odysseus. The *Odyssey* contains evidence of the low productivity of slave labour:

> *The master gone, the servants what restraints?*
> *Or dwells humanity where riot reigns?*
> *Jove fix'd it certain, that whatever day*
> *Makes man a slave, takes half his worth away.*[1]

Naturally, the Code of Hammurabi, the Bible, and Homer can be regarded by the historian and economist as sources of information about the *domestic life* of ancient peoples. Only secondarily can they be referred to as specimens of economic *thought*, which presupposes a certain generalisation of practice, speculation and abstraction. The well-known bourgeois scholar Joseph A. Schumpeter (an Austrian who spent the second half of his life living in the United States) called his book a history of economic analysis and began it with the classical Greek thinkers.

It is true that the works of Xenophont, Plato and Aristotle contain the first attempts at a theoretical explanation of the economic structure of Greek society. We are sometimes inclined to forget how many threads link our modern culture with the remarkable civilisation of that small people. Our science, our art and our language have absorbed elements of ancient Greek civilisation. About economic thought Marx said: "In so far as the Greeks make occasional excursions into this sphere, they

---

[1] *The Odyssey of Homer*, translated from the Greek by Alexander Pope, London, 1806, p. 256.

show the same genius and originality as in all other spheres. Because of this, their views form, historically, the theoretical starting-points of the modern science".[1]

The word *economy* (οἰκουομία from the words οἰκος —house, household, and υόμος — rule, law) is the title of a special work by Xenophont in which sensible rules for the management of household and estate are examined. The word retained that meaning (the science of household management) for many centuries. True, it did not have such a restricted sense under the Greeks as our household management. For the house of a rich Greek was a whole slave-owning economy, a kind of microcosm of the Ancient World.

Aristotle used the term "economy" and its derivative "economics" in the same sense. He was the first to analyse the basic economic phenomena and laws of the society of his day and became, in fact, the first economist in the history of the science.

THE VERY BEGINNING: ARISTOTLE

In 336 B. C. Philip II of Macedon was treacherously murdered at his daughter's wedding. The instigators of the crime were never discovered. If the version is true that it was the rulers of Persia, they could not have done anything more disastrous for themselves: Philip's twenty-year-old son Alexander acceded to the throne and within a few years had conquered the mighty Persian Empire.

Alexander was a pupil of Aristotle, a philosopher from the town of Stagira. When Alexander became Emperor of Macedon Aristotle was forty-eight and his fame had already spread wide throughout the Hellenic world. We do not know what prompted Aristotle to leave Macedon shortly afterwards and move to Athens. Whatever the cause it was not disagreement with Alexander: their relations did not deteriorate until much later when the talented young man turned into a suspicious and capricious tyrant. Probably Athens attracted Aristotle as the cultural centre of the Ancient World, the town

---

[1] Frederick Engels, *Anti-Dühring*, Moscow, 1969, p. 271 (Chapter X of Part II of *Anti-Dühring* was written by Marx).

where his teacher Plato lived and died and where Aristotle himself had spent his youth.

Whatever the cause, in 335 or 334 B. C. Aristotle moved to Athens with his wife, daughter and adopted son. In the following ten to twelve years, while Alexander was conquering all the inhabited lands known to the Greeks, Aristotle erected the splendid edifice of science, completing and generalising his life's work with remarkable energy. Yet he was not destined to spend a peaceful old age amid pupils and friends. In 323 B. C. Alexander died, having barely reached the age of 33. The Athenians revolted against Macedon's rule and drove out the philosopher. A year later he died in Chalcis, on the island of Euboea.

Aristotle was one of the greatest minds in the history of science. His surviving and authenticated writings cover all the spheres of knowledge existing at that time. In particular, he was one of the founders of the science of human society, sociology, within the framework of which he examined economic questions as well. Aristotle's sociological writings belong to the period of his last years in Athens. They are, first and foremost, *The Nicomachean Ethics* (his descendants called it after his son Nicomachus) and the *Politics*, a treatise on the structure of the state.

In both the natural and social sciences Aristotle was a scientist of the "new type". He formed theories and conclusions not on the basis of abstract speculation, but always on a careful analysis of the facts. His *Historia animalium* was based on extensive zoological collections. Likewise for the *Politics* he and a group of pupils assembled and examined material about the structure and laws of 158 Hellenic and barbarian states. For the most part they were city states of the "polis" type.

Aristotle has been remembered over the centuries as the wise mentor surrounded by pupils and disciples. During his last years in Athens he was in his fifties and evidently an energetic, cheerful person. He is said to have enjoyed chatting with his friends and pupils while strolling in the Peripakos, a covered walk in the Lyceum.

His philosophical school has gone down in history under the name of the Peripatetics.

The *Politics* and *Ethics* are written in the form of recorded conversations or sometimes reflections aloud. In seeking to explain an idea Aristotle frequently returns to it, approaching it from a different angle, so to say, and answering the questions of his audience.

Aristotle was a son of his time. He regarded slavery as natural and logical and a slave as a talking instrument. Moreover, he was in a certain sense conservative. He did not like the development of commerce and money relations in the Greece of his day. His ideal was a small agricultural economy (in which the slaves did the work, naturally). This economy would provide itself with almost all the essentials and the few things it lacked could be obtained by "fair exchange" with neighbours.

Aristotle's merit as an economist lies in the fact that he was the first to establish some categories of political economy and to demonstrate to a certain extent their interconnection. If we compare Aristotle's "economic system", composed from the various fragments, with the first five chapters of Adam Smith's *The Wealth of Nations* and Part I of the first volume of *Capital* by Karl Marx, we find an amazing continuity of thought. It is rising to a new stage based on the preceding ones. Lenin wrote that the urge to find the law of the formation and change of prices (i.e., the law of value) runs from Aristotle through the whole of classical political economy up to Marx.

Aristotle established two aspects of a commodity, its use value and its exchange value, and analysed the process of exchange. He posed the question which was to be the constant concern of political economy: what determines the correlations of exchange, or exchange values, or, finally, prices — their monetary expression. He does not know the answer to this question or, rather, he halts before the answer and seems to turn aside from it against his will. Yet he does produce some sensible ideas on the origin and functions of money and, finally, expresses in his own peculiar way the idea of its transformation into capital — into money which produces new money.

Such, with much digression, vagueness and repetition, is the path of scientific analysis traversed by the great Hellene.

Aristotle's scientific legacy has always been the subject of dispute. For many centuries his ideas on philosophy, the natural sciences and society, were turned into strict dogma, inviolable canon, and used by the Christian Church, pseudo-scientific scholastics and political reactionaries in their fight against the new and progressive. On the other hand, the people of the Renaissance, who revolutionised science, made use of Aristotle's ideas freed from dogma. The fight for Aristotle continues to this day. And it concerns, inter alia, his economic theory.

Read carefully the following two quotations which contain an assessment of the great Greek's economic views. The first belongs to a Marxist, the Soviet economist F. Y. Polyansky. The second to the author of a bourgeois history of economic thought, Professor J. F. Bell.

Polyansky	Bell
"Aristotle was far from taking a subjective view of value and inclined rather to an objective interpretation of the latter. In any case, he appears to have seen clearly the social need to cover production costs. True, he did not analyse the composition of costs and was not interested in this question. However, labour was probably allotted an important place in their composition."[1]	"Aristotle made value subjective, depending upon the usefulness of the commodity. Exchange rests upon man's wants.... When an exchange is just, it rests upon equality of wants, not upon costs in a labour-cost sense."[2]

It is easy to see that these assessments are diametrically opposed. Both passages speak about *value*, the basic category of political economy, which we shall be meeting time and again.

A most important part of Marxist economic theory is the *labour theory of value* developed by Marx on the basis of a critical analysis of bourgeois classical political economy. The essence of this theory is that all commodities have one basic common quality: they are all the products of human labour. The quantity of this labour is what determines the value of a commodity. If it takes five working hours to make an axe and one hour to make a clay pot, all other things being equal the value of the axe will be five times greater than that of the pot. This can be seen from the fact that one axe, as a rule, will be

---

[1] *A History of Economic Thought.* Course of lectures, Part 1, Moscow University Press, 1961, p. 58 (in Russian).

[2] J. F. Bell, *A History of Economic Thought*, New York, 1953, p. 41.

exchanged for five pots. This is its exchange value expressed in pots. It may also be expressed in meat, cloth and any other commodity or, finally, in money, i.e., in a certain amount of silver or gold. The exchange value of a commodity expressed in money is its *price*.

The interpretation of labour as something which creates value is most important. For the labour of the producer of axes to be comparable with the labour of the pot-maker, it must be regarded not as a concrete type of labour of a given profession, but simply as the expenditure over a certain amount of time of a person's muscular and mental energy — as *abstract labour*, independent of its concrete form. The use value (usefulness) of a commodity is, of course, an essential condition of the commodity's value, but cannot be the source of that value.

Thus, value exists *objectively*. It exists independently of a person's feelings, independently of the way in which he values the usefulness of a commodity subjectively. Further, value has a social nature. It is determined not by a person's attitude to an object, a thing, but by the relationship between the people who create commodities by their labour and exchange these commodities among themselves.

Contrary to this theory modern bourgeois political economy regards the *subjective usefulness* of exchanged commodities as the basis of value. The exchange value of a commodity is deduced from the intensity of the consumer's wishes and the existing market supply of the commodity in question. It thereby becomes fortuitous, "market" value. Since the problem of value is being removed to the sphere of individual preference, value loses its social nature here and ceases to be a relationship between people.

The theory of value is important not only in itself. An essential conclusion of the labour theory of value is the *theory of surplus value* which explains the mechanism of the exploitation of the working class by the capitalists.

Surplus value is that part of the value of commodities produced in capitalist society which is created by the labour of hired workers, but not paid for by the capitalist. It is appropriated by him without payment and is the source of profit-making by the class of capitalists. Surplus value is the aim of capitalist production: its creation is the general economic law of capitalism. Surplus value contains the roots of economic antagonism, the class struggle between the workers and the bourgeoisie. As the basis of Marxist economic doctrine, the theory of surplus value proves the inevitability of the development and deepening of the contradictions in the capitalist mode of production and, in the final analysis, its collapse. Attacks by bourgeois scholars on Marxism are directed primarily at the theory of surplus value. The subjective theory of value and all the related ideas of bourgeois political economy categorically exclude exploitation and class contradictions.

This explains the argument which has been going on for a good 2,400 years: was Aristotle a distant advocate of labour value or the forefather of theories which deduce exchange value from usefulness? This dispute is only possible because Aristotle did not create and could not have created a full theory of value.

He saw in exchange the equation of commodity values and searched hard for a common basis for equation. This in itself showed exceptional depth of thought and served as the point of departure for subsequent economic analysis many centuries after Aristotle. He made statements reminiscent of an extremely primitive version of the labour theory of value. It is evidently these to which F. Y. Polyansky is referring in the above passage. But perhaps even more important is the awareness of the *problem* of value which can be seen, for example, in the following passage from *The Nicomachean Ethics*:

"For, we must remember, no dealing arises between two of the same kind, two physicians, for instance, but say between a physician and agriculturist, or, to state it generally, between those who are different and not equal, but these of course must be equalised before the exchange can take place.... Hence the need of some one measure of all things.... Very well then, there will be Reciprocation when the terms have been equalised so as to stand in this proportion; Agriculturist: Shoemaker=wares of Shoemaker: wares of Agriculturist."[1]

Here in embryonic form we have an interpretation of value as the social relation between the people who produce commodities which have varying use values. It would seem to be but one step to the conclusion that in the exchange of their

---

[1] Aristotle, *The Nicomachean Ethics*, translated by D. P. Chase, London, Toronto, New York, 1920, p. 113.

products the farmer and the shoemaker relate to each other simply as the amount of work, labour time, necessary for the production of a sack of grain and a pair of shoes. But Aristotle did not draw this conclusion.

He could not, if only for the fact that he lived in an ancient slave-owning society which, by its very nature, was alien to the idea of the equality, the equal value of all types of labour. Manual labour was despised as the labour of slaves. Although there were also free craftsmen and farmers in Greece, Aristotle "overlooked" them, strangely enough, when it came to interpreting social labour.

However, having failed to lift the veil from value (exchange value), Aristotle turns, for an explanation of the mystery as if with a sigh of regret, to the superficial fact of the qualitative difference in the usefulness of commodities. He evidently senses the triviality of this statement (his idea is roughly that "we exchange things because I need your commodity and you need mine") and its quantitative vagueness, for he announces that money makes commodities comparable: "Hence the need of some one measure of all things. Now this is really and truly the Demand for them, which is the common bond of all such dealings.... And money has come to be, by general agreement, a representative of Demand." [1]

This is a fundamentally different position, which makes possible such statements as the above quotation from Professor Bell's book.

ECONOMICS AND CHREMATISTICS

Another of Aristotle's interesting ideas is his well-known distinction between economics and chrematistics, which was the first attempt in the history of the science to analyse capital. The term "chrematistics" was invented by him, but unlike "economics" it has not become established in modern languages. It was derived from the word "chrema" meaning property, estate. For Aristotle economics is the natural domestic activity connected with producing the things necessary for subsistence, use values. It also includes exchange, but only to the extent required to satisfy personal needs. The limits

---

[1] Aristotle, op. cit., p. 113.

of this activity are also natural: they are a person's sensible private consumption.

What is chrematistics then? It is "the art of making a fortune", i.e., activity directed towards making a profit, accumulating riches, particularly in the form of money. In other words, chrematistics is the "art" of the investment and accumulation of capital.

Industrial capital did not exist in the Ancient World, but a considerable role was already played by commerce and money (usury) capital. This is what Aristotle depicted: "... In the art of making a fortune, in so far as this is expressed in trading activity, there is never any limit to the attainment of the aim, for the aim here is unlimited riches and possession of money.... Everyone engaged in monetary circulation seeks to increase his capital *ad infinitum*." [1]

Aristotle regarded all this as *unnatural*, but was realistic enough to see that pure "economics" was impossible: unfortunately economics invariably develops into chrematistics. This observation is correct: we would say that capitalist relations inevitably develop in an economy in which goods are produced as commodities, for exchange.

Aristotle's idea of the naturalness of economics and the unnaturalness of chrematistics has undergone a strange transformation. In the Middle Ages the scholastics followed Aristotle in condemning usury and in part commerce as an "unnatural" means of enrichment. But with the development of capitalism all forms of enrichment began to seem natural, permissible "by natural law". It was on this basis that the figure of *homo oeconomicus* arose in the socio-economic thought of the 17th and 18th centuries, the motive of whose actions is the desire to become rich. Adam Smith announced that economic man is acting for the good of society, by striving for his own profit, and thus there emerges the best of all possible worlds known to Smith — the bourgeois world. For Aristotle the expression *homo oeconomicus* would have meant the exact opposite, a man who seeks to satisfy his reasonable needs which are by no means limitless. This hypothetical figure without flesh and blood, the hero of economic works in Smith's day, he would probably have called *homo chrematisticus*.

Leaving the great Hellene, we must now move on almost two

---

[1] Aristotle, *Politics*, St. Petersburg, 1911, pp. 25-26 (in Russian).

thousand years to Western Europe in the late 16th and early 17th centuries. This does not mean, of course, that twenty centuries passed without trace in economic thought. Hellenic philosophers developed some of Aristotle's ideas still further. Roman writers had a great deal to say about the subject which we call agricultural economy. The religious veil which learning donned in the Middle Ages occasionally concealed some original economic ideas. In their commentaries on Aristotle the scholastics developed the concept of "just price". All this can be found in any history of economic thought. But the age of the decline of slave-owning society, the growth and supremacy of feudalism did not encourage the development of economics. Political economy as an independent science arose only in the manufacturing period of the development of capitalism, when important elements of capitalist production and bourgeois relations were already forming in feudal society.

THE SCIENCE RECEIVES ITS NAME

The person who first introduced the term *political economy* in socio-economic literature was Antoine de Montchrétien, Seigneur de Vasteville. He was a French nobleman of modest means who lived under Henri IV and Louis XIII. Montchrétien's life was crammed with adventures worthy of a d'Artagnan. Poet, duellist, exile, attendant at the royal court, rebel and state criminal, he perished amid clashing swords and smoking pistols, caught in a trap set by his enemies. It was a lucky escape, however, for had the rebel been taken alive he would have faced torture and shameful execution. Even his dead body was sentenced to be profaned: the bones were smashed with iron, the corpse burnt and the ashes cast to the wind. Montchrétien was one of the leaders of the uprising of French Protestants (Huguenots) against the King and the Catholic Church. He died in 1621 at the age of forty-five or forty-six, but his *Tracte de l'Oeconomie Politique* was published in 1615 in Rouen. It is not surprising that the *Tracte* was consigned to oblivion and the name of Montchrétien besmirched. Unfortunately the main sources of biographical material about him are the partial or downright slanderous judgements of his ill-wishers. These judgements bear the stamp of bitter political and religious strife. Montchrétien was called a highwayman, forger and petty profit-seeker who allegedly changed to the Protestant religion in order to marry a rich Huguenot widow.

Almost three hundred years passed before his good name was restored and he was allotted a place of honour in the history of economic and political thought. Today it is clear that his tragic fate was no accident. His participation in one of the Huguenot uprisings, which were to a certain extent a form of class struggle by the downtrodden French bourgeoisie against the feudal-absolutist order, was the logical outcome of the life of this commoner by birth (his father was an apothecary), nobleman by chance, and humanist and fighter by vocation.

After receiving what was a good education for his day Montchrétien decided at the age of twenty to become a writer and published a tragedy in verse on a classical theme. It was followed by several other dramatic and poetic works. We also know that he wrote on *Histoire de Normandie*. In 1605, when Montchrétien was already a well-known writer, he was forced to flee to England after a duel which ended in the death of his adversary.

The four years in England played an important part in his life: he saw a country with a more developed economy and more developed bourgeois relations. Montchrétien began to take an active interest in commerce, handicrafts and economic policy. Looking at English ways he mentally transferred them to France. It is possible that his meetings with many French Huguenot émigrés in England played an important part in his future fate. Most of them were craftsmen, many highly skilled ones. Montchrétien saw that their labour and skill brought England considerable profit, whereas France, which had forced them into exile, suffered heavy losses.

Montchrétien returned to France a convinced supporter of the development of national industry and trade, a champion of the interests of the third estate. He proceeded to put his new ideas into practice. He set up a hardware workshop and began selling his goods in Paris where he had a warehouse. But his main occupation was the writing of his *Tracte*. In spite of the high-sounding title, he wrote a purely practical essay in which he sought to convince the government of the need for full patronage of the French manufacturers and merchants. Montchrétien advocated heavy duty on foreign goods, so that their import did not harm national production. He extolled labour and sang the praises, unusual for his time, of the class which he regarded as the main creator of the country's riches: "The fine and splendid artisans are most useful to a country, I would make so bold as to say, necessary and honorable." [1]

Montchrétien was one of the leading exponents of *mercantilism* which is the subject of the next chapter. He saw the country's economy primarily as an object of state management. The source of the country's and state's (king's) wealth he regarded, first and foremost, as foreign trade, particularly the export of manufactured and handicraft articles.

Immediately after the publication of his work, which he dedicated to the young King Louis XIII and his Regent Mother, Montchrétien presented a copy of it to the Keeper of the State Seal (the Minister of Finance). Evidently this loyal-looking book was well received at court initially. Its author began to play a certain role as a kind of economic counsellor, and in 1617 was appointed governor of the town of Chatillon-sur-Loire. It was probably at this time that he was made a nobleman. When Montchrétien became a Protestant and how he came to be in the ranks of the Huguenot rebels is not known. Possibly he lost hope that the royal government would put his plans into effect and was annoyed to see that instead it was fanning the flames of a new religious war. Perhaps he concluded that the principles formulated by him were more in accordance with Protestantism, and, being a man of decision and daring, took up arms on its behalf.

But let us return to the *Tracte de l'Oeconomie Politique*. Why did Montchrétien entitle his work thus and was there any special merit in it? It would appear not. The last thing he had in mind was to give a name to the new science. This and similar combinations of words were, so to say, in the air — the air of Renaissance, when many ideas and concepts of classical culture were resurrected, re-interpreted and given new life. Like any well-educated man of his day, Montchrétien knew Greek and Latin and read the classics. He frequently refers to them in his *Tracte*, in accordance with the spirit of the times. Without a doubt he was aware of the sense in which the words *economy* and *economics* were used by Xenophont and Aristotle. The 17th-century writers continued to use these words to mean housekeeping, the management of the household and private

---

[1] Quoted by P. Dessaix in *Montchrétien et l'économie politique nationale*, Paris, 1901, p. 21.

estate. A little after Montchrétien an Englishman published a book entitled *Observations and Advices Oeconomical*. The author defined economy as "the art of well governing a man's private house and fortunes" and concerned himself, for example, with such problems as a gentleman's choice of a suitable wife. According to his "economic" advice, a man should select for his spouse a lady who "may be no less useful in the day than agreeable at night".

Obviously this was not quite the same economy that interested Montchrétien. All his thoughts were directed towards the flourishing of the economy as a *state, national community*. It is not surprising that he used the attribute *political* with the word *economy*.

A good 150 years after Montchrétien political economy was regarded primarily as the science of *state economy*, the economy of national states governed, as a rule, by absolute monarchs. Only with Adam Smith and the creation of the classical school of bourgeois political economy did its character change and it became the science of the laws of economy in general, in particular, of the economic relations between classes.

Montchrétien's great service, of course, is not that he gave his book such a suitable title page. It was one of the first works in France and the whole of Europe specially devoted to economic problems. It singled out and delimited a special sphere of investigation, different from the spheres of other social sciences.

POLITICAL ECONOMY AND ECONOMICS

In recent decades the term *political economy* has gone out of fashion in the West and started to be replaced by the word *economics*. It is now used in a dual sense: in the sense of the economy, the sum total of production relations in a society, and in the sense of the science of the laws of economic development.

The terms *economics* and *political economy* should not be considered identical, however. Today the term *economics* in the sense of a branch of knowledge is understood more as the *economic sciences*. In addition to political economy these sciences now include diverse branches of knowledge about economic processes. The organisation of production, labour, sale of products, industrial financing are all the subject of the economic sciences. This applies both to capitalist and socialist economy. As we know, capitalist planning takes place within the framework of large capitalist concerns, and its methods and forms are also the subject of economic science. State monopoly regulation of the economy, without which modern capitalism is inconceivable, also needs a basis of objective knowledge about the economy as a whole and its individual branches. Thus, the practical functions of the economic sciences are increasing.

The profession of the economist in the socialist countries today includes some highly diverse functions, from very concrete engineering or planning work to the purely ideological activity of teaching and propagating Marxist-Leninist political economy.

All this can be explained by the complexity of the concept of production relations. Some of their forms are of a more general and social nature. These are the actual subject of political economy, while more concrete forms of production relations are directly connected with technology, with productive forces. Yet other economic technological problems are linked only indirectly with production relations. The importance of the concrete economic sciences is bound to grow. Their development is linked with the application of mathematics and computer technology to economic research and the practical management of the economy.

Just as philosophy, which was once the science of sciences and embraced practically all branches of knowledge, has now become only "one of the many", so political economy, which formerly embraced all economic phenomena, is now only the head of the family of economic sciences. This is quite logical.

But there is more to the matter than that. Political economy, as it emerged from the hands of Smith and Ricardo, was essentially the science of the class relations between people in bourgeois society. Its central problem was the distribution of the product (or incomes)—a social problem, and a highly controversial one at that. Many of Ricardo's followers had tried to soften the controversial social nature of his political economy. But this was not enough for the bourgeoisie: for simultaneously on the basis of Ricardo's theories there arose the political economy of Marx, which openly proclaimed social

34

production relations to be the subject of the science and concluded the logical collapse of capitalism.

Therefore in the seventies of the last century new economic conceptions appeared and took root simultaneously in a number of countries, which sought to deprive political economy of its revolutionary social content by rejecting the labour theory of value. The science was made to revolve round certain general principles void of social and historical content: the principle of the decrease in the subjective usefulness of commodities with use and the principle of economic balance. In fact, the subject of this political economy was not so much people's social relations in connection with production, as people's relations to things.

The main problem of economic science became a "technological" one void of social content, the problem of choosing between alternative possibilities for making use of the commodity in question, or, as it became accepted to say, of the factor of production in question: labour, capital or land. The problem of the optimal use of limited resources is undoubtedly an important one for any society and comes within the sphere of the economic sciences. But it cannot be regarded as the sole object of political economy.

The "social neutrality" of political economy was proclaimed. Why should science bother itself with classes, exploitation and the class struggle? But this concealed a new form of ideological defence of capitalism. In the hands of these economists—Jevons in England, Menger and Wieser in Austria, Walras in Switzerland, and John Bates Clark in the United States—"old" political economy was transformed into something beyond recognition. Now it was a set of abstract logical and mathematical schemes based on the subjective psychological approach to economic phenomena. Naturally this science soon began to require a new name. The term "political economy", which literally and traditionally possessed a social content, became a nuisance and embarrassment.

The American historian of economic thought Ben B. Seligman writes that Jevons "successfully eliminated the word *political* from political economy and turned economics into a study of the behaviour of atomistic individuals rather than of the behaviour of society at large".[1]

---

[1] Ben B. Seligman, *Main Currents in Modern Economics*, New York, 1963, p. 499.

The nature of the "revolution" which took place in the science is even clearer if we quote the following passage from another well-known bourgeois scholar, the French economist Emile James: "These great theoreticians thought above all that the object of economic science was to describe mechanisms which would operate in any economic regime and tried not to pass judgement on institutions. With regard to problems of social organisation, their fundamental theories were neutral, that is to say, one could not conclude from them either praise or blame of the existing regime".[1] The new Austrian economists "in their explanations of value by marginal utility were attacking above all the Marxist theory of labour value".[2]

In the course of the following century bourgeois economists developed techniques of economic analysis based on these principles. A vast literature arose in which the social edge of economic science was consciously or unconsciously blunted with the help of the "new" methods. The science began to forget its original function and content, although it continued to study many fascinating problems. Thus, the question of the terms *political economy* and *economics* is not a squabble over terminology, but a disagreement on fundamental principles.

---

[1] Emile James, *Histoire de la pensée économique au XX⁰ siècle*, Paris, 1955, pp. 10-11.
[2] Ibid.

CHAPTER II

THE GOLD FETISH
AND SCIENTIFIC ANALYSIS:
THE MERCANTILISTS

America was discovered as a result of the Europeans' pursuit of Indian spices, and conquered and explored because of their insatiable thirst for gold and silver. The great geographical discoveries were linked with the development of trade capital and, in their turn, greatly promoted its future development. Trade capital was historically the initial form of capital. It was from this form that industrial capital grew.

The main trend in economic policy and economic thought from the 15th to 17th centuries (and to a large extent in the 18th as well) was *mercantilism*. One might describe it in a nutshell as follows: in economic policy — the utmost accumulation of precious metals in the country and state treasury; in theory — the search for economic laws in the sphere of circulation (trade and money turnover).

"Risk your life for metal's sake," as Goethe said. The gold fetish accompanied the whole development of the capitalist system and is an integral part of the bourgeois way of life and thought. But in the age when trade capital predominated the lustre of this idol was particularly bright. Buying to sell at a higher price — that was the principle of trade capital. And the difference is seen in the form of yellow metal. The fact that this difference could arise only from production, from labour, had not yet occurred to anyone. To sell abroad more than one purchased abroad — that was the height of the state wisdom of mercantilism. And the difference was again seen by those governing the state and those who thought and wrote for them in the form of gold (and silver) pouring into the country from abroad. If there is a lot of money in the country, everything will be alright, they said.

PRIMITIVE ACCUMULATION

The age of primitive accumulation is the pre-history of the bourgeois mode of production, just as mercantilism is the pre-history of bourgeois political economy. The actual term *primitive accumulation* appears to have been coined by Adam Smith: he wrote that the primitive accumulation of capital is the condition for the growth of labour productivity through the development of many interlinked branches of production (Smith called it "previous accumulation").

Marx spoke of "the so-called primitive accumulation" as this term took root in bourgeois science and acquired a special, virtuous meaning for the bourgeoisie.

The whole process of primitive accumulation, as a result of which society became divided into the classes of capitalists and hired workers, is portrayed by bourgeois economists as an economic idyll. A long time ago there were, on the one hand, the industrious and, in particular, thrifty, sensible elect and, on the other, lazy ragamuffins who squandered all they had and even more.... Thus it happened that the former accumulated riches, while the latter were eventually left with nothing to sell but their own skins. Right and justice reign in this idyll, reward for labour and punishment for sloth and squandering.

Nothing could be further from the truth. Of course, the primitive accumulation of capital was a real historical process. But in fact it took place amid a fierce class struggle and involved oppression, violence and deception.

This was not the result of evil intent, of man's "primordial" inclination to violence, etc. During primitive accumulation the objective historical law of the transition from one social formation to another, the capitalist one, was just beginning to operate. Consequently this process was essentially progressive, for it promoted the development of the economic history of society. The age of primitive accumulation was an age of relatively rapid increase in production, the growth of industrial and trading towns, the development of science and technology. It was the age of the Renaissance, which brought a flowering of culture and the arts after a thousand years of stagnation.

But science and culture were able to develop rapidly in this age because the old feudal social relations were collapsing and being replaced by new, bourgeois relations. There can be no question of an idyll, when millions of small farmers were being ruined and semi-feudal and free landowners were being turned into urban and rural proletarians. Nor can there be any question of an idyll when the class of capitalist exploiters, whose religion was money, was being formed.

Centralised national states with a strong monarchy grew up in the 16th century in a number of West European countries — England, France and Spain. In a struggle lasting several centuries the monarchies overcame the wilful barons and subjugated them. The feudal armed retinues were disbanded and the feudal lords' warriors and retainers found themselves "out of work". If these people did not want to become farm-labourers, they joined the army and navy and set off for the colonies in the hope of finding the fabulous riches of America or the East Indies. As farm-labourers they made the farmers and landowners rich, and by going abroad they generally made the fortunes of merchants, planters and shipowners. A few "climbed up the ladder", got rich and themselves turned into merchants or planters. Some large fortunes were the result of piracy and straightforward robbery.

The towns, the handicraft and commercial bourgeoisie, were the allies and support of the kings in their struggle with the barons. The towns provided the monarchy with money, arms, and sometimes men, for this struggle. The very shift of the centres of economic life to the towns undermined the power and influence of the feudal lords. The bourgeoisie, in its turn, demanded that the state should support their interests against the feudal lords, the "common folk" and foreign competitors. And the state gave this support. The trading companies and handicraft corporations received various privileges and monopolies from the kings. Laws were promulgated, which forced the poor under pain of harsh punishment to work for the entrepreneurs, and fixed maximum wages. The economic policy of mercantilism was pursued in the interests of the urban, and particularly the commercial, bourgeoisie. In many cases mercantilist enterprises also suited the interests of the nobility, since the latter's incomes were in one way or another linked with trading and business activity.

The basis, the point of departure of any business is money which turns into money capital when the owner uses it to hire workers and purchase commodities for processing or resale. This fact lies at the basis of mercantilism, the essence and aim of which was to attract money — precious metals — into the country.

These measures were primitive in the age of early mercantilism. Foreign merchants were forced to spend on the spot all the proceeds from the sale of their goods within a given country, and special "supervisors" were even appointed, sometimes disguised, to see that they did so. The export of gold and silver was simply forbidden.

Later, in the 17th and 18th centuries, the European states changed to a more flexible and constructive policy. The rulers and their counsellors realised that the most reliable means of attracting money into the country was to develop the production of export goods and see that exports exceeded imports. Consequently the state began to promote industrial production, patronise manufactories and establish them.

These two stages in mercantilist policy correspond to two stages in the development of its economic theory. Early mercantilism, which is also called the *monetary system*, went no further than working out administrative measures to keep money in the country. Developed mercantilism sought the sources of the nation's enrichment not in the primitive accumulation of treasures, but in the development of foreign trade and favourable trade balance (an excess of exports over imports). It did not share the "administrative enthusiasm" of its predecessors. The exponents of developed mercantilism approved only that intervention by the state which, to their mind, accorded with the principles of *natural law*. The philosophy of natural law had a most important influence on the development of political economy in the 17th and 18th centuries. To a certain extent the science itself developed within the framework of the ideas of natural law. These ideas, which originated from Aristotle and other classical thinkers, received a new content in the new age. The philosophers of natural law deduced their theories from the abstract "nature of man" and his "natural" rights. Since these rights contradicted the secular and religious despotism of the Middle Ages to a large extent, the philosophy of natural law contained important progressive elements. The humanists of the Age of the Renaissance adopted the standpoint of natural law.

Turning to the state, the philosophers, with the mercantilist theoreticians following on their heels, regarded it as an organisation capable of guaranteeing man's natural rights, which included personal property and safety. The social meaning of these theories was that the state should provide the conditions for the growth of bourgeois society.

The connection between economic theories and natural law later moved from mercantilism to classical political economy. The character of this connection changed, however, for in the period of the development of the classical school (the Physiocrats in France and followers of Adam Smith in England) the bourgeoisie had less need of state tutelage and opposed excessive state intervention in the economy.

THOMAS MUN: AN ORDINARY MERCANTILIST

The English called London "the Great Wen", meaning a lump or protuberance. Like a colossal excrescence, London, once the greatest town in the world for several centuries, towers over the ribbon of the Thames, with thousands of visible and invisible threads emanating from it.

For the history of political economy London is a special town. The world centre of trade and finance was a most suitable place for the birth and development of this science. Petty's pamphlets were printed in London and his life is linked with it just as closely as with Ireland. A century later Adam Smith's *The Wealth of Nations* was published there. David Ricardo was a true product of London, its turbulent business, political and scientific life. And Karl Marx spent more than half his life in London, where *Capital* was written.

Thomas Mun (1571-1641) was a typical exponent of English mercantilism. He came from an old family of craftsmen and traders. His grandfather was an engraver at the London Mint, and his father was a mercer. Unlike his French contemporary Montchrétien, Mun did not write tragedies, did not fight duels and did not take part in uprisings. He lived a quiet, dignified life as an honest businessman and clever man.

Having lost his father at an early age, Thomas Mun was brought up in the family of his step-father, a rich merchant and one of the founders of the East India trading company, which arose in 1600 as a branch of the older Levant company that traded with the Mediterranean countries. After an apprenticeship in his step-father's shop and office, he began to work for the Levant company at the age of eighteen or twenty, spent several years in Italy, and travelled to Turkey and the countries of the Levant.

Mun soon became rich and highly esteemed. In 1615 he was elected for the first time to the committee of directors of the East India Company and soon became a skilled and active defender of its interests in Parliament and the press. But Mun was cautious and not excessively ambitious: he declined the offer to become Vice-Chairman of the company and refused to travel to India as an inspector of the company's manufactories. In those days it took three or four months to reach India and the journey was fraught with dangers: storms, illness, pirates....

On the other hand, Mun was one of the most eminent figures in the City and Westminster. In 1623 a publicist and writer on economic matters by the name of Edward Misselden described him as follows: "... his observation of the East India trade, his judgement in all trade, his diligence at home, his experience abroad, have adorn'd him with such endowments, as are rather to be wisht in all, than easie to bee found in many Merchants of these times".

Exaggeration and flattery apart, there can be no doubt that Mun was by no means an ordinary merchant. As a recent researcher has put it, he was a strategian of trade. (The word *trade*, incidentally, had basically the same meaning as the word *economy* in the England of the 17th and 18th centuries.)

Mun's mature years coincided with the reign of the first two monarchs of the house of Stuart. In 1603, the childless Queen Elizabeth died after nearly fifty years on the throne. When she became queen England was an isolated island state riven by religious and political discord. By the time of her death it was a world power with a mighty fleet and an extensive trade. The Elizabethan Age was marked by a great cultural flowering. The new ascendant to the throne James I, the son of the beheaded Mary, Queen of Scots, both feared and needed the City. He wanted to reign as an absolute monarch, but Parliament and the London merchants held the purse-string. Financial and trading difficulties which arose in the early twenties compelled the King and his ministers to turn for advice to experts from the City, and a special state commission on trade was set up. Thomas Mun joined it in 1622. He was an influential and active member of this advisory body.

In the stream of pamphlets and petitions, in the discussions of the commission on trade, the main principles of the economic policy of English mercantilism were formulated in the 1620s and continued to be applied right until the end of the century. The export of raw materials(particularly wool) was forbidden, but the export of manufactured articles was encouraged, even by state subsidies. England seized more and more new colonies which provided the manufacturers with raw materials and the merchants with profit from the transit of and intermediate trade in sugar, silk, spices and tobacco. The entry of foreign manufactured goods into England was restricted by high import duties which weakened competition and encouraged the growth of national manufactories (the policy of *protectionism*). Great attention was paid to the fleet, which had to carry cargoes all over the world and defend English trade. The most important aim of these measures was to increase the flow of precious metals into the country. But unlike Spain, which got its gold and silver straight from mines in America, the policy of attracting money proved beneficial in England because it involved the development of industry, the fleet and trade.

In the meantime a storm was gathering over the Stuart monarchy. The son of James I, the short-sighted and stubborn Charles I, antagonised the bourgeoisie who took advantage of the discontent of the broad mass of the people. In 1640, a year before Mun's death, Parliament met and openly attacked the King. Civil war broke out and the English bourgeois revolution began. Nine years later Charles was beheaded.

We do not know the political views of the elderly Mun, who did not live to see the outcome of the revolutionary events. But in his time he attacked complete absolutism in favour of restriction of the king's authority, particularly in the sphere of taxation. It is unlikely, however, that he would have approved of the king's execution. Towards the end of his life Mun was very rich. He bought considerable stretches of land and was known in London as a man able to give large loans in ready money.

Mun left two small works which, to coin a phrase, have gone down in the treasure store of economic literature. Their fate was a somewhat inordinary one. The first of these works entitled *A Discourse of Trade, from England into the East Indies Answering to Diverse Objections Which Are Usually Made Against the Same* was published in 1621 under the initials T. M. It was a polemic work directed against critics of the East India Company, who supported old, primitive mercantilism (the monetary system) and maintained that the company's operations were harming England, since it exported silver for the purchase of Indian goods and this silver was lost irrevocably by England. Efficiently, with facts and figures at his finger-tips, Mun disproved this contention, showing that the silver did not disappear but returned to England greatly increased: the goods carried on the Company's vessels would otherwise have had to be purchased at three times the price from the Turks and Levantines; moreover, a considerable portion of them were re-sold to other European countries for silver and gold. The importance of this pamphlet for the history of economic thought lies, of course, not in its defence of the interests of the East India Company, but in the fact that here for the first time was an exposition of the arguments of mature mercantilism.[1]

To an even greater extent Mun's fame rests on his second book, the title of which, as Adam Smith wrote, itself expresses the main idea: "England's Treasure by Forraign Trade, or the Balance of Our Forraign Trade Is the Rule of Our Treasure". This work was not published until 1664, almost a quarter of a century after his death. During the long years of revolution, civil war and the Republic it lay in a chest with other papers and documents which Mun's son inherited together with his father's chattels and real estate. The restoration of the Stuarts in 1660 and the revival in economic discussions prompted the rich, fifty-year-old merchant and landowner to publish the book and remind the public and the authorities of the name of Thomas Mun, now for the most part forgotten.

---

[1] For a long time English scholars tried to find a first edition of the *Discourse* which was thought to have come out in 1609. The existence of such an edition was referred to in the middle of the last century by John Ramsay McCulloch, the political economist and collector of old English economic literature. Today specialists believe that no such edition exists. Thus Mun was forestalled by the mercantilist tracts of the Italian Serra (1613) and the Frenchman Montchrétien (1615). But this by no means detracts from his merit.

As Marx says, "it continued to be the mercantilist gospel for another hundred years. If mercantilism ... has an epoch-making work 'as a kind of inscription at the entrance',[1] it is this book ...".[2]

This book, which is composed of rather diverse chapters evidently written in the period 1625-1630, gives a compact and accurate exposition of the very essence of mercantilism. Mun's style was not a flowery one. Instead of quotations from the classics he makes use of popular sayings and business calculations. Only once does he refer to an historical personage, Philip of Macedon, and this because the latter recommended that money be put into action in places which could not be taken by force.

As a true mercantilist, Mun sees riches primarily in their monetary form, in the form of gold and silver. His thinking is dominated by the viewpoint of trade capital. Just as the individual trading capitalist puts money into circulation in order to derive an increase from it, so the country should grow rich by means of trade, ensuring that exports exceed imports. The development of production is acknowledged by him only as a means for extending trade.

Economic works always pursue a more or less definite practical aim: to justify this or that economic measure, method or policy. But in the case of the mercantilists these practical tasks were particularly predominant. Mun, like other mercantilist writers, was far from the desire to create any sort of "system" of economic views. Economic thought has its own logic, however, and he was obliged to use theoretical concepts which reflected reality: commodities, money, profit, capital.... At all events, he tried to find the causal link between them.

THE PIONEERS

The new is always difficult. And in assessing the achievements of the 17th-century thinkers we should remember the enormous difficulties confronting them. The great English materialist philosophers Francis Bacon and Thomas Hobbes were in the process of formulating a new approach to nature

[1] The words in quotes are a parody on the style of E. Dühring whom Marx is criticising here.
[2] Frederick Engels, *Anti-Dühring*, Moscow, 1969, p. 274.

and society, which made it the main task of philosophy to explain their objective laws. The religious and ethic principles of many centuries' standing had to be overcome in economic thought. Previously the main question had been what *ought to exist* in economic life in accordance with the letter and spirit of the Holy Scriptures. Now it was a matter of what *really exists* and what must be done with this activity in the interests of the "wealth of society".

Although the great geographical discoveries and the growth of trade had broadened their horizons, people still knew very little about the world. To say nothing of foreign countries, even the geographical and economic descriptions of England were inaccurate, full of mistakes and nonsense. The pioneers of economic thought had very few facts and hardly any statistics at their disposal. But life demanded a new outlook on human affairs and encouraged minds questing in new spheres. During the century between Mun and Smith the number of economic works published in England grew rapidly. The first bibliography of such works composed by Gerald Massey in 1764 contained more than 2,300 titles. This was mainly mercantilist literature, although the works of Petty, Locke, North and some other writers already contained the foundations of classical political economy.

Mercantilism was not a specifically English phenomenon. The policy of accumulation of money, protectionism and state regulation of the economy was pursued throughout Europe in the 15th to 18th centuries, from Portugal to Muscovy. The *policy* of mercantilism acquired developed forms in France in the second half of the 17th century under the all-powerful minister Colbert. Its *theory* was successfully elaborated by Italian economists. Whereas in England the title of almost any mercantilist tract contained the word "trade", in the case of Italy it was the word "money": for divided Italy the problem of money and its exchange between the small states was of prime importance. In Germany mercantilism in the form of so-called "Kameralistik" was the official economic doctrine right up to the beginning of the 19th century.

But the leading role in formulating mercantilist ideas was played by English economists. This is explained by England's rapid economic growth and the maturity of the English bourgeoisie. Marx based his profound analysis of mercantilism mainly on the works of English writers.

Adam Smith introduced the view of mercantilism as a kind of prejudice. This view became established among the vulgarisers of classical political economy. Marx objected to it: "...it must not be thought that these mercantilists were as stupid as they were made out to be by the later Vulgar-Freetraders." [1] For its time developed mercantilism was a considerable scientific achievement. The most talented of these pioneers of economic thought rank with the greatest thinkers of the 17th century—in philosophy, mathematics and the natural sciences.

The national character of mercantilism as a theoretical system and as a policy had its own reasons. The accelerated development of capitalism was possible only in a national framework and depended to a great extent on the state which promoted the accumulation of capital and hence economic growth. In their views the mercantilists were expressing the genuine laws and demands of economic development.

Why does "wealth", i.e., the created, used and accumulated sum of goods—use values—grow more intensively in one country than in another? What can and must be done at manufactory level and particularly at state level to make wealth increase more rapidly? It is easy to see that the ability of political economy to provide answers to these questions justifies its existence as a science. The mercantilists tried to find the answers and sought them in the economic conditions of their day. One might say that they were the first to set the task of a "rational economy" as the most important problem of economic science. Many of their empirical conclusions and recommendations were objectively justified and in this sense scientific.

At the same time they also took the first steps towards an understanding of the laws of progression and the inner mechanism of capitalist economy. This understanding was extremely superficial and one-sided, for they sought the answer to the secrets of the economy in the sphere of circulation. They regarded production, as one critic has pointed out, merely as a "necessary evil", as a means for ensuring the flow of money into the country or, rather, into the hands of capitalist traders. Whereas in fact the foundation of any society is the production of material wealth, and circulation is secondary to this.

---

[1] Karl Marx, *Theories of Surplus-Value*, Part I, Moscow, 1969, p. 179.

This mercantilist view is explained, in its turn, by the fact that trade capital was the prevalent form of capital in general at that time. For the most part production was still carried on in the pre-capitalist mode, but the sphere of circulation, particularly foreign trade, had already been taken over by what was large capital for those days. It is no accident that the activity of such enterprises as the East India, Africa and other companies was at the centre of economic discussions in England throughout the whole of the 17th century and the first half of the 18th.

The very "wealth of nations" was regarded by the mercantilists essentially in the light of the interests of trade capital. Consequently they were bound to concern themselves with such an important economic category as *exchange value*. It was this in fact that interested them as theoreticians, for what more vivid embodiment of exchange value is there than money, gold? Yet even Aristotle's initial idea of the equation of various types of wealth and labour in exchange was foreign to them. On the contrary, they believed that exchange was unequal, unequivalent by its very nature. (This view is historically explained by the fact that they were thinking primarily of foreign trade exchange, which was often notoriously unequivalent, particularly in trade with backward and "savage" peoples.) The mercantilists, as a rule, did not develop the theory of labour value, the rudiments of which can be found in Aristotle and certain mediaeval writers.

Surplus value, which is in fact the fruit of the unpaid labour of hired workers appropriated by capitalists, appears in the form of trade profit in the mercantilists. The growth and accumulation of capital were seen by them not as the result of the exploitation of labour, but as the fruit of exchange, particularly foreign trade.

But these illusions and errors did not prevent the mercantilists from seeing many problems in their true light. Thus, they were most concerned with that as large a section of the population as possible should be drawn into capitalist production. Combined with an extremely low real wage this would increase profits and accelerate the accumulation of capital. The mercantilists attached great importance in economic development to an elastic monetary system. Their interpretation of the role of monetary factors in the economy was in certain respects more profound than Adam Smith's. Assuming a strong state in their economic projects, the later mercantilists also frequently objected to excessive and petty state regulation of the economy. This is particularly true of the English, who expressed the interests of a strong, independent and experienced bourgeoisie which needed the state only for the general defence of its interests.

Thomas Mun fought hard against strict regulation of the export of precious metals. He wrote that just as the peasant needs to cast seed into the earth in order to reap the harvest, so the merchant must export money and purchase foreign wares in order to sell more of his goods and bring the nation profit in the form of additional amounts of money.

MERCANTILISM AND OUR AGE

Mercantilism as a trend in economic theory disappeared from the scene towards the end of the 18th century. The principles of classical political economy were more in accordance with the conditions of the industrial revolution and manufacturing industry. These principles were particularly dominant in the most advanced capitalist countries — England and France. In economic policy this was reflected by a weakening in the direct intervention of the state in the economy and foreign trade.

In countries which embarked upon the path of capitalist development later, however, the ideas of the classical school could not take root fully. The bourgeoisie of these countries refused to accept that everything in economics must be left to the free play of forces. Not without justification it assumed that in this free play the English and also the French bourgeoisie had the best chance of winning. Therefore certain concrete mercantilist ideas never died, and the main points of mercantilist policy — state management of the economy, protectionism, securing an abundance of money in the country — have in many cases been actively used by governments.

Came the 20th century, and state-monopoly capitalism developed in the industrial bourgeois countries. The economic ideas which corresponded to these conditions and reflected the task of state influence on the economy were most fully expressed in the 1930s by the English theoretician John Maynard Keynes. The bourgeois economic thought of recent decades has developed to a large extent under the influence of his ideas. In many respects they determine the economic policy of modern capitalism pursued by the monopolies and the state today.

Capitalism can no longer exist by self regulation, Keynes argued. The state must take on the task of planning the economy. This task is mainly to support and stimulate the money demand which tends to lag chronically behind production. Thus it is necessary to combat unemployment and short time in factories. Individual capitalists must be constantly urged to invest, i.e., build new factories and extend production.

Non-intervention by the state in the economy, which bourgeois political economy proclaimed for a century and a half, is a false and dangerous notion. First and foremost, the state must ensure that there is an abundance of money in the country and that it is "cheap", i.e., that interest rates on loans are low. Given such a situation the capitalists will be eager to obtain bank loans, make investments, and therefore hire workers and pay them wages. Free trade is a prejudice. If it is necessary for full employment, then restrictions on the import of foreign goods are also permissible, and so are dumping (exporting goods at low prices to gain control of markets) and currency devaluation.

These recommendations are strangely reminiscent of mercantilist ideas allowing, naturally, for the difference between modern capitalist economy and the economy that existed in Western Europe 250-300 years ago. The Swedish economist Eli Heckscher (1879-1952), an acknowledged expert on mercantilism, writes: "... Keynes' view of economic relationships is in many ways strikingly similar to that of the mercantilists, despite the fact that his social philosophy was quite different...."[1] Of course it was different. Keynes is an ideologian of modern state-monopoly capitalism, whereas the mercantilists were expressing the interests of the growing trade and industrial bourgeoisie in the period of early capitalism.

Keynes expressed himself bluntly. He set himself the task of debunking "classical doctrine" (by which he meant, roughly speaking, the concepts of self-regulation and non-intervention by the state in the economy) and announced this on the very

---

[1] Eli F. Heckscher, *Mercantilism*, New York, 1955, Vol. 2, p. 340.

first page. He behaved in the same way with the mercantilists, openly acknowledging them as his predecessors. True, the critics, Professor Heckscher in particular, later proved that Keynes to some extent simply ascribed his own views to 17th and 18th century writers, interpreting them in a most strange and convenient way, to put it mildly. Nevertheless the kinship between Keynes and the mercantilists is significant. Keynes himself formulated four points linking him with them.

Firstly, the mercantilists, in his opinion, endeavoured to increase the amount of money in the country by lowering interest on loans and encouraging investment. As we have just seen, this is one of Keynes' key ideas. Secondly, they were not afraid of price increases and thought that high prices helped to expand trade and production. Keynes is one of the founders of the modern conception of "moderate inflation" as a means of supporting economic activity. Thirdly, "the mercantilists were the originals of ... the scarcity of money as causes of unemployment".[1] Keynes advanced the idea that increasing the amount of money by bank credit expansion and state budget deficits could be a most important weapon in the struggle against unemployment. Fourthly, "the mercantilists were under no illusions as to the nationalistic character of their policies and their tendency to promote war"[2]. Keynes believed that protectionism could help to solve the problem of full employment in a given country, and advocated economic nationalism.

To this one might add a fifth point which Keynes obviously took for granted: an emphasis on the important role of the state in the economy.

As mentioned above, at the end of the 19th century bourgeois political economy rejected the labour theory of value and other theoretical principles of the classical school. Today it has also renounced the economic policy which proceeds from the theories of the classical bourgeois political economists. The main reason for this is the aggravation of the contradictions in capitalism. Bourgeois economists are seeking to soften these contradictions by increasing state intervention. The conception of the omnipotence of the state in the economy was most

---

[1] J. M. Keynes, *The General Theory of Employment, Interest and Money*, London. 1946, p. 346.

[2] Ibid., p. 348.

fully expressed in the past by the mercantilists. Hence the kinship.

Not all modern bourgeois political economy has followed the Keynesian path. There are whole schools which reject the need for an increase in state intervention in the economy. They support "the freedom of private enterprise" against the inflationary enthusiasm of the Keynesians. These writers occasionally refer to attempts at state influence on the economy, production and full employment as "neo-mercantilism", using the term pejoratively. According to them, any such influence leads to the restriction of individual liberty and does not correspond to "Western ideals". These critics of "neo-mercantilism" do not see what the Keynesians are expressing (perhaps unconsciously) by their theories: that the increase in the role of the modern bourgeois state in the economy is an objective law. Otherwise capitalism would no longer be able to control the forces it has engendered.

On the other hand, the term "neo-mercantilism" is used to cast doubt on the economic policy of young developing states. The state sector of the economy, economic plans and programmes are called neo-mercantilism. The protection of national industry by customs tariffs and other measures is also neo-mercantilism. Bilateral trade agreements, financing of industry by state loans, regulating prices and restricting the profits of monopolies — all this is neo-mercantilism.

But how should these countries develop then? By freedom of trade, i.e., freedom for foreign monopolies with the benevolent non-intervention of the state. Then there would obviously be no neo-mercantilism. But nor would there be any independent economic development, for these are precisely the conditions which preserve backwardness and dependence!

Protectionism is being used in many developing countries as an instrument for promoting industrial development. In this case it is progressive and very different from the aggressive protectionism of the big developed countries, which is employed in the imperialist struggle for markets.

CHAPTER III

THE PRAISEWORTHY
SIR WILLIAM PETTY

Thomas Mun's contemporaries were Shakespeare and Bacon, the great innovators in the arts and sciences. A similar innovator in political economy, William Petty, appeared a generation later. The famous people in the generation between them, born at the turn of the century, were soldiers and preachers. Oliver Cromwell, the leader and hero of the moderate bourgeoisie, and John Lilburne, his more left-wing political rival, fought with a sword in their right hand and the Bible in their left. The political and social revolution in the 17th century assumed a religious aspect by virtue of prevailing historical conditions. It donned the austere garb of Puritanism.

The bourgeoisie exhausted its revolutionary fervour in the Cromwellian Protectorate and in 1660, in alliance with the new nobility, restored the Stuart dynasty to the throne in the person of Charles II, the son of the executed king. But the monarchy was no longer what it had been: the revolution had not been in vain. The bourgeoisie had strengthened its position at the expense of the old feudal nobility.

During the twenty years of revolution (1641-1660) a new generation of people grew up, on whose way of thought the revolution made strong, although widely differing impressions. Politics and religion (they were inseparably linked) went out of fashion to a certain extent. People whose youth had been in the forties and fifties were tired of scholastic arguments in which the Bible was the main source of wisdom. They inherited something different from the revolution: the spirit of bourgeois freedom, reason and progress. A bright constellation of talent appeared in science. The stars of the first magnitude were the physicist Robert Boyle, the philosopher John Locke and, finally, the great Isaac Newton.

It was to this generation and circle of people that William Petty belonged. He occupies a place of honour among the great scholars of his time. This English nobleman was, as Marx put it, the father of political economy and in a sense the inventor of statistics.

PETTY STRIDES ACROSS THE CENTURIES

The history of science contains cases of people being forgotten and resurrected later. Such as the somewhat mysterious figure of that remarkable economist of the early 18th century, Richard Cantillon, from whom, as Marx pointed out, such eminent economists as François Quesnay, James Steuart and Adam Smith borrowed heavily, was almost completely forgotten. He was practically discovered anew at the end of the 19th century.

Hermann Heinrich Gossen published a book in 1854 which attracted so little attention that the disappointed author withdrew it from the bookshops four years later and destroyed almost the whole edition. Twenty years later Jevons came across it by chance and proclaimed Gossen, who had long since departed from the land of the living, as the discoverer of "the new political economy". Today so-called Gossen's laws dealing with the category of utility of economic goods from a subjective, psychological standpoint occupy a considerable place in any bourgeois textbook or history of political economy.

Petty did not need to be rediscovered. He achieved fame already during his lifetime. Adam Smith was familiar with his ideas. McCulloch wrote in 1845 that "Sir William Petty was one of the most remarkable persons of the seventeenth century". He actually called Petty the founder of the labour theory of value and drew a straight line from him to Ricardo.

Nevertheless William Petty was only fully discovered for the science by Marx. Only Marx, by creating a new political economy and casting a new light on the history of the science, revealed the true place which this brilliant Englishman holds in it. Petty was the father of bourgeois classical political economy, which did not limit itself to the study and description of visible economic phenomena but proceeded to an analysis of the internal laws of the capitalist mode of production, to a search for its law of progression. In the hands of Petty and his followers this science became a powerful instrument for understanding reality and striving for social progress.

Petty's striking and unusual personality greatly attracted Marx and Engels. "Petty regards himself as the founder of a new science...", "His audacious genius ...", "A highly original sense of humour pervades all his writings ...",[1] "Even this error has genius ...",[2] "In content and form it is a little masterpiece...." — these comments in various works by Marx give an idea of his attitude to "the most brilliant and original of economic investigators...".[3]

The fate of Petty's literary heritage was an unusual one. McCulloch noted the somewhat strange fact that for all the importance of his role Petty's works were never published in full and existed only in old incomplete editions which had become a bibliographical rarity by the middle of the 19th century. McCulloch ended his note on Petty with the modest hope: "Nor could the noble successors of Petty, to whom much of his talent as well as his estates have descended, raise any better monument to his memory than the publication of a complete edition of his works."

However, Petty's "noble successors" — the earls of Shelburne and the marquesses of Lansdowne — were not overanxious to put their ancestor on general display, who had been the son of a modest craftsman, acquired riches and noble rank by none too fair means and, to quote a recent biographer, had a "loud, if somewhat doubtful, reputation".

For more than two centuries this aspect of the matter seemed more important to Petty's successors than the scientific and historical value of his writings. It was not until the very end of the 19th century that the first collection of Petty's economic works was published. At the same time one of his descendants published his biography.

---

[1] Karl Marx, *A Contribution to the Critique of Political Economy*, Moscow, 1970, pp. 52, 53.

[2] Frederick Engels, *Anti-Dühring*, Moscow, 1969, p. 275.

[3] Ibid.

Today we have a clearer idea of Petty's political views, his social and scientific activity, and his relations with the great scientists of his day. Many details of his life are now known. Great people do not need their portraits touched up or their vices and shortcomings glossed over. This applies fully to William Petty. In the history of human culture he will live on not as a large Irish landowner and adroit (although by no means always successful) courtier, but as a bold thinker who opened up new paths in the science of society. For Marxists Petty is primarily the founder of classical political economy. Bourgeois economists, while recognising Petty as a great scientist and striking personality, frequently refuse to see him as the forerunner of Smith, Ricardo and Marx. Petty's place in the science is often limited to that of the creator of the statistical method of investigation.

Schumpeter insists that Petty's work contains no labour theory of value (or concept of value in general) and no appreciable theory of wages and that, consequently, there can be no question of his having understood surplus value. He is obliged for his reputation simply to "Marx's decree to the effect that Petty was the founder of economics"[1], and also to the eulogies of certain bourgeois scholars who, Schumpeter hints, did not realise whose axe they were grinding.

Many works by bourgeois scholars regard Petty simply as an exponent of mercantilism, perhaps one of the most talented and advanced, but no more. At the most he is credited, apart from the discovery of the statistical method, with the treatment of individual economic problems and questions of economic policy: taxation and customs duties. It cannot be said that this point of view reigns supreme in modern bourgeois science. Other views are expressed, and Petty's role in economic science is seen in a more correct historical perspective. However, the main attitude is that of Schumpeter, and this is no accident.

FROM CABIN BOY TO LANDOWNER

The young Robinson Crusoe, hero of Daniel Defoe's novel, ran away from home and went to sea. Thus began his adventures which have been thrilling readers for two and a

---

[1] J. A. Schumpeter, *History of Economic Analysis*, New York, 1955, p. 210.

half centuries. A similar event took place in the family of the cloth-maker Anthony Petty in Romsey, Hampshire: his fourteen-year-old son William refused to carry on the family trade and got hired in Southampton as a cabin boy.

In the England of the 17th and 18th centuries going to sea was the usual form of protest by many young lads against a dull, humdrum life, the expression of youth's age-old thirst for adventure and independence. This was no revolt against the bourgeois way of life: on the contrary, the thirst for adventure was more or less consciously linked in these young men with the desire to get rich and assert themselves in the new bourgeois world. This feature was wholly characteristic of the young Petty too.

A year later Petty broke his leg at sea. In accordance with the harsh customs of the times he was simply put ashore at the nearest stretch of coast. This turned out to be the coast of Normandy in the north of France. Petty was saved by his practical nature, ability and good luck. In his autobiography he relates with scrupulous accuracy, again worthy of a Robinson Crusoe, what a trivial sum of money he was given before being set ashore, how he used it, and how he increased his "fortune" by purchasing various trifles and reselling them at a profit. He also had to buy a pair of crutches, which he was soon able to discard however.

Petty was a kind of child prodigy. In spite of the modest education which he received from the town school in Romsey, he knew Latin so well that he sent the Jesuits, who had a college in Caen, an "application" for admission in Latin verse. Whether they were astounded at the young man's ability or hoped to gain a valuable acquisition for the Catholic Church, the Jesuits admitted him to the college and paid for his upkeep. Petty spent two years there and as a result, to quote his own words, "I had obtained the Latin, Greek and French tongues, the whole body of common Arithmetic, the practical Geometry and Astronomy conducing to navigation..."[1]. Petty's mathematical ability was outstanding and in this sphere he kept abreast of the achievements of his day throughout his life.

In 1640 Petty earned his living in London by drawing sea charts. He then served in the navy for three years, where his talent for navigation and cartography was extremely useful.

---

[1] E. Strauss, *Sir William Petty. Portrait of a Genius*, London, 1954, p. 24.

These years were the height of the revolution. the bitter political and ideological struggle. Civil war broke out. The twenty-years-old Petty was basically on the side of the bourgeois revolution and Puritanism, but he had no desire to get involved personally in the struggle. He was fascinated by science. He went to Holland and France where he mainly studied medicine. This versatility was not only a sign of Petty's individual talent: the division into separate sciences was only just beginning in the 17th century and academic versatility was not a rarity.

Then followed three happy years of travelling, intense activity, and concentrated devouring of knowledge. In Amsterdam Petty earned his living in the workshop of a jeweller and optician. In Paris he worked as the secretary of the philosopher Hobbes who had emigrated there. By the age of twenty-four Petty was a fully developed person possessing extensive knowledge, great energy, *joie de vivre* and personal charm.

Returning to England Petty soon became in Oxford, where he continued to study medicine, and London, where he worked to earn a living, an eminent member of a group of young scientists. These scientists jokingly called themselves the "invisible college", but shortly after the Restoration they created the Royal Society, the first academy of sciences in the new age. When Petty received the degree of Doctor of Physics from Oxford University in 1650 and became Professor of Anatomy and Vice-Principal of one of the colleges, the "invisible college" began to meet in his bachelor flat which he rented in the house of an apothecary.

The political views of these scientists, including Petty, were not particularly radical. But the spirit of the revolution, which had by now led to the proclamation of the republic (May 1649) left its mark on all their activity. In science they fought against scholasticism for the introduction of experimental methods. Petty absorbed and carried all through his life this spirit of revolution and democratism, which in later years broke out from time to time in the rich landowner and nobleman, hindering his success at court.

Petty was obviously a good physician and anatomist. This can be seen from his success at Oxford, the young professor's medical writings and his subsequent high appointment. It was at this time that the event occurred which first made him known to a relatively large public.

In December 1650 in Oxford, in accordance with the barbaric laws and customs of the time, a certain Ann Green was hanged, a poor peasant girl who had been seduced by a young squire and accused of murdering her child. (It subsequently transpired that she was innocent: the child had been born prematurely and died a natural death.) After the fact of death had been established she was laid in a grave. At that moment Doctor Petty and his assistant appeared on the scene: their purpose was to take away the corpse for anatomical investigation. To their amazement the doctors discovered that there was still a breath of life in the hanged woman. By acting quickly they "resurrected" her! The subsequent development of events and Petty's actions, characteristic of many aspects of his nature, are interesting. Firstly, he carried out a series of observations not only on the physical but also on the psychic state of his unusual patient and recorded them with precision. Secondly, he showed not only medical skill but also humanity, obtaining a court pardon for Ann and organising a collection of money on her behalf. Thirdly, with his inherent flair for business, he used this happening to get publicity.

In 1651 Doctor Petty suddenly left his chair and obtained the position of doctor to the commander-in-chief of the English army in Ireland. In September 1652, he stepped on Irish soil for the first time. Why did he make such an abrupt change? Evidently the life of an Oxford professor was too quiet and unpromising for an energetic young man with a taste for adventure.

Petty saw Ireland, which had just been reconquered by the English after an unsuccessful uprising, ravaged by ten years of war, hunger and disease. The land belonging to Irish Catholics who had taken part in the anti-English uprising was confiscated. Cromwell intended to use this land to pay off the rich Londoners who had provided money for the war and also the officers and men of the victorious army. Before it could be allocated, stretches of land totalling millions of acres had to be surveyed and charted. (And this had to be done quickly for the army was restless and clamouring for rewards.) For the middle of the 17th century this was a task of colossal difficulty: there were no maps, no instruments, qualified people or transport. And the peasants kept attacking the surveyors....

This was the task that Petty undertook, seeing a rare opportunity for quick riches and advancement. His knowledge of cartography and geodesy stood him in good stead. But something else was also required: energy, drive and cunning. Petty contracted with the government and the Army command to survey Army lands. He was paid mainly with money collected from the soldiers who were to receive the land. Petty ordered new instruments from London, assembled a whole army of surveyors numbering a thousand men, and compiled maps of Ireland which were used in the courts to decide land disputes right up to the middle of the 19th century. And this was done in a little over a year. He was a man who could put his hand to anything.

The "Army land survey" turned out to be a real gold mine for Petty who was now a little over thirty. Having come to Ireland a modest physician, he turned a few years later into one of the richest and most influential people in the country.

What was legal and what was illegal in this breathtaking rise to riches? It provoked violent arguments in Petty's lifetime and to a certain extent depends on one's point of view. The actual plunder of Ireland was illegal. Petty acted on this basis, but himself always remained within the framework of formal legality: not robbing, but receiving from the existing authority; not stealing, but purchasing; driving people off their land not by arms, but by a court decision. It is unlikely that there was no bribery or corruption, but that was regarded as the natural order of things....

Petty's tremendous energy, his passion for self-assertion, adventurism ... all this found expression for a certain time in his mania to get rich. Having received, by his own figures, £9,000 of pure profit from carrying out the contract, he used this money to purchase land from officers and men who could not or did not want to wait for their plots and occupy them. Moreover, he received part of his remuneration from the government in land. We do not know exactly by what means the cunning doctor increased his property, but his success exceeded all expectations. As a result he found himself the owner of thousands of acres in various parts of the island. Later his domains extended even further. At the same time he became the trusted assistant and secretary of the Lord Lieutenant of Ireland Henry Cromwell, younger son of the protector.

For two or three years Petty flourished in spite of the intrigues of enemies and ill-wishers. But in 1658 Oliver

Cromwell died and his son's position became increasingly insecure. Against his will the Lord Lieutenant was compelled to set up a special commission to investigate the doctor's activities. True, the commission included many of Petty's friends. What is more, he fought for his fortune and good name with no less energy, brilliance and skill than he fought for his ideas. He succeeded in clearing himself not only before the commission, but also before Parliament in London (to which he had recently been elected). He emerged from the struggle if not triumphantly, at least without any losses. The political chaos of the last few months before the Restoration in 1660 put the Petty case into the shade, which suited him admirably.

Shortly before the Restoration Henry Cromwell and his confidant performed some important services for eminent Royalists who came to power when Charles II returned from exile. This enabled the Protector's son to retire gracefully into private life, and gave Petty an entrée to the court. In 1661 the cloth-maker's son was knighted and received the title of Sir William Petty. This was the height of his success. He enjoyed the favour of King Charles, he had disgraced his enemies, he was rich, independent and influential ....

It is known authentically from documents and Petty's correspondence that the crown twice offered him a peerage. He regarded these proposals, however, not without justification, as an excuse to ignore the requests with which he was pestering the King and court: to give him a real governmental post in which he could put his bold economic plans into action. His explanation of why he refused the royal favour in one of his letters is most characteristic of Petty's personality and style: that he would "sooner be a copper farthing of intrinsic value than a brass half-crown, how gaudily soever it be stamped or gilded".[1] In the many-tiered hierarchy of the court Petty had the lowest title.

Only a year after the death of Sir William Petty, his eldest son Charles was made Baron Shelburne. It was an Irish baronetcy, however, which did not confer the right to sit in the House of Lords in London. It was Petty's great-grandson who finally occupied this place and went down in English history as

[1] *Dictionary of National Biography*, ed. by L. Stephen and S. Lee, Vol. 45, p. 116.

an important politician and the leader of the Whig party under the title of the Marquess of Lansdowne.

Incidentally, in 20th-century Britain eminent economists who have performed important services to the ruling classes are now given peerages for their scientific works. The first such "aristocrat of political economy" was Keynes.

THE COLUMBUS OF POLITICAL ECONOMY

As we know, Columbus was unaware right up to the end of his life that he had discovered America, for he had set out to find a sea passage to India, not a new continent.

Petty published pamphlets with specific and occasionally even mercenary aims, as was the custom with economists of the time. The most he ascribed to himself was the invention of political arithmetic (statistics). His contemporaries, too, saw this as his main achievement. In fact he did something else as well: the ideas which he expressed incidentally, as it were, on value, rent, wages, division of labour and money became the foundation of scientific political economy. This was the true "economic America" discovered by the new Columbus.

Petty's first serious economic work was entitled *A Treatise of Taxes and Contributions* and appeared in 1662. It is perhaps his most important work too. In seeking to show the new government how it could (with his personal participation, of course, and even under his supervision) increase the revenue from taxation, he also expounded his economic views most fully.

By this time Petty had almost forgotten that he was a doctor. He occupied himself with mathematics, mechanics and ship-building only in his rare moments of leisure or meetings with some of his scientist friends. His inventive and flexible mind was turning more and more to economics and politics. His head was full of plans, projects and proposals: tax reform, the organisation of a statistics service, the improvement of trade.... All this found expression in his *Treatise*. And more besides. Petty's *Treatise* is perhaps the most important economic work of the 17th century, just as Adam Smith's book on the wealth of nations was of the 18th century.

Two hundred years later Karl Marx wrote of the *Treatise*: "In this treatise he in fact determines the *value of commodities* by the *quantity of labour* they contain."[1] In its turn "the determination of surplus-value *depends on the determination of value*".[2] These words express in a nutshell the essence of the English thinker's scientific achievement.

It is interesting to trace his line of argument.

With the keen sense of a man of the new, bourgeois age he immediately raises what is basically the question of surplus value: "... we should endeavour to explain the mysterious nature of them, with reference as well to Money, the rent of which we call usury; as to that of Lands and Houses, afore-mentioned".[3] In the 17th century land was still the main object to which human labour was applied. Consequently for Petty surplus value invariably appears in the form of land rent, which also conceals industrial profit. He also deduces interest from rent. Petty showed little interest in trade profit, which sharply distinguishes him from other contemporary mercantilists. His reference to the mysterious nature of rent is also interesting. Petty senses that he is confronted with a great scientific problem, that here the phenomenon's appearance differs from its substance.

Then comes a passage which is often quoted. Let us assume that a man (this man is to be the hero of economic treatises, not only arithmetic textbooks!) is engaged in producing corn. Part of what he produces will be used as new seed, part will be spent on satisfying his own requirements (including by means of exchange), and "the remainder of Corn is the natural and true Rent of the Land for that year". Here we have a division of the product and consequently of its value and the labour which created it into three main parts: 1) the part which represents the replacement of expended means of production, in this case seeds[4]; 2) the part which is essential for the sustenance of the worker and his family, and 3) the surplus, or net income. This latter part corresponds to the concept of the surplus product and surplus value introduced by Marx.

---

[1] Karl Marx, *Theories of Surplus-Value*, Part I, Moscow, 1969, p. 355.
[2] Ibid.
[3] W. Petty, *The Economic Writings*, Vol. 1, Cambridge, 1899, p. 42.
[4] Petty omits other expenditure of the means of production, say, manure, and also the wear and tear of a horse, plough, sickle, etc. These expenses are not reimbursed by corn in kind (this may be why Petty does not take them into account), but have to be reimbursed in value. In ten years' time, say, the ploughman will need a new horse. From each annual harvest he should set aside some part of the cost of the future purchase of this horse.

Further Petty raises the question of "... how much English money this Corn or Rent is worth? I answer, so much as the money which another single man can save, within the same time, over and above his expense, if he employed himself wholly to produce and make it; viz. Let another man go travel into a Country where is Silver, there Dig it, Refine it, bring it to the same place where the other man planted his Corn; Coyne it, and c. the same person all the while of his working for Silver, gathering also food for his necessary livelihood, and procuring himself covering, &c. I say, the Silver of the one must be esteemed of equal value with the Corn of the other: the one being perhaps twenty Ounces and the other twenty Bushels. From whence it follows, that the price of a Bushel of this Corn to be an Ounce of Silver".[1]

Obviously the attempt to equate in terms of value the parts of corn and silver which are the surplus product is tantamount to equating the whole gross product. After all, the latter twenty bushels of corn are in no way different from the other, say, thirty bushels which replace the seed and provide the farmer's subsistence. The same applies to the twenty ounces of silver mentioned above. In another passage Petty expresses the idea of labour value in pure form: "If a man can bring to *London* an ounce of Silver out of the Earth in Peru, in the same time that he can produce a bushel of Corn, then one is the natural price of the other...."[2]

Thus, Petty is essentially formulating the *law of value*. He understands that this law operates in a most complex way, only as a general tendency. This is expressed in the following truly amazing passage: "This I say, to be the foundation of equallizing and ballancing of values; yet in the superstructures and practices hereupon, I confess there is much variety, and intricacy...."[3]

Between exchange value, the size of which is determined by expenditure of labour, and the real market price are many intermediate stages which complicate the process of price formation immeasurably. With remarkable perception Petty names several price-forming factors which modern economists and planners have to take into account: the influence of

---

[1] W. Petty, *The Economic Writings*, Vol. 1, Cambridge, 1899, p. 43.
[2] Ibid., p. 50.
[3] Ibid., p. 44.

substitute commodities, novelty commodities, fashion, imitation, habits of consumption.

Petty takes the first steps towards an analysis of the abstract labour which creates value. For each concrete type of labour creates a concrete commodity, a use value: the farmer's labour — corn, the weaver's labour — cloth, etc. But each type of labour has something in common which makes all types of labour comparable and all goods — commodities, exchange values: expenditure of labour time as such, the expenditure of the productive energy of the worker in general.

In the history of economic science Petty was the first to start blazing the trail to the idea of abstract labour which became the basis of the Marxist theory of value.

One can hardly expect a balanced and complete economic theory from this founder and pioneer. Entangled in mercantilist ideas he could not get rid of the illusion that labour to extract precious metals was a special type of labour which created value most directly. Petty could not separate exchange value, which is most clearly embodied in these metals, from the very substance of value — the expenditure of universal human abstract labour. He has not the slightest idea that the degree of value is determined by the expenditure of socially necessary labour which is typical and average for the given level of economic development. Expenditure of labour in excess of that which is socially necessary is wasted labour and does not create value. With regard to the subsequent development of the science much that Petty wrote must be acknowledged as weak or downright wrong. But the main thing is that he sticks firmly to his point of view — the labour theory of value — and applies it successfully to many concrete problems.

We have already seen how he interpreted the nature of the surplus product. But in that case it was a simple commodity producer who himself appropriates the surplus product produced by him. Petty could not help seeing that in his day a considerable portion of production was already being done with the use of hired labour.

He was bound to arrive at the conclusion that the surplus product is produced not only and not so much for the worker himself, as for the owners of land and capital. The fact that he did can be seen from his reflections on wages. A worker's wage is determined and should be determined, in his opinion, only by the minimum necessary for subsistence. He should receive not more than is necessary to live, labour and multiply. Petty realises at the same time that the value created by the labour of this worker is of a totally different magnitude and, as a rule, considerably larger. This difference is the source of surplus value which appears in the form of rent in Petty's writing.

Although in undeveloped form, Petty expressed the fundamental scientific principle of classical political economy: that wages and surplus value (rent, profit, usury) are inversely related in the price of a commodity which is determined in the final analysis by expenditure of labour. Given the same level of production an increase in wages can only take place at the expense of surplus value and vice versa. From here it is only a step to recognising the fundamental opposition of the class interests of the workers, on the one hand, and the landowners and capitalists, on the other. This is the final conclusion, which was to be made by classical political economy in the person of Ricardo. Petty comes closest to this view, perhaps, not in the *Treatise*, but in the famous *Discourse on Political Arithmetick* written in the 1670s, although there too the idea is in embryonic form only.

On the whole, however, his passion for political arithmetic prevented Petty from developing his economic theory and understanding of the basic laws of capitalist economy. Many brilliant conjectures in the *Treatise* remained undeveloped. Figures now fascinated him. They seemed to be the key to everything. The *Treatise* already contains the characteristic phrase: "The first thing to be done is, to compute. ..." This was becoming Petty's motto, a kind of magic spell: compute and everything will become clear. The creators of statistics suffered from a somewhat naive belief in its power.

Of course, the foregoing does not cover the whole content of Petty's main economic works. It is far richer. His ideas expressed the world outlook of the bourgeoisie which at that time was progressive. Petty was the first to study capitalist production and assess economic phenomena from the viewpoint of production. This is his great advantage over the mercantilists. Hence his critical attitude to the non-productive sections of the population of which he singles out in particular clergymen, barristers and officials. He assumes that it would be possible to reduce considerably the number of merchants and shopkeepers who are "yielding of themselves no fruit of all" either. This tradition of a critical attitude to non-productive groups of the population is to become the lifeblood of classical political economy.

The style makes the man, as the old French saying goes. Petty's literary style is unusually fresh and original. Not because he was a master of literary niceties and subtleties. On the contrary, Petty is laconic, direct and austere. He expresses bold ideas in bold, unreserved form. He always keeps strictly to the point in simple words. The most voluminous of his works does not run to eighty pages.

The Charter of the Royal Society, of which Petty was one of the founder members, required that "... in all reports of experiments ... the matter of fact shall be barely stated, without any preface, apologies, and rhetorical flourishes". Petty regarded this splendid rule as applicable not only to the natural but also to the social sciences and sought to follow it. Many of his works remind one of "reports of experiments". (It would certainly not do modern economists and specialists in the other social sciences any harm to be guided by this rule.)

Simplicity of exposition does not prevent us from seeing behind Petty's works his striking personality, his irrepressible temperament, and political passion. This rich landowner, in his huge powdered wig and sumptuous silk robe (this is how Sir William looks in one of his later portraits), remained to a large extent the rough commoner and somewhat ironical physician. For all his wealth and titles, Petty worked unceasingly — not only mentally, but even physically. His passion was shipbuilding, and he was endlessly planning and building unusual ships. His individual features partially explain his antipathies: he could not stand idlers and parasites. Petty even adopted a strict attitude towards the monarchy. While trying to ingratiate himself at court, he at the same time wrote things which could not possibly please the King or the government: kings tend to like aggressive wars and the best way of stopping them is not to give them any money.

POLITICAL ARITHMETICK

More than anything in life the English King Charles II wanted to excel his august relative, Louis XIV of France, in some way. He organised balls and firework displays with an eye on Versailles. But he had far less money than the French ruler.

He bestowed the title of duke on some of his illegitimate sons, but Louis made his bastard offsprings marshals of France, which the Stuart could not do: his absolute monarchy was not that absolute.

Only science was left. Shortly after the Restoration at his instigation and under the patronage of the whole royal family the Royal Society was formed, of which Charles could be justly proud. Louis had nothing like that! The king himself conducted chemical experiments and studied navigation. This was in the spirit of the times. It was one of the entertainments of the "merry monarch", and so was the Royal Society.

The most interesting and witty member of the Royal Society was Sir William Petty. Among their intimates the King and the high-ranking nobility were free-thinkers, and no one could make fun of the sanctimonious of all denominations like Petty. One day the Lord Lieutenant of Ireland, the Duke of Ormonde, in a gay and probably not entirely sober company asked Sir William to demonstrate his art. Climbing onto a couple of chairs placed side by side, Petty proceeded to parody preachers of different denominations and sects amid general laughter. Carried away, he pretended to be clergymen reprimanding "some Princes and Governors", as an eye-witness puts it, for their bad management, partiality and cupidity. The laughter ceased. The Duke did not know how to quieten the spirit he had evoked.

The King and the Irish lord lieutenants enjoyed listening to Petty until he started talking about politics and trade. And he could not help doing this! For him all other conversation was just an excuse to expound his latest economic project. Each plan was bolder and more radical than the one before. This was dangerous, tiresome, unnecessary. Another Irish lord lieutenant, Lord Essex, said that Sir William was the most "grating man" in the three kingdoms (i. e., England, Scotland and Ireland). The Duke of Ormonde told him frankly that he was thought by some to be "a conjuror, by others to be notional and fanciful near up to madness, and also a fanatic".

His life was not an easy one. His natural optimism sometimes gave way to a peevish melancholy or futile rage.

Why were Petty's plans hardly ever to the liking of the Court? Some, for all their brilliant boldness, were simply utopian. Yet many were perfectly sensible for their day. The main point is that they were consciously and boldly aimed at developing capitalist economy in England and Ireland, at a more decisive break with feudal relations. But the monarchy of Charles II and his brother James II hung on to these survivals, or at the most agreed to compromise measures under pressure from the bourgeoisie. Which is why it collapsed (a year after Petty's death).

Petty always regarded the wealth and prosperity of England by comparing it with neighbouring countries. Holland was a kind of yardstick for him, and he frequently returned to the complex question of the cause for its successful development. With the years he became increasingly convinced that England's position was directly threatened not by Holland, but by a larger and more active power — France. His economic ideas assumed an increasingly open anti-French political character.

In 1676 Petty finished writing his second main economic work, the *Political Arithmetick*, but dared not publish it. Alliance with France was the basis of Charles II's foreign policy. The English King was receiving a secret financial subsidy from Louis XIV: Parliament was tight-fisted, the revenue from taxes did not reach the King, so he had to make ends meet in another way. Sir William was no coward, but he had no desire to incur the displeasure of the court.

The *Political Arithmetick* circulated in manuscript. In 1683 Petty's work was published anonymously, without his knowledge and under a different title. Only after the "glorious revolution" of 1688-89 and the related radical change in English policy did Petty's son (Lord Shelburne) publish it in full under the author's name. In the dedication he wrote that the publication of his deceased father's book had been impossible before because "the doctrine of this Essay offended France".

Petty's anti-French opinions were dictated by the interests of the English bourgeoisie. All the following century, right up to the beginning of the 19th century, England was to struggle hard with France and become firmly established as the world's first industrial power. But the most important thing in the *Political Arithmetick* are the methods by which Petty sought to prove his argument. This is the first work in the history of the social sciences to be based on the statistical method of enquiry.

Can one imagine a modern state without statistics? Obviously not. Can one imagine modern economic research without statistics? Yes, but hardly. Even if a writer uses "pure theory" in literary or mathematical form and does not quote any statistical data, he invariably assumes that they exist in principle and that the reader is more or less familiar with them.

This was not the case in the 17th century. Statistics simply did not exist (nor did the word either: it did not appear until the end of the 18th century). Very little was known about the size, distribution, age and professions of the population. Even less was known about the basic economic indices: the production and consumption of basic commodities, incomes, the distribution of wealth. Only on taxation and foreign trade were there a few facts and figures.

Petty's great service was that he raised the question of establishing a state statistical service and outlined the main methods of collecting information. He frequently returned in his writings to the creation of a statistical service and invariably, as it were, incidentally, saw himself as its head. He called this post invented by him various names, more or less high-sounding depending on his mood and assessment of his chances. Moreover, he hoped not only to calculate but to "plan" to a certain extent. For example, he compiled some estimates, remarkable for his time, on the "balance of the labour force": how many doctors and barristers the country needed (there were in fact no other specialists with higher education in the 17th century) and consequently how many students the universities should take each year.

Petty not only preached tirelessly the need for statistics, but also made brilliant use in arguing his economic views of the few and not very reliable facts at his disposal. He set himself a concrete task — to prove by means of objective numerical data that England was not poorer or weaker than France. This gave rise to a broader task — to provide a quantitative assessment of the economic position of the England of his day.

In the foreword to his work he writes about the method of political arithmetic: "The method I take to do this is not yet very usual. For instead of using only comparative and superlative words, and intellectual arguments, I have taken the course (as a specimen of the *Political Arithmetick* I have long aimed at) to express myself in terms of number, weight or measure; to use only arguments of sense; and to consider only such causes as have visible foundations in nature, leaving those that depend on the mutable minds, opinions, appetites and passions of particular men to the consideration of others."[1]

One of Petty's most eminent followers, Charles Davenant, provided the following simple definition: "By political arithmetick we mean the art of reasoning by figures upon things relating to government...." Further on he notes that this art itself is undoubtedly very ancient. But Petty "gave it that name, and brought it into rules and methods".

Petty's political arithmetic was the prototype of statistics, and his method anticipated a whole series of important trends in economic science. He wrote perceptively about the importance of calculating a country's national income and national wealth-indices which play a vast role in modern statistics and economics. He was the first to try and calculate the national wealth of England. Petty's democratism and unusual boldness are obvious from the following words: "...great care must be had distinguishing between the Wealth of the People, and that of an absolute Monarch, who taketh from the People, where, when, and in what proportion he pleaseth."[2] He was referring to Louis XIV here, but Charles II could also have seen this phrase as a strict reprimand.

Petty estimated England's material wealth at £250 million, but suggested that another 417 million be added, which he reckoned as a monetary assessment of the country's population. This paradoxical idea is more profound than may appear at first glance: Petty was seeking for a means of calculating the dimensions of the personal element of productive forces: labour skills, techniques, potential technological development.

Petty's whole economic theory begins with the question of the size and composition of the population. Marx noted in studying Petty: "Our friend Petty has quite a different 'population theory' from Malthus ... *Population-wealth...*"[3] This optimistic view of population growth is typical of the early exponents of classical political economy. At the beginning of the 19th century Malthus laid the foundations of one of the apologetic trends in bourgeois political economy by announcing that the main cause of the poverty of the working classes

---

[1] W. Petty, *Political Arithmetick*, London, 1690, p. 244.
[2] W. Petty, *The Economic Writings*, Cambridge, 1899, Vol. 1, p. 272.
[3] Karl Marx, *Theories of Surplus-Value*, Part I, pp. 354, 355.

was the natural one of excessive multiplication (for more about this see Chapter XIV).

Petty calculated the national income of England. This developed into the modern system of national accounting which makes it possible to estimate approximately a country's volume of production, the distribution of its produce for consumption, accumulation and export, the incomes of the main social classes and groups, etc. True, Petty's calculations suffered from serious defects. He estimated national income as the sum of the consumer expenditure of the population, in other words, he believed that the accumulated portion of income which goes on capital investment in building, machines, land amelioration, etc., could be dismissed. This assumption was a realistic one for the 17th century, for the rate of accumulation was extremely low and the country's material wealth was growing slowly. Moreover Petty's error was soon corrected by his followers in political arithmetic, particularly Gregory King, who made some calculations of England's national income at the end of the 17th century which are remarkable for their fullness and thoroughness.

PETTY AND GRAUNT, OR WHO INVENTED STATISTICS?

Petty's later writings deal mainly with population, its growth, distribution and employment. He and his friend John Graunt share the honour of being the founders of demographic statistics. All its powerful modern techniques developed from the modest works of these pioneers.

Each science has its disputes about authorship and priority. Occasionally these disputes are fruitless, even harmful to the discipline. Sometimes they help to clarify its history and are therefore useful. A discussion of this kind in the history of statistics centred around the "Petty-Graunt problem". Its gist is as follows.

A small modest volume was published in London in 1662 under the title of *Natural and Political Observations... Made Upon the Bills of Mortality*[1] by John Graunt. In spite of its odd, even morbid title, the book aroused considerable interest

---

[1] The title is abridged for briefness.

and ran into five editions within a few years, the second being required in the same year. The King himself showed an interest in it, and at his personal request Graunt was made a member of the newly-founded Royal Society. This was the first attempt to examine intelligently on the basis of existing scanty statistical data important problems of natural concern to people: the mortality and birth rates, the ratio between the sexes and the average life expectancy, population migration and the main causes of death.

The author of the *Observations* made the first timid attempts to approach the most important principle of statistics: that the study of a sufficiently large number of statistics on separate phenomena, each of which is fortuitous, shows that in general they are subject to extremely strict and regular laws. The birth and death of each separate individual is fortuitous, but mortality or birth rate in any given country (or even in a large town or region) is remarkably definite and slowly changing. Its changes can usually be scientifically explained and sometimes even predicted. The strict mathematical bases of statistics were laid in the following, 18th century, by the works of the great mathematicians—the creators of the theory of probability. But certain initial ideas were contained in the small book by the then unknown John Graunt.

He was born in 1620 and died in 1674, owned a haberdashery shop in the City, was self-educated and pursued his scientific investigations "in his free time". Petty became friendly with him in the late 1640s and at that time Graunt even acted as his patron. In the sixties the roles changed, but this did not cloud their friendship. Graunt was by then Petty's closest friend, his agent in London and the intermediary between him and the Royal Society. When Graunt's book attracted such interest, the rumour spread in London scientific circles that its real author was Sir William Petty who had preferred to hide behind this unknown name. This rumour grew stronger after Graunt's death. Petty's works and letters contain some passages which would appear to support it. On the other hand, he wrote quite clearly about "our friend Graunt's book".

In the 19th century the question of the authorship of the *Observations* was widely discussed in English literature. Today the "Petty-Graunt problem" can be regarded as solved. The main author of the book and its basic *statistical* ideas and methods was John Graunt. But with regard to his *socio-economic* views he was clearly under the influence of Petty who possibly wrote the preface and conclusion in which these views are expressed. It is highly likely that the general idea for the book belonged to Petty, but its execution was undoubtedly the work of Graunt.[1]

Graunt was ruined by the Great Fire of London in 1666. Shortly afterwards he became a Catholic, which also undermined his social position. Possibly all this hastened his death. As Petty's friend and first biographer John Aubrey writes, at Graunt's funeral "with tears was that ingenious great *virtuoso*, Sir William Petty, his old and intimate acquaintance".[2]

The Great Fire, which destroyed half medieval London and cleared the ground for the building of the new town, is connected with one of Petty's boldest ideas. After the fire our indefatigable deviser of schemes presented the government with a plan for cleaning and rebuilding the town. The title said that the plan was compiled on the assumption that "all the ground and rubish were someone man's who had ready mony enough to carry on the worke, together with a Legislative power to cut all Knots".[3] In other words, it obviously assumed state or municipal ownership of land and buildings as opposed to private ownership which was already hindering urban development.

One need only recall what problems and difficulties private capitalist ownership presents for the growth of London and Paris, New York and Tokyo, to fully appreciate this idea which was expressed more than three hundred years ago.

THE AGE AND THE MAN

The mercantilists did not see the objective laws in economic processes. They assumed that control of economic processes depended solely on the will of statesmen. What we now call voluntarism in economics was characteristic of the mercantilists.

[1] M. V. Ptukha, *Studies in the History of Statistics of the 17th-18th Centuries*, Moscow, 1945, p. 45 (in Russian).
[2] E. Strauss, *Sir William Petty. Portrait of a Genius*, London, 1954, p. 160.
[3] The Petty Papers. *Some Unpublished Writings of Sir William Petty ed. by the Marquis of Landsdowne*, London, 1927, Vol. 1, p. 28.

Petty was one of the first to express the idea of the existence in economy of objective, cognisable laws which he compared with the laws of nature and therefore called natural laws. This was a great step forward in the development of political economy as a science.

The actual idea of economic law could not arise until the basic economic processes — production, distribution, exchange and circulation — acquired a regular, mass form, until human relations acquired a predominantly commodity-money nature. The purchase and sale of commodities, the hiring of labour, the renting of land, and monetary circulation — only when these relations were more or less fully developed could people arrive at the conclusion that all this revealed the operation of objective laws. The mercantilists concerned themselves predominantly with one sphere of economic activity — foreign trade. Petty, on the contrary, was concerned with this least of all. He was interested in the recurring, law-governed processes which naturally determine the wage progression, rent and even, say, taxation.

By the end of the 17th century England was already becoming the most developed bourgeois country. This was basically the manufacturing stage of capitalist production, when its growth was promoted not so much by the introduction of machines and new methods of production, as by expanding capitalist division of labour on the basis of the old technology: a worker who specialises in any one operation acquires great skill in it, as a result of which labour productivity increases. The extolling of division of labour in political economy begins with certain remarks by Petty, who demonstrated its efficiency using the example of watch-making, and is particularly forcefully expressed in Adam Smith's writings, who made it the foundation of his system.

In Petty's day both industrial and agricultural production was already carried on according to capitalist principles to a large extent. The subjection of handicrafts and small-scale farming to capitalist enterprise took place slowly and in different ways in the various branches and areas. Vast regions of pre-capitalist forms of production still existed in most fields. But the trend of development had made its appearance, and Petty was one of the first to notice it.

Alongside the wool industry, which was still the basis of England's economy and trade, such branches as coal-mining and iron and steel smelting developed. In the 1680s about 3 million tons of coal was being mined annually, compared with 200,000 tons in the middle of the previous century. (But coal was still used almost exclusively as fuel: the coking process had not yet been discovered and metals were smelted with charcoal, which meant ruining the forests.) These branches developed as capitalist ones right from the start.

The countryside was also changing. The class of small landowners who carried on barter and petty trading was gradually disappearing. Their plots and the common land were becoming increasingly concentrated in the hands of large landlords who rented the land to farmers. The wealthiest of these farmers were already carrying on capitalist farming with the use of hired labour.

Let us remember that Petty himself was a large landowner. With rare exceptions, however, he did not express the interests of the landed aristocracy in his writings.

Lenin said of Lev Tolstoy that there had been no proper peasant in literature before this count. To paraphrase one might say that there had been no proper bourgeois in political economy before this landlord. Petty understood clearly that the growth of the "nation's wealth" was possible only by the development of capitalism. To a certain extent he applied these ideas on his estates. In renting out his land he made sure that the farmers improved it and the means of cultivating it. He organised a colony of English emigrant craftsmen on his land.

As a person Petty was a mass of contradictions. The great thinker appears to the impartial biographer now as the frivolous adventurer, now as the insatiable profit-seeker and persistent litigator, now as the cunning courtier, now as the somewhat naive braggart. His irrepressible thirst for life was perhaps his most characteristic feature. But the forms which it took were dictated by the social conditions and circumstances in which he lived. In a sense wealth and honours were not an aim in themselves for him, but held a sort of sporting interest. He evidently experienced inner satisfaction, showing energy, cunning and practical guile in a way logical for his age and conditions. Wealth and title had little influence on his way of life and thinking.

John Evelyn, whom Petty knew in London, describes a sumptuous dinner at Petty's house in Piccadilly in his diary for

1675: "When I have been in his spendid Palace, who knew him in meaner Circumstances, he would be in admiration himself how he ariv'd to it; nor was it his value (or) inclination to splendid furniture and the curiositie of the age: but his Elegant Lady,[1] who could indure nothing mean, and that was not magnificent; whilst he was very negligent himself and of a Philosophic temper: Lord, would he say what a deale of do is here; I can lie in straw with as much satisfaction; and was indeed rather negligent of his person...."[2]

All his life he had enemies—avowed and secret ones. They included people who envied him, political opponents, and those who hated him for the biting, pitiless gibes of which he was a past master. Some instigated physical violence against him, others wove intrigues. One day in a street in Dublin he was attacked by a certain colonel accompanied by two "assistants". Sir William put them to flight, almost losing his left eye from a blow of the colonels sharp cane. The blow fell on a sensitive spot, for Petty had suffered from weak sight ever since childhood.

He was more vexed by the enemies who intrigued against him at court, with the Irish lord lieutenants, and in the law courts. Petty's letters to his friends in the last twenty years of his life contain much bitter complaint and acrimonious disappointment. Sometimes he becomes small-minded, cursing and complaining about trifles. But his natural optimism and humour always prevail. He goes on making plans, presenting reports and ... being unsuccessful.

From 1660 his life was spent part of the time in Ireland and part in London. It was not until 1685 that he finally moved to the capital with his family and all his possessions, of which the most important were fifty-three boxes of papers. Charles II died in the same year and was succeeded on the throne by James II. The new king seemed well disposed to Petty and graciously received the projects on which the elderly Petty worked with a new bout of energy. But this too soon turned out to be an illusion.

In the summer of 1687 Petty's leg began to pain him badly. He turned out to have gangrene from which he died in

---

[1] A reference to Petty's wife, the beautiful and energetic widow of a rich landowner. Petty had five children.

[2] *The Diary of John Evelyn*, London, 1959, p. 610.

December of the same year. He was buried in his native town of Romsey.

Petty's last letters to his intimate friend Sir Robert Southwell are of great interest. They were written two or three months before his death. They symbolise his beliefs, no longer obscured by self-interest, trivial affairs and private interests. He is replying to Southwell who reproaches him mildly for being occupied with things remote from life instead of seeing to his family business (the half-blind, ailing Petty was having Newton's recently published *Mathematical Principles of Natural Philosophy* read aloud to him).

Here too Sir William is true to character. He would give £ 200 for Charles (his eldest son) to be able to understand the book. About his children, whom he loved and for whose upbringing he showed great concern, Petty wrote: "I will not sweat to make my daughter a fortune, nor to be honey for drones, and I desire my son to live within the compass of that wife's fortune which he himself best loves". And further about the meaning of life: "...you will ask me why I persist in these fruitless labours.... I say they are labours of pleasure, of which ratiocination is the greatest and the most angelical".[1]

Sir William Petty enjoyed a triple reputation with his contemporaries: firstly, that of a brilliant scholar, writer and erudite; secondly, that of an indefatigable schemer and visionary; and thirdly, that of a cunning intriguer, an avaricious man, not too fussy about the means he employed. This third reputation pursued Petty from his "accomplishments" in the division of the Irish lands right up to his death. And it was not without foundation.

Let us take a look at the latter half of Petty's life as the biography of man of property and smart dealer. The turning point in his life came in 1656-57, when he changed from a lower class intellectual into a profiteer and adventurer, and then a rich landowner. This change was an unpleasant surprise to his London and Oxford scientist friends. Petty was upset and pained by their reaction. He wrote to Boyle, whose opinion he particularly valued, begging him not to draw any hasty conclusions and to give him the chance of explaining what had happened personally. Time partially erased the estrangement, but traces of it remained.

---

[1] E. Strauss, *Sir William Petty*, London, 1954, pp. 168, 169-70.

Immediately after the Restoration Petty was obliged to fight hard to retain his lands: the former owners, some of whom enjoyed the support of the new government, were claiming them back. He threw himself into the battle with all his vigour and passion, putting a vast amount of spiritual energy and time into it. On the whole he was successful in keeping his scattered possessions and emerged triumphant. But he was persecuted by endless lawsuits.

And that was not all! Contrary to his principles and the exhortations of his friends, he threw himself into a new venture: he fell into the company of tax-farmers — rich financiers who bought the right to levy taxes from the government and robbed the country. In his works Petty attacked the system of tax-farming which stifled enterprise and production, and almost publicly called his companions swindlers and bloodsuckers. But nevertheless he paid his share. Soon afterwards he quarrelled with the "bloodsuckers", but could not get his money back. So now he was involved in yet another lawsuit — the most bitter and senseless of them all. Petty got deeply entangled in it and became furious, evoking the pity of his friends and the malicious delight of his enemies. In 1677 he even spent a short time in gaol "for contempt of court". These scandals ruined his last chances of a political career for which he was constantly striving. He was refused the appointments he required to carry out his projects.

The man of property became the slave of property. Petty himself in one of his letters compared himself to a galley slave exhausted from rowing against the wind. This was the tragedy of a talented man, whose energy and powers were spent in the harsh world of money, rent and tax-farming — *a bourgeois tragedy*.

His contemporaries sensed the tragedy, but naturally took a different view of it. They were amazed at the discrepancy between Petty's phenomenal abilities and his negligible success in the politics and government. Evelyn wrote that it was difficult to imagine anyone with a better understanding of the affairs of state. He continued: "There were not in the whole world his equal for a superintendant of Manufactures, and improvement of Trade; ... If I were a Prince, I should make him my second Counsellor at least".

Yet Petty gained nothing more than a minor post in the Admiralty.

Petty himself was by no means always blind to the triviality of the everyday affairs which exhausted his mind and energy. He sometimes laughed ironically at himself. But he could not break out of the vicious circle. The laconic brevity of his writings is to their credit and expresses his character. Yet at the same time it is the result of his preoccupation with other matters.

In 1682 Petty wrote with specific reference to the disputes on the re-minting of English coins a small work entitled *Quantulumcunque Concerning Money*. It is written in the form of thirty-two questions and brief answers. This work is as it were the steel framework of the scientific theory of money, the supporting structure, which remained to be filled in with other materials — amplifications, details, illustrations, and divisions between the various sections and problems.

Marx said of these modest notes, which were addressed to Lord Halifax and were not published in the author's lifetime, that they were "a smoothly finished work ..., which may be said to be cast in a single block.... In this book the last vestiges of mercantilist views, found in other writings by him, have completely disappeared. In content and form it is a little masterpiece ..."[1].

Adopting the standpoint of the labour theory of value, Petty treats money as a special commodity which fulfils the function of a universal equivalent. Its value, like that of all commodities, is created by labour, but its exchange value is quantitatively determined by the amount of labour expended in the extracting of precious metals. The quantity of money necessary for circulation is determined by monetary trade turnover, i.e., in the final analysis by the quantity of commodities realised, their prices and the frequency of circulation of monetary units in the various transactions (velocity of circulation). Full value money can, within certain limits, be replaced by paper money issued by a bank.

Throughout the next two centuries the theory of money and credit developed to a large extent within the framework of the ideas expressed here (and in certain other works) by William Petty, or in the polemic with these ideas.

---

[1] Frederick Engels, *Anti-Dühring*, Moscow, 1969, p. 276. (Chapter X of Part II of *Anti-Dühring* was written by Marx.)

This modest essay, in which many of the ideas are condensed and sketchy, shows what powers of theoretical thought the man possessed. He did only a small part of what he could have done. And although this can probably be said of any man, in Petty's case it is of particular relevance and importance.

CHAPTER IV

BOISGUILLEBERT, HIS AGE AND ROLE

Engels tells us that "Marx began his economic studies in Paris, in 1843, starting with the great Englishmen and Frechmen".[1] It is difficult to say what led Marx to study the works of Boisguillebert, an economist of the early 18th century by then pretty much forgotten. Perhaps chance played a role here, for in 1843 a collection of works by French economists of the first half of the 18th century was published in Paris; and the essays of Boisguillebert were republished in it for the first time after an interval of 130 years. From a conspectus of Boisguillebert's works in a mixture of French and German, Marx proceeded to short notes and then to reflections. He was led to these reflections by the remarkable ideas, well in advance of their time, of a Rouen judge in the reign of Louis XIV.

Marx probably made use of this conspectus ten years or so later in his work on the book *A Contribution to the Critique of Political Economy*, in which he first made the profound assessment of "over a century and a half of classical political economy, beginning with William Petty in Britain and Boisguillebert in France, and ending with Ricardo in Britain and Sismondi in France".[2]

---

[1] Karl Marx, *Capital*, Vol. II, Moscow, 1967, p. 7.
[2] Karl Marx, *A Contribution to the Critique of Political Economy*, Moscow, 1970, p. 52.

Boisguillebert attracted Marx not only as a scholar and writer. This clever and honest man, himself a "tiny cog" in the state machine of absolute monarchy, raised his voice in defence of the oppressed majority of the French people and had to pay for it.

THE FRENCH POOR

In the first two decades of the reign of Louis XIV Colbert was in charge of the country's economy. He realised the importance of industry and did a great deal to develop it. The growth of some branches, however, caused harm to agriculture which Colbert regarded solely as a source of financial revenue for the state. The main defect of Colbert's policy was that it left feudal relations intact, and they were hampering the country's economic and social development. Perhaps Colbert's efforts would have been more successful if the king had not given him one main task: to extort money at any price for the wars which the ambitious Louis was constantly waging and for his unprecedentedly lavish court.

After Colbert's death some of the achievements of his policy were quickly lost, but its defects made themselves felt twice as strongly. In 1701 France's most unsuccessful and ruinous war began, the so-called War of the Spanish Succession, in which it faced a coalition of England, Holland, Austria and some small states.

As he grew old Louis XIV lost the knack of finding capable people to run the state. The energetic and industrious Colbert was succeeded by mediocrities. The most important of the ministers under Louis XIV and the two Bourbon monarchs who succeeded him was the controller general of finance, who concentrated in his hands the management of state finance, the country's economy, domestic affairs, justice, and sometimes military affairs also. He was essentially a prime minister, but one who merely executed the monarch's will.

The introduction of any economic reforms depended on the controller general. Knowing this Boisguillebert constantly sought to persuade the men who occupied this post in the last decade of the 17th century and the first decade of the 18th, Pontchartrain and Chamillart, of the usefulness of his projects. But these people would not even give him a proper hearing.

Having obtained an audience with Pontchartrain, Boisguillebert began his report by saying that the Minister would think him mad at first, but would soon change his mind when he had heard his, Boisguillebert's, ideas. After listening to him for a few minutes, Pontchartrain burst out laughing and said he adhered to his original opinion and did not need to prolong the conversation.

The government would not even hear of reforms which might affect the interests of the privileged estates (the nobility and clergy), or of the tax-farmers, the rich financiers. Yet only such reforms could rescue the country's economy from prolonged crisis, and it was to this end that the importunate Rouen judge's projects were directed.

Boisguillebert's writings are a most important source of information about the disastrous state of the French economy at that time, the hard lot of the people, 75 per cent of whom were peasants. But many wrote about this. The eminent political and economic writer Marshal Vauban estimated in 1707 that 10 per cent of the total population was destitute, 50 per cent on the verge of destitution, 30 per cent in very straitened circumstances, and only 10 per cent lived well, the upper class, including several thousand people who were living in luxury.

Boisguillebert differed from other critics in that he understood to a certain extent the basic reasons for this state of affairs. Consequently he was able to do a great deal for the development of economic thought. It is no accident that he concentrated on the countryside. Here was the key to the development of bourgeois economy in France. The king, nobility and Church stubbornly kept this key locked up until the revolution at the end of the century broke all locks. The French peasant had gained his personal freedom several centuries before. But he was not the free owner of the land on which he lived and worked. The medieval principle of "no land without a seigneur" still operated in full force, although in changed forms. At the same time France did not possess the strong new class of capitalist tenant farmers which was developing in England. The peasantry was suffering under a triple burden: it paid rent and rendered all manner of feudal dues to the landowners; it supported the vast army of priests and monks by giving the Church a tenth of its income; and it was essentially the only payer of taxes to the king.

As Boisguillebert repeated many times in his works and report notes, this economic system deprived the peasant of any stimulus to improve land cultivation and expand production.

In subjecting all economic policy to the task of deriving tax revenue, the state made use of feudal survivals and delayed their destruction. The whole of France was divided into separate provinces by customs barriers, at which tolls were levied on all transported commodities. This hindered the development of the domestic market and the growth of capitalist enterprise. Another obstacle was the preservation in the towns of craft guilds with their privileges, strict rules and limited production. This was also profitable for the government, because it was forever selling the guilds the same old privileges. Even the few large manufactories which Colbert set up declined at the beginning of the 18th century. In 1685 Louis XIV revoked the Edict of Nantes which had allowed a certain amount of religious tolerance. Many thousands of Huguenot families, craftsmen and traders, left France taking with them their money, skills and entrepreneurial spirit.

THE ROUEN JUDGE

Economic projectors are a special type of people whom one can find, probably, at any time and in any country. They are similar to another peculiar tribe, inventors, and frequently face the same obstacles: the selfish interests of the strong of this world, conservatism and sheer stupidity.

Boisguillebert was one of the most passionate, honest and disinterested economic planners. He was bound to fail in the France of Louis XIV, and failure was a greater personal tragedy for him than even for Petty. Boisguillebert is perhaps not such a versatile and colourful figure as Sir William. But he commands more respect. In describing the bold judge from Rouen his contemporaries turned to classical antiquity for examples of similar civic virtues. Speaking of these two economists Marx wrote that "whereas Petty was just a frivolous, grasping, unprincipled adventurer, Boisguillebert ... stood up for the interests of the oppressed classes with both great intellectual force and courage".[1] It should be noted that

[1] Karl Marx, *A Contribution to the Critique of Political Economy*, Moscow, 970, p. 55.

Marx knew Boisguillebert only from his published works and in this description anticipated the man himself who was revealed more fully after his correspondence was discovered in the 1860s.

Pierre Le Peasant [1] de Boisguillebert was born in 1646 in Rouen. His family belonged to the Normandy *Noblesse de robe* which was the term applied in old France to noblemen who held hereditary judicial and administrative office: in addition there was the *noblesse d'épée* who served the king with their swords. The *noblesse de robe* was rapidly augmented in the 17th and 18th centuries from the ranks of the *nouveau riche* bourgeois. Such is Boisguillebert's family background.

The young Pierre Le Peasant received an excellent education for his day, after which he went to Paris and took up literature. He soon turned to the traditional family profession of law, married a young woman from his circle in 1677 and obtained an administrative legal post in Normandy. For some reason he quarrelled with his father, lost his inheritance which went to his younger brother and was forced to "go out and seek his fortune". This he did most successfully, with the result that by 1689 he was already able to pay a large sum for the highly paid and influential post of lieutenant general in the judicial district of Rouen. In the strange governmental system of the period this was something like head town judge together with the administration of police and general municipal affairs. Boisguillebert held this post all his life and passed it on to his eldest son two months before he died.

The system of selling posts was one of the most flagrant social evils of the Bourbon monarchy. In this way the treasury extorted money from the bourgeoisie, thereby preventing the latter from investing it in production and trade. New posts were often invented or old ones divided up and resold. One of Louis XIV's ministers joked that as soon as his majesty created new posts there were fools to purchase them.

Boisguillebert evidently began to study economic questions in the late 1670s. Living among the rural population of Normandy and travelling around other provinces he saw the

---

[1] This was the economist's real surname. Boisguillebert was the name of the landed estate acquired by his ancestors. This addition to the surname was generally made when a bourgeois received a title. However, Pierre Le Peasan' was always known under the name of de Boisguillebert.

desperate position of the peasantry and soon came to the conclusion that this was the cause of the country's general economic decline. The nobility and the King left the peasant just enough to prevent him from starving to death, and sometimes not even that. In such circumstances he could hardly be expected to increase production. In its turn the terrible poverty of the peasantry was the main cause for the decline of industry, since it did not have any large markets.

These ideas gradually matured in the judge's head. In 1691 he was already talking about his "system" and, obviously, setting it out on paper. The "system" was a series of reforms which we would describe today as bourgeois-democratic in character. Moreover Boisguillebert appears more as the defender of the peasants than the champion of the interests of the urban bourgeoisie. France is being treated like a vanquished country in the refrain that runs through all his works.

One might say that Boisguillebert's "system" in both its original form and the final form which it had acquired by 1707 consisted of three main elements.

Firstly, he considered it essential to introduce extensive tax reforms. Without going into details, let us say that he suggested replacing the old, obviously regressive system by proportional or slightly progressive taxation. These principles of taxation are still a matter of controversy today, so it is worth explaining them. Under the regressive system the greater a person's income the smaller the percentage of tax deducted; under the proportional system the percentage deducted for tax always remains the same; under the progressive system it increases the higher the income. Boisguillebert's proposal was exceptionally daring for his time: for the aristocracy and the Church paid practically no taxes, and he wanted to tax them at least at the same percentage as the poor.

Secondly, he proposed removing all restrictions on internal trade. He hoped that this measure would expand the home market, increase the division of labour and promote commodity and money circulation.

Thirdly, Boisguillebert demanded that a free market for corn be introduced and that its natural price should not be kept down. He regarded the policy of maintaining artificially low corn prices as extremely harmful, for these prices did not cover production costs and hampered agricultural growth. Boisguillebert believed that the economy would develop best with free competition, under which commodities would find their "true price" on the market.

He regarded these reforms as essential conditions for an economic recovery and an increase in the prosperity of the country and its people. Only in this way could the state's revenue be increased, he sought to convince the rulers. In an effort to inform the public of his ideas he published his first book anonymously in 1695-96 under the characteristic title of *Le détail de la France, la cause de la diminution de ses biens et la facilité du remède, en fournissant en un mois tout l'argent dont le roi a besoin et enrichissant tout le monde* (A detailed description of France, the reason for the decline in its prosperity, and a simple remedy which will supply in a single month all the money which the King needs and enrich the whole population).

The reference to a simple remedy and the possibility of achieving all this in one month is designed to a certain extent to catch the eye. Yet it also reflects Boisguillebert's genuine belief that all one needed to do was pass a number of laws and the economy would recover in a flash.

But the chain of disappointments had only begun. The book went almost unnoticed. In 1699 Pontchartrain's place was taken by Chamillart who knew Boisguillebert personally and appeared to be in sympathy with his views. The Rouen judge was again full of hope and worked with fresh energy, writing new works. But his main produce over the next five years was a series of long letters, memoranda to the Minister. These remarkable documents are letters, a real *crie de coeur*, as well as report notes.

Boisguillebert argues and cajoles, threatens economic disaster, begs and entreats. Confronted with a total lack of understanding, sometimes even ridicule, he remembered his dignity and fell silent. Then, consciously sacrificing personal pride for the sake of his native land, he again appealed to those in power: hurry, act, rescue.

CRIME AND PUNISHMENT

The years went by. The Minister forbade Boisguillebert publish his new writings, and the latter bided his time hoping that his ideas would be put into practice. In 1705 Boisguillebert finally received an area in the province of Orleans for his "economic experiment". It is not entirely clear how and in what conditions this experiment was carried out. In any case by the following year it had already ended in failure. In a small isolated area with the opposition of influential powers it could not have ended otherwise.

Now nothing could stop Boisguillebert. At the beginning of 1707 he published two volumes of his works. As well as theoretical treatises they also contained bitter political attacks on the government, serious accusations and ominous warnings. He did not have to wait long for the reply: the book was banned and its author exiled to the provinces.

Boisguillebert was now sixty-one. His affairs were in chaos and he had a large family — five children. His relatives tried to calm him down. His younger brother, a respected adviser of the parlement (provincial court) in Rouen, pleaded on his elder brother's behalf. He was not short of intercessors, and Chamillart himself realised the absurdity of his punishment. But the crazy inventor of schemes must submit. Gritting his teeth, Boisguillebert agreed: it was pointless to go on beating his head against a brick wall. He was allowed to return to Rouen. As a contemporary memoirist informs us, the Duc de Saint-Simon,[1] to whom we are indebted for many of the details in this story, the citizens greeted him with honour and joy.

Boisguillebert was never again subjected to direct repression. He published another three editions of his works, omitting, it is true, the most controversial passages. But morally he was a broken man. In 1708 Chamillart was replaced as controller general by Colbert's nephew, the clever and efficient Desmarets. He was well disposed towards the disgraced Boisguillebert and even tried to bring him into the administration of finance. But it was too late: Boisguillebert was a changed man and the finances were rapidly deteriorating, preparing the ground for John Law's experiment. Boisguillebert died in Rouen in October 1714.

Boisguillebert's integrated and strong personality emerges from all his works, letters and the scanty evidence of his contemporaries. In both business and private life he was obviously not an easy person to deal with: his characteristic

---

[1] An ancestor of the great utopian socialist Count Claude Henri de Saint-Simon.

features were obstinacy, persistence, and stubbornness. Saint-Simon remarks briefly that "his lively character was unique of its kind". It is clear, however, that he felt respect for Boisguillebert, bordering on awe.

His unaccommodating nature was the result of firm principles. He passionately defended his principles in both major and minor matters. And since these principles were, to put it mildly, unusual for the time, clashes were inevitable. For twenty years the modest judge from Rouen waged his hard battle, sacrificing peace of mind, prosperity and his material interests (Chamillart punished his stubbornness by imposing strange fines on him, forcing him to pay for posts he had already purchased). The ministers did not like him, but were also slightly (perhaps even more than slightly) afraid of him: Boisguillebert's superiority lay in the intrepid candour and conviction with which he defended his ideas and beliefs.

THE THEORETICIAN

Like all previous economists, Boisguillebert subordinated his theoretical constructions to practice, to substantiating the policy put forward by him. His role as one of the founders of economic science is determined by the fact that he based his reforms on an integrated system of theoretical views which was quite profound for its time. Boisguillebert's logic was probably similar to Petty's. He asked himself what determined the country's economic growth; he was specifically concerned about the causes for the stagnation and decline of the French economy. From here he proceeded to a more general question: which laws operate in the national economy and ensure its development?

We have already quoted Lenin's idea that the desire to discover the law of the formation and change of prices runs through the whole of economic theory, beginning with Aristotle. Boisguillebert made an original contribution to this long search. He approached the problem from the standpoint of what we would today call "optimal price formation". He wrote that the most important condition of economic balance and progress are proportional or normal prices.

What sort of prices are these? First and foremost, they are prices which ensure on average in every branch the defrayment of production costs and a certain profit, net income. Further, they are prices which enable the process of commodity marketing to proceed without interruption and steady consumer demand to be maintained. Finally, they are prices under which money "knows its place", promotes the payments turnover and does not acquire a tyrannical hold on people.

The interpretation of the law of prices, i. e., essentially the law of value, as the expression of the proportionality of the economy was an entirely new and daring idea. Boisguillebert's other basic theoretical ideas are linked with this one. Given this treatment of prices the question naturally arose as to how "optimal prices" could be ensured in the economy. Boisguillebert took the view that this price structure would develop naturally under free competition.

He saw the fixing of the highest possible prices for corn as the main violation of the freedom to compete. Boisguillebert believed that if maximum prices were abolished the market prices for corn would go up, which would raise the incomes of the peasants and their demand for industrial goods, production of the latter would increase, and so on. This chain reaction would also ensure the universal establishment of "proportional prices" and the flourishing of the economy.

It is still a matter of dispute to whom the famous phrase "laissez faire, laissez passer" belongs [1], which later became the motto for free trade and non-intervention by the state in the economy, and consequently the guiding principle of the classical school in political economy. It is ascribed variously in full or in part to François Legendre, a rich merchant of the time of Louis XIV, the Marquis D'Argenson (1730s), and Vincent Gournay, a trade superintendent and friend of Turgot's. But even if Boisguillebert did not invent the phrase, he expressed the idea contained in it most clearly. "Nature must be allowed to operate..." he wrote.

As Marx pointed out, Boisguillebert does not endow the concept of "laissez faire, laissez passer" with the selfish egoism of the capitalist entrepreneur, which it acquired later. In his writing "this teaching has also something *human* and *significant* in it. Human in contrast to the economy of the old

---

[1] At the end of the 19th century the German scholar August Oncken expressed the opinion that the first part of the phrase referred to freedom of production and the second to freedom of trade.

state, which was striving to increase its income by unnatural means, significant, since it was the first attempt to liberate bourgeois life. It had to be liberated to show *what it is like*". [1]

At the same time Boisguillebert did not reject the economic functions of the state; this was inconceivable for such a realistic and practical person. He assumed that the state, particularly with the help of a sensible tax policy, could promote a high level of consumption and demand in the country. Boisguillebert realised that the sale and production of commodities invariably decreased if the flow of consumer expenditure diminished. It would not diminish if the poor earned more and paid fewer taxes, for they tended to spend their income quickly. The rich, on the other hand, were inclined to save their income and thereby aggravate the difficulties of selling produce.

This line of argument is important for the development of economic thought in the following centuries. Two fundamentally different standpoints on the question of the main factors of the growth of production and wealth in capitalist society emerged in the history of bourgeois political economy. The first was briefly that production growth is determined solely by the extent of accumulation (i.e., savings and capital investment). With regard to the money demand this will "come on its own", so to say. This conception led logically to a rejection of the possibility of economic crises and general overproduction. The other standpoint emphasised consumer demand as the factor for maintaining high rates of production growth. To a certain extent Boisguillebert was its forerunner. This standpoint, on the contrary, led logically to the problem of economic crises.

It is true that Boisguillebert linked "crises" (or rather, phenomena similar to crises, the latter being characteristic of the later stage of capitalist development only) not so much with the inner laws of economics as with bad governmental policy. He can also be understood as saying that given a good policy insufficient demand and crises can be avoided. [2] Be that as it

---

[1] K. Marx, F. Engels, *Historisch-kritische Gesamtausgabe, Werke*, Schriften, Briefe, Moskau u.a., Abt. I, Bd. 3, S. 575.

[2] The incomplete and contradictory nature of Boisguillebert's views on this question allows historians of economic thought to take conflicting views on his role. The French economist Henri Denis writes that in the final analysis Boisguillebert's conception means that crises are impossible under free

may, in his main theoretical work *Dissertation sur la nature des richesses, de l'argent et des tributes* (Dissertation on the nature of wealth, money and taxes) Boisguillebert describes clearly and vividly what happens in an economic crisis. People can die from an excess of goods as well as a shortage. Imagine, he says, ten or twelve men chained at a distance from one another. One has a lot of food, but nothing else; another an excess of clothing, a third of drink, etc. But they cannot exchange with one another: their chains are the external economic forces, incomprehensible to man, which cause economic crises. This picture of disaster amid abundance calls to mind the 20th century: milk poured into the sea, corn burnt in locomotive fire-boxes — and this amid unemployment and poverty.

In theory and policy Boisguillebert's standpoint differs from mercantilist views and is to a large extent directed against them. He looked for economic laws not in the sphere of circulation but in the sphere of production, regarding agriculture as the basis of the economy. He refused to see the country's wealth in money and sought to dethrone it, differentiating between money and real wealth in the form of commodities. Finally, Boisguillebert's defence of economic freedom also meant a direct break with mercantilism.

BOISGUILLEBERT AND FRENCH POLITICAL ECONOMY

The fine and attractive feature of Boisguillebert's views is their humanism. Yet his "peasant mania" also had its reverse side from the point of view of economic theory. To a great extent he was looking backwards, not forwards, in underestimating the role of industry and trade and idealising a peasant economy. This influenced his views on fundamental economic questions.

---

competition and consequently "prepares (if not already contains) the famous 'law of markets' attributed to Jean-Baptiste Say, according to which there can *never* be general overproduction of products in a system based on the free exchange of products" (H. Denis, *Histoire de la pensée économique*, Paris, 1967, p. 151). Schumpeter, on the other hand, stresses that Boisguillebert saw lack of consumer demand and excess savings as a threat to the stability of capitalist economy and as the cause of crises, and is therefore a forerunner of the critics of "Say's law", in particular Keynes (J. A. Schumpeter, *History of Economic Analysis*, pp. 285-87).

The reasons for Boisguillebert's standpoint, which was appreciably different from Petty's, must be sought in the historical peculiarities of the development of French capitalism. The industrial and trade bourgeoisie was incomparably weaker in France than in England and capitalist relations developed more slowly. In England they were already established in agriculture as well. The English economy was characterised to a large extent by division of labour, competition, mobility of capital and labour. In England political economy was developing as a purely bourgeois system of views, while in France it was mainly petty bourgeois in nature.

English classical political economy, at the source of which Petty stands, put two most important and inter-connected problems at the centre of scientific analysis. What is the ultimate basis of commodity prices and where does the capitalist's profit come from? In order to answer these questions it was necessary to examine the nature of value. The labour theory of value was the logical basis of English economists' thought. In developing this basis they gradually approached an understanding of the difference between concrete labour which creates the various consumer values and abstract labour which lacks a qualitative characteristic, possessing only one parameter — length, quantity. This difference was never revealed and formulated before Marx, but the approach to it constitutes, to a certain extent, the history of English political economy from Petty to Ricardo.

The law of value was the true subject of its investigations. Yet, as Marx pointed out, "the full development of the law of value presupposes a society in which large-scale industrial production and free competition obtain, in other words, modern bourgeois society".[1] This society developed much later in France than in England, which made it difficult for theoreticians to observe and understand the operation of the law of value.

It is true that by his conception of "proportional prices" Boisguillebert reduced "although he may not be aware of it ... the exchange-value of commodities to labour-time".[2] But he was far from understanding the dual nature of labour and

[1] Karl Marx, A Contribution to the Critique of Political Economy, Moscow, 1970. p. 60.

[2] Ibid., p. 54.

therefore completely ignored the value aspect of wealth, which actually embodies universal abstract labour. He saw only the material aspect of wealth, regarding it merely as a mass of useful goods, consumer values.

This shortcoming in Boisguillebert's thought is seen particularly clearly in his views on money. He does not understand that in a society where the law of value operates, commodities and money are an indivisible whole. For it is in money, that absolute repository of exchange value, that abstract labour finds complete expression. Boisguillebert fought against money fanatically, distinguishing it from commodities which he regarded simply as useful goods. Since money is not in itself an object of consumption, it seemed external and artificial to him. Money acquires an unnatural, tyrannical power and this is the cause of economic disaster. He begins his *Dissertation* with bitter attacks on money: "... gold and silver, which the corruption of the heart has erected into idols.... They have been turned into gods to whom more goods, valuables and even people are still sacrificed than blind Antiquity ever offered the false divinities which have for so long formed the cult and the religion of most peoples." [1]

The utopian urge to free capitalist production from the power of money, without at the same time changing its foundations is, as Marx put it, the "national failing" of French political economy, from Boisguillebert to Proudhon.

Boisguillebert could not reveal the class, exploitatory nature of bourgeois society, which in his time was only just beginning to form within the feudal order. But he bitterly criticised economic and social inequality, oppression and force: Boisguillebert was one of the first people whose works prepared the collapse of the "old order" and paved the way for revolution. The defenders of absolute monarchy realised this already in the 18th century. Almost fifty years after Boisguillebert's death one such defender wrote that his " disgusting works" incited hatred for the government, encouraging robbery and rebellion, and were particularly dangerous in the hands of the younger generation. Yet this is one of the reasons why we find Boisguillebert's works and personality important and interesting.

---

[1] *Économistes financiers du XVIIIᵉ siècle*, Paris, 1843, pp. 394, 395.

CHAPTER V

JOHN LAW—ADVENTURER AND PROPHET

The name of Law is well-known. The first biography of the famous Scot came out during his lifetime. After the collapse of "Law's system" in France he was written about in all the European languages. No French political writer of the 18th century neglects to mention him.

The creation of modern banks and the vast development of credit and stock-exchange speculation in the 19th brought with them a new wave of interest in the activity and ideas of this passionate apostle of credit. He was regarded no longer as just a brilliant adventurer, but also as an eminent economist.

The 20th century, the "century of inflation", has discovered a new aspect of this remarkable individual. John Law hoped through an abundance of credit and paper money to secure a constant flourishing of the economy. The same idea (in a new form naturally) lies at the basis of the anti-crisis policy of the modern bourgeois state. Bourgeois researchers are finding a really mystical similarity between Law and Keynes: "The parallel between John Law of Lauriston (1671-1729), controller general of French finance, and John Maynard Keynes (1883-1946) goes so deep and covers so wide a ground, even touching some aspects of their personal life, that a spiritualist might say that Keynes was a reincarnation of Law after two centuries." [1]

---

[1] Ferdinand Zweig, *Economic Ideas. A Study of Historical Perspectives*, New York, 1950, p. 87.

Even the titles of books about Law which have come out in recent years are characteristic: *John Law. Père de l'Inflation, Der Magier des Kredits* and *La strana vita del banchiere Law.* At the same time he occupies a place of honour in weighty volumes on the history of economic thought.

A DANGEROUS CAREER AND BOLD IDEAS

John Law was born in 1671 in Edinburgh, the capital of Scotland. His father was a goldsmith and, according to the custom of the times, also lent money on interest. In 1683 he purchased the small estate of Lauriston, thereby becoming a member of the landed gentry. Possessing money, good looks and charm, John Law embarked early on the life of a gambler and swashbuckler. At the age of twenty when, to quote one of his associates, he was "nicely expert in all manner of debaucheries", Law found Edinburgh too provincial and went to London. Although Scotland and England had the same king in all other respects the former was still an independent state.

In London the young Scot soon became known by the nickname of Beau Law. In April 1694 he killed an adversary in a duel. The court passed a verdict of murder and sentenced Beau Law to be executed. Thanks to the intercession of some influential persons King William III pardoned the Scot, but the relatives of the dead man began a new lawsuit against him. Without waiting for the outcome, Law escaped from prison with the help of friends after jumping thirty feet and spraining his ankle. The only place he could go was abroad and he chose Holland.

In the three years Law spent in London he kept company not only with drunkards and women. Possessing a good practical education and a gift for calculation and all manner of financial business, he made the acquaintance of financial dealers with whom London was swarming after the Revolution of 1688-89. A few years later the Bank of England was founded, an important event in the history of English capitalism.

Law was a romanticist about banking. This sounds rather strange today: romance and banking. But at that time, the dawn of capitalist credit, its possibilities seemed unlimited and miraculous to many. It was not without reason that Law in his writings frequently compared the setting up of banks and the development of credit with the "discovery of India", i.e., the sea passage to India and America, along which precious metals and rare goods came to Europe. All his life he sincerely believed that by his bank he would do more than Vasco da Gama, Columbus or Pizarro had done! In John Law the as yet untested power of credit found its admirer, poet and prophet.

This began in England and continued in Holland, where Law studied the largest and most respectable bank in Europe at the time, the Bank of Amsterdam. In 1699 we find him in Paris. From there he set off for Italy, taking with him a young married woman, English by birth, called Catherine Seingieur. From then onwards she was to accompany him on all his wanderings. Obsessed by the idea of creating a new type of bank, Law returned to Scotland in 1704 with Catherine and their one-year-old son, to try and put this idea into practice.

The country was in the grip of economic difficulties. There was a depression in trade, unemployment in the cities, and the spirit of entrepreneurialism was crushed. All the better! Law expounded his plan for solving these difficulties in a book published in Edinburgh in 1705 under the title of *Money and Trade Considered, With a Proposal for Supplying the Nation With Money*.

Law was not a theoretician in any broad sense. His economic interests hardly ever extended beyond the problem of money and credit. But in fighting ardently for his plan he expressed on this problem thoughts which played a large and very conflicting role in economic science. Of course, Law's economic views must be seen in conjunction with his practical activity, the consequences of which were enormous. But in this activity as in his subsequent writings he merely put into practice and developed the basic ideas expounded in the Edinburgh book.

"He was a man of system," repeated the Duke of Saint-Simon, who has left us some important information about Law as an individual. Having arrived at the basic tenets of his system, Law preached and practised it with unwavering persistence and consistency.

Law maintained that the key to economic prosperity was an abundance of money in a country. It was not that he considered money itself as wealth, for he realised perfectly well that true wealth is commodities, factories and trade. But an abundance of money, in his opinion, ensured full use of land, labour and entrepreneurial talent.

He wrote: "Domestick Trade is the Employment of the People, and the Exchange of Goods..., Domestick Trade depends on the Money. A greater Quantity employes more People than a lesser Quantity.... Good Laws may bring the Money to the full Circulation 'tis capable of, and force it to those Employments that are most profitable to the Country: But no Laws ... can more People be set to Work, without more Money to circulate so, as to pay the wages of a greater number." [1]

Law obviously differs from the old mercantilists: although he too looks for the mainspring of economic development in the sphere of circulation, he does all he can to disparage metal money, rather than glorifying it. Two hundred years later Keynes called gold money a "barbarous relic". This might equally well have been said by Law. Money should not be metal. It should be credit which is created by the bank in accordance with the needs of the economy, or in other words, paper money. "The use of Banks has been the best Method yet practis'd for the increase of Money." [2]

Law's system contained two more principles, the importance of which is difficult to overestimate. Firstly, for banks he proposed a policy of credit expansion, i. e., the granting of loans many times in excess of the supply of metal money held by the bank. Secondly, he demanded that the bank should be a state one and should carry out the economic policy of the state.

We must clarify this somewhat, especially as similar problems — in different conditions and forms — are just as topical today. Imagine that the owners of a bank have invested £1 million as its capital. In addition they have received gold deposits to the value of £1 million. The bank prints notes to the value of £1 million and loans them. To anyone with even the most rudimentary idea of bookkeeping it is obvious that the bank's balance-sheet will be as follows:

ASSETS		LIABILITIES	
Gold	2 million	Capital	1 million
Loans	1 million	Deposits	1 million
		Bank notes	1 million
Total	3 million	Total	3 million

[1] J. Law, *Oeuvres complètes*, Vol. 1, Paris, 1934, pp. 14-16.
[2] Ibid., p. 46.

Obviously this bank is absolutely reliable because its gold reserve entirely covers its deposits and bank notes which could be presented for payment at any time. But, Law asks not without justification, is a bank like this much use? It is a certain amount of use, of course: it facilitates payment and prevents gold from getting lost or rubbed down. It would be incomparably more useful, however, if the bank issued notes to the value of, say, £10 million and furnished the economy with them. Then we would have the following picture:

ASSETS		LIABILITIES	
Gold	2 million	Capital	1 million
Loans	10 million	Deposits	1 million
		Bank notes	10 million
Total	12 million	Total	12 million

This bank would operate at a certain risk. What would happen, say, if the holders of bank notes presented three million of them for exchange? The bank would be ruined or, as they said in Law's day, would cease payments. But Law believes that this is a justified and necessary risk. What is more, he assumes that if the bank is forced to cease payments for a while this is not such a terrible thing either.

In our example the bank's gold reserve is only 20 per cent of the total number of notes issued and even less if one adds the deposits. This is the so-called partial reserve principle which underlies all banking. Thanks to this principle banks are able to expand loans elastically and increase circulation. Credit plays a most important part in the development of capitalist production, and Law was one of the first to see this.

But the very same principle endangers the stability of the banking system. Banks tend to "get carried away" and step up loans for the sake of profit. Hence the possibility of their collapse, which may have serious consequences for the economy.

Another danger or rather another aspect of the same danger is that the bank's abilities are exploited by the state. What would happen if a bank were forced to increase its note issue not to satisfy the real requirements of the economy, but simply to conceal a deficit in the national budget? The word "inflation" had not yet been invented, but this was what would have threatened both Law's bank and the country in which it operated.

Law saw the advantages of credit, but would not or could not see its dangers. This was the main practical weakness of his system and the ultimate cause of its collapse. The theoretical flaw in Law's views was that he naively equated credit and money with capital. He thought that by expanding loans and money issue a bank would create capital and thereby augment wealth and employment. However no credit can be a substitute for the true labour and material resources necessary to expanding production.

The credit operations which Law envisaged in his first book and which he put into practice some ten to fifteen years later on a grandiose scale lend his system an air of blatant financial adventurism. Describing Law as "the principal spokesman of credit", Marx noted sarcastically that such persons possess "the pleasant character mixture of swindler and prophet".[1]

THE CONQUEST OF PARIS

The Scottish Parliament rejected the plan to found a bank. The English Government twice refused to grant Law a pardon for the crime committed by him ten years earlier. In connection with the preparation of the Act of Union to unite England and Scotland Law was again obliged to leave for the continent where he practically led the life of a professional gambler. He lived in Holland and Italy, Flanders and France, sometimes with his family, sometimes alone, gambling everywhere and also speculating in securities, jewelry and Old Masters. In his *Lettres Persanes* (1721) Montesquieu puts the following ironical observation into the mouth of a Persian travelling around Europe: "Gambling is all the rage in Europe: being a gambler is a kind of status. The very title is a substitute for high birth, fortune and probity: it places all those who bear it in the rank of honest men...."

It was precisely in this way that Law acquired social standing and a fortune. Legends grew up around his skill as a gambler. His *sang-froid*, shrewdness, remarkable memory and good luck brought him some big wins. When Law eventually decided to settle in Paris he brought a fortune of 1,600,000 livres into France. But Paris attracted him not only by its gambling and

---

[1] Karl Marx, *Capital*, Vol. III, Moscow, 1971, p. 441.

speculating. As the financial crisis grew more acute, he felt increasingly that his project would be accepted here. The state coffers were empty, the national debt enormous, credit was low and there was stagnation and depression in the economy. All this Law proposed to rectify by the creation of a state bank with the right to issue notes.

His moment came when Louis XIV died in September 1715. Law had already been putting over his idea to a man who had a good chance of being made the country's ruler until the heir to the throne came of age, Duke Philippe of Orleans, nephew of the old king. Philippe began to believe in the Scot. After ousting the other claimants to the regency and seizing power, he summoned Law straightaway.

It took more than six months to overcome the opposition of the aristocratic advisers of the Regent and the Paris parlement who feared radical measures and did not trust the foreigner. Law had to renounce the idea of a state bank and agree to a private joint-stock bank. But this was just a tactical manoeuvre: the bank was closely linked with the state right from the start. Founded in May 1716 the Banque Générale was a great success in the first two years of its activities. A talented administrator, shrewd businessman, adept politician and diplomat, Law confidently ran the country's whole monetary and credit system with the Regent's support. Banque Générale notes, the issue of which Law successfully controlled in this period, were put into circulation and often accepted even with a premium as compared to metal money. By comparison with the Paris moneylenders the Banque granted loans at moderate rate of interest, deliberately channeling them into industry and commerce. There was a perceptible revival of the economy.

THE GREAT COLLAPSE

Law owed allegiance not to a country, but to an idea. He first offered this idea unsuccessfully to Scotland, England, the Duke of Savoy and the Republic of Genoa. When France finally accepted it he sincerely felt himself to be a Frenchman. He immediately took French citizenship and later, when he judged it necessary for the success of the system, converted to Catholicism.

There is no doubt that Law really believed in his idea and put into its realisation in France not only all his money, but his heart as well. Law was no common rogue who set out to steal as much as he could and then made off with his ill-gotten gains. Later in his "vindicatory memoranda" he frequently repeated that if that had been his plan he would not have brought all his fortune to France and would certainly have sent some assets abroad while he was still in power. We can believe the Duke of Saint-Simon when he says of Law that "there was no greed nor knavery in his nature". He was made a rogue by the very inexorable logic of his system!

In a letter written by Law in December 1715 to the Regent, in which he again explains his ideas, there is a mysterious passage which smacks of a hoax: "But the Banque is not the only idea of mine nor the greatest one; I shall produce something which will astound Europe by the changes it will make to the advantage of France, changes more important than those which have been produced by the discovery of the Indies or the introduction of credit. By this work Your Royal Highness will be able to raise the kingdom out of the sad situation to which it is reduced and make it more powerful than it has ever been, to establish order in its finances, to revive, support and develop agriculture, manufactories and commerce."[1]

Planners have always promised rulers streets paved with gold, but here is an economic alchemist who promises some sort of philosopher's stone. Two years later it became clear what lay behind these hazy promises. At the end of 1717 Law founded his second colossal undertaking—the Company of the Indies. Since it was originally created to colonise the Mississippi Basin, which belonged to France at the time, it was usually called the Mississippi Company.

Outwardly this was nothing particularly new. The East India Company had been flourishing in England for over a century and there was a similar enterprise in Holland. But Law's company differed from them. It was not an association of a narrow group of merchants who distributed the shares among themselves. The shares of the Mississippi Company were intended for sale to a relatively large section of capitalists and for active circulation on the stock exchange. The company was extremely closely linked with the state not only in the sense that it received vast privileges and monopolies in many spheres

---

[1] J. Law, *Oeuvres complètes*, Vol. 2, Paris, 1934, p. 266.

from the state. At its head alongside the imperturbable Scot sat no other than Philippe of Orleans, Regent of France. The company was merged with the Banque Générale which at the beginning of 1719 went over to the state and became called the Banque Royal. The Banque loaned capitalists money to purchase shares in the company, and ran its financial affairs. The threads of management of both institutions were concentrated in Law's hands.

Thus, Law's second "great idea" was the idea of capitalist centralisation, capitalist association. Here too the Scot appeared as a prophet, a century or more ahead of his time. Not until the middle of the 19th century in Western Europe and America did the rapid growth of joint-stock companies begin. Today they constitute almost the whole of the economy in the developed capitalist countries, particularly large-scale production. Big enterprises are not within the scope of one or even several capitalists, however rich they may be. They require the combined capital of many proprietors. Of course, the small shareholders only supply the money and do not have the slightest influence on the course of events. The real running of the business is done by the people at the top, which in the case of the Mississippi Company was Law and some of his associates. Marx said about the progressive role of joint-stock companies: "The world would still be without railways if it had had to wait until accumulation had got a few individual capitals far enough to be adequate for the construction of a railway. Centralisation, on the contrary, accomplished this in the twinkling of an eye, by means of joint-stock companies."[1]

Stock-jobbing and speculation in the buying and selling of shares invariably accompany joint-stock operations. Law's system gave rise to stock-jobbing on a scale hitherto unknown. After the company had got firmly established in the first year of its existence, Law took strong measures aimed at raising the price and expanding the sale of the shares. For a start he purchased two hundred 500-livre shares, then costing only 250 livres each, promising to pay the face-value of 500 livres for each share in six months' time whatever it cost then. Behind this absurd, as it appeared to many, transaction was some shrewd calculation which turned out to be justified. In six

---

[1] Karl Marx, *Capital*, Vol. I, Moscow, 1972, p. 588.

months the shares were worth several times their face-value and Law pocketed an enormous profit.

But this was not the main thing. The odd hundred thousand was not particularly important to him now. His aim was to attract attention to the shares, to interest buyers. At the same time he was expanding the company's business with great energy on a large scale. He combined real business with skilful publicity, thereby anticipating future practice in this too.

Law began the colonisation of the Mississippi Valley and founded town called New Orleans in honour of the Regent. Since there were not enough voluntary settlers, the government began to deport thieves, vagabonds and prostitutes to America at the company's request. At the same time Law organised the printing and distribution of all sorts of enticing literature about a fabulously rich land whose inhabitants were delighted to meet French people and brought gold, precious stones and other riches in exchange for knick-knacks. He even sent Jesuits there to convert the Red Indians to Catholicism.

Law's company devoured several French colonial companies which were doing badly and became an all-powerful monopoly. The few dozen old vessels which it owned were transformed by Law's words and his assistants' pens into vast fleets bearing silver and silks, spices and tobacco to France. In France itself the company took over tax-farming and, to be fair, did the job far more sensibly and efficiently than its predecessors. In general, all this was a strange mixture of brilliant organisation and bold enterprise with impetuous adventurism and downright fraud.

Although the company paid extremely modest dividends its shares shot up like balloons in spring 1719. This was what Law had been waiting for. Skilfully manipulating the market he began to make new issues of shares, selling them at higher and higher prices. The demand for shares exceeded their issue and when new subscriptions were announced thousands of people queued night and day outside the company's offices. And this in spite of the fact that by September 1719 the company was selling its 500-livre shares at 5,000 livres. The influential and aristocratic did not queue, but besieged Law himself and the other directors with requests to be allowed to subscribe. For a share that cost 5,000 livres on issue could be sold the next day on the stock exchange for 7,000 or 8,000! History has recorded some remarkable episodes: people trying to get into Law's office by climbing down the chimney; or a noblewoman ordering her coachman to overturn the carriage outside Law's house to lure out the gallant gentleman and make him hear her plea. His secretary amassed a whole fortune out of bribes from petitioners waiting for an audience with Law.

The Regent Philippe's mother, a caustic old lady, who left a record of this fantastic time in her letters to relatives in Germany, wrote: "They are running after Law so that he has no peace day or night. A duchess has publicly kissed his hands. If duchesses are kissing his hands what parts of his body are other women ready to honour?" In a letter dated 9 November, 1719 she relates: "Recently in the company of several ladies, he expressed the desire to leave the room. They would not let him go and he was forced to admit his reason. 'Oh, that does not matter,' they announced. 'That's nothing; relieve yourself here and we will just go on talking.' So they stayed with him." [1]

Even stranger things were happening in the Rue Quincampoix where the Stock Exchange had grown up and prospered. From dawn to dusk it was packed with crowds buying and selling, asking prices and making calculations. The 500-livre shares rose to 10,000, then 15,000 stopping at 20,000. The orgy of sudden wealth united all estates, which otherwise never mixed, not even in church. The noblewoman jostled next to the cabby, the duke haggled with the footman, and the abbot wetted his fingers settling up with the shopkeeper. The only god here was money!

People were reluctant to accept gold and silver in payment for shares. At the height of the boom ten shares were the same price as 1.4 or 1.5 tons of silver! Almost all payment was made in notes. And all this paper wealth—the shares and the bank notes—were the creation of that financial wizard Law.

In January 1720 Law officially became controller general of finance. He had in fact been managing the country's finances for a long time. But it was at this point that the first subterranean tremors were felt under his system.

Where did the company invest the vast sums which it amassed from new share issues? A small amount went on ships and commodities and the bulk on national debt bonds. In fact it shouldered the whole vast national debt (up to 2,000 million livres) by buying up bonds from their owners. This was the

---

[1] C. Kunstler, *La vie quotidienne sous la Régence*, Paris, 1960, p. 121.

establishment of order in finance which Law had promised. How was it possible to float more and more shares? Only because Law's bank kept on printing and circulating millions of new notes.

This state of affairs could not last for long. Law refused to see it, but his numerous enemies and ill-wishers, as well as simply farsighted speculators had already seen it. They naturally hastened to get rid of their shares and bank notes. Law reacted by supporting a steady price on the shares and restricting the exchange of notes for metal. But since money was necessary to support the shares, Law printed more and more of it. The numerous directives he issued in these months show signs of confusion. Law was fighting a losing battle, and the system was collapsing. By autumn 1720 the notes had turned into inflationary paper money worth only a quarter of their nominal value in silver. The prices of all commodities shot up. There was a food shortage in Paris and popular discontent grew. In November the notes ceased to be legal tender. The liquidation of the system had begun.

Law continued to fight hard to the last ditch. In July he barely escaped an enraged crowd which was demanding that the valueless papers be exchanged for legal tender, and had difficulty in finding refuge in the Regent's palace. Everyone remarked that he had become haggard, lost his customary self-assurance and courtesy. His nerves began to crack.

Many couplets, anecdotes and caricatures circulated around Paris ridiculing Law and also the Regent. The Duke of Bourbon, who was rumoured to have made 25 million livres through share speculation and invested them in material valuables, assured Law that he was now out of danger: the Parisians did not kill those they ridiculed. But Law had reason to think otherwise and never appeared without a strong bodyguard, although he had already been relieved of the post of minister. The Paris parlement, which had always opposed Law, demanded that he be tried and hanged. The Duke's trusted advisers suggested that he should at least be put away in the Bastille. Philippe began to realise that it would be better to get rid of his favourite in order to calm the unrest. His last favour was to allow Law to leave France.

In December 1720 John Law went secretly to Brussels with his son, leaving his wife, daughter and brother in Paris. All his possessions were confiscated and used to pay off creditors.

What did Law's system and its collapse mean from the social point of view? This has been a point of dispute for some 250 years.

In the 18th century Law was generally severely criticised, but there was more moral contumely in this than sober assessment. In the middle of the last century Louis Blanc in his *Histoire de la révolution française* and other socialists of similar views "rehabilitated" Law and even tried to depict him as a forerunner of socialism. Louis Blanc says that Law attacked gold and silver as the "money of the rich" and wanted to fill circulation with the "money of the poor", paper money. Through his all-embracing bank and trading monopoly Law is alleged to have been trying to assert the socialist principle of association against the bourgeois principle of cutthroat competition. Louis Blanc portrays some of Law's economic measures as a deliberate policy to ease the life of the working people.

This is somewhat remote from the truth. In the form in which Law wished to apply it the principle of association is a purely bourgeois principle. It stands in opposition not to capitalism, but to feudalism with its inert division of society into estates and absence of social mobility. Law wanted to bring together and make equal all his company's shareholders and his bank's clients, aristocrat and bourgeois, craftsman and businessman, but to bring them together as capitalists.

By his system Law prepared what capitalism was later to achieve fully: "The bourgeoisie, historically, has played a most revolutionary part.

"The bourgeoisie wherever it has got the upper hand, has put an end to all feudal, patriarchal and idyllic relations. It has pitilessly torn asunder the motley feudal ties that bound man to his 'natural superiors' and has left remaining no other nexus between man and man than naked self-interest, than callous 'cash-payments'." [1]

Law was no defender of the oppressed classes even in the limited sense that Boisguillebert was. In his writings we see none of that true compassion for the people, the peasant, which can be found in the Rouen judge. Moreover it was quite incompatible with his character of adventurer, gambler and

---

[1] Karl Marx and Frederick Engels, *Selected Works*, in three volumes, Vol. 1, Moscow, 1973, p. 111.

profiteer. Law expressed the interests of the big moneyed bourgeoisie. He placed his hopes on its entrepreneurial spirit. Such was his policy too. He supported his company's shares, which were owned by the big capitalists, to the very last, leaving the bank notes, which were distributed among a wider public, to the mercy of fate.

The system and its collapse produced a considerable redistribution of wealth and income. It undermined even further the position of the nobility, who sold estates and mansions to join in the speculating. The events of the Regency period weakened the position of the monarchy and aristocracy.

On the other hand, Law's financial wizardry hit the urban poor who suffered greatly from the rise in prices. When paper money was made illegal, it transpired that a very considerable amount had been accumulated in small sums by craftsmen, tradesmen, servants and even peasants.

One most important social result of Law's system was the rise of the *nouveau riche* who had managed to keep the wealth amassed through wild speculation.

Law lived another eight years after his flight from Paris. He was poor. Naturally not as poor as a person starving to death but as someone who did not always have his own equipage and rented a modest apartment rather than a mansion. He was homeless, but he had always led the life of an exile and wanderer. He was never again to see his wife (whom he had never actually got round to marrying) or his daughter: he was not allowed to enter France and they were forbidden to leave it.

For the first few years he still hoped to return, to vindicate himself and continue his activity. He showered the Regent with letters in which he explained and defended everything again and again. In these letters the substance of his economic ideas remained the same, except that he proposed acting with more caution and patience.

In 1723 Philippe of Orleans died suddenly. All Law's hopes for a return of his post and possessions, and even the modest pension which the Regent had begun paying him, immediately collapsed. Men came to power who did not even wish to hear of him. At this time Law was living in London. The English government thought him sufficiently influential and shrewd to entrust with a semi-secret commission to Germany. He spent about a year in Aachen and Munich.

Law was now but a shadow of the great financier and all-powerful minister. He turned loquacious, talking constantly about his affairs, defending himself and accusing his enemies. There was no lack of an audience: people thought the Scot knew the secret of turning paper into gold. Many assumed that he could not have been stupid enough not to put by part of his fortune outside France, and hoped to profit from it. The more superstitious thought he was a magician.

Law's last two years were spent in Venice. He divided his leisure between gambling (a passion of which only the grave cured him), chatting with his still numerous visitors and work on the voluminous *Histoire des Finances pendant la Régence*. This work was written in an attempt to vindicate himself to his heirs. It was first published two hundred years later. In 1728 he was visited by the famous Montesquieu on a journey round Europe. He found Law grown somewhat decrepit, but just as passionately convinced that he was right and ready to defend his ideas. John Law died of pneumonia in Venice in March 1729.

LAW AND THE 20TH CENTURY

His contemporaries thought that the monstrous excesses of Law's system could never be repeated. But they were wrong. Law's system was not the end, but the beginning or, rather, the herald of an age. His enterprises which astounded the imagination of the people of his day, now seem like children's playthings compared with what capitalism of the 19th and 20th centuries has erected.

In the middle of the last century Law's ideas, his Banque Générale and Mississippi Company, were resurrected, so to say, in the enterprises of the shrewd Pereire brothers, the Paris joint-stock bank Crédit Mobilier. Napoleon III played the same role of patron and exploiter in respect of this speculative colossus as the Regent Philippe in Law's institutions. Asking what means this bank used to "multiply its operations" and subject the whole of France's industrial development to the play of the stock-exchange, Marx replies: "Why, the same as Law used"[1], and goes on to explain the similarity in more detail.

---

[1] Karl Marx, Friedrich Engels, *Werke*, Bd. 12, Berlin, 1969, S. 32.

The Crédit Mobilier went bankrupt just before the Franco-Prussian war, but it played an historical role of some importance, laying the foundations for a new era in banking — the creation of speculative banks closely linked with industry. It was from the development of large joint-stock companies which gained the commanding heights in whole branches of industry, from the growth of the giant banks and their merging with industrial monopolies at the end of the 19th century that financial capital was formed.

But this was, so to say, "constructive" development. What about the excesses? What comparison can there be between Law's Mississippi adventure and the vast speculation of the group of businessmen who collected the money of 800,000 shareholders to build the Panama Canal and walked off with it? The word "panama" (a great swindle) became as common as the word "Mississippi" in Law's day.

And how can one compare the collapse of Law's system with the collapse of the New York Stock Exchange in 1929 or Law's inflation with the "super-inflation" of the 20th century, when money lost its value several million times over (Germany in the 1920s and Greece in the 1940s). It is difficult to overestimate the importance of the problem of inflation for modern capitalism. Inflation has become the "norm", a permanent feature of capitalist economy. It increases economic difficulties, intensifies social conflicts and promotes currency crises. Of course, modern inflation is an incomparably more complex and many-sided phenomenon than the depreciation of John Law's paper money. Modern inflation is a general economic process, which is often connected with the surplus issue of paper money, but occasionally takes place without this. In many cases the primary factor of inflation is a rise in prices, which is not directly linked with the "monetary" aspect but produced by other causes: a monopolist policy, a shortage of goods or foreign trade situation. But then the increase in the amount of money "props", so to speak, the rising level of prices, fixes it and may, in its turn, encourage inflation. Both the amount of money and the level of prices have acquired a one-way elasticity in modern conditions — they only rise, never fall. This law in embryo already existed in Law's system.

Law's personality as a financier with a fertile imagination, scope and energy has also been "repeated" many times in subsequent history. Capitalism needs such men and gives birth to them. They are sometimes real people such as Isaac Pereire or John Pierpont Morgan, or fictional characters like the stock-exchange magnate Saccard, the main character in Zola's novel *L'argent*, and Cowperwood, Dreiser's titanic and stoical financier....

Law's financial practice and ideas played an important part in establishing and developing political economy. True, he had to wait a century or more for direct disciples in the science. On the other hand, although the brilliant development of political economy in the 18th and early 19th centuries proceeded to a large extent from Law's ideas, it proceeded by rejecting them as dangerous and pernicious heresy. The struggle against this heresy was of considerable importance in forming the views of Quesnay, Turgot, Smith and Ricardo. Analysing the development of French political economy, Marx notes: "The emergence of the Physiocrats was connected both with the opposition to Colbertism and, in particular, with the hullabaloo over the John Law system"[1].

The classics' criticism of Law was progressive and aimed in the right direction. It was part of their struggle against mercantilism with which Law had much in common. Of course, he was very different from the primitive mercantilists who reduced all economic problems to money and the balance of trade. He regarded money mainly as an instrument for influencing economic development. But he did not advance beyond the superficial sphere of circulation and did not even attempt to understand the complex anatomy and physiology of capitalist production. And this was precisely what the classics of bourgeois political economy tried to do.

Relying upon monetary factors Law naturally linked all his hopes with the state. Right from the start he wanted a state bank and only temporary difficulties forced him to agree at first to a private one. His trading monopoly was a peculiar appendage of the state. Law was inconsistent in his economic policy: he abolished some state regulatory measures which were hampering the economy and immediately introduced others. He enjoyed the support of a feudal bureaucratic state, but it was against the crude and onerous intervention of such a state in the economy that the Physiocrats and Smith fought. In this respect too Boisguillebert was much closer to them than Law.

[1] Karl Marx, *Theories of Surplus-Value*, Part I, p. 59.

However, in rejecting the concept of credit as creating capital, which Law advanced and sought to put into practice, the classics underestimated the important part which credit plays in developing production. They threw the baby out with the bath water, so to say. Law's views on credit are at least more interesting than Ricardo's, although on the whole he cannot be compared with the most important exponent of classical bourgeois political economy.

Law did not believe in the predetermined harmony of the "natural order", in the omnipotence of *laissez faire*. Here too he revealed an awareness of the contradictions of capitalism. It was the aggravation of these contradictions which forced bourgeois science to review its attitude towards Law. His rehabilitation at the time of Louis Blanc and Isaac Pereira was not the last one. A new rehabilitation, from a different standpoint of course, is being carried out by the followers of Keynes, the ideologists of state monopoly capitalism.

Both Law's main ideas, i. e., that of influencing the economy through the sphere of credit and finance, and that of the great role of the state in the economy, fitted perfectly here. At the beginning of this chapter we quoted the words of a modern writer about the likeness between Law and Keynes. This is not the only paradoxical statement. In France, for example, a book has come out entitled *John Law et naissance du dirigisme*. Dirigisme is the French version of state economic planning.

In the United States changes in rates of taxation on capitalist companies and individuals can be made only with the sanction of Congress. This is an old bourgeois democratic measure which limits the executive. Today the government's economic advisers are most dissatisfied with this state of affairs: the manipulation of taxes is a most important weapon of modern economic policy and they would like to have full control of it. This reminds us of Law who was delighted at the way questions could be solved in France at that time. "It is a fortunate country where action can be considered, decided upon and carried out within twenty-four hours instead of twenty-four years like England". He was not worried by the fact that France was a despotic absolute monarchy and that was the only reason why things could be done so quickly.

Law's ideas on the positive role of an abundance of money and inflation are resurrected time and again in the different versions of bourgeois economists. They seek in "moderate inflation" a solution to economic crises, unemployment and economic depression. If pursued, however, this policy creates its own acute problems and conflicts. The profession of an economist in the West is that of a doctor at the sick bed of capitalism. The best these doctors can do is occasionally relieve the symptoms of the disease.

CHAPTER VI

PRE-ADAM ECONOMICS

In the century from Petty to Adam Smith economic science came a long way — from the first rudiments of the classical school to its formation into a system, from individual, sometimes random pamphlets to the definitive *Wealth of Nations*. The content and form of this work determined the nature of the treatises on economic theory written in the following century and even after.

As Marx wrote, "that period[1], which abounded in original thinkers, is therefore the most important for the investigation of the gradual genesis of political economy"[2]. Of course, we shall only be able to touch upon a few of the outstanding scholars and writers who, brick by brick, erected the edifice of classical political economy in England. Some of their ideas are also interesting from the point of view of modern problems.

---

[1] Marx is referring to the period from 1691 to 1752: from the publication of the works of Locke and North, which developed Petty's ideas, to the appearance of the main economic works of Hume, a close forerunner of Smith.

[2] Frederick Engels, *Anti-Dühring*, Moscow, 1969, p. 280 (Chapter X of Part II of *Anti-Dühring* was written by K. Marx).

One might say that the Britain of the new age was formed in the first half of the 18th century. This period consolidated the class compromise between the landowning nobility and the bourgeoisie. The interests of both exploiter classes merged and intertwined closely. The nobility became bourgeois and the bourgeoisie became landowners.

A political system grew up which basically remains to this very day and which for two centuries represented the bourgeois democratic ideal. It consisted of a parliamentary monarchy, where the king reigns but does not rule; two parties which replace each other from time to time in power; personal liberty and freedom of the press and speech unprecedented in the Europe of the time, which however could in fact be used only by the privileged and rich sections of society.

The Tories, the conservative party of the landowners, and the Whigs, the liberal party of the higher educated aristocracy and urban bourgeoisie, began their endless parliamentary and electoral battles. An important function of these battles was to distract the "lower classes" from the real controversial questions of the class struggle.

To a large extent the political struggle lost the religious complexion which it had in the preceding century. Alongside the official Church of England a number of former Puritan sects were also established and England became the "island of a hundred religions". But this did not hinder the socio-economic development of the bourgeois nation. As the English historian G. M. Trevelyan notes: "While religion divided, trade united the nation, and trade was gaining in relative importance. The Bible had now a rival in the Ledger."[1]

The Empire grew rapidly. North America was colonised, sugar and tobacco plantations flourished in the West Indies, India and Canada were conquered, and a large number of islands discovered in various parts of the globe. The wars waged by England were mainly successful. It became the world's undisputedly greatest maritime and trading power. In particular, English merchants practically had a monopoly on the slave trade and delivered many thousands of Negroes to America each year.

---

[1] G. M. Trevelyan, *English Social History*, London, 1944, p. 295.

Of course at the basis of all these processes lay changes in England's economy. First and foremost, the countryside was changing, English agriculture, which in the middle of the century was still producing about three times more than industry. The enclosure of land became particularly extensive at this time. Small peasant holdings and common land were gradually disappearing, giving way to large estates which were rented out in plots to rich farmers. This promoted the development of capitalism in both agriculture and industry.

There was a rapid growth in the class of hired workers without land or property, who possessed nothing but their own hands. This class was formed at the expense of the peasants who had lost their land or their ancient right of semifeudal leasing, and handicraftsmen and artisans who had been ruined by competition. But the real manufacturing proletariat still constituted an insignificant part of the "lower classes". There were many patriarchal features and vestiges of the "good old days" in capitalist exploitation. The horrors of industrial slavery were still to come.

At the other extreme the class of industrial capitalists was growing. It was joined by rich proprietor master craftsmen, merchants, and colonial planters who brought to England the fortunes they had amassed abroad. The subjection of production to capital was a complex process: often capitalists first penetrated as buyers-up and suppliers of raw material in cottage industries, then founded handicraft workshops and factories.

This was the end of the age of manufacture, i.e., handmade produce, based on the division of labour. Even with the former primitive instruments division of labour and specialisation of workers made it possible to increase productivity. Machine industry was just being born. The age of the great inventions was beginning. In the 1730s the first steps were taken towards the mechanisation of spinning and weaving and coke smelting was discovered. In the 1760s Watt invented the steam engine.

Credit was needed — by industrialists for their enterprises, merchants for foreign trade, and the government for colonial wars. This produced the emergence and rapid growth of banks and joint-stock companies which collected money capital. The national debt rose considerably. Securities and the stock exchange came into use. Alongside the industrial and trading capitalist whose main form of income was profit, there appeared the competent figure of the moneyed capitalist who received his portion of surplus value in the form of interest on loans.

Commodity and money relations already permeated the whole life of the nation. Not only trade but also production became capitalist to a large extent. The basic classes of bourgeois society stood out more distinctly. As a result of the mass repetition of social phenomena such objective categories as capital, profit, interest, land rent and wages became clearly defined. All this could now be the object of observation and scientific analysis.

On the other hand, the bourgeoisie was still the most progressive class in society. It had not yet recognised the growing working class as its main adversary. The class struggle between them was still in embryonic form. Thus the conditions were formed for the development of classical political economy in England.

POLITICAL ECONOMY LIKES ROBINSONADES

The first edition of Daniel Defoe's novel *Robinson Crusoe* appeared in London in 1719. Its fate was an unusual one. On the one hand, it is an acknowledged masterpiece of the adventure story. On the other, the literature in many languages giving a philosophical, pedagogical and politico-economic interpretation of *Robinson Crusoe* and other Robinsonades could today fill a whole library.

A Robinsonade is a situation invented by a thinker and writer in which a single person (sometimes a group of people) is placed in living and working conditions outside society. It is, if you like, an economic model in which relations between people, i.e., social relations, are excluded and only the relations of an isolated individual with nature remain. Political economy likes Robinsonades, Marx remarked. One might add that this is even truer of post-Marxian than pre-Marxian bourgeois political economy.

In spite of the success of *Robinson Crusoe*, which Defoe wrote at the age of almost sixty, and of other novels written even later, he regarded them as trifling to the end of his life. Defoe thought that the numerous political, economic and historical works which his pen had produced would bring him posthumous fame. Such illusions are not uncommon in the history of culture.

Defoe's own life was like an adventure story. He was born in London in 1660 (there is some doubt about this date) and died there in 1731. The son of a Puritan small trader, Defoe made his own way in life thanks to his natural ability, energy and wit. A participant in the Monmouth rebellion of 1685 against King James II, he managed to escape execution or deportation to the colonies only by a fortunate accident. A wealthy merchant by the age of thirty, he went bankrupt in 1692 with debts amounting to £ 17,000.

It was at this time that Defoe began writing political pamphlets and won the confidence of William III (William of Orange) and his close advisers. In 1698 he published an economic work entitled *Essay on Projects* in which he proposed a number of bold economic and administrative reforms.

Shortly after the death of the king, his patron, in 1703, Defoe was pilloried and sent to prison for a caustic pamphlet against the Church of England in defence of Puritan dissenters. He was released from prison (where he spent eighteen months and wrote prolifically) by the Tory party leader, Robert Harley. In exchange for this Defoe devoted his pen, the pen of the finest journalist of his day, to the Tory party and Harley personally. He became Harley's secret agent and travelled to Scotland and various parts of England on important and confidential missions from him.

The death of Queen Anne and the fall of Harley put an abrupt end to his career. In 1715 he was again sent to prison on a charge of political libel. He gained his freedom having once more undertaken an unenviable task — to sabotage from the inside press organs hostile to the new government.

The man who wrote *Robinson Crusoe* possessed a wealth of experience. This is what gave the story of the adventures of the seafarer from York such profundity. Defoe knew neither rest nor peace to the end of his days. It is difficult to believe that between the age of sixty and seventy a man could write several large novels, a voluminous economic and geographical description of Great Britain, a number of historical essays (including one on the Russian Emperor Peter I), a whole series of books on demonology and magic (!) and a multitude of small articles and pamphlets on the most varied topics. In 1728 he published an economic work entitled *A Plan of the English Commerce.*

Let us return to Robinsonades. At the basis of bourgeois classical political economy lay the idea of the natural man. This idea arose out of an unconscious protest against the "artificiality" of feudal society, in which man was constrained by all manner of coercive relations and restrictions. But the "natural" man of the new bourgeois society, the individualist freed from these relations and fitted for the world of free competition and equal opportunities, was regarded by Smith and Ricardo, and by their predecessors, not as the product of lengthy historical development but, on the contrary, its point of departure, the embodiment of "human nature".

In seeking to explain the behaviour of this individualist in social production under capitalism, they based themselves on the ideas of "natural law" and focussed their attention not on the actual development of society, but on the imaginary figure of the solitary hunter and fisherman. Of course, this means that a concrete Robinson Crusoe who finds himself on a desert island is turned by the authors into something allegorical and abstract, often entirely conventional.

Thus, the Robinsonade is an attempt to examine the laws of production, which is of necessity always social and linked with a concrete stage in historical development, on an abstract model which excludes the main factor—society. Marx made an extremely profound criticism of the classical political economy Robinsonade. He remarked that this inclination had moved to the "latest political economy" of the mid-19th century: it now very conveniently found the economic relations characteristic of developed capitalism in the imaginary world of the "natural man". Let us quote a single sentence from Marx: "The production of an isolated individual outside society—a rare thing which could happen to a civilised person accidentally cast into the wilderness, who *already contains social forces in himself dynamically* (my italics—A. A.)—is just as absurd as the development of a language without individuals who live and speak together."[1]

The underlined passage is interesting in connection with the plot of *Robinson Crusoe*. Remember that Robinson bears social forces to such an extent that in changed circumstances he rapidly turns from a "natural man", first into a patriarchal

---

[1] Karl Marx, *Grundrisse der Kritik der Politischen Ökonomie*, Moskau, 1939, p. 6.

slave-owner (Man Friday), and then into a feudal lord (the colony of settlers). He would have turned into a capitalist too if his society had continued to develop.

The Robinsonade was a real find for the subjective school in political economy, which attempts to examine economic phenomena in the light of individual feelings and psychology. This trend in political economy, which arose in the 1870s, focussed attention on the "atomistic individual". One can hardly imagine a more suitable figure than Robinson Crusoe.

A typical example is the Robinsonade of Böhm-Bawerk (1851-1914), an eminent economist of the Austrian subjective school. The author twice makes Robinson Crusoe serve as the point of departure for his argument—in the theory of value and the theory of the accumulation of capital.

Writers in the 17th and 18th centuries had already realised that value is a social relation, which exists only when things are produced as commodities, for exchange within society. All Böhm-Bawerk needs to introduce the concept of value is, as he himself puts it, "a colonist whose log cabin stands far from all communications in a virgin forest". This Robinson has five sacks of corn and the value of the corn is measured by the usefulness of the last of them.

Capital is the social relation between those who possess the means of production and those who are deprived of them, who sell their labour and are subjected to exploitation. It arises only at a specific stage of social development. But for Böhm-Bawerk it is simply any instruments of labour in their material form. Therefore as long as Robinson is engaged in picking wild fruit he has no capital. But as soon as he sets aside part of his labour time to make himself a bow and arrows, he becomes a capitalist: this is the initial act of accumulating capital. As we can see, capital is accumulated by means of simple economy and is not connected with any form of exploitation.

The tradition of the Robinsonade is so strong in bourgeois political economy that it has become difficult to write a book on economic theory without mentioning Robinson. The modern American economist Paul A. Samuelson opens his textbook with the dubious statement that the economic problems confronting Robinson were fundamentally no different from the problems of a large society.

THE PARADOXES OF DOCTOR MANDEVILLE

In the same London coffee houses and bookshops frequented by Defoe another colourful figure could also be found — Doctor Bernard Mandeville. A doctor without a practice, an inhabitant of the poor quarter and a lover of carousing in merry company, Mandeville enjoyed an unenviable reputation. It was said that he lived mainly on money from distillers and brewers who paid him for defending alcoholic liquor in the press.

Bernard de Mandeville was born in Holland in 1670. Shortly after leaving Leyden University in 1691 he went to live in England. He married, settled in London, became an English subject and, after living a life the details of which are little known, died there in 1733.

Mandeville owes his fame as a philosopher and writer to a single work. In 1705 he published anonymously a short poem in mediocre verse entitled *The Grumbling Hive, or Knaves Turn'd Honest*. The work attracted little attention. In 1714 Mandeville republished the same poem, adding a lengthy dissertation in prose. This time it was called the *Fable of the Bees, or Private Vices, Public Benefits*. It is under this title that Mandeville's book has become famous.

But this edition, too, appears to have gone unnoticed. It was only a new edition of the *Fable of the Bees* published in 1723, which bore the high-sounding subtitle of *A Search into the Nature of Society* that produced the reaction. Mandeville must have hoped for. The grand jury of Middlesex found the book a "nuisance", and a controversy flared up in the press around it, in which Mandeville took part with obvious relish. Another five editions came out in the author's lifetime, and in 1729 he published a second volume of the *Fable of the Bees*.

The monumental Oxford edition contains a long list of references to Mandeville in the literature of two centuries. He was written about by Marx and Adam Smith, Voltaire and Macaulay, Malthus and Keynes.

Mandeville had a great influence on the development of English political economy, particularly on Smith and Malthus (although amusingly enough they both disown him as a coarse cynic!). This influence was not on the elaboration of main categories (value, capital, profit, etc.), but more on the fundamental philosophical attitude on which the classical school was based.

Mandeville's main paradox is contained in the phrase "private vices made public benefits". Replace "vices" by the famous Smithian "self-interest" and you have Smith's main thesis about capitalist society: if each individual is allowed to pursue his own gain, sensibly, this will promote the wealth and flourishing of the whole society. In his book *The Theory of Moral Sentiments* Smith criticised Mandeville as follows: the author of the *Fable of the Bees* is wrong only in that he calls all egoistic striving and action a "vice". Self-interest, say, is not a vice at all.

But Mandeville's importance for the history of economic science does not stop at this. In his satire he made a biting criticism of bourgeois society and was one of the first to discover its basic vices. This was his alleged "amorality". Marx called him "an honest, clear-headed man".[1]

The beehive is human society, or rather, bourgeois England in Mandeville's day. The first part of the fable is a satire on it worthy of the pen of Swift. The central idea is that such a society exists and flourishes only because of the innumerable vices, absurdities and crimes that abound in it. "Flourishing" is possible in this society only because millions of people are

> ... *damn'd to Sythes and Spades,*
> *And all those hard laborious Trades;*
> *Where willing Wretches daily sweat,*
> *And wear out Strength and Limbs to eat...*

But they only have this work because the rich like comfort and luxury and spend a lot of money on things the need for which is often dictated by fashion, imagination, vanity, etc. Greedy litigious lawyers, charlatan physicians, lazy and ignorant priests, pugnacious generals, even criminals — they are all, contrary to common sense, vital in this society. Why? Because their activity engenders demand for all manner of goods and services, encouraging industry, invention and enterprise.

Thus, in this society

---

[1] Karl Marx, *Capital*, Vol. I, Moscow, 1972, p. 577.

[2] B. Mandeville, *The Fable of the Bees. Or, Private Vices, Public Benefits. With an Essay on Charity and Charity-Schools. And a Search into the Nature of Society*, 5th edition, London, 1728, p. 3.

> *...Luxury*
> *Employ'd a Million of the Poor,*
> *And odious Pride a Million more.*
> *Envy itself, and Vanity*
> *Were Ministers of Industry,*
> *Their darling Folly, Fickleness*
> *On Diet, Furniture and Dress,*
> *That strange ridic'lous Vice, was made*
> *The very Wheel, that turn'd the Trade.*[1]

(One cannot help recalling here, for example, the American automobile companies, which change their models every year for no technical reason whatsoever, only in order to play on the vanity of the buyers and increase sales at any price. The directors of these companies could well agree with Mandeville that the flourishing of the industry is based on "fickleness" and other human weaknesses, and that these weaknesses are deliberately encouraged.)

But the bees are grumbling at the prevalence of vice in their hive, and Jupiter, tired of their complaints, suddenly drives away vice and makes the bees virtuous. Thrift takes the place of extravagance. Luxury vanishes, and the consumption of everything exceeding simple natural needs ceases. The parasitic professions are abolished. Freed from chauvinism and aggressive inclinations

> *They have no Forces kept Abroad;*
> *Laugh at th' Esteem of Foreigners,*
> *And empty Glory got by Wars.*[2]

In a word, normal, healthy principles of human society prevail. But, horrors! It is this that brings ruin and collapse to the society which Mandeville has depicted in poetic form:

> *Now mind the glorious Hive, and see,*
> *How Honesty and Trade agree:*
> *The Shew is gone, it thinks apace;*
> *And looks with quite another Face,*
> *For 'twas not only that they went,*
> *By whom vast Sums were Yearly spent;*
> *But Multitudes, that lived on them,*
> *Were daily forc'd to do the Same.*

---

[1] B. Mandeville, op. cit.. p. 10.
[2] Ibid., p. 18.

> *In vain to other Trades they'd fly;*
> *All were O're-stock'd accordingly....*
> *The Building Trade is quite destroy'd,*
> *Artificers are not employ'd,*
> *No Limner for his Art is famed;*
> *Stone-cutters, Carvers are not named.* [1]

In short, an economic crisis begins: unemployment rises, goods pile up in the warehouses, prices and incomes drop and construction ceases. What a society in which parasites, warmongers, spendthrifts and rogues bring prosperity, and such unqualified virtues as love of peace, honesty, thrift, and moderation lead to economic disaster!

Mandeville's ideas, which he developed in grotesque, paradoxical form (they are expounded more soberly in the later prose section of the *Fable*) are particularly interesting in the light of the development of political economy in the succeeding centuries. Let us mention two most important facts.

The idea that all classes and strata (landowners, priests, officials, etc.) are productive and economically necessary was taken up by Malthus and his followers. In a small pamphlet contained in the *Theories of Surplus-Value* Marx uses Mandeville's ideas and even his style to disprove this view. He writes: "... Mandeville had already shown that every possible kind of occupation is productive.... Only Mandeville was of course infinitely bolder and more honest than the philistine apologists of bourgeois society." [2]

The idea that excessive thrift is harmful and that unproductive expenditure, any form of extravagance, is beneficial, even essential, as long as it creates demand and employment has been resurrected and canonised in our day by Keynes. He regarded Mandeville (and Malthus) as his precursor.

By the end of the 19th century bourgeois political economy, which refused to see any vices in the capitalist system, regarded Mandeville as a charlatan and cunning casuist. It did not even occur to anyone to criticise the thrift which Adam Smith had elevated into the greatest private and public virtue. Only the world economic crisis of 1929-33 made leading bourgeois economists start thinking along Mandeville's lines: if people start saving they will not purchase commodities, which means a

---

[1] Ibid., pp. 18-19.
[2] Karl Marx, *Theories of Surplus-Value*, Part I, Moscow, 1969, p. 388.

drop in "effective demand"; people must be made to spend their money in any way and for any purpose.

The paradoxes of Doctor Mandeville are now more than 250 years old. But they are still alive, like the society which he examined with his critical eye.

THE FORMATION OF THE CLASSICAL SCHOOL

It is generally accepted that political economy was first taught as a separate science in 1801 in Edinburgh University by Dugald Stewart, a pupil and friend of Smith's. The economics professor did not become a familiar figure until the 19th century, although an important contribution continued to be made in the science by people who were not professors at all. The talented men who created the new science in the 17th and 18th centuries fall into three main categories.

Firstly, there are the philosophers who studied economic questions within the framework of their general systems of nature and society characteristic of the particular age. The most outstanding of them are Thomas Hobbes, John Locke, David Hume and, in a sense, Adam Smith, in England, Helvetius and Condillac in France, and Beccaria in Italy.

Next come the merchants and businessmen, who moved from the narrow practice of trade to public affairs and strove to think as statesmen. Here one might mention the names of Thomas Mun, John Law, Dudley North and Richard Cantillon. In France Boisguillebert, Turgot and Gournay represented the judicial and administrative branch characteristic of that country.

Thirdly and finally, there are the intellectual commoners, people of various professions, who sometimes moved into the upper class and sometimes did not. Marx noted that medical men, William Petty, Nicholas Barbon, Bernard de Mandeville and François Quesnay, were good students of political economy. This is understandable for medicine was the only specialised natural science in those days and attracted energetic, thinking people. Churchmen appeared among the economists of the 18th century, abbots in France and Italy (including the profound and original Italian economist Fernando Galiani) and Anglican ministers in England (Tucker, Malthus).

It must be noted that these categories are most conventional and certainly do not determine the development of ideas, but they help us to understand the complicated process of the growth of the science.

The main motive behind economic writing remains the practical one of arguing or defending a particular economic policy. Yet the works of Turgot and James Steuart which appeared in the 1760s differ greatly from the merchantilist pamphlets of the 17th and early 18th centuries. They were the first attempts at a systematic and theoretical exposition of the basic principles of political economy.

Moreover the "practical motive" takes a variety of forms. In the case of some writers it is the direct defence in the press of the interests of their class and their own personal interests. In others it is the more profound process of the scientific study of social phenomena, which takes account of class interest only in a complex and mediatory form. It hardly need be said that classical bourgeois political economy was created by men of the latter kind. Adam Smith, say, was neither a merchant nor an industrialist and could not expect to benefit personally from the policy of free trade which he argued in *The Wealth of Nations.* Moreover, it was one of the paradoxes of his life that after the book came out he received a salaried post in the customs, an institution which embodied the system against which he was fighting.

For all the brilliance of his paradoxes, Mandeville stands somewhat apart in the formation of the classical school in England. It is linked first and foremost with the names of Locke (1632-1704) and North (1641-1691) who were Petty's direct successors.

A most eminent 18th-century philosopher, one of the creators of the materialist theory of cognition and the father of bourgeois liberalism, Locke occupies an important place in economic science thanks to his work *Some Considerations of the Consequences of the Lowering of Interest and Raising the Value of Money* published in 1691. At the same time Locke's philosophy as a whole served as the foundation for English political economy in the 18th and even early 19th centuries. Locke developed in the social sciences the ideas of natural law, which were a kind of equivalent to the mechanistic materialism of Newton in the natural sciences. For their time these ideas, as mentioned earlier, were progressive ones, since they introduced the principle of objective law in the sphere of social phenomena. Even Locke's important advance towards an understanding of surplus value was made from the standpoint of natural law. He writes that man should naturally have as much land as he can cultivate by his own labour and as many other goods (including, evidently, money) as he needs for private consumption. Artificial inequality in the distribution of property leads to some people having a surplus of land and money; they rent out the land and loan the money. Locke regarded land rent and interest as two similar forms of exploiter income.

Dudley North was an original personality. The younger son of an aristocratic family, he demonstrated such meagre talents for learning in childhood, that he was apprenticed (like Thomas Mun) to a merchant in the Levant Company. North spent many years in Turkey and returned getting on for forty a rich man. But, as a writer puts it, "he looked a barbarian, and was not much more cultured than one". North revealed his janissary manners when he became Sheriff of the City of London in 1683 in the period of Tory reaction under Charles II. He served the king loyally and did great harm to the Whigs, for which he was knighted and became Sir Dudley. After this he occupied several important posts, but the Revolution of 1688-89 ruined his chances of a further career.

Without possessing, say, a tenth of Locke's erudition, Sir Dudley revealed an exceptional talent for precise and bold economic thought which recognised no authorities. His small work *Discourse Upon Trade*, written at the same time as Locke's work and dealing with the same questions, is one of the finest achievements of 17th-century economic thought.

North did a great deal for the development of the basic scientific method of political economy — logical abstraction: in order to analyse an economic phenomenon, which is always infinitely complex and possesses countless relationships, one must imagine it in its "pure form", disregarding all inessential features and connections.

North took the first steps towards an understanding of capital, although it is true, that he examined it only in the form of monetary capital which yields interest. He showed that interest on loans is determined not by the quantity of money in the country (as the mercantilists and even Locke had thought), but by the relationship between the accumulation of monetary capital and the demand for it. This laid the foundation for the classical theory of interest, from which an understanding of the category of profit later emerged. North also did a great deal for the development of the theory of money.

But perhaps the main point about North was his sharp and fundamental criticism of mercantilism and his resolute defence of "natural freedom". The cause for this was his objecting (like Petty and Locke before him) to the compulsory regulation of interest. North went further than they, however, in the fight against mercantilism. In this respect he is one of the direct forerunners of Adam Smith.

Neither Locke nor North went further than Petty in the labour theory of value. But it was gradually developed and established in the numerous works of the 17th and 18th centuries, preparing the ground for Smith. The growth of the division of labour, the emergence of new branches of production, the expansion of commodity exchange — all this confirmed the idea that people were actually exchanging chunks of human labour. Consequently the ratio of exchange, the exchange values of commodities, must be determined by the amount of labour spent on the production of each commodity. There was a growing awareness that land and production instruments definitely play a part in the creation of wealth as use values, but bear no relation to the creation of value.

These ideas crystallised slowly, with great difficulty, from a chaotic confusion of concepts. Adam Smith reproduced this hard struggle of developing ideas in his own head and we shall attempt to describe it below. Among his most important predecessors in the theory of value were Richard Cantillon, Joseph Harris, William Temple, and Josiah Tucker, who wrote between the 1730s and 1750s.

A writer, about whom we can say nothing whatsoever because his name is Anonymous 1738[1], formulated the theory of value with splendid precision, excelling even Smith in a certain sense. Many economic works were published anonymously in the 17th and 18th centuries. The authors of some have long been established and others have not played a significant role in the science. Anonymous 1738 is an exception, a figure like the unknown masters of the "Life of Mary" or the "Legend of St. Ursula".

---

[1] This date, 1738, has not been fully authenticated.

Let us quote a key passage from this work which bears the modest title of *Some Thoughts on the Interest of Money in General.* For ease of analysis a commentary is given in the righthand column.

"The true and real value of the Necessaries of Life, is in Proportion to that Part which they contribute to the Maintenance of Mankind; and the Value of them when they are exchanged the one for the other, is regulated by the Quantity of Labour necessarily required, and commonly taken in producing them; and the Value or Price of them when they are brought and sold, and compared to a common Medium, will be govern'd by Quantity of Labour employ'd, and the greater or less Plenty of the Medium or common Measure. Water is as necessary for Life as Bread or Wine; but the Hand of God has poured out that upon Mankind in such Plenty that every Man may have enough of that without any Trouble, so that generally 'tis of no Price; but when and where any Labour must be used, to apply it to particular Persons, there the Labour in making the Application must be paid for, tho' the Water be not: And on that Account, at some Times and in some Places, a Ton of Water may be as dear as a Ton of Wine."[1]

The author is actually giving a definition of use value here.

A concept of exchange value is given which differs altogether from use value; the idea of socially necessary labour time is contained here in embryo.

The writer sees the difference between price and value and notes that price varies under the influence of a surplus or shortage of money.

This classic illustration of the so-called "paradox of value" shows the fundamental difference between use and exchange value.

The author states categorically that labour alone, not nature, creates value.

---

[1] Quotation taken from R. L. Meek, *Studies in the Labour Theory of Value,* London, 1956, pp. 42-43.

In connection with the development of the theory of value progress was being made in other important spheres as well. Developing Petty's idea that the wages of hired workers are determined in the final analysis by the minimum necessary for subsistence, economists came closer to an understanding of the nature of this minimum. By studying population problems they explained to a certain extent the mechanism which ensures reproduction of the labour force in such a way that competition between workers reduces wages to a bare minimum.

An important step in the understanding of capital and income from capital was the distinction between profit from trade and industry and interest on loans. Joseph Massie and David Hume, who wrote in the 1750s, already understood clearly that in normal conditions interest is a part of profit: the merchant and the industrialist are forced to share with the owner of money, of loan capital.

Thus, pre-Smithian political economy does actually examine surplus value, but treating it only in the special forms of profit, interest, and also land rent, without understanding its nature.

DAVID HUME

In March and April 1776 Hume, who was on his deathbed and knew it, hurriedly wrote the story of his life. He lived for another four months. The autobiography was published shortly after his death with a brief letter of introduction by Adam Smith, his closest friend for a quarter of a century. Smith described the philosopher's last months. Hume died with an enviable peace of mind and unusual resolution. A cheerful sociable person, he retained these qualities to the end, although sickness turned him from a corpulent man into a living skeleton.

Smith's letter played an unusual role in political economy. It left no doubt that Hume, who was already known to be an atheist, did not die a God-fearing Christian. Smith, too, shared this pagan spirit.

The fury of the Church descended on the deceased Hume and living Smith. Smith's recently published *The Wealth of Nations* was only noticed by a narrow circle of educated people at first. But the battle which raged around the names of Hume and Smith and which was an unpleasant surprise for Smith, a cautious and retiring man, attracted general attention to the book. One edition followed the other and in about ten years *The Wealth of Nations* had become the Bible of English political economy.

But Hume paved the way for Smith in another sense too. Hume's short, exquisitely composed essays, published mainly in 1752, give a concise summary as it were of the achievements of the pre-Smithian classical school in the struggle with mercantilism. They played an important role in preparing people's minds for *The Wealth of Nations*.

David Hume was born in Edinburgh in 1711, the youngest son of an impoverished nobleman. He was forced to make his own way in life, relying mainly on his masterly pen. Industry and thrift—the traditional Scottish virtues—he possessed in full measure.

At the age of twenty-eight Hume published his main philosophical work, the *Treatise of Human Nature*, which subsequently made him one of the most eminent 18th-century British philosophers. Hume's philosophy later became known as agnosticism. Like Locke Hume argued that feeling is the most important source of man's knowledge about material things, but he regarded these external things (matter) as fundamentally uncognisable in their entirety. He tried to find a place somewhere between materialism and idealism but by arguing the unknowability of the world inevitably gravitated to the latter. His criticism of religion made an important contribution to the struggle against obscurantism. But he was not a consistent atheist and his philosophy left a loophole for the "reconciliation" of science and religion.

Hume's book was not a success at first. He ascribed this to its complexity and set about popularising his ideas in short essays. In addition he turned to the philosophy of society. His initial success came with his political and economic works, and the multi-volume *History of England during the Reigns of James I and Charles I* brought him European fame. As an historian Hume supported the Tories, the landowners' party, which was also favoured by the conservative bourgeoisie. A refined intellectual, an "aristocrat of the spirit", Hume disliked the "Whig rabble", despised the coarseness of the shopkeepers and the stupidity of the Puritans, and referred to the rich London financiers as "barbarians on the banks of the Thames".

In 1763-65 Hume lived in Paris as secretary to the British Embassy. He was extremely popular in the salons and was friendly with many figures in the French Enlightenment. He then moved to an administrative post in London. His last years were spent in Edinburgh among close friends — scholars and men of letters.

Hume's economic writing contains many interesting thoughts and observations. For example, he would appear to be the first to point out, in modern economic language, the existence of time-lags in the process by which prices rise due to an increase in the amount of money in circulation. Hume noted, in particular, that of all commodity prices the "price of labour", i. e., workers' wages, was the last to rise. These important laws help us to understand the social and economic processes which take place when there is inflation of paper money.

More than anyone else in the 18th century Hume developed the idea that gold and silver are distributed naturally between countries and that each country's balance of trade strives naturally for equilibrium in the final analysis. The idea of natural equilibrium, which is typical of the whole classical school, is strongly expressed in Hume's writing. It provides the basis for his criticism of mercantilism with its policy of artificial attraction and retention of precious metals. The concept of the natural tendency of trade balances (or balances of payments, to be more precise) towards equilibrium was developed further by Ricardo. We shall return to this in the chapter on him.

Even Hume's correct observations, however, were linked with an interpretation of money which is at variance with the labour theory of value. Like the French, Hume managed without a theory of value; this may have been the result of his philosophical agnosticism and scepticism.

In political economy Hume is known primarily as one of the creators of the *quantity theory of money*. Hume and other writers who advanced similar views proceeded from the historical fact of the so-called price revolution. After gold and silver poured into Europe in the 16th to 18th centuries, the level of commodity prices there gradually rose. Hume himself estimates that prices rose three or four times on average. From this Hume drew what seemed to be the obvious conclusion: that prices had risen because there was more money (real metal money!).

But appearances are deceptive, as the saying goes. For the whole course of this process can and must be explained differently. The discovery of rich deposits caused a drop in the cost of labour to extract precious metals and, consequently, a drop in their value too. Since the value of money in relation to commodities had dropped, the price of commodities rose.

Hume thought that regardless of the amount of real metal money in circulation, the "value" of money (or commodity prices, to put it more simply) would be established during the process of circulation in which a heap of commodities encountered a heap of money.

In fact, both money and commodities go into circulation with a value which has already been determined by the socially necessary expenditure of labour. Consequently only a fixed amount of money can be in circulation at a given speed of money turnover. Any surplus will go abroad or into hoards.

Paper money is a different matter. It can never go out of circulation. The purchasing power of each unit of paper money really does depend (together with other factors) on their quantity. If more of them are issued than the quantity of real metal money necessary for circulation, they will lose their value. This, as we know, is called inflation. Hume, while examining gold and silver, was in fact describing the phenomena of paper-money circulation.

Hume's service is that he attracted attention to problems which still play an important role in political economy: how can the quantity of money necessary for circulation be determined? How does the quantity of money affect prices? What are the specific features of price formation when money loses its value?

CHAPTER VII

BENJAMIN FRANKLIN AND TRANSATLANTIC ECONOMICS

Franklin was one of the last great universal thinkers of the 18th century. The role of Franklin in North America can be compared to that of such great pioneers of learning as Lomonosov in Russia, Newton in England and Descartes in France. A physicist and one of the creators of the modern science of electricity; a philosopher and writer who gave original expression to the new bourgeois democratic views of society of his time; a political and social figure, and one of the most radical leaders of the American revolution and the new state's struggle for independence. This is a far from complete list of the spheres of activity and interests of the celebrated American who himself regarded bookprinting as his main occupation.

Within the framework of his philosophical and political activities Franklin also dealt with questions of political economy. He is one of the pioneers of economic thought in the New World.

LIFE AND WORKS

Franklin's autobiography is a remarkable historical and literary document of his age. In one of the chapters, which Franklin wrote at the age of seventy-nine, he speaks of the happiness of his life. And his was a long and happy life, indeed. He was happy as a citizen, scholar and private person. He lived to see the triumph of the cause to which the whole latter half of his life was dedicated: the independence of North America. His scientific services were recognised by the whole world. He was also happy in private life, if one discounts the fact that his only son William supported the enemies of his father and native land in the war with England.

From a poor apprentice Franklin became by the end of his life if not a rich man at least a very wealthy one. He owned several houses and pieces of land. In those days, particularly in America, this was the most important form of wealth.

Franklin was a man of the New World where, to quote Marx, "bourgeois relations of production imported together with their representatives sprouted rapidly in a soil in which the superabundance of humus made up for the lack of historical tradition".[1]

The descendants of the first settlers from England, mostly Puritans who had fled religious and political persecution, opened up the virgin lands and soon established handicrafts in the towns. But they worshipped Mammon no less than the Spanish conquistadors—although in a different way.

They created the earliest and most complete bourgeois democracy in history, defending the principles of personal liberty, elected authority and an independent judiciary. But this was a democracy in which formal equality before the law became a cover for financial and political inequality and in which unorthodox ideas were suppressed.

The Yankees did not have a decrepit feudal aristocracy, and they ridiculed titles and family privilege. In Herman Melville's novel *Israel Potter,* the hero, an American farmer and sailor who arrives in England during the War of Independence cannot bring himself to say "Your Majesty" when addressing King George III or to call English courtiers "Sir". Yet the rich landowners of Pennsylvania and the merchants of Massachusetts were no less arrogant than the English lords.

By comparison with Western Europe America was the promised land of religious freedom and toleration. Yet a few years before Franklin was born "witches" were tried and

---

[1] Karl Marx, *A Contribution to the Critique of Political Economy,* Moscow 1970, p. 55.

executed in Salem, very near his native town of Boston. The followers of the various religions lived their own isolated lives often dominated by the cruel despotism of ministers and rich parishioners. The Yankees excelled the English in religious hypocrisy. The first fighters against national oppression, they themselves ruthlessly wiped out the Red Indians and established slavery in the southern provinces.

Franklin came from this background of farmers and craftsmen, who were basically freedom-loving, brave and industrious. He absorbed all that was best in the developing nation. But his personality also reflected the contradictions of his nation's bourgeois development. He combined a profound democratism with respect for riches and power. The opponent of religious dogma and rites, he "never doubted, for instance, the existence of the Deity, that he made the world and governed it by his providence", to quote Franklin himself. The enemy of slavery and fighter for national freedom, Franklin nevertheless believed in the special mission of the Anglo-Saxon race. A simple and likeable man, he occasionally appeared to listeners and readers as a narrow-minded pedant and banal moralist.

Benjamin Franklin was born in 1706 in Boston in the large family of a Puritan soap and candle maker. He did not receive any systematic education and was a self-taught person to an even greater extent than Petty. After two years at elementary school the boy was sent as an apprentice to the printing press of his elder step-brother. Franklin relates: "...my brother was passionate and had often beaten me, which I took extremely amiss. I fancy his harsh and tyrannical treatment of me might be a means of impressing me with that aversion to arbitrary power that has stuck to me through my whole life." [1]

During these years other characteristic features of Franklin's developed: energy and push, exceptional industry and an insatiable thirst for knowledge. He read widely and made the acquaintance of educated people; his first literary ventures appeared. His attitude towards religion became fairly critical. At the age of seventeen Franklin left his home and native town. He went to Philadelphia, the Quaker capital of Pennsylvania, and worked there in a printing shop. A year later he went to England in order to improve his knowledge of printing and

---

[1] B. Franklin, *The Autobiography and Other Writings*, New York, 1961, p. 33.

buy equipment for the press. He was promised letters of recommendation and money, but neither materialised.

Franklin spent more than eighteen months in England working in London printing houses and gaining experience and knowledge. In 1726, mature well beyond his years, the young man returned to Philadelphia. He had no money, but he brought books and type faces, and most important he was brimming with ideas, optimism and confidence.

As an enterprising printer Franklin soon acquired a respectable position and became one of the most eminent citizens of Philadelphia. A circle of young people formed around him, who were interested in scientific and literary pursuits. Franklin's life and activities were strictly organised down to the last minute. It is impossible to even list everything that his indomitable energy tackled. He founded Pennsylvania University, the first scientific society, the first public library and the first fire brigade in America, he was the first to start a large national newspaper, and he improved the postal service. In 1754 he represented the province at the Albany Congress and advanced his plan for uniting the colonies under the English king but with a certain amount of self-government. In London they were mortally afraid of anything that might unite the Americans as a nation and Franklin's plan was rejected.

Franklin always took a great interest in the natural sciences and was very clever with his hands. He investigated the nature of earthquakes and invented a furnace of an ingenious design. In 1743 he saw some experiments with electricity which in those days used to be performed by travelling entertainers. He became extremely interested, took it up with his usual enthusiasm and vigour and in the space of five or six years conducted thousands of electrostatic experiments which were remarkably subtle and skilled for their day. Franklin's works laid the foundations of electrostatics. He created the unitary theory of electricity, introducing the concepts of positive and negative charge (until then many people had believed that there were two different types of electricity). Franklin proved the electrical nature of lightning, explained the phenomena of atmospheric electricity, and invented the lightning rod.

In 1757 Franklin left for England as the representative of Pennsylvania (and later of other provinces) to the English Government. The best part of the next thirty years was spent in Europe — first in England, then in France, with only two visits to his homeland. During this period Franklin was the statesman, diplomat and political writer. For many years he sought to avert an armed conflict between the colonies and the "Mother-country", searching for ways of achieving autonomy within the British Empire. But England would not agree to any concessions. Revolt became inevitable, and war broke out in 1775. The Declaration of Independence, written mainly by Jefferson, as we know, also bears traces of Franklin's hand. In the autumn of the same year Congress sent him as the representative of the insurgent colonies to France, whose military and economic help was vital for the new-born republic. In the face of enormous difficulties Franklin secured a military alliance with France. The war took an unfavourable turn for England. In the peace treaty of 1783 she recognised the independence of the United States.

Franklin died in 1790. His last work to be published in his lifetime was a letter to the editor of a newspaper on the slave trade (his letter was published 24 days before his death). He fought against slavery all through later life, as President of the State of Pennsylvania and a member of the Constitutional Convention of 1787. The form of Franklin's last piece of writing is most typical. Bagatelles, he called his satirical miniatures, the small caustic pamphlets which he frequently wrote in his last decade. These "bagatelles" fashioned by the skilled hand of the elder Franklin, stung hard.

FRANKLIN THE ECONOMIST

The labour theory of value was formulated by Adam Smith in *The Wealth of Nations*. But before this one can trace its origin in many writings in the form of more or less vague surmises over a whole century. Franklin was to a large extent a follower of Petty in political economy. In all probability he became acquainted with Petty's works during his first visit to London. Perhaps they were recommended to the enquiring 19-year-old lad by Dr Mandeville: Franklin recalls being introduced to the author of the *Fable of the Bees* in an alehouse called The Horns in Cheapside.

Some scholars link Franklin's ideas also with the influence of another of his elder contemporaries, Daniel Defoe, particularly the latter's *Essay on Projects*.

Many researchers have argued Petty's influence on Franklin comparing Petty's works with Franklin's first economic essay *A Modest Enquiry Into the Nature and Necessity of a Paper Currency*.

Franklin's work on population studies, written in 1751, a remarkable phenomenon in economic literature, also bears traces of Petty's influence. Incidentally, in his demographic works Franklin made use of the actual state of affairs in the American provinces and expressed the interesting idea that "in natural conditions" without external interference the population tended to double each twenty-five years. This estimate was subsequently used by Malthus who maintained that production of the means of subsistence was bound to lag fatally behind the growth of the population. The historical pessimism of Malthusianism was entirely alien to Franklin, however. On the contrary, he believed in the enormous possibilities of production of the means of subsistence given the rational organisation of society. He regarded a large increase in the population of America as an essential prerequisite for the development of the new continent. Concerning Great Britain, however, he wrote: "... this island, if they could be employed, is capable of supporting ten times its present number of people."[1]

Like Petty Franklin formulated the labour theory of value in the course of arguing another, more concrete question. He was trying to get into the heads of the stubborn Quakers the idea of the use of paper money, particularly when there was a shortage of precious metals.

To do this he first had to cast metal money down from its pedestal, and here his reasoning is reminiscent not so much of Petty's views as of John Law's passionate argumentation. Franklin's main idea is that labour, not money, is the true measure of value. He writes: "By labor may the value of silver be measured as well as other things. As, suppose one man employed to raise corn, while another is digging and refining silver; at the year's end, or at any other period of time, the complete produce of corn, and that of silver, are the natural price of each other; and if one be twenty bushels, and the other twenty ounces, then an ounce of that silver is worth the labor of raising a bushel of that corn. Now if by the discovery of some nearer, more easy or plentiful mines, a man may get forty ounces of silver as easily as formerly he did twenty, and the

---

[1] Benjamin Franklin, *The Works of Benjamin Franklin*, Vol. 3, London, 1806, p. 115.

same labor is still required to raise twenty bushels of corn, then two ounces of silver will be worth no more than the same labor of raising one bushel of corn, and that bushel of corn will be as cheap at two ounces, as it was before at one, *coeteris paribus*".[1]

This passage is quoted by Marx in his *Critique of Political Economy* where he gave the first and fullest description of Franklin's services in the field of political economy. Marx notes that Franklin "formulated the basic law of modern political economy",[2] i.e., the law of value.

Marx reaffirmed his high opinion of the famous American's contribution to the development of political economy in *Capital,* where Franklin is described as "one of the first economists, after William Petty, who saw through the nature of value".[3]

First and foremost, Petty's brilliant ideas needed to be skilfully disseminated, propagated and applied to concrete economic questions. And this was precisely what Franklin did. But not all. Franklin came closer than Petty to the idea of the general nature, the equivalence of all the different types of labour. Unlike Petty he did not ascribe any special qualities to the labour of mining precious metals. On the contrary, in pursuing his practical aim he did all he could to prove that this was in no way different from any other type of labour from the point of view of creating value.

The gradual progression of scientific thought to an explanation of the dual nature of labour contained in a commodity[4]

---

[1] B. Franklin, *The Works,* Boston, 1840, Vol. II, p. 265.

[2] Karl Marx, *A Contribution to the Critique of Political Economy,* London, 1971, p. 55.

[3] Karl Marx, *Capital,* Vol. I, Moscow, 1972, p. 57.

[4] The dual content of labour which creates a commodity is connected with the fact that the consumer value of a commodity is created by *concrete labour,* and the value of the commodity by *abstract labour.* Given a simple and capitalist commodity production, based on private ownership of the means of production, concrete labour is opposed to abstract labour, as private labour is to social labour. The social nature of private labour of commodity producers is seen only in the process of commodity exchange, by reducing the various types of concrete labour to qualitatively homogeneous abstract labour which appears as the expenditure of human labour power in general and forms the value of a commodity.

The contradiction between concrete and abstract labour, use value and exchange value reveals the antagonistic contradiction between private and social labour.

The dual nature of labour was discovered by Karl Marx and this discovery forms the scientific basis of the Marxist theory of labour value.

represents the development of the labour theory of value and, in connection with this, the development of the whole classical school in political economy. It was a long path and a hard one. The young Franklin took a step along this path.

Franklin's campaign for paper money had a political and class basis. On the one hand, it was aimed against the great-power policy of England who was hampering the economic development of the colonies by imposing a severely restrictive system of metal money on them. On the other, Franklin was defending the interests of the farmers and simple townsfolk against the money-lenders and merchants who wanted to have the money they loaned returned to them in hard cash. They called this money "honest" money as opposed to paper money which was "dishonest". In order to get hold of silver (there was hardly any gold in the colonies) debtors were forced to make new loans or agree to low wages. As Franklin's later works show, he was fully aware of the class interests which were involved in the dispute over money.

Franklin got carried away in his criticism of metal money and went too far, which led to theoretical weaknesses. Having observed correctly that there was no difference between silver and corn from the point of view of the creation of value, he decided that there was also no difference between them in the role which they play in exchange, in commodity circulation. He ignored the specific social role of money commodity. Silver was a universal equivalent in America at that time, i.e., a commodity which stood out from all other commodities as the result of long evolution. Corn was not such a commodity. Like all other commodities it needed silver, real money, to express its value.

Capitalist commodity economy knows no other means of expressing value. In this sense silver was a "special" commodity. Paper money could exist only as the representative of, the substitute for, silver. In this capacity their circulation was quite "legitimate" economically.

Money performs a special social function. Unlike all other commodities it acts as the universal and direct embodiment of abstract labour. It does not need another commodity to express its value: it is constantly expressed in other commodities. The emergence and evolution of money is an objective and spontaneous process, independent of human will. Franklin, however, tended to treat money as an artificial "invention", as

142

a technical instrument for facilitating exchange. Consequently he regarded metal money not as a logical form of the development of money, but merely as an artificial element imposed by an external force.

In the final analysis the reason for the shortcomings of Franklin's analysis of the basic problems of political economy lies in the underdeveloped nature of bourgeois production relations in the society which he was studying. But if one remembers that his brochure, which was published in remote, provincial Pennsylvania, preceded Adam Smith's *The Wealth of Nations* by half a century, the scientific achievements of the great American assume their true proportions.

The remarkable ideas of the twenty-three-year-old writer expressed in the brochure could not have a direct influence on the development of economic science. In his later works Franklin never raised the question of the nature of value as such, but when he happened to touch upon it, he dealt with it in various ways. Sometimes on the basis of the same labour theory, sometimes in the spirit of Physiocratic teaching by which he was influenced, and sometimes in a subjectivist way: there is no equivalence in exchange because each of the participants in a transaction receives more subjective value, *greater satisfaction.*

We have already seen that the idea of the subjective nature of value serves apologetic ends in bourgeois political economy, because the theory of surplus value, which reveals the nature of capitalist exploitation, is inconceivable on its basis. This is why the "subjectivistic" statements of thinkers of the past attract bourgeois scholars. The author of the book *Founders of American Economic Thought and Policy* published in 1958, Professor Virgle G. Wilhite of Oklahoma University, gives Franklin an encouraging slap on the back in this respect.

In many of his works Franklin also approached the question of the "economic surplus", unearned income, what is basically surplus value, from various aspects. A humanist and rationalist, he saw the "foolishness" of a social order in which some people sweat their guts out so that others can idly squander the fruits of their labour. A tirelessly hard worker, he regarded this as an insult to human justice. Franklin wrote: "What occasions then so much want and misery? It is the employment of men and women in works, that produce neither the

143

necessaries nor conveniences of life,[1] who, with those who do nothing, consume necessaries raised by the laborious.... It has been computed by some political arithmetician, that, if every man and woman would work for four hours each day on something useful, that labor would produce sufficient to procure all the necessaries and comforts of life, want and misery would be banished out of the world, and the rest of the twenty-four hours might be leisure and happiness.".[2]

Naturally Franklin had no idea how to bring about this Golden Age. His noble words are reminiscent, on the one hand, of utopias of all ages and, on the other, of the sober criticism of parasitism and unproductive labour in the works of Adam Smith and his followers.

Franklin's indignation was certainly not aimed at capitalists. He was a son of his times, when the full development of bourgeois relations was still to come. His attacks on parasites and spongers did not stop him from regarding interest on capital as highly legitimate income, a reward for thrift. He regarded land rent in the same way and tried to establish the quantitative interdependence between the amount of land rent and interest on capital. He simply assumed that there was a "fair" rate of interest. This fair, or "natural" rate he estimated at 4 per cent per annum. In his opinion, this rate reconciled the interests of creditors and debtors and promoted class peace.

Franklin certainly did not regard hired labour as exploitation of the worker by the capitalist. He did not sense the social contradiction between them, because he saw the worker of the future merely as a patriarchal farm-labourer or apprentice, side by side with whom the owner of the farm or workshop sweated and toiled.

During his lifetime Franklin was known throughout the world not only as the "tamer of lightning" and the representative of the insurgent colonies, but also as the author of the *Poor Richard's Almanack*. From 1733 to 1757 he published in Philadelphia under the pseudonym of Richard Saunders a yearly almanac which contained various parables and maxims as well as astronomical and other information. All this Franklin

---

[1] A reference to household retainers and numerous servants, officials, priests, officers, etc.

[2] Quoted from Vernon Louis Parrington, *Main Currents in American Thought*, New York, 1930, Vol. I, part 2, p. 174.

partly composed himself and partly borrowed from folklore and other sources.

Franklin provided the last issue of the almanac in 1757 with a foreword containing "Poor Richard's" maxims in condensed form. This small work entitled *Father Abraham's Speech on the Way to Wealth*, its genre difficult to determine, became extremely popular in the 18th century in America and England and was translated into many foreign languages, including Russian.

"Poor Richard's" aphorisms are the concentrated wisdom of a poor man of the people who wants to "make his way in life". Industry, thrift and prudence — these are the three pledges of prosperity and success: "God helps them that help themselves", "The Cat in Gloves catches no Mice", "If you would be wealthy, think of Saving as well as of Getting", "Many a Little makes a Mickle".

These are just a few examples. One is unlikely to find a more unusual form of economic work. But it really is an economic treatise. It consists of the simplified maxims of political economy of the age of the formation of the bourgeoisie as a class, mixed with folklore and everyday wisdom. It is the maxims about which Marx said: "Accumulate, accumulate! That is Moses and the prophets: "Industry furnishes the material which saving accumulates."[1] Therefore, save, save *i.e.*, reconvert the greatest possible portion of surplus-value, or surplus-product into capital!"[2]

Incidentally, Franklin expressed his ideas on the economic importance of accumulation in somewhat stricter form also. In articles belonging to the latter period of his life he departed from his almost inborn Puritanism and wrote that luxury could also be morally justified in connection with the need to accumulate, for, in his opinion, the hope of winning luxury could serve as a mighty impetus to work and perseverance. Some of Franklin's ideas on the "use" of luxury are reminiscent of Mandeville.

Questions of economic policy occupied Franklin all through his life. A pragmatist and realist, he frequently solved them in different ways, depending on the concrete situation and even

---

[1] Marx is quoting Adam Smith here, whose views on this question are very similar to Franklin's.

[2] Karl Marx, *Capital*, Vol. I, 1972, p. 558

the political requirements of the moment. Only his basic bourgeois democratic principles remained unchanged.

In 1760 Franklin published a pamphlet in which he argued, in particular, that the development of manufactories in the American colonies was unnecessary and even socially harmful. He wrote that agriculture alone was a truly noble' human activity, and that there were unlimited possibilities for its development in America. This is generally regarded as due to the influence of Physiocrat doctrine, with which he became acquainted at this time in Europe. Obviously this view is not without justification. But at the same time, as historians have pointed out, Franklin was being cunning in this pamphlet and trying to quieten the fears of the English Government and encourage it to join Canada, which had been conquered from the French, to the rest of the American provinces.[1]

Franklin was certainly not free of mercantilist views, which is quite logical. In other works, quite unembarrassed by the contradictions, he argues the need to develop industry in America and gives mercantilist recipes for this: import duties, an abundance of money in the economy, the active patronage of the state, the settlement of new colonies, etc.

Yet this was not the narrow-minded, provincial, shortsighted mercantilism characteristic of many of his countrymen in the 18th and 19th centuries. When thinking in terms of the world market, he assumed that international specialisation of production and free trade would not impede the development of industry in America and would also be profitable for all trading nations. The above-mentioned American writer calls these views of Franklin's by the paradoxical name of "free trade mercantilism", noting the specifically American nature of this doctrine.[2] It must be said, however, that the views of Hume and Smith were fairly close to it, although the question of the industrial development of the American colonies was not of such interest to them as to Franklin. In defending free trade they did not approach the subject dogmatically, but were governed by common sense.

This specific common sense, which is so evident in *The Wealth of Nations*, is perhaps what links Franklin most of all with the great Scot. Franklin was seventeen years older than

---

[1] P. W. Conner, *Poor Richard's Politics. Benjamin Franklin and His New American Order*, London, 1969, p. 73.

[2] Ibid., p. 74.

Smith and undoubtedly had a certain influence on him in their personal contacts. There is a story according to which Franklin was Smith's mentor and editor when the latter was working on the completion of his book in London in 1773-75. After their death (they both died in 1790) a younger friend of Franklin's, the doctor and politician George Logan, told his relatives, who subsequently made it common knowledge, the following details which he had heard from Franklin: "... the celebrated Adam Smith when writing his *Wealth of Nations* was in the habit of bringing chapter after chapter as he composed it to himself (Franklin — A. A.), Dr. Price, and others of the literati; then patiently hear their observations and profit by their discussions and criticism, sometimes submitting to write whole chapters anew, and even to reverse some of his propositions." [1]

It is difficult to say what is fact and what fiction in this curious statement. Franklin's words could have been distorted by Logan's family and his role in the completion of the work exaggerated. If their acquaintance had been so close and long-standing, more records would have remained of it.

AMERICAN POLITICAL ECONOMY AFTER FRANKLIN

Before the War of Independence (1775-1783) American economic thought had barely advanced beyond the main burning question of relations between the colonies and the metropolis. This is typical of Franklin, too, to a considerable extent.

The creation of an independent state opened up new horizons for the development of social thought. Nevertheless American political economy of the late 18th and early 19th centuries was provincial and existed largely on ideas imported from England and France. In America, however, where "full-blooded" bourgeois production relations developed about a century later than in the most advanced countries of Western Europe, there was not a sufficient basis for classical political economy, the school of Smith and Ricardo.

This showed itself in the critical attitude to both the theory and the practice of the English classics, of whom impartial class

---

[1] John Rae, *Life of Adam Smith*, London and New York, 1895, pp. 264, 265.

analysis and strictly abstract thought were typical. The main principle of economic policy advanced by the classical school, free trade and a minimum of state intervention, was also unacceptable to the majority of the bourgeoisie in the state across the Atlantic. The tone was set there mainly by protectionists who urged the defence of industry against foreign competition by means of high customs duties. This practical problem of political economy was at the centre of economic writing. As the American specialist Turner remarked, "Indeed, prior to 1880, American economics was little more than a by-product of consideration on the tariff".[1]

Franklin, a forerunner of the labour theory of value, a liberal in economics and politics, and something of a Physiocrat, could not become the founder of an influential school in the United States. A considerable influence on American economic thought of the first half of the 19th century was exerted by Alexander Hamilton, a statesman of conservative views, who supported broad intervention by the state in the economy and was the founder of American protectionism.

One of Hamilton's followers was Daniel Raymond, the author of the first American systematic treatise on political economy. His book *Thoughts on Political Economy* came out in 1820. Raymond tried to set up his "American economic system" (he was a fervent nationalist) against Smith and the whole classical school. He attacked the labour theory of value, Smith's views on profit (he saw profit as the capitalists' wage) and economic liberalism.

And, finally, there was Henry Charles Carey whom Marx called in 1852 "the only American economist of importance".[2] Marx regarded Carey as one of the most typical exponents of vulgar political economy which, unlike the classical school, aimed consciously at defending the interests of the bourgeoisie and proving that capitalism was viable and just. He was fairly well-qualified to do this.

Carey's ideas, like Franklin's, were basically closely connected with the special features of the development of capitalism in North America. However, Carey was writing a century after the founder of American economic science.

----

[1] Quoted from J. F. Bell, *A History of Economic Thought*, New York, 1953, p. 484.
[2] Karl Marx and Frederick Engels, *Selected Correspondence*, Moscow, 1965, p. 69.

During that century the face of the country and its social conditions had changed. The country of patriarchal farmers and craftsmen had turned into a land of developed capitalist relations. Towards the end of Carey's long life the United States was approaching England in volume of industrial output.

The high rates and enormous potential of capitalist economy in the United States gave rise to the optimism of Carey's views. He was full of enthusiasm and faith in the unlimited prospects for capitalist growth. The special conditions of capitalist development in North America led Carey to treat the defects and contradictions of bourgeois society as transient things not worthy of special attention. One might say that Carey's name is linked with the so-called doctrine of American exclusiveness according to which the United States could avoid the negative aspects (an acute class struggle and economic crises) which were inevitable in the capitalist development of the old continent. This doctrine has not entirely disappeared even today.

Marx credited Carey with the fact that "he expressed important American relations in an abstract form and in opposition to those of the Old World...".[1]

Carey's main method of analysis was to contrast American social relations with English ones which he regarded as abnormal and inhibited by factors which were external to capitalism "in its ideal form" (that is, in the USA version). If Carey had been referring to the vestiges of feudalism, which really were strong and onerous in England, he would have been right to a certain extent. But what he meant by factors which "distort natural conditions" were taxes, the national debt and other phenomena inherent in the very development of capitalism.

He is known primarily for his theory of the harmony of interests which denies the opposition of the class interests of the bourgeoisie and the proletariat and maintains that capitalist society creates a true association of classes. This was disproved by real events as early as in the 19th century. The powerful workers' strikes in the United States in the 1880s

---

[1] K. Marx, *Fondements de la critique de l'économie politique*, V. 2, Paris, 1968, pp. 549-50.

were one of the sources of the modern working-class movement.

Carey attacked Ricardo even more fiercely than Raymond did Smith. He called his theory a system of dissension between the classes and saw his ideas of free trade as, so to say, a personal attack on American capitalists. This English bourgeois, who was an honest man and a great scholar, appeared to him as a socialist, rebel and destroyer.

Marx regarded Carey's work as one of the most important sources of bourgeois political economy of the mid-19th century and noted that in the sphere of economic science Carey was rich in thorough studies of such questions as credit, rent, etc. In his study of the development of political economy in the USA, the Soviet specialist L. B. Alter has shown the extent and nature of Carey's influence on economic thought in France, Germany and Russia.[1]

The first anti-bourgeois trends of economic thought emerged in the 1820s and 1830s, under the influence of English and French utopian socialism, and also in connection with the growing working-class movement in the USA. The young bourgeois democratic state with its vast expanses of unsettled land was the "promised land" for many visionaries and social reformers of the Old World. Robert Owen founded his commune in the United States; and the French communist Etienne Cabet carried on practical activity and propaganda there for many years. Several communes there tried to carry out Charles Fourier's projects. This produced many publications, the authors of which regarded economic questions from the standpoint of the various trends of utopian socialism. As a rule, they did not advance beyond the main ideas of the founders of these theories in Europe (see Chapters XVIII and XIX).

The mass movement to the new lands of the West in the second third of the 19th century produced a special utopian trend in American social thought. Dreams of a happy society of independent farmers and craftsmen without heavy industry, banks or speculators, and without a political machine of coercion, were in flat contradiction to the actual tendencies of development and doomed to disillusion. Nevertheless ag-

---

[1] See L. B. Alter, *Bourgeois Political Economy of the USA*, Moscow, 1971, pp. 108-26 (in Russian).

rarian-handicraft utopias were exceptionally popular in the USA.

In the 1850s the first Marxist organisations appeared in the USA, whose leaders were friends and confederates of Marx and Engels. They were emigrés from Germany after the revolution of 1848-49. One of the first exponents of scientific socialism in America was Friedrich Sorge, the grandfather of the famous Soviet intelligence agent in the Second World War. These people and organisations began to disseminate Marxist teaching in the USA.

However, the strength and possibilities of critics of the capitalist system were extremely limited by comparison with bourgeois ideology which dominated in the universities, the press, the academic world, and politics. In the second half of the 19th and early 20th centuries a number of influential schools of bourgeois political economy grew up in the USA, which already began to "produce for export".

CHAPTER VIII

DOCTOR QUESNAY AND HIS SECT

Vocation (and reputation) come to people in different ways. François Quesnay was a doctor and natural scientist. He did not take up political economy until he was almost sixty. By then he was the author of several dozen medical works. Quesnay spent the last few years of his life in an intimate circle of friends, pupils and followers. He was a man to whom La Rochefoucauld s words applied: "Few people have mastered the art of growing old". One of his acquaintances said that he had the head of a thirty-year-old on the body of an eighty-year-old. Quesnay was the most outstanding French political economist of the 18th century.

THE AGE OF ENLIGHTENMENT

Frederick Engels wrote that "the great men, who in France prepared men's minds for the coming revolution, were themselves extreme revolutionists. They recognised no external authority of any kind whatever. Religion, natural science, society, political institutions — everything was subjected to the most unsparing criticism: everything must justify its existence before the judgment-seat of reason or give up existence." [1]

---

[1] Frederick Engels, *Anti-Dühring*, p. 25.

In the brilliant array of 18th-century thinkers a place of honour belongs to Quesnay and Turgot, the creators of classical French political economy.

The Enlighteners hoped that the ice of feudalism would gradually melt in the bright rays of the sun, the rays of liberated human intellect. This did not happen. The menacing icebreaker of the revolution loomed ever larger, and those of the younger generation of Enlighteners, including the Physiocrat economists, who lived long enough, recoiled in horror before the yawning abyss of the people's fury.

French economy in the middle of the 18th century when Quesnay took it up was not too different from the economy of the beginning of the century when Boisguillebert was writing. France was still an agrarian country and the position of the peasants had scarcely improved over the previous fifty years. Like Boisguillebert, Quesnay begins his economic works with a description of the disastrous state of French agriculture.

But some changes had taken place in those fifty years all the same. The class of capitalist farmers, who owned the land or rented it from landowners, had emerged and developed, particularly in the north of France. It was on this class that Quesnay placed his hopes for agricultural progress, and he rightly regarded such progress as the basis of the healthy economic and political development of society as a whole.

France was exhausted from senseless, devastating wars. In these wars it had lost almost all its overseas possessions and the profitable trade with them. Its position in Europe had also grown weaker. Industry mainly served the luxury and extravagance of the Court and the upper classes, while the peasantry made do with handmade articles on the whole. The sensational collapse of Law's system hampered the development of credit and banking. In the eyes of many people who expressed public opinion in mid-18th century France, industry, trade and finance had somehow been compromised. Agriculture seemed to be the last resort of peace, prosperity and naturalness.

If Law was a romantic about credit, Quesnay became a romantic about agriculture, although his personality and character contained nothing romantic whatsoever. Incidentally, the lack of this quality in the teacher was compensated for by the excessive enthusiasm of some of his pupils, particularly the Marquis of Mirabeau.

The nation became fascinated by agriculture, but fascinated in a variety of different ways. It was a fashionable topic of conversation at Court, and puppet farms were set up at Versailles. In the provinces several societies for the promotion of agriculture were set up, which tried to introduce "English", i.e., more productive, methods of agriculture. Agronomical writings began to appear.

In these conditions Quesnay's ideas produced a response, although his interest in agriculture was of a different kind. Basing themselves on a view of agriculture as the only productive sphere of the economy, Quesnay and his school drew up a programme of economic reforms of an anti-feudal nature. Turgot later sought to introduce these reforms. For the most part they were implemented by the revolution.

Quesnay and his followers were basically far less revolutionary and democratic than the main core of Enlighteners led by Diderot, to say nothing of the left wing from which utopian socialism later emerged. As a French historian of the last century, de Tocqueville, put it, they were "men of mild and calm disposition, men of substance, honest magistrates, skilled administrators...." [1] Even the ardent enthusiast Mirabeau heeded a popular remark by a contemporary wit that the art of eloquence in France consisted of saying everything without ending up in the Bastille. True, he was once arrested for a few days, but the influential Dr Quesnay soon got him out of gaol and the short imprisonment merely increased his popularity. After that he was more careful.

But objectively the activity of the Physiocrats was extremely revolutionary and undermined the foundations of the "ancien régime". Marx in his *Theories of Surplus-Value* wrote, for example, that Turgot was "one of the immediate fathers of the French revolution". [2]

MADAME DE POMPADOUR'S PHYSICIAN

The King's mistress was only a little over thirty, but she was already losing the favour of the empty-headed and pleasure-loving monarch. She later took over the management

---

[1] Alexis de Tocqueville, *L'ancien régime et la revolution*, Paris, 1856, p. 265.
[2] Karl Marx, *Theories of Surplus-Value*, Part I, p. 344.

of his harem, thus retaining her position of power to the very end. Next to these two most powerful people in France stood Dr Quesnay, Madame de Pompadour's private physician and one of the King's doctors. This round-shouldered, modestly dressed man, always calm and somewhat ironical, knew many state and intimate secrets. But Dr Quesnay also knew how to keep his mouth shut, and this quality was appreciated no less than his professional skill.

The King liked Bordeaux, but on Quesnay's orders, who considered the wine too heavy for the royal stomach, was compelled to give it up. However, he drank so much champaigne at dinner that he could sometimes hardly stay on his feet as he staggered off to Madame de Pompadour's chambers. Several times he felt faint, and Quesnay was at hand. He would relieve his patient's condition with simple remedies, while reassuring Madame who was trembling with fear at the thought of what would happen if the King were to die in her bed. She would immediately be accused of murder! Quesnay told her firmly that there was no danger of that happening. The King was only forty. If he had been sixty, Quesnay could not have answered for his life. The experienced, intelligent doctor, who had treated peasants and courtiers, shopkeepers and princesses in his time, could read Madame de Pompadour like a book.

In medicine Quesnay preferred simple, natural remedies, relying to a great extent on nature. His social and economic ideas are fully in conformity with this feature of his character. For the very word *physiocracy* means the power of nature (from the Greek *physis* — nature, and *kratos* — power).

Louis XV was favourably disposed to Quesnay and called him "my thinker". He gave the doctor a title and himself chose the coat-of-arms. In 1758 the King printed with his own hands on a manual printing-press which the Doctor had ordered for his physical exercises the first copies of the *Tableau économique*, the work which was to make Quesnay famous. But Quesnay did not like the King and secretly thought him a dangerous nonentity. He was quite unlike the Physiocrats' ideal ruler: a wise and enlightened guardian of the laws of the state. Gradually, using his constant presence and influence at Court, he tried to make the Dauphin, Louis XV's son and heir to the throne, into such a ruler, and, after his death, the new Dauphin, the King's grandson and future Louis XVI.

François Quesnay was born in 1694 in a village near Versailles, and was the eighth of Nicolas Quesnay's thirteen children. At one time it was thought that Quesnay père was a barrister or judicial official, but it later transpired that this story had been spread by the Doctor's son-in-law, a physician by the name of Hevin who published the first biography of his father-in-law shortly after Quesnay's death and tried to give him a slightly more impressive family background. Today we have documental proof that Nicolas was a simple peasant, who also engaged in small-scale trading.

Up till eleven François was illiterate. Then a kind gardener taught him to read and write. After this came lessons with the village curé and at the elementary school in the neighbouring small town. According to Hevin, all this time François had to work hard in the fields and at home, particularly as his father died when he was thirteen. The boy's passion for reading was such that he would sometimes leave the house at dawn, walk all the way to Paris, choose the book he needed and return home by nightfall, covering dozens of kilometres. This is also proof of his peasant stamina. Quesnay retained his good health right to the end, if one does not count the gout which began to torment him at a comparatively early age.

At seventeen Quesnay made up his mind to be a surgeon and became assistant to the local doctor. The main thing he had to be able to do was let blood: blood-letting was a universal remedy in those days. Although the teaching was bad, Quesnay studied hard and seriously. From 1711 to 1717 he lived in Paris, working in an engraving shop and practising in a hospital at the same time. By twenty-three he had found his feet to such an extent that he married the daughter of a Paris grocer with a large dowry, received his surgeon's diploma and began to practise in the town of Mantes, near Paris. Quesnay lived in Mantes for seventeen years and thanks to his industry, skill and a special ability to inspire confidence became the most popular doctor in the whole district. He delivered babies (he was particularly well-known for this), let blood, extracted teeth and performed some fairly complicated operations for those days. His patients gradually came to include the local aristocracy, he made the acquaintance of Parisian luminaries and published a number of medical works.

In 1734 Quesnay, now a widower with two children, left Mantes and at the invitation of the Duc de Villerois took up the post of his house physician. In the 1730s and 1740s he devoted a great deal of energy to the struggle which surgeons were waging against the "faculte"—official academic medicine. According to an old statute, surgeons belonged to the same guild as barbers and were forbidden to engage in therapy. Quesnay became the leader of the "surgeons' party" and eventually emerged victorious. It was at this time that he published his main scientific work, a kind of medico-philosophical treatise dealing with basic medical questions: the relationship between theory and medical practice, medical ethics, etc.

An important event in Quesnay's life was his move in 1749 to Madame de Pompadour who "begged" him from the Duke. Quesnay settled down in the entresol of the palace at Versailles, which was destined to play an important role in the history of economic science. By now he was a very wealthy man.

Medicine occupied a large place in Quesnay's life and activities. Over the bridge of philosophy he passed from medicine to political economy. The human organism and society. The circulation of the blood or human metabolism and the circulation of the product in society. This biological analogy directed Quesnay's thinking, and remains valuable to this very day.

Quesnay lived for twenty-five years in his apartment in the entresol of the palace at Versailles and was forced to leave only six months before his death, when Louis XV died and the new ruler swept all the vestiges of the past reign out of the palace. Quesnay's apartment consisted of one large but low and darkish room and two dark storerooms. Nevertheless it soon became one of the favourite meeting places of the "literary republic"—scholars, philosophers and writers who joined together in the early 1750s around the Encyclopaedia. Doctor Quesnay first preached his ideas not so much in the press as to the circle of friends who gathered in his entresol. Pupils and people of like mind appeared, as did those who disagreed with him. Marmontel left a vivid description of the meetings at Quesnay's: "While the storms gathered and dispersed under Quesnay's entresol, he worked hard on his axioms and calculations on agricultural economy, as calm and indifferent to the movements of the Court as if he were a hundred miles away. Down there they were discussing peace, war, the choice of generals, the dismissal of ministers, while in the entresol, we were discussing agriculture, estimating the net product, or sometimes dining gaily with Diderot, D'Alembert, Duclos, Helvetius, Turgot, Buffon; and Madame de Pompadour, unable to attract this troop of philosophers down into her salon, came herself to see them at table and chat with them."[1]

Later, when Quesnay's sect[2] gathered round him, the meetings took on a somewhat different character: those who sat down at table were mainly Quesnay's pupils and followers or people whom they were introducing to the maître. Adam Smith spent several evenings here in 1766.

What was Quesnay like?

From the multitude of fairly conflicting reports of contemporaries there emerges the picture of a cunning, wise man, who slightly concealed his wisdom under an air of simplicity; people compared him to Socrates. He is said to have liked fables with a deep and not immediately apparent meaning. He was very unassuming and not personally ambitious; without the slightest regret he often allowed his pupils the honour of publishing his ideas. In appearance he was fairly nondescript, and a newcomer to the "entresol club" could not immediately guess who was the host and chairman. "Devilishly clever", said the Marquis of Mirabeau's brother after visiting him. "Sly as a monkey," remarked a courtier after listening to one of his stories. His portrait painted in 1767 shows an ugly plebeian face with an ironical half-smile and clever, penetrating eyes.

To quote D'Alembert, Quesnay was "a philosopher at the Court, living there in solitude and study, not knowing the language of the country[3] and not making the slightest effort to learn it, having little connection with its inhabitants, a judge as enlightened as he was impartial, and free of everything he heard said or saw done there."[4]

Quesnay used his influence on Madame de Pompadour and the King in the interests of the cause to which he was now

---

[1] Oeuvres complètes de Marmontel, t. I, Paris, 1818, pp. 291-92.

[2] This was the name given to the Physiocrats' school. The word was often used without any pejorative meaning or irony, simply to indicate the close ideological link between the followers of Quesnay. Adam Smith, who had the greatest respect for Quesnay, also writes about the "sect" in The Wealth of Nations.

[3] Meaning the language of court gossip and intrigue.

[4] François Quesnay et la Physiocratie, Paris, 1958, t. I, p. 240.

devoted. Together with Turgot he helped to get the law amended slightly, organised the publication of works of like-minded friends and had Lemercier appointed to a high post where the latter tried to carry out the first Physiocrat experiment. The death of Madame de Pompadour in 1764 somewhat weakened the position of the economists, but Quesnay remained consulting physician to the King who continued to favour him.

THE NEW SCIENCE

A peasant ploughs, fertilises and sows his plot of land, then reaps the harvest. He stores some seed, sets some grain aside to feed his family, sells some to acquire the most essential town commodities and is pleased to see that he still has a surplus. What could be simpler than this story? Yet it was precisely this sort of thing that prompted Doctor Quesnay's various ideas.

Quesnay knew what would happen to the surplus. The peasant would give it in money or in kind to his *seigneur*, the King and the Church. He even calculated what proportion they would each receive: four-sevenths to the *seigneur*, two-sevenths to the King, and one-seventh to the Church. This suggests two questions. Firstly, by what right do these three appropriate a considerable part of his harvest or income? Secondly, where does the surplus come from?

Quesnay answers the first questions roughly as follows: nothing can be done about the King and the Church — that's the hand of God, so to say. With regard to the *seigneurs*, he found an interesting economic explanation: their rent can be regarded as a kind of legitimate interest on so-called *avances foncières* (land-advances) — the capital investment which they were supposed to have made long, long ago to put the land into a condition suitable for cultivation. It is difficult to say whether Quesnay himself believed this. In any case, he could not conceive of agriculture without landowners. The reply to the second question seemed even more obvious to him. The earth, nature has given this surplus! And in the same natural way it goes to the man who owns the land.

The surplus of the agricultural product, which is formed after all the expenses of its production have been deducted, Quesnay called the *produit net* (net product) and analysed its production, distribution and circulation. The Physiocrats' net product is the closest prototype of the surplus product and surplus value, although they restricted it to land rent and regarded it as the natural fruit of the earth. However their great service was that they "transferred the inquiry into the origin of surplus-value from the sphere of circulation into the sphere of direct production, and thereby laid the foundation for the analysis of capitalist production".[1]

Why did Quesnay and the Physiocrats discover surplus-value only in agriculture? Because there the process of its production and appropriation is most obvious. It is incomparably more difficult to discern in industry. The fact is that a worker in a given unit of time creates more value than the cost of his own subsistence. But a worker produces quite different commodities from the ones he consumes. He may make nuts and screws all his life, but he eats bread, occasionally meat, and most likely drinks wine or beer. In order to discern the surplus-value here one must know how to reduce nuts and screws, bread and wine to some kind of common denominator, i.e., to possess the concept of the value of commodities. And Quesnay did not have this concept. It simply did not interest him.

Surplus-value in agriculture seems to be a gift of nature and not the fruit of unpaid human labour. It exists directly in the natural form of the surplus product, particularly in grain. In constructing his model, Quesnay used in it not the poor *métayer* (sharecropper peasant), but his beloved tenant farmer who has beasts of burden and the simplest implements and also hires labour.

Reflections on the economy of this type of farmer led Quesnay to make a certain analysis of capital, although we do not find the word in his writing. He understood that, say, expenditure on land drainage, building, horses, ploughs and harrows was one type of advance, and on seed and the maintenance of hired labour another. The former expenditure is made once every few years and gradually reimbursed, the latter annually or all the time and must be reimbursed at each harvest. Accordingly Quesnay talks about *avances primitives* (which we call fixed capital) and *avances annuelles* (circulating capital). These ideas were developed by Adam Smith. Today

---

[1] Karl Marx, *Theories of Surplus-Value*, Part I, p. 45.

they are the elements of economics, but for its time this analysis was a great achievement. Marx begins his study of the Physiocrats in *Theories of Surplus-Value* with the following sentence: "The analysis of *capital*, within the bourgeois horizon, is essentially the work of the Physiocrats. It is this service that makes them the true fathers of modern political economy."[1]

By introducing these concepts Quesnay laid the foundations for an analysis of the circulation and reproduction of capital, i.e., the constant renewal and repetition of the processes of production and sale, which is of great significance for the rational management of the economy. The very term *reproduction*, which plays such an important part in Marxist political economy, was first used by Quesnay.

Quesnay gave the following description of the class structure of the society of his day. "The nation is reduced to three classes of citizens: *the productive class, the class of proprietors and the sterile class.*"[2]

A strange division at first glance. Yet it proceeds quite logically from the principles of Quesnay's teaching and reflects both its merits and defects. The productive class are, of course, the peasant farmers who not only reimburse the expenditure of their capital and feed themselves, but also create a net product. The class of proprietors are the receivers of the net product: the landowners, the Court, the Church, and all their servants, too. Finally, the sterile class is everyone else, i.e., those people, to quote Quesnay himself, "who are engaged in other services and other works than agriculture".

What did Quesnay mean by this sterility? He regarded craftsmen, workers and traders as sterile in a different sense from landowners. The former labour, of course, but by their labour which is not connected with the land, they create as much produce as they consume, merely transforming the natural form of the product created in agriculture. Quesnay thought that these people were somehow employed by the two other classes. The proprietors do not work, but they are the owners of the land, the only production factor which Quesnay regarded as capable of increasing the wealth of society. Their social function is the appropriation of the net product.

---

[1] Karl Marx, *Theories of Surplus-Value*, Part I, p. 44.
[2] *François Quesnay et la Physiocratie*, Paris, 1958, t. II, p. 793.

The defects of this scheme are enormous. Suffice it to say, that workers and capitalists both in industry and agriculture are put in the same class by Quesnay. Turgot corrected this absurd error to some extent, and Smith completely rejected it.

Or take another detail of no small importance. If a capitalist only receives a kind of wage, how, from what, can he accumulate capital? Quesnay gets round this as follows. He says that the only normal, economically "legitimate" accumulation is that from the net product, i.e., from the income of the landowner. The manufacturer and merchant can only accumulate in a way that is not entirely "legitimate", by extracting something from their "wage". Hence the origin of the apologetic theory of accumulation by capitalist abstinence. In general Quesnay saw, first and foremost, class co-operation in society. It is no accident that Schumpeter describes him as asserting the "universal harmony of class interests, which makes him the forerunner of nineteenth-century harmonism (Say, Carey, Bastiat)".[1]

Quesnay's teaching cannot be reduced to this, of course. Let us see what practical conclusions emerge from it. Naturally his first recommendation was that agriculture should be promoted in every possible way in the form of farming by large units. Yet this was followed by two other recommendations which did not seem so innocent in those days. Quesnay believed that the net product alone should be liable to tax as the only true economic "surplus". All other taxes were a burden on the economy. What did this mean in practice? That the very feudal lords on whom Quesnay was bestowing such important and honoured functions in society would have to pay all the taxes. In the France of that day the position was quite the reverse: they paid no taxes whatsoever. Moreover, Quesnay said, since industry and trade were "kept" by agriculture this should be done as cheaply as possible. Which meant abolishing or at least relaxing all restrictions and controls on production and trade. The Physiocrats came out in support of *laissez faire*.

These were the main points of Quesnay's teaching. And of the Physiocratic school. For all its shortcomings and weaknesses it was an integrated economic and social view of the world, progressive for its day in theory and in practice.

---

[1] J. A. Schumpeter, *History of Economic Analysis*, p. 234.

Quesnay's ideas are scattered about in many short works and in the writings of his pupils and followers. His own works were published in various forms, often anonymously, between 1756 and 1768. Some remained in manuscript and were not discovered and published until the 20th century. It is not easy for the modern reader to understand Quesnay's writings, although they are contained in a single not very large volume: his main ideas are reproduced and repeated with shades of meaning and variations which are difficult to catch. In 1768 Quesnay's pupil Du Pont de Nemours published a book entitled *De l'origine et des progrès d'une science nouvelle (On the origin and progress of a new science)*. This book summed up the development of the Physiocratic school. He possibly did not intend the title to be interpreted in the way we read it today, but history has shown that he hit the nail on the head. Quesnay's works really did create a new science — political economy in its classical French form.

THE PHYSIOCRATS

A feature of Physiocratic theory is that its bourgeois essence was disguised in feudal clothing. Although Quesnay wanted to make the net product alone liable to taxation, he addressed himself in the main to the enlightened interest of the powers-that-be, promising them an increase in land revenue and a strengthened landed aristocracy.

To a large extent the "trick" worked. Not only because of the blindness of the powers-that-be, but because the landed aristocracy really could only be saved by bourgeois reforms, which had already taken place — in different circumstances, it is true — in England. But in old Dr Quesnay's recipe this bitter medicine was well sweetened and disguised in attractive wrapping.

In the early years the Physiocratic school was extremely successful. It was patronised by dukes and marquises, and foreign monarchs exhibited an interest in it. At the same time it was thought of highly by the Enlightenment philosophers, including Diderot. The Physiocrats at first succeeded in attracting the support of both the most reflective members of the aristocracy and the growing bourgeoisie. From the beginning of the 1760s, in addition to the Versailles "entresol club" where only the select few had admittance, a kind of public Physiocratic centre opened in the Marquis of Mirabeau's house in Paris. Here Quesnay's pupils (he rarely visited it himself) engaged in the propagation and popularisation of the *maître's* ideas and recruited new supporters. The nucleus of the Physiocratic sect included the young Du Pont de Nemours,[1] Lemercier de la Rivière and several other people who were close acquaintances of Quesnay. Around the nucleus were groups of sect members less well acquainted with Quesnay, various sympathisers and fellow-travellers. A special place was occupied by Turgot, who belonged partly to the Physiocrats but was too great and independent a thinker to be the *maître's* mouthpiece. The fact that Turgot could not squeeze into the bed of Procrustes made by the carpenter from the "Versailles entresol" compels us to look at the Physiocrat school and its leader with different eyes.

Naturally the unity and solidarity of Quesnay's pupils, their absolute devotion to their teacher, cannot help but command respect. But it was this that eventually became the school's weakness. All its activities consisted of expounding and repeating Quesnay's views, even his actual sentences. His ideas became increasingly stultified in the form of strict dogma. On the Tuesday evenings at Mirabeau's house fresh thought and discussion gave way more and more to ritual observances. Physiocracy was turning into a kind of religion, with Mirabeau's house for its place of worship and Tuesday evenings for its services.

The sect in the sense of a group of like-minded people was turning into a sect in the pejorative sense in which we use the word today: into a group of fanatical believers in strict dogma who rejected anyone with differing views.

Du Pont who was in charge of the Physiocrats' publications, "edited" everything that came into his hands, giving it a Physiocratic slant. The funny thing is that he regarded himself as more of a Physiocrat than Quesnay ever claimed to be, and refused to publish the latter's early works (according to Du Pont, Quesnay was not yet a proper Physiocrat when he wrote them).

---

[1] After the Revolution Du Pont emigrated to the United States of America where his son founded the family business which eventually grew into the giant chemical monopoly Du Pont de Nemours and Company.

This state of affairs was assisted by certain features in Quesnay's character. D. I. Rosenberg in his *History of Political Economy* remarks that "unlike William Petty, with whom Quesnay shares the honour of being called the creator of political economy, Quesnay was a man of unshakeable principles, but with a strong tendency to dogmatism and doctrinairism"[1]. With the years the tendency increased, encouraged, of course, by the devotion of the sect. Believing the truths of the new science to be "self-evident", Quesnay became intolerant of other opinions, and the sect strengthened this intolerance greatly. Quesnay was convinced that his teaching was universally applicable regardless of conditions of place and time.

His modesty did not decrease in the least. He did not seek fame, but she herself found him. He did not belittle his pupils, but they belittled themselves. In his last few years Quesnay became unbearably obstinate. At seventy-six he took up mathematics and imagined that he had made some great discoveries in geometry. D'Alembert owned that these discoveries were rubbish. His friends unanimously tried to persuade the old man not to make a laughingstock of himself and not to publish the work in which he expounded these ideas. But in vain.

When the work came out in 1773, Turgot was most distressed: "It's the scandal to end all scandals, the sun has lost its light." To which one can only reply with the Russian saying: even the sun has its spots.

Quesnay died at Versailles in December 1774. The Physiocrats could find no one to replace him. Moreover they were already in advanced decline. Turgot's term in office from 1774-1776 revived their hopes and activity, but his retirement came as a severe blow. In fact, this was the end of the physiocrats. Moreover, 1776 was the year of the publication of Adam Smith's *The Wealth of Nations*. The French economists of the succeeding generation — Sismondi, Say and others — turned to Smith rather than to the Physiocrats. In 1815 Du Pont, now a very old man, reproached Say in a letter for the fact that he, nourished on Quesnay's milk, was spurning his wet-nurse". Say replied that after Quesnay's

[1] D. I. Rosenberg, *A History of Political Economy*, Vol. I, Moscow, 1940, p. 88 (in Russian).

milk he had consumed much bread and meat, i.e., studied Smith and other new economists.

The decline of the Physiocrats in the 1770s was not only the result of their shortcomings. They were sharply criticised, what is more, from various sides. Having lost their patronage of the Court, they became the object of attacks by reactionary feudal elements. At the same time they were criticised by writers from the left wing of the Enlightenment.

DOCTOR QUESNAY'S "ZIG-ZAG"

As we read in the memoires of Marmontel, who has left us many interesting details about Quesnay's personality, the doctor was already drawing his "'zig-zag' of the net product" in 1757. This was the *Tableau économique* which was repeatedly published and interpreted in the works of Quesnay himself and his pupils. In all its versions, however, the *Tableau* is the same: it shows with the help of statistical examples and graphs how the country's gross and net product created in agriculture circulated in its natural and monetary form between the three classes into which Quesnay divided society.

To give albeit a general idea of the modern attitude to the *Tableau économique,* let us quote Academician V. S. Nemchinov. In his work *Economico-Mathematical Methods and Models,* awarded the Lenin prize, he writes: "In the 18th century at the dawn of the development of economic science ... François Quesnay ... created his *Tableau économique,* a brilliant flight of human thought. In 1958 it was two hundred years since the publication of this table, yet the ideas contained in it have not only not faded, but have acquired even more value.... To describe Quesnay's Table in modern economic terms, it is one of the first attempts at macro-economic analysis, in which the central place is occupied by the concept of the aggregate social product.... Francois Quesnay's *Tableau économique* is the first macro-economic scheme of the natural (commodity) and monetary flows of material values in the history of political economy. The ideas contained in it are future economic models in embryo. In particular, Karl Marx paid tribute to François Quesnay's brilliant work when he created his scheme of extended reproduction...." [1]

[1] V. S. Nemchinov, *Economico-Mathematical Methods and Models,* Moscow 1965, pp. 175, 177 (in Russian).

The general idea of these quotations will be obvious to the reader, but the details should perhaps be clarified. Macro-economic analysis is the analysis of aggregate economic phenomena (social product, national income, capital investment) and related economic problems. By contrast, micro-economics is the analysis of categories and problems of commodity, value, price, etc., and also the circulation of individual capital. Quesnay's macro-economic model is a hypothetical scheme of reproduction and circulation of the social product, based on certain assumptions and postulates. It served as one of the main bearings used by Marx in his brilliant schemes of reproduction.

In a letter to Engels of 6 July, 1863, he first describes his studies in this sphere and outlines a numerical and graphic example: how the aggregate product arises from the expenditure of constant capital (raw materials, fuel, machinery), variable capital (workers' wages) and surplus-value. The formation of the product takes place in two different subdivisions of social production: the production of machinery, raw material, etc. (first subdivision) and that of objects of consumption (second subdivision).[1]

The extent to which Marx was inspired by Quesnay's ideas may be seen from the fact that right beneath his scheme he depicted the *Tableau économique* or, rather, its essence, in this letter. Marx's scheme, even in this original form, of course, was very different from Quesnay's Table: it shows the real source of surplus value — the exploitation of hired labour by capitalists. But the important thing is that Quesnay's work contained the germ of a most important idea: that *the process of reproduction and realisation can take place uninterruptedly only if certain economic proportions are observed.*

Both Quesnay in his Table and Marx in this first scheme proceeded from *simple reproduction* in which production and realisation are repeated each year in the same dimensions, without accumulation and extension. This is the natural progression from the simple to the complex, from the particular to the more general. Einstein first created a particular theory of relativity applicable only in inertial

---

[1] In this letter Marx still regards, on the contrary, the production of the means of subsistence as the first subdivision. V. S. Nemchinov notes that Marx does so "as if following the Physiocrats".

movements, and then went on to elaborate a general theory of relativity.

In the second volume of *Capital*, which was published by Engels after the author's death, Marx developed the theory of simple reproduction and laid the foundation of the theory of *expanded reproduction*, i.e., reproduction with accumulation and an increase in the volume of production. Some most important works by V. I. Lenin are also devoted to these problems.

The main problem which occupied Quesnay was, to use the language of modern economics, the problem of economic proportions which ensure the development of the economy. The mere mention of this problem should suffice to remind one of its extreme topicality and importance in the present day. One might say that Quesnay's ideas lay at the base of input-output tables in various branches of the economy today in the USSR and other countries. These tables reflect the interrelations between the different branches and are playing an increasingly large role in the management of the economy.

There has recently been a growth of interest in Quesnay in non-Marxian political economy. The bicentenary of the *Tableau économique* was most impressively celebrated. France has recognised Quesnay as one of her national geniuses.

CHAPTER IX

TURGOT — THINKER, MINISTER AND MAN

Turgot's two years as controller general under Louis XVI are a dramatic page in the history of prerevolutionary France. His reformist activity was unsuccessful: for he sought to put right by reforms what could now only be "put right" by revolution.

The man had something of a Don Quixote about him. Actually he was a Don Quixote not so much by nature as by force of circumstance: the most rational ideas and expedient actions sometimes turn out to be quixotic. But the comparison is a fitting one in another respect too. Turgot was personally a man of great spiritual nobility, unreservedly high principles and rare selflessness. These qualities were strange and out of place in the courts of Louis XV and XVI.

THINKER

Turgot was born in Paris in 1727. He came from an old Norman noble family with a long tradition of serving the state. His father held a post in Paris which corresponded to the modern appointment of prefect or mayor. Turgot was the third son and therefore traditionally destined to enter the Church. Consequently Turgot received the best possible education for his day. After graduating from the seminary with distinction and entering the Sorbonne to study for a degree, the 23-year-old abbé, the pride of the Sorbonne and rising star of Catholicism, suddenly decided not to take holy orders.

This was the decision of a mature and thinking person. Spending a lot of time on philosophy in this period and studying the English thinkers, Turgot wrote a number of philosophical works directed against subjective idealism which asserted that the whole external world was the product of human consciousness. Turgot's ability astounded his teachers and friends. He knew six languages well, studied many different sciences and possessed a remarkable memory. At twenty-two Turgot wrote a profound work on paper money, analysing Law's system and its defects. During this period, however, he was interested in economics primarily within the framework of broad philosophico-historical problems.

In 1752 Turgot became *substitut* and later *conseiller* in the Paris parlement, and in the following year used his modest inheritance to purchase the position of *maître des requêtes*. This office did not prevent him from studying hard various disciplines and also visiting salons where the intellectual life of Paris was focused. The young Turgot soon became one of the finest adornments of both society and philosophical salons. He became closely acquainted with Diderot, D'Alembert and their assistants on the Encyclopaedia. Turgot wrote several articles — philosophical and economic — for the Encyclopaedia.

A most important part in Turgot's life was played by the eminent progressive administrator Vincent Gournay, who became his mentor in the field of economics. Gournay, unlike the Physiocrats, regarded industry and trade as the most important sources of the country's prosperity. However, together with them he attacked guild restrictions on trade and supported free competition. As has already been mentioned, the famous principle of *laissez faire, laissez passer* is sometime ascribed to him. Together with Gournay, then intendant o commerce, Turgot travelled round the provinces to inspec trade and industry. On their return to Paris when Turgo began to accompany Gournay on his visits to Quesnay' "entresol club", he was already immune to the extremes o Physiocratic school. Although Turgot agreed with some o Quesnay's main ideas and had great respect for him personal ly, he went his own way in the science in many respects

Gournay died in 1759. In his *Éloge de Gournay* written immediately after his death, Turgot not only described his deceased friend's views, but systematically expounded his own economic ideas for the first time.

Turgot's scientific and literary activity was interrupted in 1761 by his appointment as intendant of Limoges. He spent thirteen years there, periodically travelling to Paris. The intendant, as the main representative of the central authority, was in charge of all the province's economic questions. But his main responsibility was the collection of taxes for the king.

Confronted with harsh reality Turgot wrote: "In the Limousin there are hardly any peasants who can read or write, and very few upon whom one can count for intelligence or probity; they are a stubborn race, opposing even changes which are designed for their own good."[1]

But Turgot did not lose heart. An energetic, even self-confident and authoritative man, he began to introduce certain reforms in his province despite all difficulties. He sought to simplify the system of tax collection; he replaced the hated *corvée*, forced peasant labour to maintain the roads, by freely hired labour and built good roads; he organised a campaign to combat cattle epidemics and pests; and he introduced the potato, setting an example by ordering his chef to prepare potato dishes each day for himself and his guests.

He had to cope with poor harvests and lack of food. Acting boldly and sensibly in dealing with these disasters, he was compelled to deviate from his theoretical principles which demanded that everything should be left to private initiative, free competition and the natural course of events. Turgot acted as a progressive and humane administrator. But in the reign of Louis XV he could do very little.

From Limoges and during his visits to Paris Turgot followed the successes of the Physiocrats. He became friendly with Du Pont and made the acquaintance of Adam Smith in Paris. However, his main writings in this period were endless reports, accounts, official notes and circulars. Only in his rare hours of leisure, at odd moments, could he study. Thus it was that in 1766, almost by accident, Turgot wrote his main economic work *Reflexions sur la formation et la distribution des richesses*: the

---

[1] Quotation taken from D. Dakin. *Turgot and the Ancien Régime in France*, New York, 1965, p. 37.

171

basic ideas had long since formed in his head and been partially set out on paper, including official documents.

This work has an unusual history. Turgot wrote it at the request of friends as a textbook or guide for two young Chinese who had been brought by Jesuit missionaries to study in France. Du Pont published it in 1769-1770. As was his custom, he "trimmed" Turgot into a Physiocrat, as a result of which a sharp conflict arose between them. In 1776 Turgot himself published a separate edition.

The *Reflexions* are written with a brilliant laconism reminiscent of the best pages of Petty. They consist of 100 concise theses, like economic theorems (some, it is true, can be taken as axioms). Turgot's theorems fall into clear sections.

Up to and including theorem 31 Turgot is a Physiocrat, a pupil of Quesnay's. Yet he gives the theory of the net product a shade of meaning which caused Marx to remark: "[With] *Turgot* [the Physiocratic system is] most fully developed." [1] Not its false initial premises, but the most scientific interpretation of reality within the framework of the Physiocratic system. Turgot is approaching an understanding of surplus value, imperceptibly moving from the "pure gift of nature" to surplus created by the farmer's labour, which is appropriated by the owner of the main means of production, land.

The next seventeen theorems deal with value, prices and money. In these pages and also in some other of Turgot's works bourgeois economists a hundred years later discovered the first seeds of the subjectivist theories which flourished so abundantly at the end of the 19th century. Like French political economy as a whole Turgot did not arrive at the labour theory of value. According to him, the exchange value and price of a commodity were determined by the relation between requirements, by the intensity of the wishes of the persons entering into the exchange, the seller and the purchaser. But these ideas of Turgot's are only slightly connected with the main body of his teaching.

It is basically the last 52 theorems that give Turgot the right to one of the most honoured places in the history of political economy.

As already mentioned, society in the Physiocratic system consisted of three classes: the productive class (farmers), the

---

[1] Karl Marx, *Theories of Surplus-Value*, Part I, p. 54.

proprietors and the sterile class (all the rest). Turgot makes a splendid addition to this scheme. The last class, according to him, "is subdivided, as to say, into two categories: that of the manufacturer entrepreneurs, the factory-owners, all possessors of large capital which they use to obtain profit by making people work by means of their advances; and the second category, composed of simple workers, who have no other possessions but their hands, who advance only their daily labour and have no other profit than their wages".[1] The fact that the wages of these workers are reduced to the minimum necessary for subsistence is mentioned by Turgot in another passage. And analogously "the class of farmers is divided like that of factory-owners into two categories, that of the entrepreneurs or capitalists who make all the advances, and that of the simple salaried workers".[2]

This model of society consisting of five classes is closer to reality than Quesnay's model which divides society into three classes. It is a kind of bridge between the Physiocrats and the English classics, who clearly divided society into the three main classes from the point of view of their relation to the means of production: landowners, capitalists and hired workers. They got rid of the fundamental differentiation between industry and agriculture, which Turgot did not dare to do.

Another of his great achievements was his analysis of capital, which is considerably more profound and productive than Quesnay's

The latter treated capital mainly as a sum of advances in various natural forms (raw material, wages, etc.), because with him capital is not linked closely enough with the problem of distribution of the product between the classes of society. Quesnay's system had no place for profit; his capitalist "managed on a wage", so to say, and Quesnay did not investigate which laws determined this "wage".

Here Turgot makes a great advance. He cannot manage without the category of profit and even, governed by true instinct, begins its examination with the industrial capitalist. The origin of profit is more obvious here, for the issue is not clouded by the Physiocrat prejudice that "all surplus comes from the land".

---

[1] Turgot, *Textes choisis et preface par Pierre Vigreux*, Paris, 1947, p. 112.
[2] Ibid., p. 114.

Turgot the Physiocrat proceeds, strangely enough, to apologise for having "somewhat reversed the natural order" and deals with agriculture in the second place only. But he need not apologise. On the contrary, his argument is most sound: the capitalist farmer who uses hired labour must receive at least the same profit on his capital as the factory owner, plus a certain surplus which is bound to give the landowner as rent.

Perhaps the most surprising theorem is the sixty-second. Capital invested in production possesses the ability of self-growth. What determines the degree, the proportion of this self-growth?

Turgot attempts to explain what constitutes the value of a product created by capital (in fact, by labour exploited by the capital in question). Firstly, the value of the product compensates for the expenditure of capital, including workers' wages.[1] The rest (basically surplus-value) is divided into three parts.

The first part is the profit equal to the income which the capitalist can obtain "without any difficulty" as the owner of money capital. This is the part of the profit which corresponds to loan interest. The second part of the profit is payment for the "labour, risk and skill" of the capitalist, who decides to invest his money in a factory or farm. This is entrepreneurial income. Thus Turgot notes a division in industrial profit, its division between the loaning and functioning capitalist. The third part is land rent. It exists only for capital which is invested in agriculture. This analysis was undoubtedly a step forward in economic science.

But immediately Turgot goes off at a tangent. He departs from the correct viewpoint that profit is the main, generalising form of surplus-value from which both interest and rent proceed. At first he reduces profit to interest: this is the minimum to which any capitalist has a right. If, instead of sitting quietly at his desk, he ventures into the smoke and sweat of a factory or sweats in the sun, keeping an eye on his farm-labourers, he should have a slight addition — a special kind of wage. Interest, in its turn, is reduced to land rent: for the simplest thing to do with capital is buy a plot of land and

---

[1] Turgot also makes special mention of an insurance fund which must be allotted from the value of the product for unforeseen expenditure (cattle plague, etc.)

rent it out. So now the main form of surplus value is land rent, and the others are merely a product of it. Again the whole of society is "living on the wages" which are produced by the land only. Turgot returns to the bosom of the Physiocrats.

As we know, even the mistakes of great thinkers are fruitful and important. This also applies to Turgot. In examining the different forms of investing capital, he raises the important question of the competition of capitals, the natural levelling out of profit due to the possibility of moving capital from one sphere of investment to another. The next important step towards solving these problems was made by Ricardo. These searchings in French and English classical economy gradually led to the solution provided by Marx in the third volume of *Capital* in the theory on the profit and price of production, the theory of loan capital and interest and the theory of land rent.

MINISTER

The Bourbon monarchs left posterity some famous sayings. Legend has it that Henry IV coined the phrase "Paris is worth a mass". Louis XIV described the absolute monarchy in a nutshell with the words "L'état, c'est moi". And Lous XV uttered the equally famous "Après nous le déluge". Louis XVI left no famous saying, possibly because he was soon beheaded, but perhaps because he was simply a fool. As Mirabeau (the son of the Physiocrat marquis) said, the only man in the family of King Louis XIV was Marie-Antoinette.

Louis XV died of smallpox in May 1774. The latter years of his life were marked by cruel reaction and financial crisis. The death of a despot is usually followed by liberal trends, even if a new tyrant is on the threshold. The death of the old king produced a sigh of relief all over France. The philosophers hoped that his 20-year-old heir, of mild and malleable disposition, would finally bring in the "Age of Reason" and put their ideas into practice. These hopes were further nurtured by the appointment of Turgot to high office, first as Minister of Marine and a few weeks later as controller general of finance, which meant in practice that he controlled all the country's internal affairs.

It is often said that Turgot became a minister by chance; his friend the Abbé de Véri had a word with Madame de

Maurepas who put pressure on her husband, the new king's favourite, etc. This is only partly true. Turgot's appointment was the result of intrigue. The wily courtier Maurepas was counting on using Turgot's popularity and well-known honesty for his own ends. He had little time for his ideas and projects.

But this is not the whole story. More than ever before the country felt the need for change. This was understood even by the feudal aristocrats at the top. A new man was needed, who was not connected with the Court clique, not tainted with the embezzlement of public funds. The man was found—it was Turgot. In taking on the cleaning of France's Augean stables of finance and economy, Turgot did not flatter himself with the illusion that it would be an easy task. He deliberately shouldered the burden and bore it without faltering. His path was that of daring bourgeois reforms, which he regarded as essential from the point of view of human reason and progress.

Marx wrote of Turgot: "He was one of the intellectual heroes who overthrew the ancien régime." [1]

What exactly did Turgot do as minister? A fantastic amount if one bears in mind the short period of his office and the enormous difficulties which he encountered. Very little if one judges by the final, long-term results. If a man like Turgot could not put through the reforms that meant reforms were impossible. Therefore a straight path leads from Turgot's reforms to the capture of the Bastille in 1789 and the storming of the Tuilleries Palace in 1792.

The most urgent task which Turgot tackled right away was to put the state's finances in order. He had a long-term programme including such radical reforms as the abolition of tax farming and the taxing of incomes from landed property. Turgot was in no hurry to make his programme generally known, realising full well how interested circles would react to it. For the time being he worked hard to introduce many individual measures, getting rid of the most blatant absurdities and injustices of the tax system, relieving the tax burden on industry and trade, and bringing pressure to bear on tax-farmers. On the other hand, he tried to restrict budget expenditure of which the main item was maintenance of the Court. Here he soon clashed with the caprice and ill-will of the extravagant Marie-Antoinette. Turgot succeeded in achieving

[1] Karl Marx/Friedrich Engels, *Werke*, Bd. 15, Berlin, 1969, S. 375.

a slight improvement in the budget and the establishment of state credit. But the minister's enemies were rapidly increasing and growing more active.

An important economic measure by Turgot was the introduction of free trade in corn and flour and the abolition of a monopoly which some cunning rogues had acquired with the support of a previous minister. This basically progressive measure, however, created great complications for him. The harvest of 1774 was a poor one, and the price of grain rose appreciably in the following spring. In certain towns, particularly Paris, there was popular rioting. Although no one has been able to prove it, there are grounds for thinking that these riots were to a large extent provoked and organised by Turgot's enemies with the aim of undermining his position. The Minister quelled them with a firm hand. He may have assumed that the people did not understand their own interests and that these interests should be explained to them in a different way. All this was used against Turgot by his ill-wishers, to whom Maurepas now secretly belonged: as time passed, he feared and envied Turgot more and more.

Yet Turgot went on without hesitating. In early 1776 he received the King's approval of his famous Six Edicts, which more than any of his previous measures undermined feudalism. The most important of them were the two about the suppression of the *corvées* and the abolition of the *jurandes* and *maîtrises*, the privileged trade corporations. The latter was considered by Turgot not without justification to be an essential condition for the rapid growth of industry and the estate of capitalist entrepreneurs. The edicts met with bitter resistance, the core of which was the Paris parlement. They could not become law until they had been registered by parlement. The fight went on for more than two months. It was not until 12 March that Turgot obtained registration and the edicts became law.

It was a Pyrrhic victory. All the forces of the ancien régime now rallied against the reformist minister: the Court clique, the upper echelons of the Church, the nobility, the judiciary and the corporation bourgeoisie.

The people understood the democratic nature of Turgot's reforms to a certain extent. The peasants were overjoyed to be free of the hated *corvées*, but hardly knew his name. The more literate Parisian apprentices and journeymen rejoiced and wrote couplets in praise of Turgot. But the people were far below, and his enemies close at hand. The gay couplets of the journeymen and the practical articles of the Physiocrats were drowned in the vile stream of spiteful pamphlets, mocking rhymes and caricatures which flooded Paris. The lampoonists depicted Turgot sometimes as France's evil genius, sometimes as a helpless and unpractical philosopher, and sometimes as a puppet in the hands of the "economists' sect". Only Turgot's incorruptibility and honesty were left unquestioned: no one would ever have doubted them.

The whole campaign was directed and financed by the Court clique. Other ministers hatched plots against Turgot. The Queen histerically demanded that Louis send him to the Bastille. The King's brother was one of the most vicious slanderers.

In this uproar the inexorably firm, proud and solitary Turgot was a truly majestic and tragic figure.

His fall was now inevitable. Louis XVI finally gave way to the pressure which came from all sides. The King did not dare tell his minister about retirement to his face: the order to vacate his post was brought to Turgot by a royal messenger. This took place on 12 May, 1776. Most of the measures initiated by him, particularly the edicts mentioned above, were soon fully or partially revoked. Nearly everything went on as before. Turgot's supporters and assistants whom he brought into government service retired with him, some being forced to leave Paris. The hopes of the Physiocrats and Encyclopaedists were crushed.

MAN

Although Turgot was not yet fifty he suffered from bad health. His attacks of gout were particularly painful. Of the twenty months he was in office seven were spent in bed. Yet his work was never interrupted, not for a single day. He went on dictating draft laws, reports and correspondence, receiving officials and giving instructions to his assistants. He was sometimes carried into the King's cabinet in a sedan chair.

He continued to despise ill health, although it pursued him doggedly. Sometimes he could only get about with the aid of crutches, which he referred to ironically as his "paws". He died from a disease of the liver in May 1781, exactly five years after his retirement.

His friends were struck by the calmness with which Turgot reacted to his fall from favour and the failure of his reforms. He could even ridicule censors opening his letters. He seemed to enjoy having retired into private life: in the fifteen years that he was intendant and minister he had no time for reading, private study and contact with his friends. Now he was given the time.

In his letters Turgot discusses literature and music, and talks about his studies in physics and astronomy.

In 1778 as president of the Académie des Inscriptions et Belles Lettres he officially made his new friend, Benjamin Franklin, an academician. It was for Franklin, as ambassador for the resurgent American colonies, that he wrote his last economic work *Mémoire sur l'impôt*. Like the rest of French society he took a passionate interest in American affairs during this period. With his inherent optimism he hoped that the Republic across the ocean would avoid the mistakes and shortcomings of decrepit feudal Europe.

Turgot was a constant visitor to the salons of his old friend the Duchesse d'Enville and Madame Helvetius, the philosopher's widow, where the most freethinking and enlightened people gathered. The intellect of this great admirer of human reason remained sharp and clear right up to the end.

Turgot was a somewhat stern and forbidding person in private life. He was occasionally accused of lacking flexibility and being too single-minded. This obviously made personal contact with him difficult, even for those who were close to him, and frightened those who did not know him well.

He was particularly irritated by hypocricy, thoughtlessness, and inconsistency. Turgot never learnt the manners of the Court. His biographer writes that residents of Versailles were embarrassed and scared by his appearance, "his piercing brown eyes, his massive forehead, his majestic features, the very poise of his head, a dignity like that of Roman statuary."

He did not fit into the court at Versailles. Among his many talents he did not possess the gift described by Talleyrand — of using language not to explain one's thoughts, but to conceal them.

CHAPTER X

ADAM SMITH
THE SCOTTISH SAGE

Political economy is celebrating two dates connected with the name of one of its founders: 1973 was the 250th anniversary of the birth of Adam Smith and 1976 will be the bicentenary of the publication of *The Wealth of Nations*. Once again attention is focused on this great Scot and his eminent role in the science.

Walter Bagehot, an English economist and publicist of the Victorian era, wrote in 1876: "Of Adam Smith's Political Economy almost an infinite quantity has been said, but very little has been said as to Adam Smith himself. And yet not only was he one of the most curious of human beings, but his books can hardly be understood without having some notion of what manner of man he was."[1]

The study of Smith has advanced greatly since then, of course. Nevertheless in 1948 the British specialist Alexander Gray said: "Adam Smith was so pre-eminently one of the master minds of the eighteenth century and so obviously one of the dominating influences of the nineteenth, in his own country and in the world at large, that it is somewhat surprising that we are so ill-informed regarding the details of his life.... His biographer therefore is almost perforce driven to eke out

---

[1] *Bagehot's Historical Essays*, New York, 1966, p. 79.

his scanty material by writing not so much a Biography of Adam Smith as a History of his Times." [1]

The needs of the age produce the man required. Determined by the actual development of capitalist economy, political economy in England reached the stage at which the need arose for the creation of a system, the systematisation and generalisation of economic knowledge. Smith was excellently equipped for the job both personally and academically. He was fortunate in combining an ability for abstract thought with the gift of being able to talk about concrete things vividly; encyclopaedic learning with exceptional conscientiousness and academic honesty; the ability to use other men's ideas with a great independence and criticalness of thought; a certain academic and civic boldness with professorial calm and orderliness.

A characteristic of economic science is that it makes it possible, or at least tries to understand and interpret the meaning of phenomena which appear simple and ordinary, but are of vital importance to man. Money is such a phenomenon. There is no one who has not held it in his hands, or does not know what it is. But money contains many secrets. For economists this problem is inexhaustibly complex, and will undoubtedly continue to occupy their minds for many years to come.

Smith had a remarkable feeling for the romance of everyday economic phenomena. Under his pen all the acts of buying and selling, renting land and hiring workers, paying taxes and discounting bills acquired a special meaning and interest. It emerged that without understanding them one could not begin to fathom what happening in the "dignified" higher sphere of politics and state government. The fact that political economy aroused such interest in the age of Byron and Pushkin is due to Smith.

Another important fact is that Smith, in expressing the interests of the growing industrial bourgeoisie, was by no means its unconditional apologist. He not only strove subjectively for academic impartiality and independent judgment, but to a large extent achieved them. These qualities enabled him to create a system of political economy. To quote Marx, "he attempted to penetrate the inner physiology of bourgeois

---

[1] A. Gray, *Adam Smith*, London, 1948, p. 3.

society ...".[1] Smith's book is an important achievement of human culture and the apex of 18th-century economic thought.

SCOTLAND

It has become a platitude that one can only understand Smith's political economy if one takes into account that he was a Scot, and what is more a typical Scot with a pronounced national character.

The French writer André Maurois begins his biography of another great Scot, Alexander Fleming, the discoverer of penicillin, with the words: "Scotsmen are not Englishmen. Far from it." Industry, thrift and economy are generally regarded as typical features of the Scottish national character. The Scots are considered to be sober, taciturn and businesslike. And inclined to discuss abstract subjects, to "philosophise".

However, the point is not the extent to which this somewhat trite description of Scottish national character is true. For Smith and an understanding of the individual nature of his views it is important to explain the position of his country and the Scottish people during his lifetime.

In 1707 the Act of Union between England and Scotland was passed. It benefited the English and Scottish industrialists, merchants and rich farmers whose influence increased perceptibly at this time. The customs barriers between the two countries were removed, the sale of Scottish cattle in England increased, and the Glasgow merchants gained access to trade with English colonies in America. For the sake of all this the Scottish bourgeoisie was prepared to sacrifice its patriotism somewhat: for Scotland was bound to play a subordinate role in the new United Kingdom. On the other hand, the majority of the Scottish aristocracy was opposed to Union. With the help of loyal and ferocious Highlanders, who still lived in a feudal order with relics of the tribal system, they rose up several times in revolt. The population of the economically more developed Scottish lowlands did not support them, however, and each uprising failed.

---

[1] Karl Marx, *Theories of Surplus-Value*, Part III, Moscow, 1968, p. 165.

After Union the economic development of Scotland accelerated, although certain branches suffered from English competition and others from surviving feudal customs. The town and port of Glasgow grew particularly rapidly, and a whole industrial area developed around it. The existence of cheap labour from the village and highland areas and of large markets in Scotland, England and America promoted the growth of industry. The big landowners and rich tenant farmers began to introduce improvements in agriculture. In the seventy years between Union in 1707 and the publication of *The Wealth of Nations* in 1776 Scotland changed considerably. True, economic progress was limited almost exclusively to the Scottish lowlands, but it was here, in the triangle between Kirkcaldy, Glasgow and Edinburgh, that nearly all Smith's life was spent.

By the time Smith reached maturity, economy had bound the fate of Scotland indissolubly with that of England. To Smith, who saw everything in terms of the development of productive forces and the "wealth of the nation", this was particularly obvious. As for Scottish patriotism, in his case, as with many other enlightened Scots, it took a "cultural", emotional, but not political form.

The influence of the Church and religion on social life and learning was gradually diminishing. The Church had lost control of the universities. Scottish universities differed from Oxford and Cambridge in their spirit of freethinking, the importance of the secular sciences and their practical bias. In this respect Glasgow University, where Smith studied and later taught, stood out in particular. The inventor of the steam engine, James Watt, and one of the founders of modern chemistry, Joseph Black, worked with him and were his friends.

Around the 1750s Scotland entered upon a period of great cultural activity which can be seen in various branches of science and the arts. The brilliant array of talent which little Scotland produced over fifty years is most impressive. In addition to those already mentioned it includes the economist James Steuart and the philosopher David Hume, the historian William Robertson, and the sociologist and economist Adam Ferguson. Smith was well acquainted with such people as James Hutton, the geologist, William Hunter, the celebrated doctor, and Robert Adam, the architect. The influence of these people and their works extended far beyond the confines of Scotland, and of the British Isles.

Such was the environment, the atmosphere, in which Smith's talent developed. Naturally he did not absorb Scottish culture alone. English learning and culture, particularly English philosophical and economic thought, moulded him no less than purely Scottish influences. In the practical sense the whole of his book is aimed at exerting a specific (antimercantilistic) influence on the economic policy of the United Kingdom, the London government. Finally, one must mention another line of influence — the French. In Scotland, which had maintained traditional links with France since the time of Mary Stuart, the influence of French culture was felt more strongly than in England. Smith was well acquainted with the works of Montesquieu and Voltaire, and welcomed Rousseau's early works and the early volumes of the Encyclopaedia most enthusiastically.

PROFESSOR SMITH

Adam Smith was born in 1723 in the small town of Kirkcaldy, near Edinburgh. His father, a customs official, died several months earlier. Adam was the only child of the young widow, and she devoted her whole life to him. The boy grew up delicate and sickly, avoiding the boisterous games of other children of his age. The family lived modestly, but did not know real poverty. Fortunately Kirkcaldy possessed a good school and teacher, who did not believe in stuffing the children's heads with nothing but Biblical quotations and Latin conjugations, as so many others did. What is more, Adam was surrounded by books right from the start. Such were the beginnings of the immense learning which later distinguished Smith.

True, he did not receive, for obvious reasons, such a brilliant education as the aristocrat Turgot. In particular he never had a good teacher of French and never learned to speak it properly, although he read it fluently. The classical languages, which were a must for an educated person in the 18th century, he did not really study until he was at university (particularly Greek).

Smith went to Glasgow University very early, at fourteen (as was the custom in those days). After the logic course (first year), which was compulsory for all students, he went on to study moral philosophy, thereby choosing the humanities. He also studied mathematics and astronomy, however, and always remained remarkably knowledgeable in these spheres. By seventeen Smith had the reputation among the students of being a scholarly and somewhat strange fellow. He would fall deep in thought in a noisy crowd or began to talk to himself, oblivious of all around him. These slight eccentricities remained with him all his life. After graduating from Glasgow, Smith was awarded an exhibition to continue his studies at Oxford University. The exhibition was paid from a bequest by a wealthy philanthropist. Smith spent six years in Oxford almost uninterruptedly.

The professors and tutors kept a careful eye on the students' reading, banning freethinking books. Smith's life at Oxford was a miserable one, and he always recalled his second university with hatred. He was lonely and frequently suffered from ill health. Again his only friends were books. Smith's reading ranged very wide, but he showed no special interest in economic science at this time.

In 1746 he left for Kirkcaldy where he spent two years, continuing his self-education. During one of his visits to Edinburgh he made such a strong impression on the rich landowner and patron, Henry Home (later Lord Kames), that the latter suggested organising a cycle of public lectures on English literature for the young scholar. Later the subject matter of his lectures, which were a great success, changed. They began to deal mainly with natural law; in the 18th century this concept included not only jurisprudence, but also political doctrines, sociology and economics. The first signs of a special interest in political economy belong to this period.

In 1750-51 he seemed to have been expressing the main ideas of economic liberalism. At all events, in 1755 he wrote in a special note that these ideas belonged to his lectures in Edinburgh: "Man is generally considered by statesmen and projectors as the material of a sort of political mechanics. Projectors disturb nature in the course of her operations in human affairs; and it requires no more than to let her fair play in the pursuit of her ends that she may establish her own designs.... Little else is requisite to carry a state to the highest degree of opulence from the lowest barbarism, but peace, easy taxes and a tolerable administration of justice; all the rest being brought about by the natural course of things. All governments which thwart this natural course which force things into another channel, or which endeavour to arrest the progress of society at a particular point are unnatural and to support themselves are obliged to be oppressive and tyrannical."[1]

This is the language of the progressive bourgeoisie of the 18th century with its strict attitude towards the state which had not yet fully discarded its feudal clothing. In the passage one can already feel the bold, energetic style characteristic of Smith. This is now the same Smith who in *The Wealth of Nations* refers with wrathful sarcasm to "that insidious and crafty animal, vulgarly called a statesman or politician, whose councils are directed by the momentary fluctuations of affairs".[2] This would appear to be not only the negative attitude of a bourgeois ideologist to the state of his day, but also simply the profound hatred of a democratic intellectual for bureaucracy and political intrigue.

In 1751 Smith moved to Glasgow to take up the post of professor at the university. At first he received the chair of logic, then moral philosophy, i.e., social sciences. He lived in Glasgow for thirteen years with regular visits of two to three months a year to Edinburgh. In old age he wrote that this was the happiest time of his life. He lived in a very familiar and intimate environment, enjoying the respect of professors, students and eminent citizens. He was able to work without any interference, and a great deal was expected from him academically. He acquired a circle of friends and began to assume the characteristic features of the British bachelor and club man, which remained with him all his life.

As in the case of Newton and Leibniz, no woman played a conspicuous role in Smith's life. There exist, it is true, vague and unauthenticated rumours that he was twice on the verge of marriage — in the Edinburgh and Glasgow years — but each time nothing came of it for some reason. This does not appear to have disturbed his peace of mind, however. At least there are no traces of such disturbance in either his correspondence (most scanty, incidentally) or the reminiscences of contemporaries.

---

[1] Quoted from W. R. Scott, *Adam Smith as Student and Professor*, Glasgow, 1937, pp. 53-54.

[2] A. Smith, *The Wealth of Nations*, Vol. I, London, 1924, p. 412.

All his life his mother and cousin, an old maid, kept house for him. Smith outlived his mother by only six years, and his cousin by two. As one of Smith's visitors remarked, the house was "absolutely Scottish". Scottish national dishes were served and Scottish traditions and customs observed. This familiar way of life became a necessity to him. He did not like going away for long periods and always hurried back home.

In 1759 Smith published his first large scientific work, the *Theory of Moral Sentiments*. Although this book on ethics was a progressive work for its time, worthy of the age and ideals of the Enlightenment, it is important today mainly as a stage in the formation of Smith's philosophical and economic ideas. He attacked Christian morality, based on fear of retribution in the hereafter and the promise of heavenly bliss. A prominent place in his ethics is occupied by the antifeudal idea of equality. All men are naturally equal, therefore moral principles apply equally to all.

Smith was proceeding from absolute, "natural" laws of human conduct, however, and a very vague sense that ethics was basically determined by the socio-economic order of the society in question. Therefore, having rejected religious morality and "innate moral sense", he put another abstract principle in their place, the "principle of sympathy". He tried to explain all man's feelings and actions in relation to other people by his ability to "get into their skin", to imagine himself in their position and feel for them. However cleverly and sometimes wittily this idea is developed, it could not become the foundation of scientific materialist ethics. Smith's *Theory of Moral Sentiments* did not outlive the 18th century. It did not immortalise the name of Smith. Quite the reverse, the fame of the author of *The Wealth of Nations* saved it from oblivion.

In the meantime the direction of Smith's scientific interests had already changed perceptibly in the course of his work on the *Theory*. He was making an increasingly profound study of political economy. He was encouraged to do this not only by personal inclination, but also the demands of the times. Economic problems were making themselves felt with special force in commercial and industrial Glasgow. It had an interesting club of political economy, where people discussed trade and duty, wages and banking, land rent conditions and the colonies. Smith soon became one of the club's most eminent members. His meeting and friendship with Hume also stimulated his interest in political economy.

At the end of the last century the English economist Edwin Cannan discovered and published some important material which throws light upon the development of Smith's ideas. This was notes of Smith's lectures made by a student at Glasgow University and then slightly corrected and rewritten. Judging by the contents, these lectures were given in 1762-63. It is clear from them that the course of moral philosophy on which Smith lectured to the students had turned by then into a course of sociology and political economy. He expressed a number of remarkable materialist ideas, for example: "Till there be property there can be no government, the very end of which is to secure wealth, and to defend the rich from the poor".[1] In the economic sections of these lectures one can see in embryonic form ideas later developed in *The Wealth of Nations*.

Another interesting find was made in the 1930s: a draft of the first few chapters of *The Wealth of Nations*. British scholars date this document 1763. It too contains several of the important ideas in the future book: the role of the division of labour, the concept of productive and unproductive labour, etc. These works also contain an extremely biting criticism of mercantilism and an argument for *laissez faire*.

Thus, by the end of his period in Glasgow, Smith was already a profound and original economic thinker. But he was not yet ready to produce his main work. The three-year visit to France (as tutor to the young Duke of Buccleuch) and his personal meeting with the Physiocrats completed his preparation.

SMITH IN FRANCE

Fifty years after the events described, Jean Baptiste Say asked the old Du Pont about Smith's stay in Paris in 1765-66. Du Pont replied that Smith had visited Doctor Quesnay's "entresol club". But he had sat quietly and said little at the Physiocrat gatherings, so one could not have suspected that this was the future author of *The Wealth of Nations*. A. Morellet, a scholar and writer, with whom Smith became friendly in Paris, says about Smith in his memoirs that "M. Turgot ... had a

---

[1] A. Smith. *Lectures on Justice, Police, Revenue and Arms*, Oxford, 1896, p. 15.

high opinion of his talent. We saw him many times; he was introduced to Helvetius: we talked about commercial theory, banking, national credit and many points of the great work which he was planning."[1] From his letters it is also known that Smith became friendly with the mathematician and philosopher D'Alembert and the great fighter against ignorance and superstition, Baron Holbach. Smith visited Voltaire at his estate on the outskirts of Geneva and had several talks with him. He regarded him as one of the greatest Frenchmen.

As early as 1775 Smith published an article in the *Edinburgh Review*, which shows the author's exceptional knowledge of French culture. From his lectures it is obvious that he had a detailed knowledge of the ideas and activity of John Law. He was probably only slightly acquainted with the works of the Physiocrats, although he had read Quesnay's articles in the Encyclopaedia. His knowledge of their ideas was gained mainly in Paris, from personal encounter and from the Physiocrat literature which had begun to appear in abundance.

One might say that Smith went to France just at the right time. On the one hand, he was already a sufficiently mature scholar and person with views of his own. On the other, his system had not yet developed fully and he was able to absorb the ideas of Quesnay and Turgot.

The question of Smith's dependence on the Physiocrats, and Turgot in particular, has a history of its own. Smith penetrated more deeply the inner physiology of bourgeois society. Following the English tradition, he based his economic theory on the labour theory of value, whereas the Physiocrats did not actually have a theory of value. This enabled him to take a most important step forward by comparison with the Physiocrats; he proved that all productive labour creates value, not only agricultural labour. Smith had a clearer idea of the class structure of society than the Physiocrats.

At the same time there are spheres in which the Physiocrats were more advanced than Smith. This applies in particular to Quesnay's brilliant ideas about the mechanism of capitalist reproduction. Smith followed the Physiocrats in believing that capitalists could accumulate only by self-deprivation, by abstinence and refraining from consumption. But the Phisioc-

---

[1] A. Morellet, *Mémoires sur le dix-huitième siècle, et sur la revolution française,* t. I, Paris, 1822, p. 244.

rats at least had the logical basis that, in their opinion, capitalists accumulated "out of nothing", since industrial labour was "sterile". Smith does not even have this justification. He is inconsistent in his thesis about the equality, the economically equal value of all types of productive labour. He could clearly not rid himself of the idea that agricultural labour still took preference from the point of view of the creation of value: here nature "works" with man.

Smith's attitude to the Physiocrats was quite different from his attitude to the mercantilists. He regarded the mercantilists as ideological adversaries and, for all his professional restraint, did not spare the sharpest (sometimes even excessive) criticism for them. Generally speaking he saw the Physiocrats as allies and friends who were advancing to the same aim by a different path. His conclusion in *The Wealth of Nations* is that "this system, however, with all its imperfections is, perhaps, the nearest approximation to the truth that has yet been published upon the subject of political economy".[1] In another passage he writes that it "never has done, and probably never will do, any harm in any part of the World".

The last remark could be taken as a joke. Adam Smith jokes almost imperceptibly, preserving an imperturbable seriousness. He was evidently like this in life too. One day during an official dinner at the University in Glasgow the person sitting next to him, who had come from London, asked in surprise why everyone was so respectful to a certain person there obviously not overblessed with intelligence. Smith replied: "We know that perfectly, but he is the only lord in our College." His neighbour could not tell whether this was a joke or not.

France exists in Smith's book not only in the ideas connected directly or indirectly with the Physiocrats, but also in a multitude of different observations (including personal ones), examples and illustrations. The general tone of all this material is critical. For Smith France with its feudal, absolutist system and fetters on bourgeois development was a vivid example of the contradiction between existing orders and the ideal "natural order". It could not be said that everything was perfect in England, but on the whole its system came much closer to the "natural order" with its freedom of the individual, conscience and, most important, enterprise.

---

[1] A. Smith, *The Wealth of Nations*, Vol. III, London, 1924, p. 172.

What did the three years in France mean for Smith's private life? Firstly, his material position greatly improved. By agreement with the Duke of Buccleuch's parents he was to receive three hundred pounds a year not only during the journey but also as a pension all his life. This enabled Smith for the next years to devote himself exclusively to his book: he did not return to Glasgow University. Secondly, all his contemporaries noted a change in his character: he had become more disciplined, efficient and energetic, and even acquired a certain skill in dealing with different people, including his superiors. He was never to acquire social poise, however, and remained in the eyes of most of his acquaintances a somewhat eccentric and absent-minded professor. Rumours of his absent-mindedness grew quickly with his fame and became part of it for the man in the street.

THE "ECONOMIC MAN"

Smith spent about a year in Paris — from December 1765 to October 1766. But he did not occupy the same place in the Paris salons as his friend Hume had for the last three years, or Franklin was to in ten years' time. Smith was not made to shine in society and he knew it.

Of particular importance for him was his acquaintance with Helvetius, a man of great personal charm and brilliant intellect. In his philosophy Helvetius strove to free ethics from religious and feudal fetters. He announced that egoism was a natural human quality and a factor in social progress. The new, essentially bourgeois ethics proceeded on the assumption that each person strives naturally for his own gain and that this is limited only by the similar striving of other people. He compared the role of self-interest in society with the role of gravity in nature. This is connected with the idea of natural equality: each person, irrespective of birth and position, should be given an equal right to pursue his own gain, and the whole of society will profit from it.

Smith developed these ideas and applied them to political economy. His view of human nature and the relationship between man and society lay at the root of the views of the classical school. The concept of *homo oeconomicus* arose slightly later, but its inventors based themselves on Smith. The famous passage about "the invisible hand" is perhaps the most quoted one from *The Wealth of Nations*.

Smith's line of reasoning is roughly as follows. The main motive behind human economic activity is self-interest. But man can pursue this interest only by performing services for others, by offering to exchange his labour and the products of his labour. Thus division of labour develops. People help one another and in so doing promote the development of society, although each of them is an egoist and cares only for his own interests. The natural human striving to improve one's material position is such a powerful stimulus that if allowed to act freely it is capable of carrying society to prosperity. What is more, "drive nature out of the door and it will come in through the window" as they say in Russian: this stimulus is even capable "of surmounting a hundred impertinent obstructions with which the folly of human laws too often incumbers its operations...".[1] Here Smith is attacking mercantilism, which restricts man's "natural freedom", the freedom to buy and sell, rent and hire, produce and consume.

Each individual strives to use his capital (as we can see, Smith is talking basically about the capitalist, not just man in general) so that its product will have the highest value. Usually in so doing he does not think of the public good and does not realise the extent to which he is promoting it. He has in view only his own gain, but is "led by an *invisible hand* (my italics — A. A.) to promote an end which was no part of his intention.... By pursuing his own interest he frequently promotes that of the society more effectually than when he really intends to promote it".[2]

The "invisible hand" is the spontaneous operation of objective economic laws. These laws act independently of and often contrary to human will. By introducing the concept of economic laws into the science in such a form Smith made an important step forward. He put political economy on a scientific basis. The conditions under which self-interest and spontaneous laws of economic development operate most efficiently Smith called "the natural order". With Smith and subsequent generations of political economists this concept has a dual meaning, as it were. On the one hand, it is the principle

---

[1] A. Smith, *The Wealth of Nations*, Vol. II, London, 1924, p. 40.

[2] Ibid., Vol. I, p. 400.

and goal of economic policy, i.e., the policy of *laissez faire* (see below), and on the other, it is a theoretical construction, a "model" for the study of economic reality.

In physics the abstract concepts of ideal gas and ideal liquid are used as a convenient way of obtaining knowledge. Real gases and liquids do not behave "ideally" or behave so only in certain circumstances. However it is worth while to ignore these deviations in order to study phenomena "in their pure form". The abstraction of the "economic man" and free (perfect) competition is somewhat similar in economics. The real man cannot be reduced to self-interest. Just as there never has been and never can be absolutely free competition under capitalism. However, the science could not study mass economic phenomena and processes if it did not make certain assumptions which simplify, model, infinitely complex and diverse reality, accentuating the most important features in it. From this point of view the abstraction of the "economic man" and free competition was totally justified and played an important role in economic science. In particular it corresponded to the real nature of 18th- and 19th-century capitalism.

Let us quote two examples from Marxist economic theory.

The law of value operates in a commodity economy based on private ownership as a spontaneous regulator and motive force of production. If, for example, due to some technical innovation, a commodity producer reduces expenditure of labour time on the production of each commodity unit, the *individual value* of the commodity drops. But the *social value*, which is determined by the average social expenditure of labour time, does not change, all things being equal. Your skilled commodity producer will sell each unit of his commodity at its former price, which is determined in principle by the social value, and receive an additional income, for in one working day, say, he is producing 25 per cent more units of the commodity than anyone else. Obviously competing commodity producers will try to copy new techniques. This is the first principle of the mechanism of "stimulating technological progress". The operation of the spontaneous factors described, which are independent of human will, brings about a reduction in socially necessary expenditure of labour per unit of commodity and a drop in social value. It is easy to see that the commodity producer is acting as an "economic man" here, striving to maximise his income, and the conditions under which this takes place are those of free competition.

Another example—the formation of the average rate of profit under free competition capitalism. It is inconceivable that over any lengthy period the rate of profit in different branches of business would be substantially different. The levelling out of the rate of profit is an objective necessity. The mechanism which ensures this levelling is competition between the various branches and the flow of capital from branches with a low rate of profit to those with a higher one. Again it is obvious that here the capitalist is seen from one angle only—as the personification of the striving for profit. The condition about the possibility of the unrestricted flow of capital is the same as the condition about free competition. In reality there have always been factors restricting the free flow of capital and Marx was well aware of them. But these factors are to be introduced into the model only after it has been examined "in its ideal form".

The capitalist, as Marx put it, is personified capital. In other words, the personal qualities of an individual capitalist cannot be of significance to political economy. He is of interest to the science only because and to the extent that he expresses the social relations of capital. Here one senses a certain kinship with Smith's ideas. But the conclusion is quite different. With Smith the capitalist, by pursuing his self-interest, is unconsciously strengthening capitalism. With Marx, by acting in much the same way, he is not only developing the productive forces of capitalism but also objectively preparing its logical collapse. There is also another fundamental difference linked with this. Marx examines man from the viewpoint of historical materialism as the product of lengthy historical development. This man, as the object of political economy, exists only within the framework of a given class society and acts in accordance with its laws. For Smith, however, the *homo oeconomicus* is the expression of eternal and natural human nature. He is not the product of development, but rather its point of departure. Smith shared this extra-historical and consequently false concept of human nature with all the eminent thinkers of his day, Helvetius, in particular.

With the concept of the "economic man" Smith raised a question of immense theoretical and practical importance: that of the motives and stimuli of human economic activity. He gave an answer which was fruitful and profound for its time, if one bears in mind that his "natural" man disguised the real man of bourgeois society.

Socialism also came up against the problem of motives and stimuli when it turned from a scientific theory into a socio-economic fact. With the collapse of capitalism and the total abolition of exploitation of man by man bourgeois stimuli for human economic activity also disappeared.

But what stimuli have replaced people's urge to get rich which, as Adam Smith said, in the final analysis drives on capitalist production? Are they simply socialist consciousness, labour enthusiasm, patriotism? For there are no capitalists, the factories and fields belong to the people, and the people are working for themselves....

Yes, socialism does produce new and powerful stimuli for labour and activity. This is its great advantage over capitalism. These stimuli do not appear out of thin air, however, but develop in the socialist transformation of society and of the people themselves, their psychology, morals and consciousness. In a society where the principle of distribution according to labour operates, material interest rightly remains a most important stimulus to labour. The principles of cost accounting, which were formulated on the basis of Lenin's ideas, have become the main method of socialist management. The economic reform carried out in the USSR in recent years develops and deepens these principles in the new conditions of a developed socialist society.

LAISSEZ FAIRE

The policy of *laissez faire* or, as Smith put it, natural freedom, follows directly from his views on man and society. If the economic activity of each person eventually leads to the good of society, it is clear that this activity must not be hampered in any way.

Smith believed that given free movement of commodities and money, capital and labour, society's resources would be used in the most rational way possible. The idea of free competition was the alpha and omega of his economic doctrine. It runs right through *The Wealth of Nations*. Smith even applied this principle to doctors, university professors and ... clergymen. If the clergymen of all denominations and sects were given the right to compete freely among themselves and no single group received privileges or, of course, a monopoly, they would be most harmless (and this, he hints, is the most one can hope for from them).

Smith's achievement was not that he discovered the principle of *laissez faire*, but that he argued it so consistently and systematically. Although the principle was born in France, it needed a Britisher to develop it to its logical conclusion and make it the basis of economic theory. England, which had become the most developed industrial country in the world, was already objectively interested in free trade. The fashion for Physiocracy in France was to a large extent a whim of enlightened and liberal aristocrats and soon passed. The "fashion" for Smith in England turned into the creed of the bourgeoisie and embourgeoisified nobility. The economic policy of the English government throughout the following century was to a certain extent the implementation of Smith's programme.

The first steps were taken while Smith was still alive. There is an amusing story in this connection. Towards the end of his life Smith was a famous man. On a visit to London in 1787 he arrived at the house of a very aristocratic person. There was a large company in the drawing room, including the Prime Minister William Pitt. When Smith entered, everyone rose to their feet. According to his professorial habit he raised a hand and said: "Be seated, gentlemen." To which Pitt replied: "No, we will stand till you are first seated, for we are all your disciples." Possibly this is just a legend. But it is a plausible one. Pitt did pass a series of measures in the sphere of trade which corresponded in spirit to the ideas of *The Wealth of Nations*.

Smith nowhere set out his programme point by point, but this is not a difficult task. In practice *laissez faire* as he understood it implies the following.

Firstly, he demanded the repeal of all measures restricting labour mobility, to use a modern term. Above all, this applied to such feudal survivals as compulsory apprenticeship and the settlement laws. Obviously the objective aim of this demand was to ensure freedom of action for capitalists. But one must bear in mind the age when Smith was writing: the British working class at that time was still suffering not so much from capitalism as from its insufficient development. Consequently Smith's demand was a progressive and even humane one.

Secondly, Smith advocated completely free trade in land. He was against the holding of large estates and proposed a repeal of the law of primogeniture which forbade the division of inherited lands. He wanted land to be in the hands of owners who were capable of making the most economic use of it or agreeable to put it into circulation. All this was directed towards the development of capitalism in agriculture.

Thirdly, Smith proposed abolishing the relics of governmental regulation of industry and domestic trade. The excise levied on the sale of certain commodities on the home market should be introduced only for the sake of budget income and not to influence the economy. England no longer had any taxes on the movement of commodities within the country. But Smith's criticism was all the more telling and relevant for France.

Fourthly, Smith made a detailed criticism of the whole of English foreign trade policy and drew up a programme of free foreign trade. This was his most important demand, and it was most directly aimed against mercantilism. Thus the free trade movement was born, which became the banner of the English industrial bourgeoisie in the 19th century.

The whole of mercantilist policy came under fire from Smith: the striving for a compulsorily active balance of payments, the bans on the import and export of certain commodities, the high import duties, subsidies for export, and monopolistic trading companies. He was particularly critical of English colonial policy, and stated openly that it was dictated by the interests not of the nation, but of a small group of traders. Smith considered the policy of suppressing industry and restricting trade pursued by England in Ireland and particularly in the North American colonies, both shortsighted and absurd. He wrote: "To prohibit a great people, however, from making all that they can of every part of their own produce, or from employing their stock and industry in the way that they judge most advantageous to themselves, is a manifest violation of the most sacred rights of mankind." [1]

This was published in 1776 when England was already at war with the insurgent colonists. Smith sympathised with American republicanism, although he remained a good Britisher and supported not the secession of the colonies, but the creation of union between England and the colonies on the basis of full

---

[1] A Smith, *The Wealth of Nations*, Vol. II, London, 1924, p. 78.

and equal rights. He expressed himself no less boldly on the East India Company's policy of plunder and oppression in India. It must also be remembered that Smith wrote many biting and harsh words in his book about the Church and the university education system. True, in England he was not risking either his head or his liberty and was not likely to be sent to prison, where some of his French friends, Voltaire, Diderot, Morellet and even Mirabeau, had been at various times. But he knew how vicious the hatred and attacks of the English clergy, the university authorities and newspaper hacks could be. He feared all this and did not conceal his fear.

Smith's attraction as a person is that, although a naturally cautious and wary man, he nevertheless wrote and published a daring book.

CHAPTER XI

ADAM SMITH THE CREATOR OF A SYSTEM

THE WEALTH OF NATIONS

In spring 1767 Smith retired to Kirkcaldy and lived there almost continuously for the next six years, which he devoted entirely to work on his book. In one of his letters he complains that the monotony of life and the excessive concentration of energy and attention on a single object were undermining his health. Leaving for London in 1773, he felt so ill that he considered it necessary to give Hume the formal rights to his literary heritage in case he should die. Smith thought he was travelling with a finished manuscript. In fact it took him about another three years to finish the work. A quarter of a century separates *The Wealth of Nations* from his first economic essays in the Glasgow lectures. It was indeed his magnum opus.

An Inquiry into the Nature and Causes of the Wealth of Nations was published in London in March 1776.

The work consists of five books. The basic principles of Smith's theoretical system, which completes and generalises many ideas of English and French economists of the preceding century, are expounded in the first two books. The first contains, in essence, an analysis of value and surplus value, which Smith examines in the concrete forms of profit and land rent. The second book bears the title "Of the Nature, Accumulation, And Employment of Stock". The remaining three books are the application of Smith's theory partly to history but mainly to economic policy. The small third book deals with the development of European economy in the age of feudalism and the formation of capitalism. The extensive fourth book is a history and critique of political economy; eight chapters are devoted to mercantilism and one to the Physiocrats. The largest book, the fifth, deals with state finance — receipts and expenditure. It is in the books with denser concrete material that some of Smith's most characteristic statements on basic economic problems lie.

The Wealth of Nations is undoubtedly one of the most absorbing books in the history of political economy. As Walter Bagehot remarked, it is not only an economic treatise but also "a very amusing book about old times". It is very different from Quesnay's dry analytical studies, Turgot's theorems and Ricardo's Principles with their rarefied atmosphere of profound abstraction. Smith's work combines vast erudition with subtle observation and original humour. From The Wealth of Nations one can learn a mass of interesting facts about the colonies and the universities, warfare and banking, silver mines and smuggling ... and a great deal more. From the modern point of view, a great deal of this has little to do with economic theory. But for Smith political economy was the almost all-embracing science of society.

The basic method of investigation in political economy is that of logical abstraction. By establishing in economics a series of basic initial categories and connecting them by fundamental dependences, one can proceed to analyse increasingly complex and concrete social phenomena. Adam Smith developed this scientific method. He sought to construct his system by basing it on such categories as division of labour, exchange, exchange value, and proceeding to the incomes of the main classes. In this sense his numerous digressions and descriptions can be regarded as factual illustrations possessing a certain demonstrative value. But Smith could not maintain this high level of scientific inquiry. He was often carried away by description and superficial ideas and abandoned his more profound analytical approach. This duality was determined objectively by the features of the age and Smith's place in the science, and subjectively by the peculiarities of his intellect.

In this connection Marx wrote: "Smith himself moves with great naïveté in a perpetual contradiction. On the one hand he traces the intrinsic connection existing between economic categories or the obscure structure of the bourgeois economic system. On the other, he simultaneously sets forth the connection as it appears in the phenomena of competition and thus as it presents itself to the unscientific observer just as to him who is actually involved and interested in the process of bourgeois production. One of these conceptions fathoms the inner connection, the physiology, so to speak, of the bourgeois system, whereas the other takes the external phenomena of life as they seem and appear and merely describes, catalogues, recounts, and arranges them under formal definitions. With Smith both these methods of approach not only merrily run alongside one another, but also intermingle and constantly contradict one another." [1]

Further on Marx says that Smith's duality is justified because his task really was a dual one. In striving to arrange economic knowledge into a system, he had not only to give an abstract analysis of intrinsic connections, but also to describe bourgeois society and select a system of definitions and concepts. This duality of Smith's, his inconsistency in pursuing the basic scientific principles, was of great importance for the future development of political economy. David Ricardo was probably the first to criticise the Scot, defending Smith the analyst against Smith the describer. Yet authors who, unlike Ricardo, were developing Smith's superficial, vulgar ideas, could also quote *The Wealth of Nations*.

Smith had a profound understanding of the subject of political economy as a science, an understanding which retains its importance to the present day. Political economy has two aspects. First and foremost, it is a science which studies the objective laws of the production, exchange, distribution and consumption of material goods in a given society, laws which exist independently of human will. When Smith describes the subject matter of the first two books of his inquiry in the introduction, he is in fact expounding this understanding of political economy. He is proposing to examine the *causes* of the growth of the productivity of social labour, the *natural* order of the distribution of the product between the different *classes* and groups of people in society, the *nature of capital* and the means of its gradual *accumulation*.

This is the *positive*, analytical approach to the economic structure of society. It studies what exists in reality and also

---

[1] Karl Marx, *Theories of Surplus-Value*, Part II, Moscow, 1968, p. 165.

why this reality develops. It is important that Smith sees political economy primarily as the analysis of *social* problems, relations between the social classes.

But there is also another aspect. In Smith's view, political economy should solve practical questions on the basis of objective analysis: it should argue and recommend an *economic policy* to "provide a plentiful revenue or subsistence for the people, or more properly to enable them to provide such a revenue or subsistence for themselves".[1] Political economy should, therefore, see that an order obtains in society which creates the most favourable conditions for the growth of productive forces.

This is the *normative*, practical approach. In such an approach the economist tries to answer the question of what should be done for the "growth of wealth" and how.

As a rule both methods are closely interconnected and in any economic conception the one complements the other. However, as we shall see below, the prevalence of either the first or the second approach was typical subsequently for many well-known scholars: whereas "Say's school" prided itself on its "positivism" and stressed the rejection of normative recommendations, Sismondi, on the contrary, saw political economy primarily as the science of how to transform society in the way he desired. Smith, however, with his characteristic many-sidedness, combined both approaches most organically.

DIVISION OF LABOUR

Adam Smith depicts the division of labour as the main factor in the growth of the productivity of social labour. He connects the actual invention and improvement of instruments and machines with the division of labour. Smith quotes his famous example of the pin factory where the specialisation of workers and the division of the operations between them made it possible to increase production many times over. Throughout the whole book the division of labour is a kind of historical prism, through which he examines economic processes.

Smith notes that the "wealth" of society, i.e., the volume of production and consumption of products depends on two

---

[1] Adam Smith, *The Wealth of Nations*, Vol. I, London, 1950, p. 395.

factors: 1) the proportion of the population engaged in productive labour, and 2) the productivity of labour. He farsightedly believed that the second factor was incomparably more important. Having asked what determines the productivity of labour, he gives a reply which is perfectly logical for his day: division of labour. And it is true that at the manufacturing stage of capitalist development, when machines were still rare and manual labour predominated, division of labour was the main factor in the growth of productivity.

Division of labour is of a dual nature. Workers employed in one factory specialise in different operations and together produce a finished article, pins, for example. This is one type. The other is quite different — the division of labour in society between individual enterprises and branches. The cattle-breeder breeds cattle and *sells* it for slaughter, the butcher slaughters it and *sells* the hide to the tanner, the latter processes the leather and *sells* it to the shoe-maker....

Smith confused these two types of division of labour and did not see the fundamental distinction between them: in the first case there is no buying or selling of the commodity, but in the second case there is. He regarded the whole of society as a gigantic factory, and the division of labour as the universal form of human economic collaboration in the interests of "the wealth of nations". This is connected with his general view of bourgeois society, which he regarded as the only possible, natural and eternal one. In fact the division of labour which Smith saw was specifically capitalist, which determined its main features and consequences. It did not simply promote the progress of society, but developed and strengthened the subjugation of labour to capital.

Two-faced on this question, as on many others, Smith sings the praises of capitalist division of labour at the beginning of the book, yet in another passage argues its bad influence on the worker: "In the progress of the division of labour, the employment of the far greater part of those who live by labour, that is, of the great body of the people, comes to be confined to a few very simple operations, frequently to one or two.... his [the worker's — A. A.] dexterity at his own particular trade seems, in this manner, to be acquired at the expense of his intellectual, social, and marital virtues. But in every improved and civilised society this is the state into which the labouring poor, that is, the great body of the people, must necessarily fall, unless government takes some pains to prevent it."[1] The worker turns into the helpless appendage of capital, capitalist production, into what Marx called the "partial worker".

The last sentence in the passage catches one's eye. It is somewhat unexpected from an unconditional supporter of *laissez faire*. The fact is that here Smith sensed a dangerous tendency in capitalism: if everything is left to take its natural course, there is the danger that a considerable part of the population will degenerate. He can see no other force apart from the state which could prevent this.

Having described the division of labour and the process of commodity exchange, Smith raises the question of money, without which regular exchange is impossible. In the small fourth chapter he conscientiously discusses the nature of money and the history of its emergence from all other commodities as a special commodity—universal equivalent. Smith returns frequently to money and credit, but on the whole these economic categories play a minor role in his writing. He sees money only as a technical instrument facilitating the course of economic processes, and calls it "the great wheel of circulation". Credit he regards solely as a means of activising capital and devotes little attention to it. The value of Smith's views lies in the fact that he evolved money and credit from production and saw their subordinate role in relation to production. But these views were also one-sided and restricted. He underestimated the independence which monetary and credit factors acquire and their great converse influence on production.

The first four chapters of *The Wealth of Nations* read easily and their contents are quite entertaining. They serve as a kind of introduction to the central part of Smith's teaching—the theory of value. Smith embarks upon it by earnestly entreating the reader's "patience and attention" in view of the "extremely abstracted" nature of the subject.

LABOUR VALUE

Smith's first critics generally made use of his methods and ideas. Consequently his influence, particularly combined with

---

[1] A. Smith, *The Wealth of Nations*, Vol. II, London, 1924, pp. 263, 264.

that of Ricardo, was immense right up to the 1860s. Then the situation changed. Marxism emerged, on the one hand. And, on the other, the subjective school in political economy, which soon became the dominant school in the bourgeois science.

The attitude towards Smith became "strict" and the first victim was, of course, his theory of value. This did not happen immediately, though. Alfred Marshall, the well-known English bourgeois economist of the second half of the 19th century, who retained a link with Ricardo and tried hard to reconcile him with the new subjectivist ideas, wrote about Smith that his "chief work was to combine and develop the speculations of his French and English contemporaries and predecessors as to value." [1]

The standpoint of the eminent American economist Paul H. Douglas, writing forty years later, was a different one. He accused Smith of having rejected that which was of most value in his predecessors and by his theory of value of sending English political economy up a blind alley, from which it did not manage to emerge for a whole century. Schumpeter in his *History of Economic Analysis* reinforces the outwardly respectful, but basically very sceptical attitude to Smith. Indeed he actually doubts whether one can say that Smith supports the labour theory of value. Finally, in a somewhat mediocre American textbook on the history of economic thought (J.F. Bell) one reads: "Smith's contributions to a theory of value are more confusing than enlightening. Errors, inaccuracies, and contradictions plague his statement." [2]

From all this one thing is unquestionably true: that Smith's theory of value suffers from serious defects. But, as Marx pointed out, these defects and contradictions were logical and productive in their own way for economic theory. Smith tried to advance from the initial, simplest formulation of the labour theory of value, in which it seems a mere commonplace, to the real system of commodity-money exchange and price formation under capitalism in the conditions of free competition. In this investigation he came up against some insoluble contradictions. Marx believed that the ultimate cause of this was the absence in Smith (and Ricardo) of an historical view of

[1] Quoted from J. A. Schumpeter, *History of Economic Analysis*, p. 307.

[2] J. F. Bell, *A History of Economic Thought*, p. 188.

capitalism, their acceptance of the relations between capital and hired labour as eternal ones, the only ones possible. Apart from them Smith knew only the "rude state of society" which he viewed almost as myth. Nevertheless he approached the problem of value with great scientific depth.

Smith defined and delimited the concepts of consumer and exchange value more precisely than anyone before him. Renouncing Physiocrat dogma and basing his argument on his own theory of the division of labour, he recognised that all types of productive labour are equivalent from the point of view of the creation of value. In so doing he grasped the fact that exchange value is based on the substance of value, to quote Marx, i.e., on labour as all productive human activity. This paved the way for Marx's discovery of the dual nature of labour as abstract and concrete labour. Smith realised that skilled and complicated labour creates more value per unit of time than unskilled and simple labour, and can be reduced to the latter with the aid of certain coefficients. He also understood to a certain extent that the magnitude of the value of a commodity is determined not by the actual expenditure of labour of the individual producer, but by the expenditure which is necessary on average in the given state of society.

Smith's distinction between the natural and market price of a commodity was a productive one. By natural price he understood basically the monetary expression of exchange value and believed that in the long run market prices gravitate towards it as a kind of centre of fluctuation. Given equilibrium of demand and supply in free competition market prices coincide with natural prices. He also laid the foundations for an analysis of the factors capable of producing long-run divergences of prices from value; he considered monopoly to be the most important.

Smith's profound intuition may be seen in the fact that he posed the problem which remained at the centre of the theory of value and price formation throughout the following century. In Marxist categories this is the transformation of values into the price of production. Smith knew that profit must tend to be proportional to capital and understood the nature of the average rate of profit on which he also based his natural price. His weakness lies in the fact that he could not connect and combine this phenomenon with the labour theory of value.

As Engels wrote, in Smith we find "not only two but even three, and strictly speaking even four sharply contrary opinions on value, running quite jollily side by side and intermingled".[1] Evidently the main cause for this is that Smith could not find sufficiently logical links between the labour theory of value as it was developed at that time and recorded by him, and the complex concrete processes of capitalist economy. He therefore began to modify and adapt his initial conception.

Firstly, alongside value, which is determined by the quantity of necessary labour contained in a commodity (first and main view), he introduced a second concept in which value is determined by the quantity of labour which can purchase the given commodity. In a simple commodity economy, where there is no hired labour and commodity producers are working with means of production which belong to them, this is one and the same in terms of magnitude. A weaver, for example, exchanges a piece of cloth for a pair of boots. One might say that the piece of cloth is worth a pair of boots, or that it is worth the labour of the bootmaker for the time it took him to make the boots. But quantitative coincidence is not proof of identity, for the value of a given commodity may be quantitatively determined in one way only — in the known quantity of the other commodity.

Smith completely lost the ground under his feet when he tried to apply this, his second interpretation of value to capitalist production. If a bootmaker works for a capitalist, the value of the boots made by him and the "value of his labour", that which he receives for his labour, are entirely different things. This means that the employer who buys the worker's labour (he is in fact buying labour power, the ability to labour, as Marx proved) receives more value than he pays for this labour.

Smith could not explain this phenomenon from the standpoint of the labour theory of value and wrongly concluded that value was determined by labour only in the "rude state of society", where there were no capitalists or hired workers, i.e., to use Marxist terminology, in a simple commodity economy. For the conditions of capitalism Smith constructed

---

[1] Frederick Engels, *Anti-Dühring*, p. 275.

a third version [1] of the theory of value: he decided that the value of a commodity was simply composed of costs, including workers' wages and the capitalist's profit (land rent as well in certain branches). He was also reassured by the fact that this theory of value seemed to explain the phenomenon of average profit on capital, "natural rates of ... profit", as he put it. Smith simply equated value with the price of production, not seeing the complicated intermediate links between them.

This was "theory of prices set by production costs" which was to play an important role in the following century. Here Smith adopted the practical standpoint of the capitalist who thinks that the price of his commodity is determined mainly by costs and average profit, and also by supply and demand at any given moment. This concept of value offered great scope for depicting labour, capital and landed property as equivalent creators of value. Say and other economists who sought to use political economy to defend the interests of capitalists and landowners, soon deduced this from Smith.

CLASSES AND INCOMES

As we know, the theory of value was to provide the answer to two related questions: the ultimate basis of prices and the ultimate source of income. Smith gave a partially correct answer to the first question, but could not reconcile it with reality and adopted a vulgar standpoint. In developing the labour theory of value he also contributed to the scientific solution of the second question, but again proved inconsistent.

What does Smith understand by the "rude state of society"? Although he regarded it almost as a myth, it was a myth with an important meaning. Did he think of it as a society without private property? Probably not. Smith did not see a "golden age" in either the past or the future of mankind. He probably had in mind a society with private property but without classes. Whether such a society is possible or has ever existed is an entirely different question.

Let us imagine a society with a million farmers each of whom possesses just enough land and instruments of labour and

---

[1] A fourth version — the subjectivist interpretation of value as the result of the *burden* of labour — is found in Smith in embryonic form only.

produces just enough for personal consumption and exchange for his family's subsistence. In addition the society has a million independent craftsmen, each of whom works with his own instruments of labour and raw materials. There is no hired labour in this society.

From Quesnay's point of view, this society has two classes, from Smith's only one. And Smith's approach is more correct because classes differ not according to the branch of the economy in which the people constituting them are employed, but according to the relation which these people have to the means of production. In these conditions, Smith says, the exchange of commodities takes place according to labour value and the whole product of labour (or its value) belongs to the worker: fortunately he does not yet have anyone with whom to share it. But these days are long since past. The land has become the private property of landowners, and the work-shops and factories are in the hands of capitalist owners. Such is modern society. It is composed of three classes: hired workers, capitalists and landowners. Smith is sufficiently realistic to see various intermediate strata and groups as well. But in fundamental economic analysis one can ignore this and proceed from the three-class model.

Thus as a rule the worker today works on someone else's land and with the aid of someone else's capital. Therefore the whole product of his labour no longer belongs to him. The landowner's rent is the first deduction from this product or from its value. The second is the profit of the capitalist employer who hires workers and gives them instruments and materials for their work.

Smith came close to an understanding of surplus value as the expression of the exploitation of labour by capitalists and landowners. However, like all economists before Marx, he did not single out surplus value as a special category but examined it only in the concrete forms which it assumes on the surface of bourgeois society: profit, rent and interest. Paul Douglas has discovered five passages in *The Wealth of Nations* where Smith speaks of the full product of labour which once belonged to the worker and was later taken from him. To quote Douglas, this phrase is "of great importance in the history of socialist thought, and it is most significant to find it in Adam Smith...."[1]

---

[1] Adam Smith, 1776-1926. "Lectures to Commemorate the 150th Anniversary of the Publication of *The Wealth of Nations*", Chicago, 1928, p. 96.

This is quite true. Incidentally, I should mention that scholars have subjected the text of *The Wealth of Nations* to scrupulous investigation and analysis. There are few great literary works that contain so many different and even contradictory statements.

Another stream in Smith's thought proceeded from his treatment of value as a sum of incomes: wages, profit and rent. In fact profit and rent cannot be deducted from the full value of a commodity if they themselves form this value. Here we find a completely different view of the distribution of incomes: each factor of production (the term appeared later), i.e., labour, capital, and land, takes part in the creation of the value of a commodity and naturally claims its share. From here it is not far to the "divine right of capital" proclaimed in the 19th century by the apologist economists.

Having formed value from incomes, Smith decides to examine how the natural rate of each income is determined, i.e., by what laws the value of the individual commodity and of the whole product is distributed between the classes of society.

When Smith examines each of the three main incomes he again returns to his theory of surplus-value to a certain extent. His view of wages remains of interest even today. Of course, his theory *of wages* is unsatisfactory in many respects, for he did not understand the true nature of the relations involved in the worker's sale of his labour power to the capitalist. He assumed that the actual labour was the commodity and that consequently it had a natural price. But he actually defined this natural price in the same way as Marx defined the value of labour power — by the value of the means necessary for the subsistence of the worker and his family. Smith made a series of realistic and important additions to this.

Firstly, he already realised that the value of labour power ("natural wages", to use his term) is not only determined by the physical minimum of the means of subsistence, but depends on conditions of place and time, i.e., includes an historical and cultural element. Smith quoted the example of leather footwear, which had become an item of necessity for men and women in England, for men only in Scotland and for neither sex in France. One is bound to conclude that with the development of the economy the circle of requirements expands and the value of labour power expressed in real commodities should increase.

Secondly, Smith saw clearly that one of the main reasons for low wages, their proximity to the physical minimum, was the weak bargaining position of the worker in relation to the capitalist. He wrote about this in very strong terms. One is bound to conclude here that the organisation and solidarity of the workers, their resistance, can limit the greed of the entrepreneurs.

Thirdly and finally, he linked the wage trend with the state of the country's economy, distinguishing three cases: a progressive economy, a regressive economy and a stationary economy. He believed that in the first case wages should rise because labour is in great demand in an expanding economy. The subsequent development of capitalist economy has shown that an expanding economy really does help the workers' struggle for higher wages.

Smith completed the singling out of *profit* as a special economic category in political economy. He fundamentally rejected the assertion that profit is only wages for a special type of work of "inspection and direction". The amount of profit, he shows, is determined by the amount of capital and in no way connected with the hypothetical difficulty of this labour. Here and in several other passages Smith is in fact interpreting profit as exploiter income, as the main form of surplus value.

Side by side with this view we find the superficial bourgeois view of profit as the capitalist's natural reward for risk, for advancing the worker his means of subsistence, for so-called abstinence.

CAPITAL

Economists of the pre-Marxian period, the classical bourgeois political economists included, regarded capital simply as an accumulated reserve of instruments, raw material, means of subsistence and money. This meant that capital always had existed and always would, for no production is possible without such a reserve. Marx challenged this with an interpretation of capital as an historical category which arises only when labour power becomes a commodity, when the main figures in society are the capitalist, who possesses the means of production, and the hired worker, who possesses nothing but the ability to labour. Capital is the expression of this social relation. It has not always existed and is by no means eternal. Even if capital can be regarded as a sum of commodities and money, it is only in the sense that they embody the unpaid (surplus) labour of hired workers which is appropriated by the capitalist and that they are used to appropriate new portions of this labour.

In the passage about which Marx said that Smith had grasped the true origin of surplus value here, the latter writes: "As soon as stock has accummulated in the hands of particular persons, some of them will naturally employ it in setting to work industrious people, whom they will supply with materials and subsistence, in order to make a profit by the sale of their work, or by what their labours add to the value of the materials."[1] Here Smith is referring to the historical process of the emergence of capital and the exploitatory essence of the social relations which it engenders. Proceeding in the second book to a special analysis of capital, however, Smith abandons this profound point of view almost entirely. His "technical" analysis of capital is similar to that of Turgot. But Smith examines such questions as fixed and circulating capital, different spheres of capital investment, loan capital and loan interest more systematically and in more detail than Turgot or anyone else.

What distinguishes Smith and gives his whole exposition a certain ring of authority is the emphasis on *the accumulation of capital* as the decisive factor of economic progress. Adam Smith strives with great consistency and perseverance to prove that accumulation is the key to the nation's wealth, that everyone who saves is the nation's benefactor and every spendthrift its enemy. This shows his profound understanding of the basic economic problem of industrial revolution. According to the estimates of modern English scholars, the savings-ratio (the accumulated portion of the national income) in England during the second half of the 18th century was no more than 5 per cent on average. It probably did not begin to rise until about 1790 when the industrial revolution entered its most intense period. Five per cent is very little, of course. Today it is customary to regard the situation as more or less satisfactory if the savings-ratio is from 12 to 15 per cent, 10 per cent is the danger signal, and 5 per cent means catastrophe. Increase the

---

[1] A. Smith, *The Wealth of Nations*, Vol. II, p. 42.

savings-ratio at all costs. That is what Smith urges, put in modern terms.

Who can and should accumulate? Capitalists, of course, the wealthy farmers, industrialists, and merchants. Smith regards this as their important social function. Already in his Glasgow lectures he noted with approval the "ascetism" of the local knights of capital: in the whole town it was difficult to find a rich man who kept more than one manservant. A person gets rich from hiring productive workers and poor from hiring servants, Smith wrote. This also applies to the nation as a whole: one must strive to reduce to a minimum the section of the population not engaged in productive labour. Smith's concept of productive labour was aimed hard at the feudal elements in society and everything connected with them: state bureaucracy, the military, and the Church. As Marx noted, the critical attitude to this crew who are a burden on production and hinder accumulation expresses the point of view of both the bourgeoisie of that period and the working class.

Smith wrote: "The sovereign, for example, with all the officers both of justice and war who serve under him, the whole army and navy, are unproductive labourers. They are the servants of the public, and are maintained by a part of the annual produce of the industry of other people.... In the same class must be ranked, some both of the gravest and most important, and some of the most frivolous professions: churchmen, lawyers, physicians, men of letters of all kinds; players, baffoons, musicians, opera-singers, dancers, etc." [1]

The sovereign and buffoons in the same company! Officers and churchmen are parasites! Academic scrupulousness makes the author also acknowledge "men of letters of all kinds", to whom he himself belongs, as unproductive workers from the economic point of view. These phrases undoubtedly contain some daring and telling irony, but it is well concealed behind a professorial seriousness and objectivity. Such is Adam Smith.

SMITHIANISM

Smith's teaching exercised most influence in England and France, countries where industrial development was at its

---

[1] A. Smith, *The Wealth of Nations*, Vol. I, London, 1924, p. 295.

height in the late 18th and early 19th centuries and where the bourgeoisie possessed state power to a considerable extent.

In England, however, there were no important and independent thinkers among Smith's followers until Ricardo. Smith's first critics were men who expressed the interests of the landowners. The most eminent of them in England were Malthus and the Earl of Lauderdale.

In France Smith's teaching had at first received a cool reception from the late Physiocrats. Then the revolution diverted attention from economic theory. The turning point came at the very beginning of the 19th century. The first competent translation of *The Wealth of Nations*, made by Germain Garnier and furnished with his commentaries, was published in 1802. In 1803 Say and Sismondi published books in which both economists appeared mainly as followers of Smith. Say interpreted the Scot in a way which suited the bourgeoisie more than "pure" Smith did. To the extent that Say fought energetically for capitalist industrial development, however, many of his ideas were close to those of Smith.

If Smith's teaching was progressive in England and France, this was even more obvious in countries where feudal reaction prevailed and bourgeois development had just begun — Germany, Austria, Italy, Spain and, of course, Russia. It is said that Smith's book was originally banned by the Inquisition in Spain. Reactionary German professors who lectured in the spirit of the German brand of mercantilism, Kameralistik, refused to recognise Smith for a long time. Nevertheless it was in Prussia, the largest of the German states, that Smith's ideas had an influence on the course of events: the people who introduced liberal bourgeois reforms there in the period of the Napoleonic Wars were his followers.

In speaking of Smith's teaching and influence, one must bear in mind that his inconsistency, the presence in his books of heterogeneous and even contradictiory conceptions, enabled people of entirely different views and principles to draw on him and regard him as their teacher and forerunner. The English socialists of the 1820s to 1840s who sought to turn Ricardo's teaching against the bourgeoisie regarded themselves and were in fact the spiritual heirs of Adam Smith. These people based themselves mainly on Smith's theories of the full product of labour and deductions from it for the capitalist and landowner. On the other hand, "Say's school" in

France, which represented the vulgar apologetic trend in bourgeois political economy, also regarded itself as followers of Smith. It was based on another stream in Smith's thought: the collaboration of production factors in creating the product and its value. They also borrowed Smith's argument for free trade, but endowed it with a crude commercial character.

The most important line of theoretical influence from Smith leads to Ricardo and Marx.

Smith's teaching possessed different aspects from the point of view of theory and that of concrete economic and social policy. Some of Smith's followers borrowed only one of these aspects: free foreign trade, the struggle against protectionism. These arguments were of a progressive or fairly reactionary nature depending on the concrete situation. In Prussia, for example, it was the conservative Junker circles who campaigned for free trade: they had an interest in the importation of cheap foreign industrial goods and the free export of their own corn.

But we know full well that in Smith's case free trade was only a part of a broad anti-feudal programme of economic and political freedom. Smith's great role in the history of civilisation is that his ideas (very often almost inseparably fused with the ideas of other leading 18th-century thinkers) can be felt in many progressive and liberating movements of the first half of the 19th century.

SMITH'S PERSONALITY

Little remains to be said about Smith's life. Two years after the publication of *The Wealth of Nations* he received, thanks to the efforts of the Duke of Buccleuch and other influential acquaintances and admirers, the comfortable post of Scottish commissioner of customs in Edinburgh with an annual salary of six hundred pounds. This was a great deal at that time. Smith spent the rest of his days in the customs, supervising duty collection, corresponding with London and from time to time sending soldiers to catch smugglers. He moved to Edinburgh and rented an apartment in the old part of the town. Continuing to lead his former modest way of life, he spent considerable sums on charity. The only thing of value which he left was his extensive library. Smith himself once said: "I am a beau in nothing but my books."

In the 18th century state posts like the one Smith obtained were given only through protection and were regarded as splendid sinecures. But Smith, conscientious and somewhat pedantic, took a serious view of his duties and spent a considerable amount of time at his desk. This alone (plus age and illness) excluded any further serious study. And it would appear that Smith had no particular desire for it. True, at first he had a plan to write his third big work, a kind of universal history of culture and learning. But he soon abandoned this intention. After his death some interesting notes on the history of astronomy and philosophy and even the fine arts were found and published. The new editions of his works took up a great deal of his time. During his lifetime six editions of the *Theory of Moral Sentiments* and five of *The Wealth of Nations* were published in England. For the third edition (1784) Smith made some important additions, in particular, the chapter on the "Conclusion of the Mercantile System". He also kept an eye on the foreign editions of his books; two French translations were published, one German, one Danish, and an Italian one was in preparation. *The Wealth of Nations* was published in English in Ireland and America. The editions of *The Wealth of Nations* in the first fifty years after its publication would fill a small secondhand bookshop. The first Russian edition came out in 1802-1806. Altogether there have been eight Russian editions of Smith's book, including four after the October Socialist Revolution of 1917.

The Scottish capital was the country's second cultural centre after London and in certain respects not inferior to it. On the other hand, it was a comparatively small, intimate town. True to his old customs, Smith had his own club here too, where he met regularly with a close circle of friends and acquaintances. In addition friends dined with him every Sunday. He had already become a European celebrity, one of the sights of Edinburgh, as it were. Travellers from London and Paris, Berlin and St. Petersburg sought an introduction to the Scottish sage.

In appearance Smith was in no way remarkable. He was slightly over average height and bore himself erect. The simple face had regular features, greyish-blue eyes and a large, straight nose. He dressed so as not to attract attention. Wore a wig to the end of his days. Liked walking with a bamboo cane over his shoulder. And was in the habit of talking to himself to such an extent that one day two market women took him for a madman. "Hegh sirs!" said one, shaking her head significantly. "And he's weel put on too!" rejoined the other. He was very absentminded. In his dealings with others he was benevolent and loquacious. One of his contemporaries writes, perhaps somewhat exaggeratingly: "He was the most absent man in company that I ever saw, moving his lips and talking to himself, and smiling in the midst of large companies. If you awaked him from his reverie and made him attend to the subject of conversation he immediately began a harangue, and never stopped till he told you all he knew about it, with the utmost philosophical ingenuity."[1]

Smith died in Edinburgh in July 1790 at the age of sixty-seven. For almost four years before this he had been gravely ill.

Smith possessed considerable intellectual, and sometimes also civic, courage, but was in no sense a fighter. He was humane and hated injustice, cruelty and violence, but resigned himself to them with comparative ease. He believed in the triumph of reason and culture, but feared greatly for their fate in this coarse and evil world. He hated and despised bureaucrat officials, but himself became one of them.

Smith had great sympathy for the poor labouring population, the working class. He advocated the highest possible wage for hired labour because society could not prosper and be happy if its greater part was poor and unhappy. It was unfair that the people who supported the whole of society by their labour should live in poverty. But at the same time he assumed that "natural laws" destined workers for the lowest place in society and thought that "though the interest of the labourer is strictly connected with that of the society, he is incapable either of comprehending that interest or of understanding its connection with his own".[2]

Smith regarded the bourgeoisie as the rising, progressive class and objectively expressed its interests, its broad, long-term interests, not narrow, temporary ones. But, himself a lower-class intellectual, he did not feel the slightest liking for capitalists as such. He believed that the thirst for profit blinded

---

[1] C. R. Fay, *Adam Smith and the Scotland of His Day*, Cambridge, 1956, p. 79.
[2] A. Smith, *The Wealth of Nations*, Vol. I, London, 1924, p. 230.

and hardened these people. They were prepared to act in any way against the interests of society for the sake of profit. They strove with all their power to raise the price of their goods and lower the wages of their workers. The industrialists and merchants invariably sought to suppress and restrict free competition and create monopolies which were harmful to society.

In general, the capitalist for Smith was the natural and impersonal instrument of progress, the growth of "the nation's wealth". Smith defends the bourgeoisie only to the extent that its interests coincide with the interests of the growth of society's productive forces.

CHAPTER XII

DAVID RICARDO
THE GENIUS FROM THE CITY

In 1799 a wealthy member of the London Stock Exchange was staying in the spa of Bath where his wife was taking the waters. Dropping into the public library he happened to leaf through Adam Smith's *The Wealth of Nations*, became interested in it and asked to have the book sent to his rooms. Thus Ricardo first turned his attention to political economy.

This incident is related by Ricardo himself, but it is anecdotal, like the stories about Newton's apple and Watt's kettle. Being an educated person he must have known about Smith's book. Ricardo already possessed extensive practical knowledge of economics, and also a certain ability for abstract thought, for he was interested in the natural sciences. Nevertheless the Bath library could, of course, have acted as a stimulus.

Ricardo continued to make money, studying mineralogy in his spare time. But his main activity, his labour of love was now political economy. Among Ricardo's merits the most striking is perhaps his selfless passion for science which he studied not for money, professional success or fame; his constant and disinterested search for truth. The study of political economy was for him an inner, organic need, the logical way of his expressing his vivid and original personality. Ricardo was a modest man and all his life considered himself something of a dilettante in the science. But this dilettante was to complete the creation of English classical political economy.

Ricardo's great service was that he elaborated methods of scientific economic investigation. His contemporaries spoke of "the new science of political economy" which had emerged from the pen of Ricardo and to a certain extent they were right: it is true that in his works for the first time political economy acquired the features of a science as a system of knowledge about the economic basis of society. Ricardo tried to find the answer to the question which has always occupied economists — what are the most favourable (optimal) social conditions of production and distribution for the growth of the material wealth of society. He expressed a number of ideas on this problem which retain their significance to this very day. An important feature of Ricardo's theoretical views was their monism, i.e., the existence of a single general conception forming the basis of a scientific interpretation of all the varied facts of economic reality. Following his great predecessor Adam Smith Ricardo sought to study economy as a complex system and to define the basic conditions of equilibrium. This was connected with his conviction that objective laws exist in economy and that there are mechanisms which ensure the operation of these laws as prevailing tendencies. The problem of the "mechanism of self-regulation" in economics still retains its theoretical and practical importance. A considerable role was played by Ricardo's works in the development of such concrete spheres of economics as monetary circulation and credit, international economic relations, and taxation. On the theories of land rent and international division of labour Ricardo expressed ideas which have become part of the treasury of economic thought. A profound theoretician, he was at the same time closely involved with the economic problems of his time and his country. He was a skilled polemicist and talented publicist on economic and social questions. Ricardo maintained high principles of scientific ethics which merit respect and emulation.

Even for the age in which Ricardo lived, when the profession of economist did not yet exist, his path in the science was remarkable and evoked the admiration of his contemporaries. One of his disciples wrote in 1821: "Could it be that an Englishman, and he not in academic bowers, but oppressed by mercantile and senatorial cares, had accomplished what all the universities of Europe, and a century of thought, had failed even to advance by one hair's breadth?" [1]

THE INDUSTRIAL REVOLUTION

England had been at war almost continuously for a quarter of a century. At first with the Jacobites, then with General Bonaparte and finally with Emperor Napoleon. The war ended in the summer of 1815 with the victory of Waterloo. England could now enjoy the fruits of victory. The Continental Blockade, with which Napoleon had hoped to stifle English trade, collapsed. European markets opened up for English goods — the best and most varied in the world at that time.

The war was waged far from English shores, on the continent of Europe, in the colonies, and on the high seas. It helped rather than prevented England from growing rich. The last third of the 18th century and the first third of the 19th was the age of the English industrial revolution. Capitalism left the manufacturing stage and entered the stage of machine industry. Cottage workshops were replaced by factories employing hundreds of people. The gloomy, begrimed industrial towns sprang up: Manchester, Birmingham, Glasgow.... The cotton industry was at the hub of the industrial revolution. Branches which produced machinery and fuel for it also developed. The age of coal and iron began. Steam became the main source of motive power. In 1822 Ricardo travelled to the continent on a steamboat, and two years after his death the first steam locomotive appeared.

The English countryside was changing. The small independent peasant holdings on their own or rented land were disappearing, giving way to large estates and the units of capitalist tenant farmers. An agricultural proletariat was forming, which swelled the ranks of the miners, navvies, masons, and factory workers.

The English grew wealthy, but with this wealth came inequality in distribution. Class distinctions became more acute and pronounced. For the workers it was a monstrously cruel world — the world that staggered the young Engels when he

---

[1] Quoted from M. Blaug, *Ricardian Economics. A Historical Study*, New Haven, 1958, p. V.

first came to England in 1842. The working day was 12-13 hours long, sometimes even longer. Wages provided just enough food to keep people from starving. Unemployment or illness doomed the worker and his family to starvation. Machines enabled factory owners to make use of the even cheaper labour of women and children, particularly in the textile industry.

Any association or union of workers was banned by law and regarded as rebellion. The first demonstrations by the workers against these terrible conditions were spontaneous outbursts of despair and fury. The Luddites destroyed machines, naively believing them to be responsible for their suffering. In 1811-12 their movement swelled to considerable proportions. Byron raised his solitary voice in the House of Lords in defence of these desperate souls. Ricardo could not, of course, approve of the actions of the Luddites, but he fought for the legalisation of workers' unions and was the first to provide in his works a sober analysis of the social consequences of the use of machines. In 1819 troops fired on a large demonstration by Manchester workers in the Petersfield area. Contemporaries referred to this slaughter jokingly as the "victory of Peterloo" (an allusion to Waterloo).

Nevertheless the class antagonism of the bourgeoisie and the proletariat at the beginning of the 19th century was not yet the main conflict in society, a conflict which determined all social relations and ideology. The bourgeoisie was still the ascendant class, and in general its interests corresponded to those of the development of productive forces. The working class was still weak and disorganised. It was the object, rather than the subject in social relations and in politics.

The interests of the bourgeoisie were threatened more by the encroachments of the landowners. The increased price of corn brought the latter an increase in land rent, and after the war they managed to get the Tory Parliament to pass the Corn Laws, which greatly restricted the import of foreign corn into England and helped to keep the price of bread high. This was unprofitable for factory owners, because they were forced to pay higher wages to their workers to keep them from starving. The battle around the Corn Laws was an important part of English political life throughout the first half of the 19th century and to a great extent determined the theoretical positions of economists. In this struggle the interests of the landowners were opposed to a certain extent by the joint interests of the industrial bourgeoisie and the working class.

Such was the historical background against which Ricardo's teaching developed and the English classical school reached its height. This background partly explains why Ricardo was able to analyse the basic socio-economic problems with such scientific objectivity and impartiality, particularly the relations between capital and labour. Naturally, the personality of Ricardo the scholar also played an important part in this.

THE WEALTHIEST ECONOMIST

There is an English joke that goes like this. What's an economist? A man who hasn't got a penny in his pocket and gives other people advice which leaves them without a penny in their pockets if they follow it. There is always an exception to the rule, however. Ricardo amassed a considerable fortune and occasionally gave his friends, Malthus in particular, such good advice about investing their money that they had no grounds for complaint.

Ricardo's ancestors were Spanish Jews who fled from the persecution of the Inquisition to Holland and settled there. The great economist's father came to England in the 1760s, where he first engaged in wholesale trading and then began dealing in bills of exchange and securities. David was the third of his seventeen children. He was born in London in April 1772, went to an ordinary elementary school and was then sent for two years to Amsterdam where he began to learn the secrets of commerce in his uncle's office.

After his return David continued his studies for a short time, but his systematic education stopped at the age of fourteen. His father allowed him to take lessons from private tutors. However, it soon transpired that the young man's interests exceeded what his father considered necessary for a business man. This displeased him and the lessons came to an end. By sixteen David was already his father's most trusted assistant in the office and at the stock exchange. He was mature beyond his years. Observant, inventive, energetic, he soon became noticed in the stock exchange and the business offices of the City. His father began entrusting him with independent commissions.

However such a person could not endure the despotism and

conservatism of his father. He was indifferent to religion, but at home he was compelled to observe all the dogma of Judaism strictly and perform its rituals. The conflict came out into the open when Ricardo informed his father that he intended to marry a Christian. The young lady was the daughter of a Quaker physician, the same type of domestic tyrant as Ricardo senior. The marriage took place against the will of both families. Marrying a Christian meant that Ricardo was expelled from the Jewish community. He did not become a Quaker, but chose Unitarianism, the freest and most flexible of the sects which had broken away from the established Anglican Church. In all probability this was simply a decorous cover for his atheism.

The happy ending to this romantic story could have been clouded by poverty, for the young couple naturally did not receive anything from their parents. And at the age of twenty-five Ricardo was already the father of three children (he had eight altogether). He knew no other trade than gambling on the stock exchange and now proceeded to do so not as his father's assistant but independently. He was lucky and was also helped by connections, reputation and ability. Five years later he was already very wealthy and conducting large operations.

Today it is mainly the shares of large private companies that are sold on the stock exchanges of Britain, the United States and other countries. At the end of the 18th century there were still very few joint-stock companies. Transactions involving the shares of the Bank of England, the East India Company and other companies constituted a trifling fraction of stock exchange operations, and Ricardo hardly engaged in them at all. The gold-mine for him, as for many other shrewd businessmen, was the national debt and transactions involving state loan bonds. In the first ten years of the war, from 1793 to 1802, the funded debt of Great Britain rose from £238 million to £567 million, and by 1816 it was more than £1,000 million. In addition, foreign loans were floated in London. The prices of bonds fluctuated under the influence of various economic and political factors. Playing the market became the prime source of getting rich for the young businessman.

As his contemporaries testify, Ricardo possessed phenomenal acumen and instinct, speed of reaction and at the same time great caution. He never got carried away, never lost his presence of mind and sober judgment. He knew how to sell in time and sometimes made do with a modest gain on each bond, obtaining a profit through big turnovers.

Rich financiers formed small groups and obtained contracts from the government to float newly issued loans. To put it more simply, they purchased all bonds of the new loan wholesale from the government and then sold them retail. The profits from these operations were enormous, although they sometimes entailed great risk: the prices of the bonds might suddenly drop. The loan was allotted to the group of financiers which made the highest bid at auctions organised by the Treasury. In 1806 Ricardo and two other businessmen bid unsuccessfully at the auction and the loan was given to another group. Next year Ricardo and his group obtained the right to float a loan of twenty million. He invariably took part in auctions over the next ten years and floated several loans.

By 1809-10 David Ricardo was one of the most prominent figures in the London financial world. He bought a sumptuous house in the most aristocratic part of London, then a large estate at Gatcomb Park in Gloucestershire, where he set up his country residence. After this Ricardo gradually withdrew from active participation in the world of business and became a large landowner and rentier. His fortune reached a million pounds, which was a great deal for those times.

This is the biography of a talented financier, shrewd businessman, and knight of profit. What about science?

This wily stock-exchange expert and respected *père de famille* was a man with a most enquiring mind and an insatiable thirst for knowledge. At twenty-six Ricardo, having acquired financial independence and even a certain degree of wealth, suddenly turned to the disciplines which circumstances had prevented him from studying in his youth: the natural sciences and mathematics. What a contrast! In the morning at the Stock Exchange and the office—the businessman, cool and self-possessed beyond his years. And in the evening at home—the likeable, enthusiastic young man who demonstrates experiments with electricity and his collection of minerals with naive pride to his relatives and acquaintances.

Ricardo's keen intellect developed under the influence of these studies. They helped to produce those qualities which played such an important role in his economic works: his thought was remarkable for its strict, almost mathematical logic, extreme clarity, and dislike of excessively general arguments. It was at this time that Ricardo first became acquainted with political economy as a science. Smith still reigned supreme, and the young Ricardo could not help falling under his influence. Yet he was strongly impressed by Malthus, whose *Essay on the Principle of Population* was first published in 1798. Later, when he became personally acquainted with Malthus, Ricardo wrote to him that on reading this book he had found Malthus' ideas "so clear and so satisfactorily laid down that they excited an interest in me inferior only to that produced by Adam Smith's celebrated work".[1]

At the beginning of the century a young Scot by the name of James Mill appeared in London, a controversial publicist and writer on socio-economic questions. Ricardo became acquainted with him, an acquaintance which soon turned into a close friendship lasting until Ricardo's death. At first Mill played the role of mentor. He introduced Ricardo to a circle of scholars and writers and encouraged him to publish his early writings. Later the roles were reversed to a certain extent. After the appearance of Ricardo's main works Mill became his pupil and follower. True, he did not develop the strongest aspects of Ricardo's teaching or give him the best defence from critics, which actually contributed to the collapse of Ricardian economics. Nevertheless we must not mention Mill without a kind word: a true admirer of Ricardo's talent, he was constantly urging him to write, edit, publish. Sometimes he played the slightly comic role of setting Ricardo "tasks" and demanding "accounts" of the results. In October 1815 he wrote to Ricardo: "I expect you are by this time in a condition to give me some account of the progress you have been making in your book. I now consider you as fairly pledged to that task."[2]

Some talented people have great need of such friends.

Ricardo always suffered from lack of confidence in his powers, from a certain literary timidity. Nor did he have the sense of duty, the "devotion", with which Smith worked for many years on his book. Outside his business Ricardo was a

---

[1] Quoted from J. H. Hollander, *David Ricardo. A Centenary Estimate*, Baltimore, 1910, pp. 47-48.

[2] Quoted from D. Ricardo, *The Works and Correspondence*, Vol. 6, Cambridge, 1952, p. 309.

mild and even somewhat shy man. This can be seen in his everyday life, in contact with other people. In 1812 he went to Cambridge where his eldest son Osman was in his first year at university. And in this unaccustomed environment he, a rich and respected man of forty, felt awkward and unsure of himself. Describing the visit to his wife in a letter, he wrote: "I am endeavouring to conquer every thing that is shy and reserved in my disposition, that I may contribute as much as I can to procure a few agreeable acquaintances for Osman."

AT THE APPROACHES: THE PROBLEM OF MONETARY CIRCULATION

As Marx writes, in the Parliamentary debates on the Bank Acts of 1844 and 1845 the future Prime Minister Gladstone once remarked that even love has not made as many fools as philosophising about money.[1]

The theory of money is one of the most complex spheres of economic science. In England at the beginning of the 19th century the question of money and banking was at the centre of a passionate polemic and struggle between party and class interests. It was only natural that Ricardo, who was well acquainted with credit and monetary practice, should first try his strength as an economist and publicist in this arena. He was thirty-seven at that time.

In 1797 the Bank of England was allowed to stop giving gold in exchange for its notes. Notes became inconvertible paper money. In a number of articles and pamphlets published in 1809-1811 Ricardo argued that the increase in the market price of gold in this paper money was the result and indication of its depreciation due to excessive issue. His opponents maintained that the rise in the price of gold was explained by other causes, in particular, the demand for gold to export abroad. Ricardo's talent revealed itself in these works, that of the skilled polemicist and writer, capable of highly logical and consistent argument. This was by no means an academic discussion. Those who denied the depreciation of notes were backed by the governors of the Bank of England, the

---

[1] Karl Marx, *A Contribution to the Critique of Political Economy*, Moscow, 1970, p. 64.

conservative majority in Parliament, the ministers, and the whole "war party". In the final analysis it was the expression of the class interests of the landowners whom the war and inflation had brought increased rents. Ricardo, on the other hand, was expressing, as in all his subsequent activity, the interests of the industrial bourgeoisie, whose role at that time was a progressive one. Politically he was close to the Whig (liberal) opposition, the "peace party".

Ricardo did not limit himself to criticism of the existing system of monetary circulation, but produced a positive programme which was supplemented in some of his later works. What he proposed was a monetary system which conformed as far as possible to the demands of the development of capitalist economy. And it must be said that Ricardo's ideas were to a large extent put into practice in the 19th century. From 1819 to 1914 England was on the gold standard.

Briefly, these ideas were as follows: 1) stable monetary circulation is the most important condition of economic growth; 2) this stability is only possible on the basis of the gold standard — a monetary system based on gold; 3) gold in circulation can be largely or even wholly replaced by paper money exchanged on fixed parity with gold, which is a great saving for the nation. In his last work which he did not have time to complete, Ricardo proposes depriving the Bank of England, then a private company, of the right to issue notes and control state finance. To this end he proposed the establishment of a national bank. For its time this was an extremely bold proposal.

The Ricardian theory of money reflected both the strength and the weakness of classical political economy. Ricardo tried to base the theory of money on the labour theory of value, but was not so consistent and in fact rejected it in his analysis of concrete economic processes.

The value of gold money, as of all commodities, is determined in principle by the cost of the labour of producing it. Both commodities and money enter circulation with fixed values. This means that in order to maintain the circulation of a given amount of commodities a certain amount of money is required. If, let us say, the total annual amount of commodities is 1,000 million working days of average labour, and one gramme of gold is equal to one working day, 1,000 million grammes of gold are necessary for circulation. Let us assume, however, that each gramme of gold can serve ten transactions in a year, circulate ten times. Then one-tenth of the gold would be enough — 100 million grammes. In addition, part of the gold can be saved by transactions made in credit. This in broad outline is the conception later expounded by Marx.

But Ricardo did not follow this line of argument. He proceeded from the assumption that any amount of gold, no matter how it came to be there, could circulate in a given country. In circulation a quantity of commodities simply meets a quantity of money, and in this way commodity prices are established. If there is more gold prices are higher, if there is less they are lower. This is the quantity theory of money which we already know from Hume. Ricardo differs from Hume in that he is striving to reconcile it with the labour theory of value. But naturally he has little success in this.

Ricardo's thinking was dominated by the experience of inconvertible paper money circulation. The purchasing power of paper money is determined in the main by its quantity. No matter how much of this money is issued, it always represents the amount of full-value gold money which is necessary for circulation. When, say, there are twice as many paper dollars as gold ones, each paper dollar loses half its value.

Why, however, did Ricardo automatically apply the phenomena of paper money circulation to gold? Because he did not see the fundamental difference between the two and believed gold to be a token of value as well. He saw money only as a means of circulation and did not take into account all the complexity and variety of its functions.

Ricardo thought that his theory of money could also become the key to an explanation of the fluctuations in international economic relations. He reasoned thus. If a given country has too much gold, commodity prices rise and it becomes profitable to import goods from abroad. The country's trade balance shows a deficit, which has to be covered with gold. Gold leaves the country, prices go down, the flow of foreign goods stops and everything returns to equilibrium. When there is not enough gold in a country the reverse takes place. Thus an automatic mechanism operates which naturally restores equilibrium to trade balances and distributes gold among the various countries. Hence Ricardo drew important conclusions in favour of free trade. There is nothing to worry about, he said, if the import of commodities exceeds their export. This is no reason for restricting exports. It simply means that there is too much gold in the country and that prices are too high. Free import helps to lower them.

The demand for free trade in England was a progressive one in Ricardo's day as in Smith's time. But his theory of automatic adjustment contradicted reality. Firstly, it was based on the quantity theory of money and wrongly asserted that changes in the quantity of money in a country directly determine price levels. Secondly, gold moves between countries not only under the influence of relative levels of commodity prices. Ricardo's critics pointed out, not without justification, that during the Napoleonic Wars gold left England not because prices in England were higher (on the contrary, prices for industrial goods were considerably lower there), but because of high military expenditure abroad, purchase of corn after poor harvests, etc.

For all its defects the Ricardian theory of money nevertheless played an important role in the development of economic science. It formulated many questions about which people had most confused notions before and which subsequently became increasingly important: the velocity of money in circulation; the "demand for money", i.e., the factors determining the economy's requirements for money; the role of the convertibility of paper money into gold; the mechanism of the international movement of gold and the influence of commodity price levels on trade and payments balances.

The latter is particularly interesting in the light of the present currency crisis in the capitalist world. Ricardo was extremely interested in the question of the influence of different price levels in the various countries on balances of payments (or, to use his terms, on trade balances and the movement of precious metals between countries), and of the inverse influence of the ebb and flow of world money on price levels. For all the changes which have taken place since then in monetary systems and the role of precious metals as world money, both these problems remain important and controversial ones to this day. The topical nature of the first can be seen, for example, from the previous years' discussions on deficits in the balance of payments of the United States (to what extent these deficits are the result of "revaluation of the dollar", that is, of a higher level of prices in the United States than in the other major capitalist countries given the existing rates of exchange). The significance of the other problem is well illustrated by the experience of West Germany with its huge, surplus accumulation of gold and dollar reserves as a result of the inflow of short-term capital (how this fact influences the growth of inflationary tendencies in the economy of the Federal Republic of Germany).

In 1809 Ricardo was still completely unknown as an economist. By 1811 he was already a recognised authority, the leader of the movement to re-establish the convertibility of bank notes. Partly through Mill, partly in other ways, Ricardo made the acquaintance of eminent politicians, journalists and scholars. Controversial questions on politics, economics and literature were debated in his hospitable home at a good table. Without any special effort on his part Ricardo found himself at the centre of a circle of intellectuals. The reason was his tact, calm and composure, as well as his brain.

The English writer Maria Edgeworth has left a penetrating description of Ricardo as a conversationalist. "Mr. Ricardo, with a very composed manner, has a continual life of mind, and starts perpetually new game in conversation. I never argued or discussed a question with any person who argues more fairly or less for victory and more for truth. He gives full weight to every argument brought against him, and seems not to be on any side of the question for one instant longer than the conviction of his mind on that side. It seems quite indifferent to him whether you find the truth, or whether he finds it, provided it be found. One gets at something by conversing with him; one learns either that one is wrong or that one is right, and the understanding is improved without temper being ever tried in the discussion; ... He is altogether one of the most agreeable persons, as well as the best informed and most clever, that I ever knew." [1] The friendship between Ricardo and Malthus is a strange paradox in the history of economic science. It was a very close one. Ricardo and Malthus met often, visited each other and corresponded very frequently. Yet it is difficult to imagine two more different people. The whole history of their friendship is one of ideological argument and disagreement. They could rarely find anything on which to agree. This is not surprising, for their theories represented the

---

[1] Quoted from D. Ricardo, *The Works and Correspondence*, Vol. 10, Cambridge, 1955, pp. 168-169, 170.

interests of different classes: Malthusian political economy was subordinated to the interests of the landowning class, which was quite unacceptable to Ricardo. In his turn, Malthus could not accept Ricardo's most important ideas: the labour theory of value, the portrayal of rent as parasitic income, free trade, and the demand to repeal the Corn Laws.

Possibly one explanation of their friendship is that Ricardo possessed great scientific objectivity and self-criticism. Always dissatisfied with what he had achieved and how he had expressed it, Ricardo sought in Malthus' sharp criticism a means of polishing, clarifying and developing his own ideas. And in criticising Malthus he himself advanced.

THE PRINCIPLE OF COMPARATIVE COST

Ricardo reflected a great deal on the factors which determine the flow of international trade. This is understandable: for England foreign trade had always played a particularly important role, and still does. He asked himself why certain commodities were exported by a given country and others imported, and how foreign trade contributed to the growth of production, to economic progress.

Adam Smith had given a simple and rather trite answer to these questions. Perhaps one can conceive of wine being produced in Scotland, but the cost of labour would be excessively high. It is more profitable to produce, say, oats, in Scotland and exchange it for wine from Portugal where wine production involves low labour costs and oats high labour costs. In all probability both countries benefit. This explanation could not satisfy Ricardo. Surely trade could not be profitable only in such obvious cases when profit is determined by natural factors.

He reasoned thus. Even if one could imagine that Scotland produced both oats and wine at less cost, but oats more cheaply than wine, with a given ratio of costs and given proportions of exchange, it would be more profitable for her to produce oats *only*, and Portugal wine *only*. This is the principle of comparative cost, or comparative advantage. Ricardo based this principle on the labour theory of value and sought to prove it with the help of numerical examples; he was very fond of such examples and made constant use of them.

Let us try to illustrate Ricardo's ideas with a numerical example which is as close as possible to the conditions of the early 19th century. Imagine that England and France produce two commodities only — cloth and corn. In England the production of one metre of cloth requires an average ten hours of labour, and one ton of corn twenty hours. In France cloth requires twenty hours and corn thirty. In accordance with the law of value one ton of corn will be exchanged for two metres of cloth in England, and one and a half metres of cloth in France. It should be noted that in this example England has an absolute advantage in the production of both commodities, but a *relative* advantage only in cloth. France has a relative advantage in corn. This can also be put as follows: in France the production of cloth is twice as expensive as in England, and the production of grain only one and a half times as expensive. This "only" constitutes the relative advantage.

Let us assume that both countries follow Ricardo's advice and specialise: England in cloth and France in corn. One might think that the ratio of the exchange of cloth for bread would be somewhere between the English and the French, say, 1.7 (i.e., 1.7 metres of cloth for one ton of corn). The rest of the argument is best given in the form of a table:

	England	France
Total expenditure of labour hours on I metre of cloth and I ton of corn	30	50
Before specialisation		
Production and consumption of cloth (metres)	I	I
Production and consumption of corn (tons)	I	I
After specialisation		
Production of cloth (metres)	3	–
Production of corn (tons)	–	1.67
Consumption of cloth (metres)[1] . .	I	0.67×I.7=I.I
Consumption of corn (tons)[1]	2: I.7=I.2	I
Gain from specialisation for consumption	0.2 tons corn	0.1 metre cloth

---

[1] For the sake of simplicity it is assumed that after specialisation England consumes the same quantity of cloth and exchanges the rest. France consumes the same quantity of corn and exchanges the rest. The figures are expressed in round numbers.

As we can see, for each thirty hours of social labour the English economy gains 0.2 tons of corn and for each fifty hours of labour the French gains 0.1 metres of cloth. Thanks to the specialisation and development of foreign trade both countries can in principle increase consumption of both products.

Ricardo also realised that this gain is, as a rule, appropriated by a certain class — the capitalists. But it was characteristic of his thinking to regard this as meaning that the profit from foreign trade "affords ... incentives to saving, and to the accumulation of capital". The accumulation of capital is a guarantee of economic growth and, in particular, it could have a beneficial influence on the position of the working class since it produces an increase in the demand for labour power. In its abstract form the principle of comparative cost is applicable to the international division of labour in general. The question is simply which class receives the economic gain from specialisation. It is only logical that in recent years, in connection with the increased importance for the socialist countries of the problem of the international division of labour and specialisation of production, this principle has attracted the attention of Marxist economists.

Sometimes Marxist literature stresses the fact that these ideas of Ricardo's were subsequently used by bourgeois political economy for apologistic aims. It must be remembered, however, that the initial principle is one thing, and its ideological application in different historical circumstances is quite another.

In his criticism of Ricardo's theory of foreign trade, Marx nevertheless pointed out that *in principle* specialisation can be profitable even for a comparatively backward country, since such countries "thereby receive commodities cheaper than it could produce them".[1] It is true that Ricardo was already drawing conclusions from the principle of comparative cost which fitted in with his theory of the harmonic and balanced development of international economic relations under free trade. He argued basically that trade profits all who participate in it and binds together "the universal society of nations throughout the civilised world", and bread, wine and other agricultural products in other countries. Metal articles and other industrial commodities would be produced in England.

---

[1] Karl Marx, *Capital*, Vol. III, Moscow, 1971, p. 238.

Thus the principle of comparative cost served as an argument and justification for the "natural" dominion of England in industrial production and its role as the world's main industrial power. Subsequently the link between the principle of comparative cost and the labour theory of value was broken. It began to be used to justify one-sided specialisation of economically backward and developing countries in production of raw material and foodstuffs, as an argument against their industrialisation.

The whole idea of free trade, which was an important part of bourgeois classical political economy, underwent a change. Although free trade was particularly advantageous for the English bourgeoisie, it was mainly a progressive trend at that time: it was aimed at the destruction of feudalism in England and other countries, at the drawing of new areas into world trade, the creation of a capitalist world market. Today the principle of free trade, at least in relation to the developing countries, is often reactionary. Many economists from Western Europe and the United States even admit that free trade would doom the developing countries to the eternal role of raw material suppliers and simply preserve their backwardness. Only active intervention in the sphere of foreign trade (as in other spheres of the economy), the imposition of duty on the import of foreign industrial goods, promotion of national export of such goods, etc., can help these countries overcome their backwardness.

THE MAIN BOOK

Ricardo's main work appeared in quite a different way from Smith's *The Wealth of Nations*. Neither the turbulent age, nor the author's temperament permitted him many years of work in quiet seclusion.

Ricardo's scientific interests were very closely linked with problems of the moment. One such problem was the Corn Laws, which had even ousted the topics of banking and money. Ricardo, by now already an eminent economist and publicist of the liberal camp, threw himself into the battle. The immediate reason for his going into action was the polemic with Malthus who defended the Corn Laws and the high prices of bread. Out of this polemic a theoretical system emerged from

Ricardo's pen. His works written in 1814-17 are the highest expression of classical bourgeois political economy in England.

Smith's system could no longer claim to be a complete explanation of economic reality. Too much had changed over the last forty years. The classes of bourgeois society had formed and their economic interests had crystallised. The fight over the Corn Laws was waged openly from the positions of the main classes, basically the industrial bourgeoisie and the landowners. The problem of the distribution of the national income between the classes came to the fore in economic science. For Smith it had been only one of several important problems. For Ricardo it was the subject of political economy. He writes: "To determine the laws which regulate this distribution is the principal problem in Political Economy: much as the science has been improved by the writings of Turgot, Stuart, Smith, Say, Sismondi, and others, they afford very little satisfactory information respecting the natural course of rent, profit, and wages." [1]

Ricardo tried to establish laws of *distribution* by proceeding from the conditions and interests of *production*. What did this actually mean? Firstly, he based his system on the theory that the value of commodities is created by labour in the process of production and is measured by the quantity of this labour. Further, he examined production in its concrete capitalist form and asked himself how value is formed and incomes are distributed when the means of production are in the hands of landlords (land) and capitalists (factories, machines, raw materials). Finally, he saw increased production of material goods as the main function of capitalism.

On the question of the relations between the classes and the development of capitalism Ricardo drew the following main conclusion. If economic development is left to itself, prices for agricultural produce will rise steadily, in connection with population growth and the gradual transition to the cultivation of less fertile land. All the profit from this goes to the landowners, whereas the profit rate on capital drops. The workers also suffer from this, for there is a relatively lower demand for their labour. As Ricardo wrote, "the interest of the landlord is always opposed to the interest of every other class in

---

[1] D. Ricardo, *The Principles of Political Economy and Taxation*, London, 1937, p. 1.

236

the community".[1] What can counter this tendency? The import of cheap corn from abroad. Hence the harm of the Corn Laws: they benefit only the parasite landlords.

In a letter to Say of August 1815 Ricardo first mentions his intention of expounding his views in a book. All that autumn he worked extremely hard, becoming more and more absorbed in it. Business, travelling and visiting were reduced to a minimum.

In the course of this work he soon came up against the main difficulty — the problem of value (which we shall analyse below). Smith's theory did not satisfy him, but he was not able to replace it by another. The search became agonising. In one of his letters he wrote that he had known no peace for two weeks until he thought out some important point. Ricardo's letters in general are full of complaints and doubts at this period. Mill tried everything to cheer him up including flattery: "...you are already the best *thinker* on political economy, I am resolved you shall also be the best writer." Ricardo's complaints form a somewhat amusing contrast to the phenomenal speed with which the book was written.

In April 1817 the *Principles of Political Economy and Taxation* was published in an edition of 750 copies. Ricardo's book shows all the signs of haste. He sent the manuscript to the publishers section by section, simultaneously supplementing and amending it. Another two editions came out in his lifetime. They differ little from the first, with the exception of the first chapter "On Value" in which Ricardo strove hard to be precise and convincing.

The third edition of the book consists of 32 chapters clearly divided into three parts. The main principles of the Ricardian system are expounded in the first seven chapters. All the most important points are contained in the first two chapters — on value and rent. Marx said that here Ricardo penetrates the very essence of the capitalist mode of production and gives "some quite new and startling results. Hence the great theoretical satisfaction afforded by these first two chapters..."[2]. The seven theoretical chapters are followed (not consecutively) by fourteen dealing with tax. The remaining eleven chapters contain various additions which arose after

---

[1] *Economic Essays by David Ricardo*, London, 1966, p. 235.

[2] Karl Marx, *Theories of Surplus-Value*, Part II, Moscow, 1968, p. 169.

completion of the main chapters, reflections on and criticism of other economists, mainly Smith, Malthus and Say.

The historical importance of Ricardo for economic science can be reduced to two points. He adopted a single guiding principle, the *definition of value by labour*, by labour time, and sought to erect the whole edifice of political economy on this basis. It was this that enabled him to penetrate further behind the external appearance of phenomena and discover a number of elements of the true physiology of capitalism. He proved and formulated the *economic opposition of the classes* in bourgeois society and thereby got to the very root of historical development.

Both central points of Ricardo's system were used by Marx in his economic theory which produced a revolution in political economy. It is primarily these achievements of Ricardo's that made English classical political economy one of the sources of Marxism. Bourgeois economics, on the other hand, rejected both of Ricardo's main propositions. Very shortly the first point brought down on Ricardo the accusation of excessive abstraction and scholasticism, and the second of cynicism and incitement to class hatred.

Ricardo was devoid of all sentiment. His political economy was cruel, for so was the world which it sought to describe. Therefore those who, like Sismondi, criticised Ricardo from the viewpoint of the humaneness and goodness of separate individuals, are wrong. The scientific nature of Ricardo's views, like Smith's, is determined by the fact that he analysed the interests of classes from the viewpoint of the development of production, the growth of national wealth. He also defended the interests of the industrial bourgeoisie only to the extent to which they corresponded to this high principle. Ricardo did depict the workers as living robots in the production process. The capitalist chooses what is most profitable to him — to hire workers or install new machines. There is no room for sentiment here. Marx wrote: "This is stoic, objective, scientific. In so far as it does not involve *sinning* against his science, Ricardo is always a philanthropist, just as he was in practice too." [1]

Ricardo certainly did not think that philanthropy could cure the ills of society. But in real life he was a kind and generous

[1] Karl Marx, *Theories of Surplus-Value*, Part II, p. 119.

man. Maria Edgeworth describes how she looked round the school not far from Gatcomb Park where 130 children were taught on his money under the supervision of Mrs. Ricardo. He donated money for hospitals and helped many poor relations. There is an interesting correspondence about a poor girl, a former servant in the Ricardos' home, whom a certain young rake lured to London and tried to seduce. This took place at the beginning of 1816 just when Ricardo was working hard on his book. Thanks to the efforts of Ricardo, who did not begrudge his time and even risked being challenged to a duel by the young man, the girl was returned to her parents. A truly Dickensian interlude.

CHAPTER XIII

DAVID RICARDO
THE CROWNING OF THE SYSTEM

THE PUZZLE — VALUE

Ricardo strove hard for a clear understanding of the nature of value. He frequently acknowledged his former views to be unsatisfactory and revised them. As soon as he seemed to have overcome one difficulty another took its place. His last work, *On Value*, was cut short by illness and death. By absolute value he meant what Marx called the substance of value, the amount of labour contained in a commodity. By relative value he meant the exchange value, the quantity of another commodity which should by virtue of natural laws be exchanged for one unit of the commodity in question. Ricardo's weakness was that although he recognised absolute value, he did not seek to penetrate its nature or study the character of the actual labour embodied in this value. What invariably interested him was simply the quantitative aspect of the matter: how is the actual magnitude of exchange value determined and with what can it be measured. Hence his search for the "ideal measure of value", a search for a chimera, a wild fancy.

Occasionally the impossibility of reconciling his theory of value with all the real economic processes drove Ricardo to despair. In one such moment of weakness he wrote in a letter that perhaps it would be simpler to do away with the problem of value altogether and study the laws of distribution without it. But the weakness passed and he again returned to his main task, searching for a way out of the impasse.

As in many other questions, Ricardo began where Smith had stopped. He gave a more precise delimitation of the two factors of a commodity—use and exchange value. The exchange value of all commodities, apart from a minute number of unreproduceable goods, is determined by the relative expenditure of labour on their production.

As we know, Smith was inconsistent in his labour theory of value. He believed that the definition of value by labour, labour time, was applicable only to the "rude state of society", when there was no capital or hired labour. In modern society value was determined by the sum of incomes in the form of wages, profit and rent received from the production and realisation of a commodity. Such inconsistency was unacceptable to Ricardo's strictly logical mind. He was not happy with Smith's typically free treatment of basic principles. Such a fundamental law as the law of value could not be entirely discarded with the development of society. No, said Ricardo, the definition of value by labour time is an absolute, universal law.

Here one must add: in any society in which goods are produced as commodities for exchange and sale for money. But Ricardo could not imagine any other society. Even if he knew history well he certainly did not take seriously, say, production conditions in primitive society. With regard to a possible future society, he could imagine it only in the form of "Mister Owen's parallelograms",[1] which he regarded as wild fantasy although he respected Owen personally. Ricardo did not possess Smith's historical sense and therefore did not see the vast difference between a society of independent hunters who exchange their spoils and the system of factory production and hired labour which obtained in his day. In short, he did not know any society other than a capitalist one, and regarded the laws of this society as natural, universal and eternal.

Nevertheless his theory of the universal application of the law of labour value to developed capitalist society was Ricardo's great service to economic science. From the views of Smith and his disciples it followed, in particular, that a rise (and indeed any change) in money wages produced a corresponding

---

[1] A reference to the workers' settlements (communes) which Robert Owen proposed building in the form of geometrically regular shapes.

change in the value and prices of commodities. Ricardo firmly rejected this statement: "The value of a commodity, or the quantity of any other commodity for which it will exchange, depends on the relative quantity of labour which is necessary for its production and not on the greater or less compensation which is paid for that labour."[1]

If wages rise without any change in labour productivity, this does not change the value of a commodity. All things being equal it does not influence the price either, which is only a reflection of value in gold. What does change then? The distribution of value between the worker's wages and the capitalist's profit. In free competition capitalists cannot compensate for a rise in wages by increasing the prices of their commodities.

This problem was destined to play a great role. From the very start it was acutely political and closely linked with the struggle of the working class for higher wages. Marx based himself on Ricardo, in particular, in his special analysis of the relationship between wages, prices and profits aimed at refuting the view, harmful to the working-class movement, that the struggle for higher wages was pointless because any rise would soon be negated by a rise in prices. Marx explained that "A general rise in the rate of wages would result in a fall of the general rate of profit, but, broadly speaking, not affect the prices of commodities."[2]

These propositions are still important today in connection with bourgeois conceptions which maintain that a rise in workers' money wages is the sole or main cause of the rising cost of living and growing inflation. At the same time one must bear in mind that the views of Ricardo and Marx were expressed in conditions different from those of the present day, when capitalism had certain features which have since disappeared or changed. The most important of them were, firstly, free competition, which excluded the possibility of an individual entrepreneur influencing the market prices of his commodities, and, secondly, a stable monetary circulation on the basis of the gold standard, which limited the possibility of adjusting credit and money to the rising level of prices.

---

[1] D. Ricardo, *The Principles of Political Economy and Taxation*, London, 1937, p. 5.

[2] K. Marx and F. Engels, *Selected Works*, in three volumes, Vol. 2, p. 75.

As we know, the predominance of monopolies possessing a considerable amount of control over markets and prices, and one-sided elasticity of monetary circulation and credit in the direction of increasing volume are typical of modern capitalism. In these conditions entrepreneurs are able to shift higher wages onto commodity prices, which they do constantly in order to maintain and increase profits. Naturally, the possibility to do this is not unlimited and depends on the degree of monopolisation of the market and many other factors. The problem of the relation between wages and prices is playing an important role in the political life of modern capitalist countries. The increase in prices by monopolies, which is usually represented as the result of an increase in real wages, is one of the main factors of modern inflation. Naturally this question merits the most concentrated attention of Marxist economists.

The conclusion about the inverse relation between wages and profit occupies an important place in Ricardo's views on the future of capitalism and in his political programme. It will be remembered that Ricardo believed prices of agricultural produce had a chronic tendency to rise. This would produce an increase in real wages: since workers always received the bare minimum, they would simply die of hunger if there were no increase. But capitalists' profits would be reduced correspondingly, for they cannot raise the prices of industrial goods. Expensive corn is bad for industrialists and at a certain stage deprives them of the stimulus to accumulate capital, which, from Ricardo's point of view, means economic catastrophe!

Ricardo was as aware as Smith of the main difficulties encountered by the labour theory of value.

The first was to explain the exchange between the worker and the capitalist. A worker's labour alone creates the value of a commodity, and the quantity of this labour determines the amount of the value. But in exchange for his labour the worker receives less value in the form of wages. Thus it follows that the law of value is violated in this exchange. If it were observed the worker would receive the full value of the product created by his labour, but then the capitalist would have no profit. Thus a contradiction arises: either the theory does not correspond to reality, or the law of value is constantly being violated in the most important sphere of exchange.

This contradiction was resolved by Marx who showed that the worker sells the capitalist not his labour, which is only a process, an activity, the expenditure of human energy, but his labour power, i.e., his ability to labour. In buying it the capitalist ordinarily pays the worker the full value of his labour power, for this value is determined not by what labour creates, but by what the worker needs for subsistence and reproduction. Thus, the exchange between capital and labour takes place in complete accordance with the law of value, which does not exclude the exploitation of the worker by the capitalist.

The second difficulty was how to reconcile the law of value with the fact that in real life capitalists' profit is determined not by the value of the commodities produced in their factories, but by the amount of capital involved. If value is created by labour alone and commodities are exchanged roughly at their value, the various branches of production are in entirely different positions. Branches and enterprises, where a lot of labour power is used but little machinery and materials, should have high-value commodities, sell their commodities at high prices and, consequently, receive a high profit. The same applies to branches where capital has a quick turnover and yields a quick profit. On the other hand, in branches and enterprises where a great deal of capital has to be invested in the means of production or where the turnover of capital is slower, the value of commodities, prices and profits should be lower.

But this is impossible. It contradicts the real facts of capitalism, for it is a well-known fact that capital tends to yield a standard rate of profit. Otherwise it would leave branches yielding low profit. So it would seem that the law of labour value is incompatible with the absolute, operating law of average profit.

Adam Smith ignored this contradiction, in effect rejecting labour value and forming value from incomes, one of which is average profit. Ricardo could not do this, for he linked his conception more consistently with the labour theory of value. He attempted to force the fact of equal profit for equal capital into the framework of this theory. To stop the frame from cracking he strove, with a skill and determination that deserved more worthy ends, to belittle the importance of the differences in the composition and circulation of capital. In a somewhat naive fashion Ricardo is basically trying to convince the reader that even if average profit does change the law of value this is a minor point and can be overlooked.

He was trying to argue the unarguable, of course. When commodities are produced in conditions of capitalism, the law of value operates (here Ricardo was right), but it cannot operate as it does in simple commodity production (here he was wrong). Value is transformed into the price of production, which includes average profit on capital, and thus the differences in the composition and circulation of capital are balanced out. This is performed by the mechanism of capitalist competition between branches. It is not a rejection, but a development of the law of value. This in general outline is the answer which Marx provided.

The price of production is a fundamentally different category from value. It is pure chance if they happen to coincide. Ricardo tried to prove that they are one and the same, however, and that deviations can be overlooked. This position very soon proved to be extremely vulnerable to criticism by his theoretical opponents.

SHARING OUT THE CAKE, OR RICARDIAN SURPLUS VALUE

Ricardo possessed what was basically a mathematical mind. The age when economics and mathematics were to work hand in hand was still far off, which is why there are no formulae or equations in his works. But his mode of thought and manner of exposition are reminiscent of strict mathematical proof.[1] Ricardo possessed the remarkable ability of singling out simple elements and principles from the complex of economics and developing them to their logical conclusion, leaving aside everything that seemed to him to be secondary, not essential. The strictness and logic of his thought impressed his

---

[1] As early as 1838 A. A. Cournot, the pioneer of mathematical methods in economics, noted this feature of Ricardo's thought and not without justification pointed to a weakness in Ricardian "mathematics" with its unwieldy numerical examples: "There are authors, like Smith and Say, who have written about political economy while retaining all the embellishments of purely literary form; but there are others, like Ricardo, who, in dealing with more abstract questions or seeking a greater precision, have not been able to avoid algebra, and have only disguised it under arithmetical calculations of exhausting prolixity" (A. A. Cournot, *Recherches sur les principes mathématiques de la théorie des richesses*, Paris, 1838, p. IX).

contemporaries greatly. He was a brilliant polemicist. "Don't meddle with Ricardo," James Mill wrote to a friend. "It is not easy to find him in the wrong, I can assure you. I have often thought that I had found him in the wrong, but I have eventually come over to his opinion." [1]

His mathematical approach had its own faults, however. In distribution as in value, Ricardo saw primarily the quantitative aspect. He was interested in the shares and proportions but not so much in the actual nature of distribution, its connection with the structure and development of society.

For the most part Ricardo developed Smith's views on wages, profit and rent as the primary incomes of the three main classes in society. The definition of wages as the cost of the means of subsistence of the worker and his family was borrowed by Ricardo from his predecessors. He thought that he was improving this theory by basing it on the Malthusian theory of population: he accepted the main principles of this theory, which would seem to be the only important point on which he agreed with Malthus. Basing his argument on Malthus, Ricardo believed that wages were kept within the strict limits of the physical minimum not by virtue of the specific laws of capitalism, but of a natural, universal law: namely, that as soon as the average wage exceeds the minimum means of subsistence workers need to produce and bring up more children, competition on the labour market grows stronger and wages fall again.

The views of Malthus and Ricardo became the basis of the so-called "iron law of wages" which was later advanced by Ferdinand Lassalle and other petty-bourgeois socialists. This "law" suggests the futility of the working class's struggle for its economic interests, since wages, it is asserted, are inevitably linked to the physical minimum of the means of subsistence. Although Marx has been and still is accused in the West of adhering to the "iron law", such ideas are in fact alien to Marxism.

Ricardo's theory was to a large extent a static one. Although he noted and even extolled the growth of labour productivity, he nevertheless did not see that in the course of this process the working class itself changes. In particular, two important

---

[1] J. B. Hollander, *David Ricardo. A Centenary Estimate*, Baltimore, 1910, p. 120.

factors change: 1) the normal, socially accepted demands of the worker increase, and 2) there is a growth in the organisation and solidarity of the working class, its ability to fight for a higher standard of living, and as its consciousness grows the class struggle becomes stronger.

Ricardo saw the distribution of the national income in society as the sharing out of a cake which is generally speaking of one fixed size. The workers receive a more than modest slice. All the rest goes to the capitalists who are compelled to share it with the landowners, however. The latter's share is constantly increasing, moreover.

This idea — that rent (and also interest on loans paid by the industrialists to the monetary capitalist) is simply a deduction from profit — was an important one. It meant that profit was treated as the primary, basic form of income, the foundation of which is capital, i. e., as surplus value. Ricardo's equation of profit and surplus value was, of course, connected with his equation of the price of production and value. His theory of distribution had the same merits and defects as his theory of value.

The value of an individual commodity and of all commodities forming the national income is determined objectively by expenditure of labour. This value is divided into wages and profit (including rent). Hence Ricardo concludes the fundamental contradiction underlying the class interests of the proletariat and the bourgeoisie. Many times he wrote that wages and profit can change in inverse proportion only: if wages rise, profit falls, and vice versa. This is why the fervent American apologist of capitalism Carey called Ricardo's theory a system of strife and enmity between the classes.

Again Ricardo was interested only in proportions, in the quantitative side of the matter. He was not concerned with the nature, genesis and future of the relations which produce the contradiction between wages and profit. Therefore he could not discover "the secret of surplus value", although he came close to it by realising that the capitalist appropriates from the worker a part of the value created by the latter's labour.

One of Ricardo's finest scientific achievements was his analysis of the nature and magnitude of land rent. Unlike his predecessors, he constructed his theory of rent on the firm basis of the labour theory of value. He explained that the source of rent was not Nature's bounty, but the labour applied to the land. Since land resources are limited, not only the best tracts are cultivated, but also middling and poor ones. The value of agricultural produce is determined by the expenditure of labour on relatively poor stretches of land, and the best and middling ones yield a higher profit. Since profit has to average out, capitalist tenants are forced to give this excess to landowners in the form of rent.

Ricardo believed that the poorest stretches did not yield rent. Marx showed that this was wrong: given private ownership of land the landowner will not rent out even the poorest plot for nothing. Marx called Ricardian rent *differential* (i. e., connected with the natural differences in the land) and this special rent, overlooked by Ricardo, *absolute rent.*

A great role was played by the analysis of processes applied by Ricardo (in undeveloped form) from the viewpoint of small increments in economic numbers: the value of agricultural produce is determined by the expenditure of labour on the last (marginal) plot of land which it is expedient to cultivate at the given level of technology and demand. The method of small increments (margins) was to play an important role in economics.

WHITHER CAPITALISM?

A modern American populariser of science, R. L. Heilbroner, writes about the Ricardian system: "This is as basic, bare, unadorned and architectural as Euclid, but, unlike a set of pure geometrical propositions, this system has human overtones: it is a *tragic* system." [1] The tragedy which Ricardo saw in the capitalist order, and his pessimism in relation to the future of this order were well-founded and reflected real trends in capitalist development. True, the idle landowners did not devour England. The "under-accumulation" sickness which Ricardo prophesied for English capitalism proved to be not so terrible after all. The working class did not passively reconcile itself to its gloomy Malthusian-Ricardian fate. The tragic nature of the capitalist order turned out to be somewhat different from what Ricardo had expected.

---

[1] R. L. Heilbroner, *The Great Economists*, London, 1955, p. 78.

Nevertheless the great thinker saw many features of capitalism in their true light. He was absolutely right in thinking that capitalism tended to keep the proletariat in the position of an appendage to production and reduce workers' wages to the bare minimum. He was also right to fear the destructive influence of large-scale land-owning on economic progress. If not the experience of England, that of a number of other countries has confirmed these fears.

Ricardo's pessimism was tempered by at least two considerations. Firstly, he believed that free trade, particularly the free import of corn from abroad, could and would change the position basically by stopping the rise in rent and fall in profit. Secondly, he accepted unreservedly the principle that general overproduction and economic crises were impossible, later called "Say's law". From this quarter at least, he thought, capitalism was not threatened.

Society's requirements for goods and services are limitless, Ricardo said. Even if the human belly cannot contain more than a certain amount of food, there is no limit to demands for various "conveniences and ornaments". Was he not confusing requirement with effective demand? No, he was not that naive. He realised that demands which are not backed up by ready money mean little, economically speaking. But, like Say, Ricardo thought that by generating incomes production itself automatically creates effective demand for goods and services and that this demand inevitably ensures the realisation of all goods and services.

He regarded capitalist society as an ideally regulated mechanism in which any difficulty with sales was solved quickly and easily: the producers of a commodity which is being produced in an excessive quantity soon receive the corresponding signal from the market and switch to the production of another commodity. Ricardo expressed the thesis about the impossibility of general over-production as follows: "Productions are always bought by productions, or by services; money is only the medium by which the exchange is effected. Too much of a particular commodity may be produced, of which there may be such a glut in the market as not to repay the capital expended on it; but this cannot be the case with respect to all commodities."[1]

---

[1] D. Ricardo, *The Principles of Political Economy and Taxation*, p. 194.

Scarcely had the ink dried with which these lines were written, than events firmly disproved them: the first general crisis of overproduction broke out in England as early as 1825. It is possible that Ricardo, with his scientific impartiality and self-criticism, would have revised his views subsequently. But by then he was no longer in the land of the living.

Thus, the system of classical bourgeois political economy (the classical school) found its fullest expression in the works of Ricardo. Let us try to set out its main features.

1. Characteristic of the classical school was the desire to penetrate, using the method of scientific abstraction, the essence of economic phenomena and processes. It analysed these processes with great objectivity and impartiality. This was possible since the industrial bourgeoisie, whose interests the classical school expressed in the final analysis, was at that time a progressive force, and the class struggle between the bourgeoisie and the proletariat had not yet become the main factor in society.

2. At the basis of the classical school lay the labour theory of value and the whole edifice of political economy was erected upon this. However, the classical school was unable to explain the laws of capitalism by proceeding from the labour theory of value in the form in which this theory was developed by the classical economists. The classical school regarded capitalism as the only possible, eternal and natural social order.

3. The classical school saw the problem of production and distribution in society from the point of view of the position of the main classes. This enabled it to come close to the conclusion that the source of the incomes of capitalists and landowners was the exploitation of the working class. It could not explain the nature of surplus-value, however, because it did not have a clear understanding of the specific nature of labour power as a commodity.

4. The classical school's views of the reproduction of social capital were based on the principle of natural equilibrium in the economic system. This was connected with a belief in the existence of objective, spontaneous economic laws, independent of human will. But the conception of the self-regulatory nature of capitalist economy also concealed the latter's contradictions. Of particular importance was the classical school's rejection of general overproduction and crises.

5. Bourgeois classical political economy advocated maximum restriction of state intervention in the economy (the principle of *laissez faire*), free trade. To a large extent its economic liberalism was combined with liberalism in politics and the propagation of bourgeois democracy.

MEMBER OF PARLIAMENT

Ricardo's *Principles of Political Economy and Taxation* was by no means a best seller. It was a book for economists, not for the general public. And at that time there were hardly any economists. Sismondi quotes Ricardo as saying that there were not more than twenty-five people in England who understood his book.

But a year after its publication McCulloch published a long eulogistic review in which he tried to put Ricardo's ideas in more popular form and picked out his statements on current questions of economic policy. The efforts of Mill and certain other persons brought Ricardo's book to the attention of the public which was already quite familiar with his name. Malthus was already writing his *Principles of Political Economy* in which he challenged Ricardo on basic questions of theory and policy. Ricardo could feel that he had achieved what he had set out to do.

In 1819, when the second edition came out, he finally retired from business and gave up membership of the Stock Exchange. His fortune was by then invested in land, real estate and safe, unspeculative bonds. Ricardo's children were brought up as the heirs of a rich landowner, an English gentleman. (His family, i. e., widow and children, did not allow Moses Ricardo, his closest brother, to publish a biography of the great economist: they did not want to draw attention to his Jewish origin and Stock Exchange career.)

Parliamentary activity was natural for a man of Ricardo's position and inclinations. His friends advised him to enter this arena. There was only one way for Ricardo to get into the House of Commons—to buy a parliamentary seat from some impoverished landlord, the owner of one of the many "rotten boroughs". And this was what he did. Elected by a remote Irish constituency, Ricardo never went there and never saw any of his electors, which was quite in keeping with the times.

He spent only four years in Parliament but played a fairly eminent role there. Ricardo did not belong formally to either the ruling Tory party or the Whig opposition. The latter was more acceptable to him, and he enjoyed considerable authority among left-wing and radical opposition circles. But he maintained an independent position in the Commons and frequently voted against the Whig leadership. Economic problems naturally played an important part in Ricardo's parliamentary activity. He continued to campaign against the Corn Laws for free trade, a reduction in the national debt and the improvement of banking and monetary system. But among his speeches we also find some in defence of freedom of the press and against restrictions on the right of assembly. Like Adam Smith Ricardo supported the fullest possible bourgeois democracy in politics.

All eyewitnesses agree that members listened attentively when Ricardo was addressing the House. He was not a brilliant orator in the usual sense of the word. However, the urge to penetrate the social essence of phenomena and problems and the logic and efficiency of his writing can also be found in his parliamentary speeches.

Parliament took up nearly all Ricardo's time when it was in session. During these months he lived in London. He spent the mornings at home reading papers, writing letters and draft speeches, receiving visitors, and occasionally going to Westminster for committee meetings. In the afternoon the House sat and Ricardo was one of its most conscientious members. Almost all his writings from 1819 to 1823 were connected with Parliamentary activity. The main ones dealt with the Corn Laws and the national debt.

He could only pursue his studies in the summer months in Gatcomb Park, of which he had become increasingly fond. There he wrote a criticism of Malthus' book, prepared the third edition of his *Principles*, and continued to ponder on the problems of value, land rent and the economic consequences of the use of machines. He carried on an intense correspondence with Malthus, Mill, McCulloch and Say. At this time Ricardo was at the centre of European economic science. Regular meetings of economists at his home led in 1821 to the founding of the London Club of Political Economy, of which Ricardo was the generally recognised leader. He performed this function with great tact and modesty.

Death overtook Ricardo suddenly amid this intense activity. He died at Gatcomb Park in September 1823 from inflammation of the brain. He was only fifty-one.

What sort of a person was Ricardo in real life?

His appearance is described as follows: below medium height, lean but well-built and very active; a pleasant face with an intelligent, benevolent and sincere expression; dark, attentive and alert eyes; simple and engaging manners. Judging by what we know, he was a likeable and pleasant person in his dealings with others. He was physically incapable of quarrelling with his friends, although he frequently disagreed with them on questions of economics and politics.

Ricardo possessed to a high degree the qualities of the family man, the head of the family. Not only his children, but also his younger brothers and sisters, and even his wife's relatives looked upon him as a wise and just elder. (His wealth might also have had something to do with this.) In the latter years of his life he spent much time on the upbringing of his children, married his elder son and daughters, and smoothed over various trivial family conflicts. In spite of his by no means advanced years, he felt like an Old Testament patriarch when his children gathered in the hospitable house at Gatcomb Park with grandchildren and other relatives. The large house was always packed not only with relatives, but guests of all kinds — acquaintances from London with their acquaintances, neighbouring landowners, and friends of the children.

Ricardo was a well-educated person, but he did not have the same breadth of knowledge and interests as the encyclopaedic mind of Adam Smith. It is difficult to call this a failing. In order to carry out his historic mission in economic science Ricardo required tremendous intellecutal concentration in one field. If he had tried to be an all-rounder he would probably not have been able to do what he did for political economy in a short space of time.

RICARDO AND MARX

Marx wrote: "... my theory of value, of money and of capital, is in its fundamentals a necessary sequel to the teaching of

Smith and Ricardo."[1] At the same time he subjected the teaching of both British economists to profound criticism and constructed the new proletarian political economy on its basis.

Marx's criticism of Ricardo's theory is a model of conscientiousness and constructivity. Approximately one-third of the lengthy *Theories of Surplus-Value* is devoted to Ricardo. In his criticism Marx makes frequent use of the device of showing how Ricardo should have reasoned if he had developed his own correct initial premises consistently. Marx reveals the objective, historically conditioned limitations of the classical school. Ricardo was a genius, but no genius can break the bounds of age and class. And Marx criticises Ricardo not for being a bourgeois economist but for being inconsistent in his scientific conception, which could not help being a bourgeois one.

What did Marx create on the basis of Smith's and Ricardo's teaching?

He turned the labour theory of value into a profound and logical system on the basis of which he erected the whole edifice of a fundamentally new political economy. He freed the labour theory of value from the contradictions and impasses which had tormented Ricardo. The most important factor in all this was Marx's discovery and analysis of the dual nature of the labour contained in a commodity — concrete and abstract labour. Proceeding from the labour theory of value Marx also created a theory of money which explained the phenomena of metal and paper money circulation.

Having explained the nature of labour power as a commodity and outlined the historical conditions of the buying and selling of labour power, Marx created the theory of surplus value on the basis of the labour theory of value and in full accordance with it. For the first time it was scientifically explained that what actually took place within the framework of a "fair", equivalent exchange between capital and labour was the exploitation of the working class.

Marx made surplus-value the universal form of the appropriation by capital of unpaid labour and its product. The seeds of this idea which we find in Ricardo were fully developed and moulded into a single system. The concrete forms of unearned income — profit, rent and interest — found their places in this

---

[1] Karl Marx, *Capital*, Vol. I, p. 26.

system. The class nature of the problem of distribution emerged with great strength and clarity.

By the theory of average profit and price of production Marx, as has already been mentioned, solved Ricardo's "fatal" contradiction. But not only this. In so doing he reached a conclusion of tremendous importance: although each capitalist directly exploits "his" workers, all capitalists as it were put their surplus value into a kitty and share it out according to capital. Economically the capitalist class as a single whole is opposed to the working class.

By making use of the scientific elements contained in Ricardo's theory of land rent Marx created the profound conception which explains rent as a form of income of landowners and the laws of capitalist development in agriculture.

Marx rejected the views of Ricardo and Say on the impossibility of general overproduction and crises. He was the first to elaborate the principles of the theory of reproduction and to show the inevitability of periodic crises in capitalist economy.

Ricardo's social pessimism, which he partly took from Malthus, gave way to the Marxist universal law of capitalist accumulation, which proceeded logically from all his teaching. Marx proved both the existent possibilities for the forward development of capitalism and the inevitability of capitalism's ultimate revolutionary collapse and replacement by socialism.

CHAPTER XIV

AROUND RICARDO — AND LATER

Just as Quesnay's pupils had talked about the creation of a "new science" half a century earlier, so in the latter years of Ricardo's life and after his death it became accepted to speak of the "new science of political economy".

It is true that Ricardo's works outlined the subject of political economy (human social relations in connection with the production of material goods) and elaborated its method (scientific abstraction). It seemed to have acquired to some extent the features common to the precise and natural sciences. But political economy is a class science. Whatever the subjective intentions of the specialist, his ideas always serve directly the interests of a certain class to a greater or lesser extent. Ricardo's teaching was openly and frankly bourgeois. But it was precisely this openness and frankness that ceased to please the bourgeoisie when the class struggle in England became more acute: in the 1830s and 1840s, the period of Chartism, it became the centre of all social and political life.

In this new situation Ricardo's followers, who occupied a leading place in English bourgeois political economy right up to the middle of the century and even later, began to renounce the bolder and more radical aspects of his teaching and adapt it to the interests of the bourgeoisie. They either limited themselves to simple commentaries on Ricardo or gave his ideas an apologetic twist.

In 1851 Marx, after making a thorough study of new English economic literature in the British Museum Library, wrote to Engels: "Au fond, since A. Smith and D. Ricardo this science has made no progress, although much has been done in specific investigations, including some very sophisticated ones."[1]

The abundance of specialised economic studies reflected the rapid development of capitalism and the objective need to study individual aspects of the economy. The skeleton of economic science was taking on flesh. Statistics became very advanced, in particular the indexing method. The growth of individual branches of industry was described and analysed. Concrete research was carried out in the sphere of agrarian economics, price movement, monetary circulation and banking. An extensive literature emerged on the position of the working class. By the middle of the century political economy was firmly ensconced in university syllabuses.

All this applies to the bourgeois, official science. But alongside it in the 1820s to 1840s one finds other writers in England whom Marx called the proletarian opponents of the political economists. They borrowed from Ricardo's teaching those elements which could be turned against the bourgeoisie.

English political economy of the 1820s to 1840s played an important role in the development of Marx's economic doctrine. A considerable part of the *Theories of Surplus-Value* is devoted to a critical analysis of the views of English economists of that period. This criticism played an important role in Marx's substantiation of the labour theory of value and price formation, the theory of profit and the universal law of capitalist accumulation.

THE 19TH CENTURY

Nowhere did the "age of bourgeois wealth" show itself with such cynicism and hypocrisy as in England. Money became the one and only connection between people in society. A person was now judged solely from the point of view of whether he had capital and how big it was. The poor man, who a mere fifty or hundred years ago was still linked with his native parts by a

---

[1] Karl Marx/Friedrich Engels, *Werke*, Bd. 27, S. 228.

multitude of ties and who could in the last resort rely upon the help of the community, sometimes even the protection of the landlord, now had nothing whatever to lean on. He was now a worker, whose only possession was his worker's hands, and whose only source of subsistence was to sell these hands to the capitalist.

Capitalists demanded and obtained full freedom to exploit workers. "Anarchy plus the constable" was how Thomas Carlyle, an ardent critic of bourgeois customs in the first half of his career, described the system. He meant that the state gave capitalists full freedom to make money and compete between themselves as they saw fit, but performed the function of guarding this "freedom" and private property with the help of the police.

It was the same Carlyle who first called political economy the "dismal science". What did he mean by this? Firstly, Ricardian political economy, as we know, was totally devoid of all sentiment. It made no secret of the terrible position of the workers, but regarded it as natural. Secondly, and in this respect it was close to Malthus, it regarded the age-old gap between population and natural resources as the main cause of poverty and therefore took a pessimistic view of the future.

But for the English moneybags political economy was anything but a dismal science. They thought that the science founded by Smith and Ricardo should help them to find ways of getting rich more quickly. The popularity of political economy interpreted in this light assumed humoristic forms. Maria Edgeworth relates that in the 1820s it became very fashionable for London ladies to talk about political economy. Rich gentlewomen required that their daughters' governesses should teach the subject. One governess who thought she was quite well enough equipped with her knowledge of French, Italian, music, drawing, dancing, etc., was astounded by this request and answered hesitatingly: "No Ma'am, I cannot say I teach political economy, but I would if you think proper try to learn it." "Oh dear no, Ma'am — if you don't teach it you won't do for me", was the retort.

The English bourgeoisie needed a philosophy which would directly support the "science of getting rich". This philosophy was utilitarianism in ethics and positivism in epistemology (the theory of knowledge). The father of utilitarianism was Jeremy Bentham. Bentham's utilitarianism (the philosophy of use, from the Latin *utilitas*) is historically connected with the views on nature and human behaviour which were developed by Helvetius and Smith. Man is an egoist by nature. The essence of any decision, including economic ones, is that he mentally weighs up the advantages and disadvantages (satisfaction and pain, gain and loss), striving to maximise the former and minimise the latter. He is most successful when he makes a free and sensible choice. The aim of society, the state and the legislators is to create the most favourable conditions for this. Society is merely a number of individuals. The more gain, satisfaction and happiness there is for each individual, the more "total happiness" there will be in society. Bentham advanced the notorious slogan "the greatest happiness for the largest number of people". From this philosophy proceeded the principle of individualism which has been fully assimilated by bourgeois political economy: each man for himself in the competitive struggle. The capitalist must have the chance to purchase labour power freely, and the worker to sell it freely. It is assumed that each will conclude this transaction to his maximum benefit.

This idea of the "man calculator" was taken up a few decades later by the subjective school in political economy. For this school the main economic problem is comparison of the degrees of satisfaction obtained from the consumption of various commodities, the comparison of the utility of wages with the disutility (burden) of labour, etc.

At first Bentham's utilitarianism was progressive, generally speaking, for it advanced the ideas of bourgeois freedom as opposed to feudalism. When the modest liberal demands of the Benthamites were met for the most part, however, and when, on the other hand, the class struggle between the bourgeoisie and the proletariat grew more acute, utilitarianism lost the ground from under its feet and merged with capitalist apologetic trends.

Positivism was a broad trend in 19th-century West European philosophy. In England it was connected with traditions that went back to Hume's agnosticism. According to these ideas, the aim of science is simply to describe and systematise facts and any advance beyond this is futile "metaphysics". This is the consciously down-to-earth, prosaic philosophy of the age of bourgeois money-grubbing. The most eminent positivist philosopher was John Stuart Mill. The philosophy of positivism became the basis of the economic theory of Mill and his age (mid-19th century), and also of the subsequent development of bourgeois political economy.

MALTHUS AND MALTHUSIANISM

Malthus is an odious figure in the history of political economy. About 180 years has passed since the publication of his *Essay on the Principle of Population*, but the ideas and the author's name are still the object of heated ideological and political discussion. Malthus laid the foundations of Malthusianism, the population theory which maintains that all human disasters are the result of overpopulation regardless of the social order. Today Malthusianism is playing a considerable role in the ideological struggle between capitalism and socialism for the developing countries. The reactionary Malthusians maintain that the central problem for these countries is a surplus and excessively rapid growth of population: solving this problem and passing a minimum of essentially bourgeois reforms would give them an entrée into "high society" (capitalist, of course). Marxists maintain that in order to get rid of economic backwardness as quickly as possible it is essential to have some radical social transformations. Within this framework a certain policy of controlling the birth rate and population growth could be effective. It is obvious that these standpoints are diametrically opposed.

Malthus' place in the science is determined by two main factors: his "law" of population and his strange role as Ricardo's critic and helper, opponent and friend.

Thomas Robert Malthus was born in 1766 near Guildford, Surrey, and was the second son of an educated squire. Since the estate in English families is not divided between the children he received nothing, but he did have a good education, at first at home and then at Jesus College, Cambridge. After graduating from college Malthus took orders in the Anglican Church and received the modest post of curate in a rural parish. In 1793 he was made a fellow of Jesus College and remained so until his marriage in 1804: one of the conditions of fellowship was bachelorhood.

The young Malthus spent a great deal of time at the home of his father, with whom he engaged in endless talks and disputes on philosophical and political subjects. Strange though it may seem, the father was the enthusiast and optimist, and the son the sceptic and pessimist. Searching for arguments in the disputes with his father, he came across the idea in some 18th-century writers that people reproduce more quickly than the means of subsistence increase, and that if its growth is not checked the population doubles every 20-25 years. It seemed obvious to Malthus that food production could not grow at such a pace. That meant the forces of nature would not allow mankind to extract itself from poverty. Exessive reproduction by the poor — that was the main cause of their wretched position in society. And there was no way out of this impasse. Revolution was no use here.

In 1798 Malthus published anonymously a small pamphlet entitled *An Essay on the Principle of Population as It Affects the Future Improvement of Society*. He expounded his views sharply and uncompromisingly, even cynically. For example, he wrote: "A man who is born into a world already possessed, if he cannot get subsistence from his parents on whom he has a just demand, and if the society do not want his labour, has no claim of *right* to the smallest portion of food, and, in fact, has no business to be where he is. At nature's mighty feast there is no vacant cover for him. She tells him to be gone, and will quickly execute her own orders." [1]

Malthus obviously belonged to the breed of English gentlemen who are firmly convinced of the superiority of their class and nation, who despise all babbling about the poor, unfortunate and crippled, who in their imperturbable composure, white gloves and immaculate frock coat can attend factory riots and sepoy executions. These people regard cruelty as necessary commonsense and humanity as dangerous fancy.

Incidentally, as many of Malthus' contemporaries relate, he was a sociable, even likeable man: his friendship with Ricardo bears this out. He was remarkably composed and calm. Nobody ever saw him angry, overjoyed or downcast. It was this feature which enabled him to exhibit indifference (perhaps feigned) to the criticism to which he was subjected for his harsh views.

---

[1] Malthus considered it necessary to remove this passage from a number of subsequent editions. Quoted from J. M. Keynes, *Essays and Sketches in Biography*, New York, 1956, p. 26.

Malthus' book was just what the English ruling class, terrified of the influence of the French revolution on the English people, wanted. Malthus himself was amazed at its success and set about preparing a second edition. He went abroad to collect material in support of his theory. The second edition was very different from the first: it was an extensive treatise with historical excursions, criticism of various writers, etc. In all there were five editions of the *Essay* in Malthus' lifetime, the last one five times the size of the first!

In 1805 Malthus was appointed professor of modern history and political economy in the recently founded college of the East India Company. He also performed the functions of the college clergyman. He regularly attended the meetings of the Political Economy Club where he invariably opposed Ricardo and James Mill. In 1815 Malthus published his work on land rent, and in 1820 the book *Principles of Political Economy*, which contains his polemic with Ricardo for the most part. Malthus' lectures and speeches were notable for their dry and doctrinaire tone. They were also difficult to listen to because he had suffered from a speech defect since childhood. In his political views he was a Whig, but a very moderate one who always strove for the golden mean, as an English biographical dictionary says of him. Malthus had three children. He died suddenly in December 1834 from heart failure.

MAN AND THE EARTH

It would be wrong to write off the Malthusian theory of population as nonsense or crude apologetics. Such men as David Ricardo and Charles Darwin spoke of its influence on their thinking. Marx and Engels wrote that it reflected, although in distorted form, the real defects and contradictions of capitalism.

Malthus maintained that the population tends to increase more quickly than the means of subsistence. In order to "prove" this he knocked the reader smartly on the head with the hammer of his notorious progression: each twenty-five years the population could double and, consequently, increase as a series of numbers in geometrical progression 1, 2, 4, 8, 16, 32, 64 ... whereas the means of subsistence, according to him, could at best increase over the same periods of time in arithmetical progression: 1, 2, 3, 4, 5, 6, 7, ... "In two centuries the population would be to the means of subsistence as 256 to 9; in three centuries as 4,096 to 13, and in two thousand years the difference would be almost incalculable." [1]

Malthus was a good psychologist and realised the force of such simple and startling illustrations. The reader was inclined to forget that this was only a tendency and his hair stood on end at the apocalyptic vision of a world where people had no room to stand, to say nothing of live or work. The author calmed his imagination somewhat by saying that in fact it was impossible: nature herself sees to it that this tendency does not become reality. How does she do that? With the help of wars, disease, poverty and vice. Malthus regarded all this as man's natural punishment for his sinfulness, for his indestructible sexual urge. Surely there must be some other solution. Yes, there is, said Malthus in his book, beginning with the second edition: "preventive checks" or, to put it more simply, sexual continence. Malthus praised late marriages, celibacy, and widowhood. But in spite of all his assurances Malthus himself did not really believe in the effectiveness of these measures and again returned to the inevitability of positive restrictions. It is interesting that he was not in favour of contraceptive devices, which were already being discussed at that time. He rejected such a restriction of the birth rate as interference with the competence of nature, i. e., God. In Malthus' system overpopulation is not only the Scourge of mankind but also a kind of blessing, a Divine whip urging on the naturally lazy worker. Only constant competition between workers, of whom there are always too many, will force them to work hard for low wages.

Malthus' theory was extremely rigid and dogmatic. It sought to present the limited and by no means authentic experience of a certain stage in capitalist development as a universal law valid for any age and social order.

Above all, it is not true that the tendency to unchecked reproduction can be checked simply by insufficient means of subsistence and the Malthusian demons which proceed from this. Malthus maintained that a growth in the means of

---

[1] T. R. Malthus, *An Essay on the Principle of Population*, Vol. I, London, 1862, p. 11.

subsistence immediately produced a reaction in the form of an increase in the birth rate and size of the population, until this in its turn neutralised the growth in the means of subsistence. In fact this tendency is by no means an absolute one. At a definite stage in society's development it readily gives way to the directly opposite tendency: a growth in the means of subsistence and the standards of life tends to reduce the birth rate and the rates of natural population growth. Today the rate of this growth in the rich countries of the West is a mere one half to one-third of that in the poor countries of Asia, Africa and Latin America. As is known, over the past 20 to 25 years Japan has made spectacular economic progress, while the birth rate there has dropped by half.

Socialism does away with the "fatal" relationship of poverty of the masses to overpopulation. The new social system secures an unprecedentedly steep growth in the production of goods and services, as well as their more equitable distribution. Furthermore, it guarantees personal well-being and freedom, genuine equality of men and women, rapid cultural advance, thereby opening the way to a reasonable and humane regulation of population size. Under socialism and communism it is possible to solve one of the most formidable problems mankind has ever faced—one of maintaining an optimum population *size*, i. e., a population growth commensurate with a maximum in production and consumption, which in the final analysis, if you like, would ensure a happy and prosperous life for all.

Let us now turn to the second Malthusian entrant in the perpetual contest between population and resources—the means of subsistence growing in arithmetic progression. On this point Malthus is even further from the truth.

Indeed, he painted a picture, which is roughly as follows. Imagine a piece of land providing a livelihood to one person. He puts in 200 man-days of labour per annum and receives, say, ten tons of wheat from his plot, which is just enough for him. Then a second man comes along (a grown-up son perhaps) and puts another 200 man-days into the same plot. Does the harvest double, to twenty tons? Probably not, Malthus assumes; it would be good going if it increased to fifteen or seventeen tons. If a third man appears, they will receive an even lower return for the additional 200 man-days. Someone will have to go.

This in elementary form is the so-called law of diminishing returns, or law of diminishing fertility of the soil, which lies at the basis of Malthus' teaching. Does such a law exist? Not as an absolute and universal law of the production of material goods. In certain economic conditions situations and phenomena may arise when the growth of expenditure does not yield a proportional increase in production. But this is by no means a universal law. It is more a signal to economists and engineers that something is wrong in the given sector of the economy.

The example quoted above depicts a completely hypothetical and artificial situation and certainly does not exhaust the problem of man's exploitation of natural resources. In real life the labour which is mentioned there is applied in conjunction with certain means of production. If this combination is properly selected the return for the given quantity of working hours does not decrease. Of particular importance is technological progress, which equips labour with increasingly productive instruments and methods. The plot in question could be joined with several neighbouring ones and most probably the return would increase with an increased scale of production, better organisation, specialisation and more effective application of technology.[1]

The subsequent history of agricultural development in capitalist countries disproves Malthus and his forecasts. This was constantly pointed out by V. I. Lenin in his works on the agrarian question: technological progress in agriculture during the second half of the 19th century made it possible to increase agricultural output considerably with a relative (and even in

---

[1] Taking into account these obvious objections to the "law of diminishing returns", modern bourgeois economists greatly limit its sphere of action by comparison with Malthus. They say that this "law" operates only when an increased quantity of the factor in question is added to a fixed quantity of other production factors. What is meant by basic factors of production is, as we know, labour, capital and land. The above example describes such a situation — as we can see, a totally unrealistic one. It assumes that land and capital (the other means of production) are unchanged, and only the amount of labour changes. Nevertheless, Malthusians still use the "law of diminishing returns" in some form or other. In rejecting this "law" Marxist economists by no means ignore the real and important problem of return (growth of production in its natural form) for production costs. This return varies depending on the above-mentioned factors (and many others). The task of increasing the return per rouble of capital investment, per man-hour of labour and per hectare of land is a most important one to improve the efficiency of socialist economy.

some cases absolute) reduction of the labour force engaged in agriculture. Equally striking changes in the same direction have been taking place in the agriculture of North America and Western Europe since the Second World War. This is further confirmation of the fact that the threat to capitalism as a system comes not from "underproduction" of means of subsistence, but from the social contradictions to which the system gives rise.

In concentrating attention on overpopulation Malthus was reflecting the tendency inherent in capitalism to transform part of the proletariat into a "surplus", to create a constant reserve of unemployed. But, contrary to what Malthus maintains, this overpopulation is not an absolute surplus of people compared to natural resources, but a relative surplus of workers under capitalism.

The objective meaning of Malthus' writings can be reduced largely to defence of the interests of landowners. In acknowledging the difference between himself and Ricardo, Malthus himself noted the paradox: "It is somewhat singular that Mr. Ricardo, a considerable receiver of rents, should have so much underrated their national importance; while I, who never received, nor expect to receive any, should probably be accused of overrating their importance." [1] If this means anything it is only that the vulgar sociological approach cannot explain a person's psychology and thought: this complex sphere is not determined by his social position. (It must not be forgotten, incidentally, that Ricardo only *became* a landowner, whereas Malthus *was* one by birth and only subsequently became a clergyman and professor.)

This class standpoint and his personal qualities made Malthus' point of view in economics very different from that of Ricardo. In particular, whereas Ricardo gazed as it were into the distance, overlooking contradictions and problems which seemed to him to be individual and transient ones, Malthus stopped and took a closer look. This was the case with the problem of crises which Ricardo ignored, but Malthus did not.

As has already been mentioned, bourgeois political economy was divided into two main trends on this question. Smith and Ricardo believed that the key problem for capitalism was

---

[1] T. R. Malthus, *Principles of Political Economy*, Oxford, a.o., 1951, pp. 216-17.

accumulation, which would ensure the growth of production, whereas there were no serious difficulties from the point of view of demand and realisation. Malthus (together with Sismondi) attacked this point of view and was the first to place the problem of realisation at the centre of economic theory. In so doing he showed a remarkable awareness of the contradictions of capitalist development. Ricardo assumed that the realisation of any number of commodities and services could be ensured by the combined demand of capitalists (including the demand for commodities designed for production) and workers. And he was right in principle. But the possibility of such realisation does not mean that in practice it proceeds smoothly and without conflict. Certainly not. The process of realisation is interrupted by crises of overproduction which become increasingly destructive as capitalism develops. Malthus sought a solution to the problem of realisation in the existence of social classes and strata unrelated to capitalists or workers. It was only their demand, he maintained, that could ensure the realisation of the whole mass of produced commodities. Thus, the saviours of society, according to Malthus, were the very landowners and their servants, officers and clergymen whom Smith referred to as parasites.

Keynesianism, the leading trend in 20th-century bourgeois political economy resurrected and adopted Malthus' ideas on the question of realisation and the factors of "effective demand". Keynes' statement that it would have been far better for capitalism if economic science had followed Malthus' line instead of Ricardo's approach was not fortuitous. In modern economic policy the consumption of commodities by various intermediate strata and the encouragement of this consumption by the state is an important anticrisis measure. Bourgeois economic thought, incapable of providing a scientific explanation of the basic laws of capitalism, still finds certain methods of softening the concrete contradictions of the capitalist system pragmatically, under pressure of circumstances.

THE DISINTEGRATION OF RICARDIANISM

The writings of James Mill and McCulloch in the 1820s and 1830s represented the most painstaking reproduction and popularisation of the letter of Ricardo's teaching. With regard to the spirit of this teaching, they did not understand it and could not develop it. The mediocrity of Ricardo's closest followers is recognised even by modern bourgeois economists. Schumpeter writes that Ricardo's doctrine "wilted in their hands and became stale and unproductive practically at once". But he sees the reason for this mainly in the sterility of the doctrine itself.

What is the real reason for the sad fate of this great economist's legacy? Ricardo left a profound system of ideas, but it was also full of glaring contradictions and lacunae. He himself was more aware of this than anyone else. In order to develop Ricardo properly it was necessary to master the principles of his teaching and then find a scientific solution to these contradictions.

Naturally it was most important that the people surrounding Ricardo were personally incapable of solving such a task. But this was not all. However important the role of the individual in science, it is subject to the same laws as the role of the individual in history: the age, historical necessity, produces people capable of solving the tasks of the moment. The point is that the creative development of Ricardo's teaching required a transition to the standpoint of a different ideology. It was basically impossible within the framework of bourgeois ideology. This is why Ricardo's true heir was Marxism.

Let us recall the two main contradictions which confronted Ricardo. *Firstly*, he could not explain how the exchange of capital for labour (more simply, the hiring of workers by a capitalist) was compatible with his labour theory of value. If a worker receives the full "value of his labour" (we know that this expression is wrong, but Ricardo put it this way), i. e., if his wage is equal to the value of the commodity created by his labour, it is impossible to explain profit. If, however, a worker receives less than the "value of his labour" what about the exchange of equivalents, the law of value? *Secondly*, he could not reconcile labour value with the phenomenon of equal profit for equal capital. If value is created by labour alone, commodities on which an equal amount of labour is expended should be sold at approximately equal prices, regardless of the amount of capital used in their production. But this would mean different rates of profit for capital, which was obviously impossible as a long-term phenomenon.

We already know how Marx solved these contradictions. Let

us see how English economists of the 1820s and 1830s approached them. We shall not go into detail on individual writers, but simply indicate the general trend. Ricardo's pupils could not find a solution to these contradictions and sought to get round them as follows.

Capital is accumulated labour. Mill, McCulloch and others began again from this very Ricardian beginning. Hence the value of a commodity produced by labour with the help of capital should include the value of the latter. If this means that the value of a commodity includes the transferred value of machinery, raw materials, fuel, etc., it is true. But we are still no closer to finding out where the profit comes from. For a capitalist will not advance capital, i. e., buy these means of production, only in order to have their value reproduced in the ready commodity.

No, said the economists, this is not what we mean. The worker works in the factory, but so does the machine. By analogy one might say that cotton, coal, etc., "work" too. For it is all accumulated labour. By working they create value. The portion of the value created by them is profit. It naturally goes to the capitalist and is in proportion to the capital.

This is a pseudo-solution of Ricardian contradictions. According to this argument the worker receives the "full value of his labour", since everything that he does not receive from the newly created value was created not by him, not by his living labour, but by past labour embodied in capital. The value of a commodity created by this combined labour brings the capitalist the average profit on capital when the commodity is realised. This conception removes the scientific basis from Ricardo's teaching, the labour theory of value, of which only the shell remains. The value of a commodity is now formed from the capitalist's expenditure on the means of production and wages and from profit. In other words, value is equal to production costs plus profit.

But this is banal, you will say, a mere truism. Without necessarily being a capitalist, you can see that the capitalist determines the prices of his commodities roughly as follows: by calculating his expenses and adding on top of them a reasonable profit. This theory does in fact describe the most superficial, commonplace things, without going any deeper. But it is where the appearance of things does not reveal their essence that science ends.

And how splendid this scheme is for the capitalist! So the worker receives a wage which is a fair reward for his labour. The capitalist receives a profit which is again a legitimate reward for the "labour" of the buildings, machinery and materials belonging to him. And it is easy to add that the owner of land is fully justified in receiving rent: for land also "works". The antagonism of the classes which emerged from Ricardo's teaching, disappears here, giving way to the peaceful collaboration of labour, capital and land. A similar scheme was put forward earlier in France by Say, except that he did not bother to try and fit it into the labour theory of value. Labour — wages; capital — profit; land — rent. This triad, which links the factors of production and their respective incomes, had become established in English political economy by the middle of the 19th century.

There was an obvious weakness in this theory of value, which is often called the theory of production costs. The value of a commodity was explained by the expenses, i. e., the value of commodities taking part in its production. In fact, prices were explained by prices. It is true that cloth costs so many shillings and pence a yard because the labour costs so much, the machinery so much, the cotton so much, and so on. But why does the machinery cost so much, and no more or no less? And so on. The question of the ultimate basis of prices, which has always been a central one in political economy, is simply ignored here, and the closely related question of the ultimate source of income is resolved in an apologetic fashion.

In order to try and overcome this difficulty, economists in the 1830s to 1850s argued as follows, moving further and further away from Ricardo and increasingly preparing the way for the conceptions of Jevons and Marshall. On the one hand, expenses began to be treated not as objective values which in the final analysis depend on the cost of labour, but as the subjective sacrifices of the worker and the capitalist. On the other, value became regarded less as the function of a single variable production costs, and more as the function of many variables, particularly the demand for a given commodity and its utility for the purchaser. Value ceased to be regarded as the natural basis, the centre of price fluctuation. Now it was a question giving a direct explanation of prices, and prices, of course, are fixed and changed under the influence of many factors.

Further steps towards the vulgarisation of Ricardo were made also by explaining capitalist profit in terms of the so-called "abstinence" of capitalists. This conception is closely connected with the name of the English economist N. W. Senior (1790-1864). The explanation of profit as something produced by working machinery, buildings and materials did not satisfy many economists. Consequently a theory was advanced that profit is produced by the "abstinence" of the capitalist who could spend his capital on consumption but "abstains" from so doing.

Let us imagine two capitalists both with monetary capital of £10,000 each. The first invests his capital in a brewery, say, sits in his office and supervises the work. At the end of the year he had £1,000 profit, or ten per cent on his capital. The second capitalist also has £10,000, but does not like the smell of brewed beer or the worries of supervision. At the same time he does not want to spend his money on a new house, carriage, etc. He makes the following suggestion to the first capitalist: "Add my £10,000 to your capital, extend your brewery and pay me 5 per cent a year, £500." The first capitalist agrees. Obviously the other man's capital will yield the same rate of profit as his own. But half of this profit he gives to the owner of the capital.

"Could the second capitalist have spent his money on the above-mentioned or any other goods?" ask the authors of the "abstinence" theory. Yes, he could. But he abstained. He preferred to wait a year and receive interest on his capital, to wait two years and receive more interest (moreover, the capital remains intact and can be spent at any time he likes!). Man naturally prefers to enjoy things here and now, rather than in the future. By agreeing to renounce things now for things in the future, our capitalist is making a sacrifice and thereby acquiring the right to a reward.

And what about the first capitalist? He could sell his brewery and spend the money too. He does not do so and therefore has exactly the same right to be rewarded for his abstinence. But he has the advantage over his colleague of brewing the beer "himself." He must receive his wage for this labour of supervision, management, and direction. So he is actually receiving not a profit of £1,000, but two different incomes for his capital: £500 as interest for abstinence and another £500 as wages for management.

Profit as an economic category disappears altogether here. Alfred Marshall was logical in a way when he replaced the triad (labour, capital, land) half a century later by a combination of four factors: labour — wage, land — rent, capital — interest "organisation" — entrepreneurial income. "Abstinence", which did not sound quite decent (you see, the millionaire abstains from spending his money and does not satisfy his needs fully!), he replaced by the more decent "waiting". At the same time attempts were made to explain on the basis of new, subjective marginalist theories how the size of the reward for each factor is determined. Other economists picked out yet another element of capital, risk, and correspondingly yet another form of reward for the capitalist, a kind of payment for taking a risk. To this very day it is still disputed whether the reward for risk comes under loan interest or entrepreneurial income (or both).

How did Marx solve the problem? The division of profit into interest and entrepreneurial income is a real one, and with the development of credit this phenomenon acquires increasing importance. Consequently the capitalist who is using his own capital divides the profit into two parts: the fruit of capital as such (Marx called this *capital-property*) and the fruit of capital directly employed in production (*capital-function*). But this does not mean that in both these forms capital — whether by abstinence or labour — creates value and legitimately appropriates the part which it creates. This dual nature of capital is an essential condition for the exploitation of labour by capital, the production of surplus value. When surplus value is created and turned by the process of competition into average profit, the question arises of its division between the owners of capital and the capitalists who are actually making use of it (if these are not the same people). But this question is important only from one point of view: how the two types of capitalists share the fruits of the worker's unpaid labour between them.

The thesis that profit can be reduced to interest on loans and "wages for management" is disproved by the practice of joint-stock companies. They pay interest on loaned capital, give dividends to shareholders (this is also a type of interest) and pay extremely high salaries to hired managers who are in charge of production, sales, etc. But apart from this they have undistributed profit which is used for accumulation. I shall say nothing of the taxes paid to the state. To explain from the point of view of bourgeois theories of profit where the money comes from for undistributed profit and taxes is somewhat difficult.

JOHN STUART MILL

In the 1850s and 1860s England reached the peak of its economic and political power. The bourgeoisie could, and were obliged to, share the fruits of this prosperity with the working class, particularly as emigration has somewhat reduced the pressure of England's relative overpopulation. This affected, first and foremost, the higher qualified groups of the working class, the so-called "working-class aristocracy". By the end of the century working conditions had improved, and the standard of living of the working class as a whole had also risen. A series of factory acts were passed, trade unions were made legal and soon grew fairly powerful. However, the class struggle of the proletariat moved increasingly into the sphere of purely economic interests, which generally suited the bourgeoisie.

The policy towards the working class was also determined by the alignment of forces and the struggle between the ruling classes and their factions. In the minds of many representatives of the liberal bourgeoisie this struggle was a struggle for the eternal ideals of humanism and progress, for the collaboration of people enjoying equal rights to achieve this progress, for freedom and tolerance as absolute values. This would appear to be the explanation of the psychology and academic and social activities of John Stuart Mill. The heartless world of money was certainly not to his liking, but he hoped that gradually the darker sides of this world would become a thing of the past. He was even interested in socialism, evolutionary socialism, of course, without revolution or class struggle. Mill turned out, however, in the final analysis to be an exponent of the idea of "steering a middle course", a master of compromise and eclectics. He sought to coordinate the political economy of capital with the claims of the working class, which could no longer be ignored.

Mill's personality is not without interest. He was born in London in 1806 and was the elder son of James Mill, the philosopher, economist and friend of Ricardo's. A man strict to

273

the point of harshness and principled to the point of dogmatism, James Mill had his own system of upbringing and decided to apply it to his son. The boy's "work day" was strictly regulated. The list of books which he had read by the age of eight is quite astounding. There were no toys, stories or games with other children. Walks with his father, during which he was tested on the books he had read, and later lessons with his young brothers and sisters took the place of all that. The boy turned into a real infant prodigy whose knowledge never ceased to amaze his father's friends and acquaintances. The habit of reading and intellectual activity soon became part of his nature. He made an independent study of higher mathematics and the natural sciences. But his favourite subject was history. He wrote essays expounding or criticising ancient and modern writers. His father's strictness increased rather than decreased. James Mill demanded mature and independent thought from the boy. He was fond of setting him impossible tasks. His son must always think that he knew, understood and was capable of very little. And his son did think so, because he was almost totally deprived of the company of children and young people of his own age. Only later when he went out into the wide world did he realise his superiority and tragic shortcomings.

At thirteen the young Mill studied a course of political economy with his father. His father gave him lectures, they discussed complex questions in detail and the boy wrote essays. John Stuart Mill later recalled: "My being an habitual inmate of my father's study made me acquainted with the dearest of his friends, David Ricardo, who by his benevolent countenance, and kindliness of manner, was very attractive to young persons, and who after I became a student of political economy, invited me to his house and to walk with him in order to converse on the subject." [1]

In 1822 Mill published his first works on political economy, two small articles on the theory of value. He dreamed of a political career, but his father decided otherwise. The following year he took the post of the lowliest clerk in the department of the East India Company which was run by his father and began to make his way up the ladder. At first office work did not interfere very much with his feverish intellectual activity.

---

[1] J. S. Mill, *Autobiography*, London, 1940, p. 45.

Accustomed to working fourteen hours a day, he continued to read and write for himself and for publication, and to tutor his brothers and sisters. Mill called himself a thinking machine. But the rarified intellectual atmosphere could not take the place of all the complexity of life, the natural world of emotions, desires and impressions. The result was a nervous breakdown, disillusion, and thoughts of suicide.

In 1830 he made the acquaintance of Mrs. Harriet Taylor, the beautiful and clever wife of a rich London merchant and the mother of two children. His acquaintance and friendship with Mrs. Taylor cured Mill of his black melancholia. With Mill's help and participation a circle of thinking and liberally inclined people formed around her. Harriet Taylor gradually became Mill's closest helper, the first reader and critic of his works.

In the 1830s Mill published a political journal which was the mouthpiece of the "philosophical radicals", the most left-wing group of Whigs in Parliament at that time. In 1843 his most important philosophical work *A System of Logic* was published and in 1844 *Essays on Some Unsettled Questions of Political Economy*. The latter contains Mill's original contribution to the science, whereas his voluminous *Principles of Political Economy* (1848) is simply a skilled compilation. In spite of this, or rather precisely because of it, Mill's book was an unparalleled success, had seven editions during his lifetime and was translated into many languages.

The death of her husband enabled Harriet Taylor to marry Mill in 1851. Throughout the eight years of life that remained to her Mrs. Mill was seriously ill. Mill, whose own health was poor, was a model of self-sacrifice and stoicism. Reading the *Autobiography*, Mill's correspondence and the memoires of people who knew him, one experiences conflicting emotions. He was a weak man; possibly the upbringing and domineering personality of his father made him so. In fact, for twenty years his life was a constant, sometimes painful and humiliating compromise. He simultaneously challenged the rules of society and did not want to go against them too much. This is most typical of Mill's personality. In private life, as in learning and politics, Mill could not face up to difficulties and fell them with a single blow. He preferred to live, burying his head in the sand like an ostrich. He created his own special, isolated intellectual world and managed to feel more or less at peace in it. As Carlyle once remarked, he was an unhappy man who thought himself to be happy.

On the other hand, Mill's moral character cannot help but evoke a certain respect. He was high-principled and consistent in his own way. One must remember that Mill and Harriet Taylor belonged not to the bohemian literary set, but to respectable bourgeois society of the Victorian age which did not forgive violations of "decorum".

In 1858 Mill stopped working in the East India Company whose authority in India was taken over directly by the English Government after the sepoy rising. The company was liquidated. In the following years Mill published several political and philosophical works, but ceased to engage in political economy, if one does not count the new editions of the *Principles.* He developed the ideas of bourgeois democracy (*On Liberty*) and defended women's rights (*The Subjection of Women*). For several years he was a Member of Parliament. After being defeated at an election he went to France and died in Avignon in 1873.

THE POLITICAL ECONOMY OF COMPROMISES

Quoting the passage in which Mill speaks of the injustice of distribution under capitalism, Marx states in the first volume of *Capital*: "To avoid misunderstanding, let me say that although men like John Stuart Mill are to blame for the contradiction between their traditional economic dogmas and their modern tendencies, it would be very wrong to class them with the herd of vulgar economic apologists." [1]

Mill is scientific to the extent to which he strives to adhere to the principles established by Smith and Ricardo and consciously refrains from distorting real processes to please the bourgeoisie. But he did not develop the classicists. On the contrary, he adapted them to the existing level of vulgar political economy. He was strongly influenced by Malthus, Say and Senior. In connection with this Marx wrote of Mill's eclecticism, the absence of a consistently scientific point of view in his writing, and described Mill's works as the "bankruptcy of bourgeois political economy". Mill gave developed and precise form to "compromise political economy" which sought to

---

[1] Karl Marx, *Capital*, Vol. I, p. 572.

combine the interests of capital with the demands of the working class.

An important feature of Mill's *Principles* is that it was the best specimen of a mid-19th century treatise in which the science of political economy is surveyed as a whole. It remained the most authoritative exposition of bourgeois political economy right up to Marshall's *Principles of Economics* published in 1890. Schumpeter admires the free spirit of the Victorian age, when a work which expressed a certain sympathy for the working class, censured the cult of money and did not denounce socialism could become the gospel of the bourgeoisie. The most important thing in Mill's book was not that he criticised capitalism, but that he saw in it the opportunity for improvement and peaceful development into a kind of evolutionary socialism that did not threaten the bourgeoisie. John Stuart Mill's service to the bourgeoisie was probably greater than those of most diehard conservatives and downright apologists of whom these have always been plenty. Mill was the forerunner of the economic and social ideas of the 20th-century British Labour movement.

Marx frequently returned to the idea that after the 1820s bourgeois political economy divided into two main streams: on the one hand, patent apologetics, on the other, attempts to find a middle way between the "divine right of capital" and the interests of the workers. Moreover these tendencies are not homogeneous. The latter provided certain opportunities for objective scientific investigation. This investigation could even be essential for substantiating reformist programmes.

The concept of "vulgar political economy" was closely linked by Marx with the theory of production factors (the notorious triad) and with the apologetic treatment of incomes — wages, profits and rents — as the natural fruit and reward of these factors and quite unconnected with the exploitation of hired labour by capital. In this connection Soviet specialists, in preparing a new edition of the *Theories of Surplus-Value*, included sections of Marx's manuscript dealing with this problem at the end of the three-volume edition under the heading of "Revenue and Its Sources. Vulgar Political Economy". In particular, Marx writes: "In fact, the vulgar economists — *by no means to be confused with the economic investigators we have been criticising* — translate the concepts, motives, etc., of the representatives of the capitalist mode of production who are held in thrall to this system of production and in whose consciousness only its superficial appearance is reflected."[1] Yet for all the decisive importance of the problem of incomes and their sources political economy cannot be reduced to this alone. Such questions as accumulation and consumption, crises and the economic role of the state have come to occupy an increasingly important place in the science. Concrete studies of a number of spheres of economic activity became necessary. Mill basically shared the vulgar point of view on incomes, but again one cannot limit his views to this alone.

His main economic work consists of five books (parts). They deal respectively with production, distribution, exchange, the progress of capitalism and the role of the state in the economy. They are all written in excellent English, clear, logical and smooth. Too smooth! There are none of Ricardo's brilliant contradictions here, simply an attempt to unite different points of view eclectically.

The theory of value with which Ricardo and Smith began their books is here relegated to the third part. This is no accident: the labour theory of value is by no means the basis of Mill's economic teaching, although he does not reject it formally.[2] In Mill's system value bears little relation to production as such, and is simply a phenomenon in the sphere of exchange, circulation. Value is merely the relation characteristic for the exchange of a given commodity for other commodities, in particular, for money. This relation is established on the market.

The bourgeois classics from Petty to Ricardo regarded the question more or less as follows: the ultimate basis of exchange values and prices is expenditure of labour, and the operation of all other factors produces this or that deviation from this basis. Mill in effect did away with the ultimate basis of prices.

---

[1] Karl Marx, *Theories of Surplus-Value*, Part III, p. 453.

[2] The structure of exposition adopted by Mill can be traced right up to modern Anglo-American economic textbooks. P. Samuelson's textbook is arranged in such a way that the first two parts contain a general "theory of production" and deal with its growth factors, and only in the third part is the problem of value introduced, which is concealed under the guise of "price formation". Naturally there is no trace here either of the labour theory of value, but the factors of price formation are again examined *á la Mill*, although a later technique of analysis is used: rejecting the search for the ultimate basis of prices and replacing it by a number of factors operating in connection with demand and supply.

The Ricardian stream in his thought can be seen in the fact that he regarded the determination of prices by production costs as applicable for the basic mass of goods. These goods "naturally and permanently exchange for each other according to the comparative amount of wages which must be paid for producing them, and the comparative amount of profits which must be obtained by the capitalists who pay those wages".[1]

However, in striving to avoid the impasse into which Ricardo's closest pupils had strayed by treating value in such a fashion, he in fact departed from it and reached the conclusion that the exchange value (and price) of a commodity is established simply at the point at which supply and demand are equal. Mill sought to reconcile both approaches by maintaining that expenses should be regarded as the most important fact in determining the supply of a commodity.

As already mentioned, the eclectic treatment of value was mastered by subsequent bourgeois political economists. The classics' question as to the ultimate basis of prices was, in fact, replaced by another: how are prices which correspond to the conditions of economic equilibrium determined. The Marxist conception answers this question by basing it on, not divorcing it from, the firm foundation of labour value (the theory of the competition and price of production). Mill, however, helped to divorce the second question from the first. This was the beginning of the formal analysis of price formation on the basis of supply and demand, which was developed at the end of the century by other bourgeois economists.

Mill's theory of value is almost totally void of the social content which it has with Smith and Ricardo. This can be seen from the fact that he deals with the questions of distribution and incomes before examining value. For Smith and Ricardo this would have been quite impossible, for they were dealing with the distribution of value created and measured by labour. This is why they came close to an understanding of surplus-value as a deduction from the full value of the product to the benefit of the capitalist and the landowner.

This approach is not totally lacking in Mill. Like Ricardo, he wrote that the capitalist's profit proceeds from the fact that labour produces more value than it costs. But this again is

---

[1] J. St. Mill, *Principles of Political Economy with Some of Their Applications to Social Philosophy*, London, 1873, p. 291.

merely lip service to his teacher. In fact he accepts the explanation of profit as the result of the capitalist's thriftiness. With regard to the quantitative aspect of distribution, the shares of each of the three factors, i. e., in fact, classes, Mill had no clear ideas whatsoever on this question. He sought to adhere to the Ricardian viewpoint and said that the share of rent was determined by the law of diminishing fertility of the land and the changeover to cultivating poorer land, and therefore tended to rise. The level of wages was practically stable, since it was determined by the so-called wages fund. Profit was basically a remnant of the value of a product, quantitatively very indeterminate.

The theory of the wages fund dominated in all post-Ricardian political economy right up to the end of the 19th century. Its supporters compared the economy of a large country to a farm the owner of which sets aside enough food for a year to feed his labourers. He cannot possibly give them more than he has stored. Nor will he store more food than his labourers need to work his land. When this model was applied to society it transpired that society always has a very rigid and in fact stable reserve of vital supplies which are stored ("saved") by capitalist in order to keep their workers. Wages are determined by a simple division of this fund by the number of workers. The resultant picture was reminiscent of the above-mentioned "iron law of wages": if the labour reserve is a fixed constant no struggle can win the working class any improvement in its position: at the very most one group of workers can gain only at the expense of another. As the author of the article on the labour reserve in Palgrave's *Dictionary of Political Economy* (a solid work published at the end of the 19th century) remarks, this theory contributed greatly to make the doctrines of political economy unpopular with the English working class.

True to himself, John Stuart Mill gives a concise formulation of the theory of the wages fund on one page and on another talks about the possibility of a considerable rise in the standard of living of the working class under capitalism. In 1869 in one of his articles he openly rejected this theory, but in a new edition of the *Principles* let his old viewpoint stand.

Compromise and the urge to reconcile the irreconcilable characterised this man to the very end.

CHAPTER XV

ECONOMIC ROMANTICISM
SISMONDI

The works of the Swiss economist Sismondi occupy an important place in the history of political economy and in certain respects retain their scientific significance today in spite of the distance which separates us from the age in which he lived and worked. In his *Characterisation of Economic Romanticism (Sismondi and Our Native Sismondists)* V. I. Lenin wrote: "Sismondi occupies a special place in the history of political economy ... he stands apart from the main trends, being an ardent advocate of small-scale production and an opponent of the supporters and ideologists of large-scale enterprise." [1]

The role of Sismondi and his ideas is determined first and foremost by the fact that in the age of the industrial revolution and the triumphant advance of capitalism he was the first to give a profound and penetrating criticism of this social system and its economic mechanism. It was criticism from a *petty-bourgeois* standpoint, but precisely this ideological position enabled him to see the contradictions and problems in capitalist development, which had been overlooked by his brilliant contemporary and opponent, Ricardo, the most eminent exponent of classical *bourgeois* political economy. Sismondi was the first important economist of the pre-Marxian

---

[1] V. I. Lenin, *Collected Works*, Vol. 2, p. 133.

period to cast doubt on the prevailing dogma of the natural and eternal nature of capitalism. He saw political economy not as the science of bourgeois wealth and means of augmenting it but as the science of improving the social mechanism in the interests of human happiness. Sismondi's works are full of sincere sympathy for the hard fate of the new-born proletariat and other sectors of the working population. He introduced the word *proletariat* into socio-economic literature of the new age, resurrecting and reinterpreting the Latin term. Petty-bourgeois ideology is still sometimes one of the sources of comparatively objective knowledge of the mechanism of capitalist economy.

Sismondi's writings, which have a vivid and lively literary style, reflect his personality of the humanist and radical who sought ways of solving urgent social problems.

Sismondi was not the forerunner of Marx in the sense in which Ricardo was. In the sphere of the theory of surplus value Sismondi showed little originality and, in fact, proceeded no further than Smith. But his criticism of capitalism, his analysis of crises, undoubtedly played a part in the formation of Marxism. In many of Marx's works we find profound and pithy assessments of the Geneva economist.

THE CITIZEN OF GENEVA

Jean Charles Leonard Simonde de Sismondi was born in 1773 on the outskirts of Geneva. His ancestors came from Northern Italy, lived for a long time in France and later, after converting to Calvinism and fleeing religious persecution, settled in Geneva. The economist's father was a Calvinist pastor; the family was wealthy and belonged to the Geneva aristocracy.

In the 18th century Geneva was a small independent republic linked with the other Swiss cantons by a rather tenuous union. Like Rousseau, his great fellow-countryman and to a certain extent teacher, Sismondi was, to quote one of his biographers, a citizen of Geneva by both birth and sentiment, but a Frenchman by the cast of his mind and the direction of his writings. Sismondi's academic works were all written in French and generally published in Paris. He can be regarded largely as a representative of French economic thought.

The roots of Sismondi's ideas can to some extent be seen in the peaceful patriarchal atmosphere in which his childhood and youth were spent. All his life he retained the conviction that happiness usually visits the homes of honest working craftsmen and farmers and flees from the big towns with their factories, trading offices and banks. But it was precisely this patriarchal life which was becoming a thing of the past, destroyed by the industrial revolution, in the course of which handicrafts were giving way to factory production, and the independent craftsman, who took pride in his skill and modest prosperity, to the poverty-stricken worker.

Without finishing his education Sismondi was compelled at the age of eighteen to go to Lyon and work there as a clerk for a merchant who was a friend of his father's. The Jacobin revolution soon reached Lyon and then spread to Geneva, always closely linked with neighbouring France. The Sismondi family embarked on a period of wanderings. At the beginning of 1793 they emigrated to England and lived there for eighteen months. Shortly after their return they were again compelled to flee, this time to Northern Italy which, however, was soon occupied by the French too. For five years Sismondi fils managed a small farm in Tuscany purchased with money which had been brought with him. During these turbulent years he was often in prison as a politically suspect person. The Sismondi family returned to their native land after Geneva officially became part of France (in 1798) where the first consul Napoleon Bonaparte "established law and order".

By this time the abilities and inclinations of the young Sismondi were fairly well-defined. The first fruit of his literary activity was a book on Tuscan agriculture. In 1803 he published a work on political economy *De la richesse commerciale* in which he appeared as a pupil of Adam Smith and advocate of his ideas.

Sismondi joined the circle of scholars and writers grouped round the famous banker, politician and thinker, Necker, and his daughter Madame de Staël, the writer and social figure. He lived and worked for a long time on the estate of Necker and Madame de Staël and accompanied her on her travels. The literary romanticism of Madame de Staël and the writers of her circle obviously had a certain influence on Sismondi. He wrote his multi-tomed *Histoire de la renaissance de la liberté en Italie* and gave a brilliant series of lectures on the history of Romance literature. In 1813 Sismondi went to Paris where he saw the fall of Napoleon, the restoration of the Bourbons and the tragedy of the Hundred Days. These events suddenly changed him from an opponent into a supporter of Napoleon: he hoped that the new empire would realise his somewhat vague ideals of freedom and happiness.

After Waterloo and the Congress of Vienna (1815) Sismondi returned to Switzerland, of which Geneva had again become a part. He also went to England and some other countries. During these years his socio-economic ideas formed which he expounded in the book *Nouveaux principes d'économie politique ou de la richesse dans ses rapports avec la population.* This is Sismondi's main contribution to economic science. The book soon made him an economist of European fame. In 1827 he published a second edition in which his polemic with the Ricardo school in England and the Say school in France was even more acute. He regarded the economic crisis of 1825 as proof of his rightness and the fallacy of the ideas that general overproduction was impossible. The foreword to this edition bears a note of triumph over his opponents. This did not prevent him, incidentally, from always having the greatest respect for Ricardo.

This book, as Sismondi writes, arose not so much as the result of detailed study of the works of other economists, as of real observations which convinced him that the very principles of the "orthodox" science, i. e., Smith's teaching, as it was developed by Ricardo, on the one hand, and Say, on the other, were wrong.

As we know, Ricardo regarded all social phenomena from the point of view of the interests of production, the growth of national wealth. Sismondi announced that production was not an end in itself, that national wealth was not really wealth at all, because the overwhelming majority of the population received only a few miserable crumbs from it. The path of heavy industry was a perilous one for mankind. He demanded that political economy should see the real man behind its abstract schemes.

In 1819 he married a young Englishwoman. They did not have any children. The rest of his life was spent peacefully on his small estate near Geneva, absorbed in the work on his grandiose *Histoire des Français.* Although he produced 29 volumes Sismondi did not live to finish this work. He also published a number of other historical and political works. His economic writings of this period are of little interest.

Sismondi was an incredibly industrious person. Right up to the end of his life he invariably spent eight hours a day, often more, at his writing desk. His collected works fill seventy volumes! His pastimes were walking and conversing with the numerous friends and visitors who gladly gathered in his hospitable home. The declining years of this famous citizen of Geneva were as joyful as his childhood and adolescence. He died in 1842 at the age of 69.

Portraits of Sismondi show a massive, broad-shouldered man. As one of his contemporaries relates, Sismondi was remarkably awkward and clumsy from his youth. This is even said to have kept him away from society and turned him into an academic recluse. He was extremely mild, kind and responsive. Writers describing Madame de Staël's circle call him "good soul Sismondi". He was a loyal friend, model husband and solicitous son and brother. At the same time his mild disposition did not prevent him from being a man of principle, bold and resolute in his views and actions when the occasion demanded. The contemporary referred to above writes: "Though he was apparently pacific by nature, he on more than one occasion confronted formidable aggressions rather than compromise a friend. He was connected with a celebrated Review in which was inserted an article that wounded the feelings of a man who was too vain of his nobility. He accused Sismondi of its authorship and required him to acknowledge the charge or name the real author. Sismondi refused him any answer. A challenge was sent; Sismondi accepted it, received the fire of his adversary, and fired his own pistol into the air, declaring for the first time, that he was not the writer of the article. He retired from this ridiculous conflict with all the honours of war." [1]

CRITICISM OF CAPITALISM

Let us return for a moment to Aristotle. The reader may remember that the great Hellene contrasted economics and chrematistics. Economics was natural economic activity aimed

---

[1] A. Stevens, *Madame de Staël, a Study of Her Life and Times: the First Revolution and the First Empire*, Vol. II, London, 1881, p. 19.

at satisfying human needs. Chrematistics was the striving for unlimited wealth, economic activity not for the sake of consumption, but for the sake of the accumulation of wealth. We have seen the changes which this idea has undergone since the time of Aristotle.

It is the natural basis of any criticism of capitalism, because from this standpoint capitalism is pure chrematistics. Sismondi's ideal was not a seminatural slave-owning economy, but a patriarchal economy of independent farmers and craftsmen, the embodiment of chrematistics was not Athenian traders and money-lenders, but English factory-owners, merchants and bankers whose customs were already taking over his native Geneva and his beloved France.

Sismondi's criticism of capitalism was petty-bourgeois, but this must not be understood in the primitive sense. It was not that he regarded shopkeepers or handicraftsmen as the acme of perfection but he knew no other class on which he could place his hopes for a better future for mankind. Sismondi saw the hardships of the industrial proletariat and wrote a great deal about its wretched state, but had no understanding whatsoever of its historic role. He was writing in an age when the ideas of utopian and petty-bourgeois socialism were developing. He himself was not a socialist, but the age imparted a socialist character to his criticism of capitalism in spite of his intentions. He became the founder of petty-bourgeois socialism, primarily in France, but also to a certain extent in England.

Sismondi had an organic hatred of the cult of money inherent in capitalism. When Madame de Staël was preparing to go to the United States (this visit did not take place), he wrote indignantly that everything was measured in terms of money there and quoted an article from an American newspaper which talked only about how wealthy Necker's daughter was and did not say a word about her talent, wit and literary achievements. Sismondi's criticism of capitalism reveals with great clarity many of the most important contradictions and defects of capitalism. He centred his theory on the problem of markets, realisation and crises, and linked it closely with the development of the class structure of bourgeois society, with the tendency to turn the working people into proletarians. In so doing he hit the nail on the head, grasping the contradiction which was developing historically and which turned from a small sore into capitalism's most dangerous defect. It would be no exaggeration to say that the problem of economic crises has been the subject of thousands, many thousands of works on political economy. Sismondi's writings have not disappeared in this great mass. He did not solve the problem of crises, of course. But by the very fact that he raised it (in 1819!) he made a great step forward by comparison with his contemporaries. In estimating Sismondi's contribution to the science V. I. Lenin wrote in the above-mentioned work: "Historical services are not judged by the contributions historical personalities *did not make* in respect of modern requirements, but by *the new contributions they did make* as compared with their predecessors."[1]

For Ricardo and his followers the economic process was an endless series of states of equilibrium, and the transition from one state of equilibrium to the next took place smoothly, by means of automatic "adaption". They were interested in these states of equilibrium, but paid little attention to the transitions. Sismondi however announced that the transitions were not smooth but took the form of acute crises, the mechanism of which was of great importance for political economy.

Sismondi's model of capitalism is roughly speaking the following one. Since the motive force and aim of production is profit, capitalists strive to squeeze the greatest possible profit out of their workers. Owing to the natural laws of reproduction (Sismondi basically followed Malthus) the supply of labour is chronically in excess of demand, which enables capitalist to keep wages down to the bare minimum. In order to live workers were compelled to work 12-14 hours a day, as Sismondi pointed out. The purchasing power of these workers was extremely low and limited to a small amount of bare necessities. Their labour, however, was capable of producing more and more commodities. The introduction of machines simply increases the disproportion: they increase labour productivity and at the same time make workers redundant. The inevitable result is that more and more social labour is employed in the production of luxury articles for the rich. But the demand of the latter for luxury articles is limited and unstable. Hence the inevitability of overproduction crises

---

[1] V. I. Lenin, *Collected Works*, Vol. 2, Moscow, 1971, pp. 185-86.

emerges from Sismondi's logic almost without any intermediate links.

Hence also Sismondi's recipes emerge. A society, in which there exists more or less "pure" capitalism and two classes prevail, capitalists and hired workers, is doomed to serious crises. Sismondi seeks salvation, like Malthus, in "third persons" — intermediate classes and strata. Only for Sismondi, unlike Malthus, these are primarily the small commodity producers — peasants, handicraftsmen, artisans. What is more, Sismondi assumes that the development of capitalist production is impossible without an extensive foreign market which he treats in a one-sided way: as the sale of commodities of the more developed countries to the less developed ones. He explains the fact that England had not yet choked under the burden of its wealth by the existence of foreign markets.

Sismondi demanded extensive intervention by the state in the economy. Only with the assistance of the state he hoped to establish in economic life the natural and healthy standards which the spontaneous process of development was constantly undermining. Sismondi proposed a number of measures which seemed dangerously socialist at the time, but are quite acceptable to capitalist today: social insurance and security for workers, workers' sharing in the profits of an enterprise, etc.

But in many respects Sismondi looked backwards rather than forwards. He sought a solution to the evils of capitalism in the artificial retention of old customs, in preventing the concentration of wealth in the hands of a few people. Sismondi did not want to return to the Middle Ages, of course, to feudalism. But he wanted the inhuman advance of capitalism to be checked by means of establishing social institutions which, under the guise of something new, would restore "the good old days". In order to give the workers material security he proposed introducing a system reminiscent of the old handicraft guilds. He would have liked to resurrect small land holdings in England. This economic romanticism was utopian and essentially reactionary, for it rejected the progressive nature of the development of capitalism and looked for inspiration to the past, not the future. Explaining why the term *reactionary* was applicable to Sismondi's theories, V. I. Lenin wrote: "This term is employed in its *historico-philosophical* sence, describing only the *error* of the theoreticians who take models for their theories from *obsolete* forms of society. It does not apply at all to the personal qualities of these theoreticians, or to their programmes. Everybody knows that neither Sismondi nor Proudhon were reactionaries in the ordinary sense of the term." [1]

In many respects Sismondi was a progressive thinker and person. This is seen primarily in his understanding of the historical process as the replacement of less progressive social orders by more progressive ones. Arguing with Ricardo and his followers who did not see any possibilities for social development other than capitalism, Sismondi asked his opponents the following question: "...can we conclude on the basis of the fact that capitalism is more progressive than the formations which it replaced that we have now reached the truth, that we shall not discover the fundamental vice of the system of hired labour as we discovered it in the systems of slavery, feudalism and guild corporations... The time will undoubtedly come when our grandsons will judge us no less barbarous for having left the working classes without defence, as they judge, and as we ourselves judge, nations who reduced the very same classes to slavery." [2]

This fine passage shows that Sismondi foresaw the replacement of capitalism by a higher and more humane social order, the features of which, however, he could simply not envisage.

CRISES

"So nations run dangers which seem to be contradictory. They can be ruined equally by spending too much and spending too little." [3] Sismondi's perception is quite remarkable. Neither Smith nor Ricardo would have dreamed of putting the question like that. From their point of view a nation, like an individual, could be ruined only when expenditure exceeded income and therefore "devoured capital". How could it be ruined by spending too little?

In fact this idea of Sismondi's conceals a great deal of truth and is most applicable to modern capitalism. To a certain

---

[1] V. I. Lenin, *Collected Works*, Vol. 2, Moscow, 1971, p. 217.

[2] J.-C.-L. Simonde de Sismondi, *Nouveaux principes d'économie politique, ou de la richesse dans ses rapports avec la population*, t. 2, Paris, 1827, p. 435.

[3] Ibid., t. 1, p. 123.

extent it is true that crises begin because a nation is "spending too little". Commodities without purchasers pile up in the warehouses, production is decreased and employment and incomes drop. The modern bourgeois society seeks to combat crises with measures aimed at encouraging people to buy more. Or it begins to spend hard itself, getting the money with the help of national credit. If there is not sufficient effective demand in the economy to absorb the mass of commodities produced, this demand must be encouraged or even artificially created. This is a truism of modern anticrisis policy. It reflects, if not a theoretical understanding of the causes of crises, practical methods born of experience and the generalisation of this experience, which may be effective in combating crises within certain limits.

But Sismondi's theoretical system contained some profound errors which ultimately led to a reactionary utopia, to the defence of the patriarchal order, backwardness and manual labour. In outlining Sismondi's views above, we spoke all the while of personal consumption and its objects. This is no accident. Like Smith Sismondi reduced the product of labour to the sum of incomes — profits, rents, and wages. This produced the strange idea which Marx called *Smith's dogma*, namely, that a nation's annual product may be reduced in its natural form to a mass of consumer goods. For incomes are spent mainly on consumption. Everything else produced by the national economy can be ignored for the purposes of "pure analysis". Sismondi gave this dogma a special interpretation, making it the basis of his ideas on the causes of economic crises.

In fact, however, the annual product of a society consists not only of consumer objects but also of means of production: machinery and transport, coal, metal and other materials. Part of them, it is true, are later embodied in consumer objects. But this may well happen next year or even later. What is more, even within the framework of the year in question one cannot talk only about the realisation of cloth, say. One must also talk of the realisation of the cotton from which the cloth is produced, etc. Even if no new capital investment is made, the same machines have to be produced to replace redundant ones and premises built to replace decrepit ones. Capitalism is characterised not by simple reproduction but by extended reproduction in which new capital investment is constantly being made.

With the increasing complexity of production, the development of new branches, and the growth of automation, the proportion of the means of production in the annual product increases to a certain limit. It is particularly high when there is a high rate of accumulation, i. e., when the volume of capital investment is high in relation to the product. The economy's demand for means of production creates a special market, largely independent of the consumer capacity of society. This is why crises cannot be continuous, but are always periodic. To a certain extent capital supports itself, circulating in a closed circle, so to speak. Coal is mined, but it is used in blast furnaces, not in people's fireplaces. Metal is smelted, but it is made into machinery for the mining industry, not into knives and forks. The spontaneous nature of capitalist economy does not reveal straightaway that too much coal, metal and machinery is being produced.

It is wrong to look for the cause of crises only in the poverty of the vast mass of the population, which is incapable of creating effective demand for consumer goods. Both theory and practice show that production can also increase considerably when the standard of living is extremely low. This is particularly obvious when a considerable military demand is added to production demand in the economy. Finally, it should be recalled that there were no crises before capitalism, although the overwhelming majority of the population was just as poor then as in the 19th century or still poorer.

The contradiction between production and consumption inherent in capitalism also plays an important part in economic crises. But, contrary to Sismondi's view, there is more to it than that. As Marx proved, this very contradiction is a manifestation of a more general one — *the contradiction between the social character of production and the private capitalist form of the appropriation of its results.* This contradiction means that in a capitalist economy production is socialised, i. e., is carried on mainly by large specialised companies producing for a wide market. This production is subordinated not to the aims and interests of society, however, but to the profit of the capitalists who own the companies. Large-scale social production develops in accordance with its own laws. It is not concerned, so to say, with the fact that capitalists regard it not as an end, but only as a means of making money. It is this conflict which is resolved in crises.

Each capitalist strives to increase production at his factory and at the same time to keep workers' wages down to the bare minimum. On the other hand, each capitalist increases production of his commodity without regard for the overall situation in the given branch and in other branches. As a result commodities are produced in relative excess (by comparison with effective demand) and the proportions necessary for development of the economy are disturbed. With the growth of the role of fixed capital in industry increasing significance attaches to the fact that decisions about capital investment are made by private entrepreneurs in an uncoordinated and arbitrary fashion in capitalist economy. There can be no guarantee that they will make sufficient capital investment to use all the resources available.

A crisis is the natural and inevitable form of progression of capitalist economy, a form of transition from one temporary state of equilibrium to another. To use the language of cybernetics, capitalist economy is a self-programming system with very complex feedback and no central control. The programming of this system to optimal conditions (for the moment in question) is done by the method of trial and error. Crises are these "trials and errors", to put it mildly, but their cost to society in economic and social terms is very high. It can be measured by the amount of underproduced and, consequently, underconsumed commodities, the number of lost working man-years, and in social terms by the growth of working-class poverty.

THE HISTORICAL FATE OF SISMONDISM

In the 1890s the name and ideas of Sismondi were at the centre of the struggle being waged by Russian revolutionary Marxists against the liberal Populists. This struggle saw the formation of V. I. Lenin's talent as a profound economic thinker and brilliant polemicist. It played an important role in the development of Russian revolutionary social democracy. The Populists maintained that capitalism had no basis for development in Russia because it would not solve the problem of realisation the people were too poor to buy the mass commodities which large-scale capitalist industry was capable of producing. Unlike other countries which had embarked on the capitalist path of development earlier, Russia could not rely on foreign markets, which had been captured long before. The Populists advocated a "special" path of development for Russia: to a peasant-communal "socialism", bypassing capitalism. This petty-bourgeois utopia was based, as V. I. Lenin showed, on theoretical views very close to those of Sismondi who also prophesied the collapse of capitalism from "underconsumption" and placed his hopes on artisans and peasants.

At the beginning of the twentieth century the laws of the monopoly stage of capitalism became the most important theoretical problem for Marxism. Within the framework of this problem there arose questions of the new forms and tendencies of the accumulation of capital and the contradictions of this process under imperialism. In 1913 a book appeared by one of the leaders of the German Social Democrats, Rosa Luxemburg, *Die Akkumulation des Kapitals*. Since Sismondi was the first thinker to see the possibilities and limits of capitalist production and accumulation, an important place in this book was devoted to an analysis of his ideas. Rosa Luxemburg demonstrated most skilfully the strong points in Sismondi's disputes with Say and the Ricardo school.

In her theoretical conception, however, Rosa Luxemburg accepted Sismondi's thesis of the impossibility of the accumulation of capital and the advance of production in a "purely capitalist" society. This abstraction, which is the basis of Marx's schemes of realisation of the social product, she called "an anaemic theoretical fiction". According to her, Marx's analysis proved the impossibility of economic crises. Like Sismondi, Rosa Luxemburg maintained basically that the advance of capitalism was possible only at the expense of the breakdown of precapitalist forms of economy. The completion of this process threatened to "asphyxiate" capitalism. This led her, in particular, to a false interpretation of imperialism. Rosa Luxemburg in fact reduced imperialism to the policy of seizing colonies, believing that this policy was dictated simply by the shrinking of home markets and the aggravation of the problem of realisation.

After the Second World War Marxist thought faces new problems in assessing the possibilities and prospects for the economic growth of capitalism. It is impossible to overestimate the importance of correct estimates of this kind for the strategy and tactics of the anti-imperialist struggle. In this connection the views of such thinkers as Sismondi and Rosa Luxemburg, who, for the best possible motives, belittled the real possibilities for the development of capitalism "in depth", with the help of its inner forces and sources, are of more than historical significance. To quote the Soviet Academician N. N. Inozemtsev: "In the late forties and early fifties false ideas on the question of the scale and potential rates of capitalist economic development became fairly widespread. The authors of these ideas were in fact ignoring Lenin's point that the struggle of two tendencies, towards progress and towards regress, is characteristic of imperialism, and that the presence of the second of these tendencies by no means excludes the more rapid growth of capitalism than before.... The direction of attention to the "self-jamming" of capitalist production forces, to severe world economic crises of the 1929-33 type, led objectively, in the new situation which had arisen by the 1940s, to a false assessment of the condition of the class forces on the world arena.... It justified a certain passivity, the expectation of some extraordinary cataclysms which were felt to be a necessary condition for the success of the further development of the world revolutionary process." [1]

Capitalism is doomed historically, not because it cannot develop any further, but because this development engenders a complex of contradictions which logically and inevitably create the material and political prerequisites for the revolutionary replacement of capitalism by a higher social order — socialism.

A knowledge of Sismondi's ideas also helps one to understand certain tendencies in the development of modern bourgeois political economy. Traces of his views, a certain "kindred light" in which socio-economic phenomena are examined can be seen in many writers who appear as "heretics" in relation to the orthodox doctrines of the late 19th and early 20th centuries. These "heresies" were of two kinds: some contained a more or less penetrating social criticism of the bourgeois system itself: others limited themselves to a criticism of the complacency of the "neo-classical" school in respect of economic crises and brought this problem to the fore. In certain cases both these aspects were combined.

---

[1] *The Political Economy of Modern Monopoly Capitalism*, Vol. 2, Moscow, 1970, pp. 373-75 (in Russian).

The most important example of this remote similarity is perhaps the economic theory of John Hobson.

While remaining within the framework of the bourgeois world outlook, Hobson made a serious criticism of capitalism at the turn of the century and official political economy of the present day, particularly English political economy. He noted that capitalist production was by no means subordinated to the aim of improving the lot of the masses, but rather increased the wealth, the fruits, which these masses could not enjoy. He wanted production and wealth to be assessed from the point of view of "human utility". Hobson advocated a programme of social reform which included, together with a fixed minimum wage and high progressive taxation on capitalists, strict state control of monopolies. He wrote: "... substitution of direct social control for the private profit-seeking motive in the normal processes of our industries is essential to any sound scheme of social reconstruction." [1]

A certain kinship with Sismondi's ideas can also be seen in Hobson's theory of crises, in which he is most critical of "Say's law" and maintains that crises of general overproduction in capitalist economy are not only possible but inevitable. He sees the cause of crises in the constant striving for excessive accumulation, a product of the social structure of bourgeois society, and the equally constant lagging behind in the consumer capacity of the population. The resultant excess of capital and shortage of domestic demand for both capital investment and consumer goods, Hobson regarded as the main cause of foreign economic expansion of large capital in the developed capitalist countries and condemned the "aggressive imperialism" of these countries.

In the field of the theory of accumulation and crises Keynes regarded Hobson as one of his closest forerunners. In this connection many bourgeois writers discuss the existence of ideological links between Keynes and Sismondi. However, the link would appear to be limited to the fact that Keynes regarded the fall of the so-called marginal propensity to consume as one of the causes of potentially surplus savings and a shortage of effective demand. Given such a broad interpretation Sismondi's "influence" may be found in almost all theories

---

[1] Quoted from Ben B. Seligman, *Main Currents in Modern Economics*, New York, 1963, p. 238.

of economic crises where the problem of private consumption and consumer demand plays a part. Sismondi is often linked with Albert Aftalion, the eminent French economist of the early 20th century, who is regarded as the discoverer of the principle of acceleration, i.e., the theory that changes in demand and production of consumer goods produce relatively more sharp changes in capital investment and machinery production, and therefore play an important part in crises. The acceleration principle contains some rational elements, reflecting the links between the subdivisions of social production in the economic cycle.

On the broader scale the objectively determined evolution of bourgeois political economy over recent decades has been advancing in a direction certain features of which were astutely perceived by Sismondi. Let us quote the following passage from James: "It is macro-economics and no longer micro-economics, the urge to study economic phenomena from a dynamic point of view, belief in the frequency and 'normality' of disequilibrium, a rejection of *laissez faire* and the development of interventionist ideas which are the main features characterising 1950 by comparison with 1900."[1] As we have seen above, each of these elements (in different terms and often with different conclusions) can be found in embryo in Sismondi's works. All this goes to show the fruitful nature of his theoretical thinking.

Yet this is by no means the limits of his legacy and historical significance. Bourgeois economic science, the main ideological task of which in the present day is to defend monopoly capitalism, has not and could not have inherited the spirit of social protest which is present in Sismondi's writing. He was a staunch defender of the working people against the capitalists, an opponent of exploitation and oppression, a critic of apologetic trends in bourgeois political economy, and an outstanding thinker and humanist.

PROUDHON

It is no accident that Sismondi's name is linked with that of the Frenchman Pierre Joseph Proudhon. Like Sismondi, Proudhon criticised capitalism strongly from a petty-bourgeois

---

[1] E. James, *Histoire de la pensée économique au XXe siécle*, Paris, 1955, p. 18.

standpoint. Like Sismondi, he sought a solution in the abolition of the "evils" of capitalism without the destruction of its foundations. But he was writing twenty to forty years after Sismondi, when the growth of the class struggle had already led to the broad expansion of various trends of socialism. In the history of political economy and sociology Proudhon is regarded as the main representative of *petty-bourgeois socialism.*

Marx admired Proudhon's bold criticism of the bourgeoisie, his outstanding intellect, and his talent as a publicist. But the petty-bourgeois utopias in which Proudhon indulged were harmful and dangerous for the young working-class movement. On receiving Proudhon's recently published book *Système des contradictions économiques ou la philosophie de la misère* in Brussels, Marx strongly attacked it in his work *The Poverty of Philosophy* (1847). The significance of this book extends far beyond its critique of Proudhon: it contains the main principles of Marx's economic theory.

Proudhon came from a poor family. As a youth he worked as a shepherd and compositor, then as the joint owner of a small printing press, and a clerk. He had no systematic education and was a talented self-educated man. His life was a hard one, full of toil and material deprivation, struggle and persecution. Under King Louis Philippe he was taken to court for his bold writings and under the dictator president Louis-Napoleon spent three years in prison and was then forced to emigrate. In Brussels he almost became the victim of an enraged crowd who thought he was an agent of Louis-Napoleon (by then Emperor Napoleon III).

Proudhon's life and activity abounds in contradictions. He fought the bourgeoisie and its ideologists in scholarship and literature, particularly economics, but at the same time strongly attacked communism. In politics he was an opportunist: castigating Napoleon III one day and writing him penitent and eulogistic letters the next. A fighter against all forms of oppression and inequality, he regarded the subordinate position of women in society as both natural and normal and, to a certain extent, applied it in his own family. In one of his works he wrote that women's mental powers, as well as physical, should be considered as equal to only two-thirds those of men.

Proudhon's personality reflects, as it were, the contradictions of the petty bourgeoisie as a class, its intermediate and unstable position between the main classes of capitalist society.

He became a socialist on the wave of the 1848 Revolution which suddenly cast him into the maelstrom of political events and forced him to give clear expression to his views on society and the economy. For all his inconsistency and confused ideas, Proudhon was an honest and brave man. After the suppression of the June uprising of Paris workers he became a member of the Constituent Assembly to which he was elected as one of the few defenders of the people. His speech of 31 July 1848, in which he castigated the ruling classes and demanded measures to relieve the poverty of the working people, was called an "act of great courage" by Marx. But this was the climax of Proudhon's activities. During his period of imprisonment (1849-52) he moved perceptibly to the right, embracing ideas of a fairly passive anarchism. The writings of his later years contain increasingly little of importance and originality.

Proudhon had a lively, vivid style and made use of bold paradoxes and neat aphorisms. This is one of the secrets of his popularity. He has gone down in literature as the author of the famous paradox "Property is theft", which made him immortal, and completed his activity with another bold paradox "Right is strength". Both are true to a certain extent of bourgeois society.

Proudhon's main economic works came out in 1846-50. Apart from the critique of capitalism reminiscent of Sismondi, the main subject of these writings is the idea of a *people's exchange bank*. In 1849 Proudhon made an unsuccessful attempt to put this idea into practice.

Bourgeois society, wrote Proudhon, determines the value of commodities spontaneously and unfairly. The realisation of this value is inconceivable without money, hence all evils: sharp price fluctuations, cutthroat competition, crises, unfair distribution of goods. All this can be rectified without touching the foundations of capitalist commodity economy by creating the mechanism for direct social establishment of value according to labour expended. The bank proposed by Proudhon was to establish value. It would accept commodities from producers without restriction and give them a kind of cheque to exchange for commodities which they needed. Proudhon thought this centralised moneyless exchange would operate smoothly and easily, and that each man would receive a just reward for his labour.

This utopian scheme was obviously intended for small-scale owner commodity producers. But how could fair dealings be established between capitalists and hired workers? Proudhon's reply to this question was equally naive and vague. He thought that the essence of capitalist exploitation lay in loan interest. The abolition of money would deprive capitalists of the opportunity to receive interest. On the other hand, the bank was to credit workers (in goods?) without interest, which would ensure that they received the "full product of their labour".

In fact Proudhon had no answer to the social and economic problems confronting mankind in the age of industrial capitalism. But he gave a vivid portrayal of many of capitalism's vices and, by his own contradictions, demonstrated the need for a truly socialist solution of these problems. In this sense he was forerunner of scientific socialism. The name of Proudhon rightly occupies a place among those of the creators of socialism, which since 1918 have adorned the obelisk in the Alexandrovsky Garden by the Kremlin wall.

CHAPTER XVI

THE SAY SCHOOL AND COURNOT'S CONTRIBUTION

Official economic science in France in the first half of the 19th century was represented by the Say school. Initially the antifeudal trend was strong in this bourgeois school. But as the class struggle between the bourgeoisie and the proletariat became more acute, official ideology was directed increasingly against the working class, against socialism. The Say school extolled the capitalist entrepreneur, preached the harmony of class interests and attacked the working-class movement. Its main principle in economic policy was *laissez faire*.

Criticism of Say's apologistic views, according to which the capitalists' profit is engendered by capital without any exploitation of the workers, was most important for the elaboration of Marx's theory of surplus-value. The posing in bourgeois political economy of the important problem of the mechanism of realisation of the social product is linked with the name of Say. In this sphere criticism of Say, who denied the inevitability of overproduction crises played an appreciable role in the development of Marxist economic doctrine.

Considerable progress was made in the specialised spheres of economic science in France and in England. Cournot's attempt to apply mathematical methods of analysis to economic theory was of particular importance for the future.

1789—the beginning of the French Revolution. 1799-1815—the Consulate and Empire of Napoleon Bonaparte. 1815—the Bourbon restoration. 1830—the July Revolution, the overthrow of the Bourbons and the establishment of Louis Philippe's constitutional monarchy. 1848—the February revolution and the proclamation of the Republic. 1851—the counter-revolutionary Bonapartist coup. 1852—the founding of the Déuxieme Empire.

These are the milestones of French history in the period in question. But they are merely the superficial outline, the changes in the political superstructure of society. The most important factor is the changes in the economic basis. During this period in France the industrial revolution gained force and machine industry began to develop. The relations between capitalist and hired workers became the main form of social relations, particularly in the towns, but also to a certain extent in the country. The bourgeoisie replaced the nobility economically and politically as the ruling class in society.

This age found artistic reflection in one of the most remarkable works of world literature, Balzac's *La comédie humaine*. Like all great writers Balzac was interested in *man*. Yet he not only expressed spontaneously in this work the principle that man always exists only within the framework of a definite age and concrete social group, but consciously made it the basis of this magnum opus. Balzac wrote that *La comédie humaine* was both the history of the human heart and the history of social relations.

French economists estimate that the country's national wealth more than tripled from 1815 to 1853. During these years the number of operating spindles in the cotton industry increased four times over. There was an even more rapid increase in the amount of cotton processed annually, although at the middle of the century it was still one-fifth that in England. Although it lagged behind England in this and many other respects (particularly the application of machinery), France nevertheless passed quickly through the main stages of the industrial revolution. The value of its exports increased almost four times between 1815 and 1855. French silks, Parisian clothes and fancy goods, glass and a number of other industrial goods were exported in large quantities to many countries. Paris became an important industrial and financial centre. The number of joint-stock companies and the volume of stock exchange transactions grew, banks developed and savings banks appeared.

Paris was a lively hub of politics and ideology. Its newspapers and journals were read all over Europe. Emigrés from Germany, Poland, Russia and Italy formed an important element of the Paris intelligentsia. France had a strong intellectual influence on other countries. Ideas born in Paris were received in Europe and America with the same interest and respect as Paris fashions. Consequently the ideas of the Say school also spread far beyond the borders of France, often expounded by skilled publicists.

SAY—MAN AND SCHOLAR

Jean Baptiste Say was born at Lyon in 1767. He came from a bourgeois Huguenot family. As a child he received a good education, but started work in a trading office at an early age. He read a great deal to extend his knowledge. In his study of political economy, Say concentrated first and foremost at Smith's *The Wealth of Nations.*

He welcomed the revolution most enthusiastically. His patriotic fervour was strong enough to make him volunteer for the revolutionary army which fought the monarchs of Europe. But the Jacobin dictatorship was too much for him. He left the army and returned to Paris where he became the editor of a respectable journal. The rule of the conservative bourgeoisie, who came to power in these years after the fall of the Jacobins, was, generally speaking, acceptable to Say, although he criticised many of the government's actions.

Bonaparte's Consulate first brought Say further promotion. He received a post as a member of the Tribunal on the Finance Committee. At the same time he continued to write a large work which came out in 1803 under the title of *Traité d'économie politique ou simple exposition de la manière dont se forment, se distribuent et se consomment les richesses.* This book, which Say subsequently revised and supplemented many times for new editions (there were five in the author's lifetime) was his principal work.

Say's treatise was a simplified exposition of Smith, schematised and, as he saw it, free of unnecessary abstractions and complexities. The labour theory of value, which Smith had followed albeit not entirely consistently, was replaced by a "pluralist" treatment in which value was made dependent on a number of factors: the subjective utility of a commodity, the cost of its production, supply and demand. Smith's ideas on the exploitation of hired labour by capital (i. e., the elements of the theory of surplus-value) completely disappeared in Say, giving way to the factors of production theory which is discussed later. Say followed Smith in his economic liberalism. He demanded a "cheap state" and advocated minimum state intervention in the economy. In this respect he was close to the Physiocratic tradition. Say's economic liberalism was of special significance for the fate of the book and its author.

The economic policy of the Consulate and Empire, although bourgeois in its general nature, was firmly opposed to Smith's free trade. Napoleon needed industry for his wars and the struggle with England, but he thought it would develop more rapidly through strict protectionism and all-round regulation of the economy. This opened the door to bureaucracy and favouritism. Napoleon regarded the economy, finance and trade simply as instruments for his policy of conquest. The only economic theory he needed was one which would justify and support his policy.

Say's book attracted the attention of the public and came to the notice of Napoleon. The lowly official was invited to the First Consul to discuss the questions treated in his book. Say was given to understand that if he wanted to find favour with the authorities he would have to revise the *Treatise* to suit Napoleon's views and policy. He refused to do so, however, and was forced to retire.

Being an energetic, practical and enterprising person, he turned to what was for him the new sphere of industrial business and bought shares in a textile factory. He became rich. This affected the whole of his subsequent academic and literary activity. Now he was not just the bourgeois intellectual but the practising bourgeois, a specialist in the concrete needs and requirements of his class. His dislike of abstractions grew more intense and he increasingly regarded economic science as a source of practical wisdom for the bourgeois entrepreneur. He now tended to reduce political economy to the problems of production and sale organisation and business management. He assigned a particularly important role in capitalist economy to the figure of the entrepreneur whom he endowed with the features of the bold innovator, eminently capable of uniting capital and labour most efficiently in the production process.

In 1812 Say sold his shares in the factory and moved to Paris as a wealthy rentier. The fall of Napoleon and the Bourbon restoration enabled him at last to publish a second edition of the *Treatise*. This earned him the reputation of the most eminent French economist. He was favoured by the new government. Say easily renounced the republicanism of his youth and became a loyal servant of the Bourbons: for the bourgeoisie had retained its power and economic policy was now inclining towards free trade.

Say was a typical member of the third estate, the French bourgeois third estate which made the revolution and then recoiled from it in horror, rushed headlong into the embrace of General Bonaparte and then renounced the Emperor Napoleon when he did not justify the hopes of the bourgeoisie. Say's personal fate reflects this historical and class turning point in the attitude of the French bourgeoisie.

With his cult of sober common sense and commercial shrewdness Say was made for this age in which the bourgeoisie consolidated its position. He began to give public lectures on political economy and in 1819 received the chair of "industrial economics" at the National Conservatoire of Arts and Trades. Say's lectures were extremely popular. As in his writing, he simplified economic problems, reducing them to the level of the man in the street. A skilled systematiser and populariser, he created the illusion of clarity and simplicity for his audience. Political economy is indebted primarily to Say for the fact that in the 1820s it was almost as popular in France as in England. Say's works were translated into many languages, including Russian. He was a foreign member of the St. Petersburg Academy of Sciences.

In 1828-1830 Say published his six-volume *Cours complet d'économie politique pratique* which, however, contained nothing new theoretically by comparison with the *Treatise*. He took up the chair of political economy specially created for him at the Collège de France. Say died in Paris in November 1832.

Say was not a very likeable person in his later years. Basking in fame, he ceased to probe further and simply reiterated his old ideas. His printed works are characterised by boastfulness and lack of modesty, and in polemics he used unfair methods and a rude manner.

For Marxists Say is primarily the founder of 19th-century vulgar political economy. Making use of Smith's weak points and in direct polemics with Ricardo, he replaced their striving for a profound analysis of the basic laws of capitalism by a superficial treatment of economic phenomena. Nevertheless (and to a certain extent precisely because of this) Say holds an important place in the history of bourgeois economics. He was the first to express in clear form the idea of the equal participation of the factors of production — labour, capital and land — in creating the value of the product. After this idea had been developed in the works of many writers, all that remained for economists of the 1870s to 1890s was to create a single theory of the principles according to which the "services" of each factor are remunerated. Thus Say is the father of the bourgeois apologetic theory of distribution.

FACTORS OF PRODUCTION AND INCOMES

Labour — wages, capital — profit, land — rent. Let us recall this triad, or triune formula, which plays such an important part in bourgeois political economy.

Say's factors of production theory was an attempt to answer the basic question, which both Smith and Ricardo painstakingly sought to solve. With the development of capitalism material goods are increasingly produced with means of production belonging to a special social class. Consequently, the value of commodities should in some way contain a portion belonging to the class of capitalists. How does this portion arise and how is it determined?

For Smith and Ricardo (and, as we have seen, for Ricardians right down to Mill Jr.) this was simultaneously a problem of value and distribution. With Say it is all much simpler. In fact his theory of distribution is separate from the theory of value, and the latter holds little interest for him. As a result, all that remains of the production process is one aspect — the creation of utilities, use values. Presented in this way it is obvious that production requires the combination of natural resources, the means and instruments of labour, and labour power, i. e., land, capital and labour. It is this obvious fact that Say emphasises.

It may be objected that this is a general feature of all production processes and therefore cannot explain the specific nature of capitalist production. But this objection could not have occurred to Say, because for him the capitalist mode of production was, to an even greater extent than for Smith, the only conceivable, eternal and ideal one. He regarded the existence of capitalists and landowners as a kind of law of nature, like the rising and setting of the sun.

In Say's theory profit is the natural product of capital and rent, the natural product of the land. Both are totally independent of social order, class structure and form of ownership. Capital yields profit like apple trees yield apples and black-currant bushes black currants.

This conception is diametrically opposed to the labour theory of value and the theory of surplus-value. It denies the exploitation of workers by capitalists and landowners and presents the economic process as the harmonic collaboration of equal factors of production. The main work of Frédéric Bastiat, the most well-known of Say's followers, was actually called *Les harmonies économiques*.

The factors of production theory in the form in which it was expounded by Say and his pupils has earned the reputation of being oversimplified and superficial even in bourgeois economics.

Indeed, the answers which Say gave to the basic economic questions of his day to a large extent evaded the issue. How is value formed and what determines commodity prices in the final analysis? What determines the formation of the proportions of the distribution of created value — the incomes which correspond to each factor of production? Say and his followers had basically nothing to say about this. They got round it with banalities and commonplaces.

In his works Say examines each type of income separately, but only his treatment of profit is of interest. As we already know, profit is divided into interest on loans and entrepreneurial income. The first is appropriated by the capitalist as the owner of capital, the second by the capitalist as the director of the enterprise. For Say entrepreneurial income is not simply a type of wage which a hired manager could also receive. It is the reward for a special and highly important social function, the essence of which is the rational combination of the three factors of production. The entrepreneur's incomes, Say wrote, are a reward for his "industrial skills, that is to say, his judgement, his natural or acquired talents, his activity, and his sense of order and conduct".[1]

This explanation of entrepreneurial income in terms of the organising role of the entrepreneur was taken up by Marshall. Schumpeter made use of another of Say's points, the role of the entrepreneur as the innovator, the bearer of technological progress. Finally, the American Frank Knight wrote that the entrepreneur bears the "burden of uncertainty" or, to put it more simply, the risk, for which he should be specially rewarded; Say also hints at this.

The problem of combining natural elements, materialised and living labour in the production process, also exists independently of the apologetic treatment which the Say school gave it and which it is still receiving from bourgeois political economy. It is not only a social problem, but also a most important technico-economic one.

The given aim of, say, increasing the wheat harvest by 50 per cent can be attained in a number of ways: by expanding the area under crops or increasing the amount of labour and material expenditure (capital) applied to the same area, by adding more capital with the same amount of labour or by adding more labour. Naturally in real life the task is solved by a combination of the growth of elements (factors). But in what proportions are they best combined? What account must be taken of the concrete position in the given country or area, in particular, the extent to which there is a shortage of the various types of resources? It is one thing if there are large unused tracts of land, another if there is no extra land, but a lot of unemployed labour, and so on. Obviously all these are important practical questions which confront economists. They may arise on the scale of an individual concern (the micro-economic level) or on the scale of the whole country (the macro-economic level).

A country's national income or social product may be regarded as the sum total of use values produced in a given year. The monetary estimate of these commodities is a means of gauging by a single measure the physical volume of this infinitely varied aggregate: cement and trousers, cars and sugar.... Their changes reflect the growth in the physical volume of production, i. e., the growth of wealth, prosperity. Such an approach fully justifies the question of the share of the national income (or product) attributable to each of the factors which take part in production and the portion of the growth of these magnitudes produced by the growth of each of the factors. A study of the functional dependencies between the expenditure of the factors is of great significance for increasing the efficiency of the economy. Naturally it is an oversimplified hypothesis to assume the independence of each factor in the creation of products (seen as the sum of use values) and the divisibility of these factors, etc. But bearing this in mind and taking into account the restrictions placed on analysis by real conditions we can use the "factor" analysis of production with a certain degree of effectiveness. One of the methods of this

---

[1] J.-B. Say, *Traité d'économie politique...*, Paris, 1841, pp. 368-69.

analysis, which is widely applied at the present time, is that of production functions.[1]

Generally speaking this means that the volume of production (of a given commodity or series of commodities at a given enterprise or in a given country, etc.) is the function of a series of variables, the number of which may be as large as you like. In mathematical symbols this can be expressed as follows:

$$Y = F(x_1, x_2 \ldots x_n)$$

where Y is production and $x_1, x_2 \ldots x_n$ are the various factors, for example, the number of workers, the level of their qualifications, the amount of machinery, the quality of the raw material, etc.

Many variations of this function have been advanced with varying combinations of arguments. The most well-known is the Cobb-Douglas function, named after two American scientists of the 1920s, which is as follows:

$$Y = AK^\alpha L^\beta$$

Here it is assumed that the volume of production is determined by two main factors: K (amount of capital, i. e., means of production employed) and L (amount of labour). The power indices A and β show the percentage of increase in production if the amount of capital and labour are raised by 1 per cent respectively, the other factor remaining constant. A is the proportionality coefficient; it may be treated also as taking into account all qualitative factors of production which are not expressed in the amount of capital and labour.

Many economists have tried to develop and improve the Cobb-Douglas function, to introduce dynamic elements into it, particularly technological progress. Of particular importance in this connection is the work of the Dutch economist Jan Tinbergen who was the first to be awarded the Nobel prize in economics for 1969. There are statistico-mathematical studies

---

[1] The historical emergence of this method is connected with the bourgeois apologetic theory of distribution which goes back to Say. However, subsequently the practical needs of capitalist economy determined its use to solve concrete tasks of a technical economic nature with the aid of mathematics and statistics. From the fact of the original connection between the method of productive functions and the factors of production theory as a theory of distribution it by no means follows that it is necessary to reject the actual apparatus of production functions as well, which can be separated from this bourgeois basis and, given a corresponding scientific interpretation, used to analyse important aspects of production growth.

which give more or less plausible estimates of the quantitative share of the main factors (including the "technological progress" factor) in the growth of production.

"SAY'S LAW"

We have already several times come across Say's "law of markets" or, simply, "Say's law". The problem of realisation and crises, which it deals with, plays an enormous role in the development of capitalism and political economy. The history of "Say's law" is somewhat reminiscent of the story of Malthus' "law of population". In the first edition of the *Treatise* (1803) Say wrote four pages on sale of commodities. They express in most imprecise form the idea that general overproduction of goods and economic crises are fundamentally impossible. Production itself engenders incomes with which commodities of corresponding value are bound to be purchased. Total demand in the economy is always equal to total supply. Only partial disproportions may arise: overproduction of one commodity and underproduction of another. But this is corrected without a general crisis. Like Malthus' basic idea, this simple proposition appears to be self-evident. But it is obviously excessively abstract and deprives Say's idea of any meaning.

A heated controversy soon flared up around "Say's law" (which at the time did not bear this high-sounding title). The most eminent economists of the day took part in it, including Ricardo, Sismondi, Malthus and James Mill. Defending and arguing his idea, Say inflated his exposition of the "law" with each new edition of the *Treatise*, but did not make it any the more precise.

Today the debate on "Say's law" in the West is mainly a discussion between the supporters of the so-called neo-classical and Keynesian trends in political economy. The former, even if they do not refer to the "law", in fact adopt a position which goes back to Say. They maintain that, given flexible prices, wages and other basic elements, the economy can avoid serious crises automatically. Consequently they usually oppose large-scale intervention by the bourgeois state in the economy. In terms of views on economic policy the neo-classicists frequently tend towards "neo-liberalism".

Keynes and his followers, on the other hand, argue the inevitability of crises in a freely developing capitalist economy and criticise "Say's law". Keynes wrote that the adherence of professional economists to this "law", which is disproved by real life, has made the ordinary man increasingly unwilling "to accord to economists that measure of respect which he gives to other groups of scientists whose theoretical results are confirmed by observation when they are applied to the facts".[1] The Keynesian trend supports widespread state intervention in the economy.

In the period under review, i. e., the first half of the 19th century, "Say's law", or what was understood by it at that time, played a dual role. On the one hand, it reflected the Say school's inherent belief in the pre-established harmony of bourgeois society and economy. The school could not see or would not see the contradictions leading inevitably to over-production crises. "Say's law" assumes that commodities are produced simply for the satisfaction of people's demands and exchanged with money playing a completely passive role in the exchange. This is extremely far from the case. But "Say's law" also contains an aspect which was progressive for its time. It was aimed against Sismondi's thesis about the impossibility of the progressive development of capitalism. It expressed the thesis, albeit in most imprecise form, that capitalism creates its own market in the course of its development and does not need the notorious "third persons" of Malthus and Sismondi to solve the problem of realisation. Using Say's arguments, the bourgeoisie advanced the progressive demands of curtailing the bureaucratic state apparatus in favour of free entrepreneurism and free trade. This explains partly why Ricardo accepted Say's theory of markets.

THE SCHOOL

In 1873 Marx wrote his preface to the second edition of Capital (Volume I), in which he gave a brief outline of the development of bourgeois political economy in the 19th century. Noting the achievements of the classical school at the

---

[1] J. M. Keynes, *The General Theory of Employment, Interest and Money*, London, 1946, p. 33.

beginning of the century and the heated discussions of the 1820s he continued: "With the year 1830 came the decisive crisis.

"In France and in England the bourgeoisie had conquered political power. Thenceforth, the class-struggle, practically as well as theoretically, took on more and more outspoken and threatening forms. It sounded the knell of scientific bourgeois economy. It was thenceforth no longer a question, whether this theorem or that was true, but whether it was useful to capital or harmful, expedient or inexpedient, politically dangerous or not. In place of disinterested inquirers, there were hired prize-fighters; in place of genuine scientific research, the bad conscience and the evil intent of apologetic."[1]

This applied above all to the Say-Bastiat school. Marx wrote further that after 1848 vulgar economy underwent new changes as a result of which "prudent, practical business folk, flocked to the banner of Bastiat, the most superficial and therefore the most adequate representative of the apologetic of vulgar economy".[2]

Engrossed in its service of bourgeois practice, the Say school did practically nothing for the development of economic theory. This is pointed out not only by Marxists but also by the more serious bourgeois historians of economic thought, particularly Schumpeter.

Almost right up to the end of the century the centre of the school was the chair of political economy at the Collège de France which Say held in his later years. One of his followers was the comparatively well-known economist Michel Chevalier who, together with Bastiat, was the main exponent of the free trade movement in the school and played an active role in the sphere of economic policy. The members of the school published books on political economy inspired by Say and written in his style. They were popular in their day, but have hardly left any trace in the science.

One can regard Jérôme-Adolphe Blanqui as belonging to the school, the brother of the revolutionary and utopian communist Louis Auguste Blanqui. Blanqui the economist was, on the contrary, a highly respectable bourgeois professor. He is known mainly for his *Histoire de l'économie politique en Europe*

---

[1] Karl Marx, *Capital*, Vol. I, Moscow, 1972, pp. 24-25.
[2] Ibid., p. 25.

(1839), one of the first detailed histories of economic thought, which for a long time was regarded as a kind of model and translated into many languages, including Russian.

Mention must be made of Charles Dunoyer, yet another ardent "optimist", champion of "economic freedom" and defender of the existing capitalist system against all criticism. Dunoyer is a good illustration of the above-mentioned difference between the normative and positive approach in political economy. It was most logical that Dunoyer, who believed passionately in the inner powers of capitalism and rejected state intervention in the economy, should be (unlike Sismondi) a supporter of the positive approach. He expressed his views on this question in the following aphoristic form: "Je n'impose rien; je ne propose même rien; j'expose" (I do not impose anything; I do not even propose anything; I expound).

One could add many other names: as already mentioned, the Say school prevailed in orthodox economics and the French economists had their own scientific society and journal. But we have named enough. The important point to emphasise is that the Say school and its views were formed in the 1830s and 1840s in the bitter struggle against socialist ideas which were spreading widely in France. This determined the school's features to a large extent. Bastiat, in particular, carried on a fierce polemic with Proudhon. In Chapter XVIII we shall be dealing with the economic teaching of the great socialist utopians, Saint-Simon and Fourier, whose pupils and followers were the main ideological opponents of the Say school.

COURNOT: HÍS LIFE AND WORK

Many economic phenomena and processes are quantitative by their very nature. There usually exist some quantitative relations between economic variables: if one changes, the other or others connected with it also change by some law or other. For example, if the price of a given commodity rises, the demand for it will most likely drop to a certain extent. The nature of this dependence can usually be expressed as a function. It was this sort of reasoning that led certain enquiring minds as early as the 18th century to wonder whether mathematics might not be applied to the study of economic phenomena. Attempts were made accordingly. However, it was not until about the middle of the 19th century that the development of theoretical economics led to the mathematical formularisation of some basic economic problems.

The first scientist to apply mathematical methods to economic research deliberately and consistently was the French economist Antoine Augustin Cournot. The work which was later to make Cournot famous came out in 1838 and was entitled *Recherches sur les principes mathématiques de la théorie des richesses*. Because this work aroused little interest in his lifetime, it has become accepted in histories of economic thought to write that Cournot was a talented failure, a "martyr of the science". This is not quite true. Cournot lived the quiet and prosperous life of a college professor and administrator of academic institutions. He was the author of a number of mathematical works which were successful in their day. Cournot was on good terms with all the regimes which replaced one another in France throughout his long life and held an eminent position in orthodox science and in state service.

At the same time it is true that Cournot was painfully aware of the lack of recognition of his scientific services in a much profounder sense. He was attempting to find with the help of mathematics and philosophy a synthesis of the natural and social sciences. His writing in the last two decades of his life dealt mainly with the philosophy of the natural sciences. Without using formulae, Cournot attempted also in two works in the 1860s and 1870s to return to economics, but they did not attract the attention of the public either. These works did not possess the originality of his first book and, unlike it, were fated to gather dust on library shelves. Cournot's biographer writes: "There is a vivid contrasts between his brilliant official career and his complete lack of recognition during his lifetime as a scientist.... In his memoirs he writes sadly and bitterly that however badly his works sold, particularly in France, they nevertheless contained some more or less new ideas capable of explaining the general system of the sciences more than before." [1]

Cournot was born in 1801 in the small town of Gray in eastern France in a wealthy petty-bourgeois family, some

---

[1] Quoted from H. Reichardt, *Augustin A. Cournot. Sein Beitrag zur exacten Wirtschaftswissenschaft*, Tübingen, 1954, S. 8.

members of which were well-educated. His grandfather was a notary and had a great influence on the boy's upbringing. Cournot was an unusually quiet and assiduous boy, fond of reading and reflection. Possibly this was encouraged by his acute shortsightedness which developed at an early age. He went to school until fifteen and then lived at home for about four years, reading and educating himself, with occasional visits to the college in Besançon. In 1821 he began to study natural sciences at the École Normale Supérieure in Paris where his passion for mathematics revealed itself to the full. Shortly afterwards, however, the École was closed temporarily by the government because of the antiroyalist views of the students, and Cournot, in spite of his indifference to politics, found himself for a while, like the other students, under police surveillance.

From 1823 to 1833 Cournot lived in the family of Marshal Saint-Cyr as his son's tutor and secretary to the Marshal who was writing his memoirs about the Empire period. During this period Cournot spent a great deal of time studying various sciences, and attending lectures at various academic institutions. He published several articles. In 1829 he was awarded a doctorate degree by Paris University for his work on mathematics. He made the acquaintance of many eminent scientists, particularly the mathematician Poisson who regarded Cournot as one of his most talented pupils and remained his patron all his life. Thanks to Poisson's protection Cournot was appointed professor at Lyon and began to teach higher mathematics there. A year later he was made Rector of the Grenoble Academy, where he showed himself to be an efficient administrator. In 1838 he obtained an even higher post in the educational system as inspector general of studies. His main mathematical works were also published in the early 1840s.

It is something of a mystery for the biographer how Cournot's economic work appeared so suddenly and unexpectedly amid these most varied writings. Nothing has yet come to light to indicate that he had shown any interest in political economy earlier. It must be remembered, however, that Cournot was a person of encyclopaedic knowledge and very broad interests. His reading must have included Say's works which were most popular at the time. It is possible that he became acquainted with the writing of Smith and Ricardo through Say. To this must also be added the common sense and economic intuition which are very obvious in Cournot's book. Dissatisfied with the imprecise, vague and inconsistent nature of the main tenets of economic science, he sought to apply strict logic and mathematical methods to it. Carried away by this task, a new one for him and for economic science, Cournot, who was an extremely systematic, even pedantic person, pursued it to the point at which he considered it possible to publish. He evidently thought his book would attract attention and stimulate the minds of other scholars. Here he was to be disappointed.

Cournot's successful official career continued until 1862. In the period of the Second Republic (1848-1851) he was a member of the commission on higher education and in the Second Empire, a member of the imperial council on education. For eight years he was Rector of Dijon University where he earned the respect of students and professors alike for his high principles and breadth of vision. During this period his scientific interests shifted from the sphere of pure and applied mathematics to that of philosophy. Upon his retirement Cournot settled in Paris and lived a strictly regimented life to the end of his days: he always got up and went to bed at a certain time and invariably spent the morning studying. At first glance he seemed a strict and severe man, but with friends and close acquaintances he was sociable, talkative and not without a sense of humour. Cournot died in Paris in 1877.

COURNOT'S CONTRIBUTION

It is interesting for whom Cournot's economico-mathematical book was intended. He was afraid it might seem too complex for the ordinary reader and at the same time fail to attract the attention of professional mathematicians. He wrote, however, that "there is ... a large number of people who, after making some advanced studies in the mathematical sciences, have directed their efforts towards the applications of sciences in which society is particularly interested (he evidently has in mind technology and the natural sciences.— A. A.).The theories of social wealth should attract their attention. And in examining them they should feel the need, as I have myself, of making clearer by the signs that are familiar to them an analysis so vague and often so obscure in writers who have thought it proper to limit themselves to the resources of everyday language." [1]

Cournot was possibly the first of the type of mathematicians, engineers and natural scientists characteristic of his day who became interested in the fascinating and controversial problems of the social sciences and attempted to apply the precise language of mathematics to them. Like many mathematicians after him he accepted economic science and its tasks for the most part as he found them in the existing literature. It is characteristic of Cournot, however, that in seeking to overcome the dogmatism and limitations of the prevailing schools he retained an objective and social approach to the main problems, particularly that of value. This distinguishes him from the economist mathematicians of the second half of the 19th century for whom the subjective, psychological approach was typical. Cournot, for example, rejected the Robinsonade right from the start and constructed his own theory for a society with developed commodity production and exchange.

Basically Cournot examined one important problem in his work: the interdependence of the price of a commodity and the demand for it in different market situations, i. e., with different relations between the power of buyers and sellers. In so doing he showed a keen sense of the nature and limits of applying mathematics in economic research. He did not claim to elaborate the basic socio-economic questions with the help of mathematics, but limited himself to tasks which were more or less suitable for mathematical formularisation.

In studying the question of the relation between demand and price, Cournot introduced into economics the important concept of *elasticity of demand*. As already mentioned, everyday experience tells us that when the price of a given commodity rises the demand for it drops, and vice versa. This "law of demand" was expressed in the form of the following function by Cournot, in which D is demand and p is price:

$$D = F(p)$$

Cournot noted that this dependence varies for different commodities. Demand may change considerably with a relatively slight variation in price. And, conversely, demand may react only slightly to a change in price—this is low elasticity of demand. Cournot noted further that the latter, strange though it may seem, applies both to certain luxury articles and to vital necessities. For

---

[1] A. Cournot, *Recherches sur les principes mathématiques de la théorie des richesses*, Paris, 1838, p. X.

example, the price of a violin or an astronomical telescope may drop by half, but there is unlikely to be a perceptible rise in demand: demand is limited to a narrow circle of enthusiasts for whom the price is not the main consideration. On the other hand, the price of firewood may double, but the demand will certainly not drop to the same extent, for people are prepared to cut down on other expenditure rather than live in unheated homes. Thus the function of demand can have different forms and, consequently, be represented by different curves. Less obvious, but more important mathematically, is Cournot's thesis that this function is constant, i. e., that any infinitely small variation in price corresponds to an infinitely small variation in demand. Not without justification he assumes that economically this principle is realised more fully, the wider the market and the more possible combinations of demands, conditions and even caprices among the consumers. The constancy of the function means that it can be differentiated and makes it possible to use differential and integral calculus in the analysis of demand.[1]

Proceeding from the above annotations the gross receipts from the sale of a certain amount of a given commodity may be expressed as the product pD or $pF(p)$. Cournot differentiates this function and looks for its maximum, proceeding on the assumption that any commodity producer, being an "economic man", is striving to maximise his income. Hence by means of transformations, Cournot finds the price which corresponds to the maximum gross receipts (income).

This price depends on the type of demand function, i. e., on the nature of its elasticity. It is also obvious that it is not the highest price which yields the maximum gain, but a concrete price which the seller determines by trial and error. Cournot begins his analysis with what he regards as the simplest situation — a natural monopoly. Let us assume, he says, that someone is the owner of a source of mineral water with unique properties. What price should he put on this water to ensure maximum income? After attempting to answer this question, he proceeds to more complex situations, introducing new factors (production costs, competition, and other restrictions). He examines the cases of duopoly (two competing monopolists), a limited number of competitors and, finally, free competition. Thus, Cournot's model is constructed in reverse order to the actual historical process of development in the 19th century which went from free competition to monopoly.

---

[1] The application of these branches of mathematics (together with analytical geometry) was characteristic of the whole of mathematical economics in the 19th and early 20th centuries. In 1908 the Italian economist Barone wrote that although mathematics was becoming indispensable to the economic theorist, any normal and reasonably educated person could acquire what was needed of it in about six months of studying in his spare time. Today the mathematical apparatus of economic research is considerably more complex. As two Soviet writers remarked, one of them a most eminent mathematician and economist, "the mathematical apparatus which arose in connection with problems of mathematical physics and theoretical mechanics, was also used for the investigation and solution of economic tasks. Naturally, this could only be of use in the early stages. Later on the need arose for the creation of mathematical methods specially adapted to the problems of economic analysis". (L. V. Kantorovich and A. B. Gorstko, *Mathematical Optimal Programming in Economics*, Moscow, 1968, p. 6, in Russian).

His whole analysis is based on the use of a single method — determination of the extremal values of the functions of demand which assume different forms depending on the market situation. The mathematical strictness and logic of this investigation is most impressive. Cournot's work is very different from other works by eminent exponents of bourgeois economic thought in his day. His language was totally unfamiliar and foreign to them. No wonder he was not understood.

Cournot's conception suffers from some fundamental flaws. In the most general sense it must be regarded as a bourgeois apologetic one: Cournot ignores the exploitation of labour by capital, crises and other basic laws of capitalism. The only things he examined directly in his model are prices, which he sees as being formed in the sphere of circulation and almost completely unconnected with production. In his treatment of monopoly and competition he distorts many important elements of real capitalist economy.[1] Cournot's "pure political economy", which ignored the contradictions of capitalism, was one of the sources of the subjective school. It was the representatives of this school who, after Cournot's death, "rediscovered" him and depicted him as their forerunner. To a certain extent he was. What concerns us here, however, is not the logical limitations of Cournot's philosophy, but the methodology created by him for examining concrete economic problems. In this respect he was a true pioneer who blazed a new trail in the science.

Cournot realised that his mathematical model would be a more valuable instrument of knowledge if it were supplemented with empirical material which reflected economic reality in numerical form. He merely expressed this idea, which had to wait about a century before it was seriously put into practice.

But almost at the same time as Cournot (even a little earlier) a German by the name of Johann Heinrich von Thünen constructed another economic model and partly achieved what Cournot wanted to do, supplemented it with empirical

---

[1] The fullest Marxist criticism of Cournot is given by Blyumin (see I. G. Blyumin, *A Critique of Bourgeois Political Economy*, Vol. I, "The Subjective School in Bourgeois Political Economy", Moscow, 1962, pp. 491-532 (in Russian).

material. Thünen was a North German Junker (landowner) and spent all his life peacefully engaged in agriculture on his small estate. This landowner was a born thinker, however. He was seeking to solve a different economic problem. He presupposed the existence of an isolated economic area in the form of a circle with uniformly fertile land all over it and a town (the natural source of demand for agricultural produce) in the centre. In examining this model he reached the interesting conclusion that the optimum would be to arrange the various branches of agriculture in the form of concentric circles of diminishing intensity. For ten years Thünen kept an account of the expenditure and results in his economy with amazing industry and accuracy.

In particular, he estimated at what distance from the town in the case of an agricultural commodity with a fixed price transport costs would be equal to net profit (gross receipts minus production costs) and production would consequently be unprofitable. Whereas Cournot's book was the beginning of abstract mathematical economics, Thünen's calculations are sometimes regarded as the prototype of econometrics, mathematical economics which includes statistical information and the elaboration of empirical models based on factual quantities.

Thünen's only work bears the title of *Der isolierte Staat in Beziehung auf Landwirtschaft und Nationalökonomie*. The first volume came out in 1826 and part of the second in 1850. The rest of the second volume and the third volume were published posthumously, in 1863. Thünen was hardly noticed and little appreciated by his contemporaries. In modern bourgeois science he is particularly valued as the forerunner of marginalism.

Contrary to the Ricardian theory of labour value and class distribution, Thünen believed that the value of a product was created by labour and capital, and sought to establish the proportion of natural distribution between them with the aid of the marginal principle. The income of labour and capital is determined by the marginal productivity of the former and the latter, i.e., by the productivity of the last unit which it is expedient to use in production. These ideas were not developed in bourgeois political economy until half a century later.

MATHEMATICAL METHODS IN ECONOMICS

The discussion on the role of mathematical methods in economics is at least a century old. All possible points of view have been expressed in it, from "antimathematical obscurantism" to statements that without mathematics there can be no economics at all. Today such extreme positions are unlikely to find any support. But the place, forms and limits of mathematics in the various fields of economic knowledge are still, and will undoubtedly remain, an object for discussion. Basically the question of mathematical methods in economics is decided, like any other scientific question, mainly on the basis of the criterion of practice, or, to put it more simply, real life. The objective needs of the economy at a certain stage of development demanded the mathematisation of economics. When the basic production unit was the small firm, all that was required of its directors was practical know-how. But the management of the production, sale and finances of a large-scale modern enterprise is quite a different matter. You cannot get along without science here and that science is to a considerable extent economic cybernetics, i. e., the mathematical discipline which studies relations, direction and control in economic systems. Direct economic needs also produced new mathematical methods of solving the economic tasks of a certain class. The main type of economic task is the selection of the optimal, most rational version of a programme of production, capital investment, material supplies, etc. The scientific solution of these tasks on the basis of economico-mathematical methods is becoming possible only with the use of modern electronic computers. It is becoming, as it were, the third component of the system economics — mathematics — computers, which is already playing an important role in increasing economic efficiency and will acquire increasing significance.

The application of economico-mathematical methods in the economy has long since advanced beyond the limits of individual enterprises and even the large-scale producing and financing complexes of modern concerns in capitalist countries. The practical needs of state-monopoly capitalism are encouraging bourgeois scholars to elaborate mathematical models of the functioning of the national economy (macro-models). It is typical that the authors of such models and investigations include the most eminent Western economists of recent decades. Features common to those works are, on the one hand, the use of bourgeois politico-economic methodology and, on the other, the broad application of mathematics, from the simplest symbols and algebra to complex modern methods. These works are usually of an econometrical nature, i. e., they contain or presuppose the supplementing of the model with statistics. The works of the American scholar W. Leontief in the sphere of input-output analysis is of great scientific and practical importance. They were, incidentally, preceded by the elaboration of a similar method in Soviet planning bodies in the 1920s. The essence of this method is the tabular portrayal of the economy as a system of more or less aggregated (i. e., uniting homogenous production) branches linked with one another by quantitative relations which reflect the transfer of goods and services from branch to branch.

Mathematical models play a most important part in forecasting the development of the economy, and the forecasting boom is not an accidental or passing feature of the present situation in capitalist countries. The changeover to economic programmes and their control by the state is being effected with the use of mathematical methods and models. The developing countries, for whom increased rates of growth and the elaboration of optimal proportions in the economy is a matter of vital importance, are showing considerable interest in scientific methods of planning and management.

There is no doubt that scientific methods of control with the use of mathematical models and methods can be applied most effectively and fruitfully in socialist planned economy. Soviet planning bodies have accumulated a considerable amount of experience in this sphere, and recent years have been particularly rich in the introduction of new methods. The specialists of the other socialist countries are making a substantial contribution to the elaboration of the theory and practice of planning. The Soviet Academician V. S. Nemchinov, and the Polish economist O. Lange were eminent specialists and propagandists of economico-mathematical methods.

Soviet scientists are paying great attention to the study of economico-mathematical works by Western economists. The *objective-cognitive* and *practical* function of bourgeois economic science frequently prevails in these works and develops parallel

321

to another main function — the *ideological and apologetic* one. The distinction between these two functions in modern bourgeois political economy, which is accepted at the present time by the majority of Marxist economists, was proposed by the Soviet specialist L. B. Alter. It does not refer only to economico-mathematical works, of course, but is particularly useful in estimating them.[1]

The ideological function in economico-mathematical works reveals itself in an interesting way. On the one hand, the conditions of the tasks in the sphere of the economic system are formulated in such a way that the specific class features of bourgeois society disappear. The economic behaviour of the individual is created independently of the class to which he belongs; economic decisions of entrepreneurs independently of the form of ownership of the means of production; the actions of the bourgeois state independently of its class essence. (As we have seen, such features were already characteristic of Cournot.) On the other hand, it is often based on the unsubstantiated thesis of the practically unlimited ability of the state to manage the development of the economy, and spontaneous forces in the economy are played down. Soviet specialists take this aspect of the matter into account in analysing bourgeois economico-mathematical works and reveal and criticise there apologetic elements.

The most controversial question in the sphere of economico-mathematical methods is that of the use of mathematics in theoretical studies on political economy where the aim is to discover the basic qualitative, socio-economic laws of a given social system be it capitalism or socialism. Mathematics is a method and instrument of obtaining knowledge like logic, abstraction and experiment. In itself it is neutral, just as electronic computers are neutral, say. At the basis of all theoretical economic research there lies a philosophical conception determining the qualitative analysis which precedes

---

[1] In considering the various types of economico-mathematical works, some writers suggest the existence of three functions in bourgeois economic science using mathematical methods: the ideological, i.e., the function of the theoretical defence of capitalism; the function of objective cognition and scientific substantiation of governmental economic policy; and the primarily technical function of solving concrete tasks and serving individual firms and enterprises (see S. Avgursky, "Econometry and Modern Capitalism", *Economics and Mathematical Methods*, No. 5, 1969, p. 646, in Russian).

any application of mathematics and formulates the conditions and limits of the task. Marxist economic research differs from non-Marxist independently of whether mathematics is used in one or the other. The question of its use is decided by scientific expediency. In some spheres important results may be obtained without formal mathematic devices. In others they are useful, even essential. Criticising those who feared that the use of formal mathematical methods would harm the purity of Marxist-Leninist theory, V. S. Nemchinov wrote: "Reference is often made to the possibility of abusing mathematics. Such abuse is, of course, possible. But it can be reduced to nought if a proper preliminary qualitative analysis of the economic phenomena under review is made."[1]

It should be recalled that Marx believed the application of mathematics in economic theory to be both possible and expedient. Many quantitative laws in Marx's theory are expressed with the help of algebraic formulae which often contain direct and inverse proportionality. There is the well-known remark of Marx's recorded by Paul Lafargue, that a science is not properly developed until it can make use of mathematics.[2] In 1873 Marx wrote to Engels that he thought it possible by means of the mathematical processing of reliable statistical material on economic cycles "to deduce ... the main laws of crises"[3]. He is referring here, of course, not to the causes of crises, but to the laws of their progression.

The mathematisation of all spheres of knowledge and the development of the cybernetics, information system approach is inevitably having a great influence on economic science.

---

[1] V. S. Nemchinov, *Economico-Mathematical Methods and Models*, p. 12.
[2] Paul Lafargue et Wilhelm Liebknecht, *Souvenirs de Marx*, Paris, 1935, p. 9.
[3] Karl Marx/Friedrich Engels, *Werke*, Bd. 33, Berlin, 1966, S. 82.

CHAPTER XVII

ECONOMIC NATIONALISM FRIEDRICH LIST

LIST AND GERMAN HISTORY

From the 18th century German political economy inherited *cameralistics*, a method which arose in the mediaeval universities of the descriptive exposition of all social sciences with the emphasis on the theory and practice of management of the state. The official economic doctrine was mercantilism, even when it had long since given up the ghost in England and France. Smith's ideas began to take root in Germany at the beginning of the 19th century and the result was a strange mixture of his doctrine and old-fashioned cameralistics.

This was a period of turbulent political events and economic transformations. Napoleon's conquests were attended by the collapse of feudal relations in the kingdoms and principalities which constituted Germany. The personal dependence of the serfs was abolished. The urban craft guilds broke up. In a number of German states, particularly Prussia, the strongest, bourgeois reformers came to power who were prepared to following the example of England and France in certain respects.

Yet even after the Napoleonic Wars Germany remained an economically backward and politically disunited country. The princes and landowners used the patriotic upsurge of the struggle against the foreign invaders for their own ends. Reaction triumphed and proved to be invincible up to the turbulent events of 1848 which shook Germany as they did the rest of Europe.

In terms of level of economic development Germany was far behind England and France. By 1840 its population was roughly equal to that of England (about 27 million), but Germany produced $1/14$th her coal, $1/8$th her iron and consumed $1/16$th her cotton.[1] Nevertheless, its industrial growth was advancing fairly rapidly, particularly after the signing of the Zollverein in 1834, the economic union of the German states.

Industry had already appeared in Germany, which has not yet cast off the yoke of feudalism and patriarchal ways. The powerful uprising of Silesian weavers (1844) showed the ruling classes the growing might of the working class. The German bourgeoisie did not have time to manifest itself as a progressive class, the bearer of new and daring ideas, and quickly resorted to an alliance with the landowners and all reactionary forces. It was this alliance which shortly gave birth to Kaiser Germany.

Political economy in Germany in the 1820s to 1840s was the handmaid of the Prussian monarchy and the German princes. The economists who emerged from the cameralistics school wrote textbooks which were a poor transposition of Anglo-French models in patriotic German form and contained just enough knowledge to pass the examination for a post in the civil service.

But the new times demanded new policies. Friedrich List, by no means an important theoretician, but a colourful writer and public figure, expressed with great force the striving of the German bourgeoisie, progressive to the extent that they were linked with the unity and industrial development of Germany, retrograde in that their realisation was made dependent on a semifeudal monarchy. In many questions List succeeded in rising above the general level of university and civil service scholarship of his day. He followed a different path from the English classics who also represented the interests of the bourgeois class but in different historical and socio-economic conditions.

---

[1] L. A. Mendelson, *The Theory and History of Economic Crises and Cycles*, Vol. II, Moscow, 1959, p. 523 (in Russian).

OFFICE, PRISON, EMIGRATION

Friedrich List was born in 1789 in the Württemberg town of Reutlingen (South Germany). His father was a wealthy artisan, a tanner. The family did not belong to the town aristocracy, but held an hereditary place of honour in the middle class. List's schooling finished at fifteen, after which he helped his father for two years in his workshop. He soon won the reputation of a lazybones and daydreamer among the apprentices. The family decided to apprentice him to a clerk. Here the young List made great strides and began the ascent of the ladder of official posts in the Württemberg Kingdom, which was a vassal of the French Empire until 1814. In his ten years of service List held many different posts: he studied law for eighteen months at Tübingen University and finished his official career in the rank of *Rechungsrat* in the Württemberg capital of Stuttgart. In 1817, thanks to the protection of the liberal minister Wangenheim, he was appointed professor of the "practice of state management" in Tübingen University.

A brilliant career! This high appointment of the 28-year-old List was no mere accident. By then he not only had the reputation of being a capable administrator, but was also well known as an eminent liberal publicist. Nurtured on the ideals of the French revolution and the German liberation movement, List became the firm supporter of radical bourgeois democratic reforms.

His political ardour, boldness and clarity of thought, vivid language and biting sarcasm, all that is typical of his mature writing, can be found in these early articles. By nature he was a keen, expansive and extraordinarily energetic, a sanguine person and an optimist. Without abandoning the political struggle in Württemberg and continuing his literary and professorial work, List threw himself into a new struggle in 1819, this time on a national scale. He founded an association of traders and industrialists, the main task of which was to fight for the economic unity of Germany, more concretely, for the abolition of internal tariffs.

But in the same year clouds began to gather over his head. The other university professors intrigued against him, denouncing him to the authorities as a man of "dangerous political tendencies". Wangenheim could no longer protect List: he was now in retirement and reactionary circles were in power in Württemberg. List was accused of his activity in the association: as a state employee he should have discussed it beforehand with his superiors. List replied with a proud and highly dignified notice of his intention to resign from the university. In the   hile the citizens of Reutlingen had elected him to the lower chamber of the new Württemberg parliament. The government managed to have the election annulled on the grounds that the successful candidate was under thirty, which did not conform to the age qualification laid down in the constitution. But six months later List was re-elected.

His parliamentary activity was brief and hectic. Shortly after his election he presented the chamber with a petition from the citizens of Reutlingen, drafted by him, proposing a broad programme of democratic reforms. The document was written in the challenging language of a rebel and soon brought the wrath of the government on his head. He was charged with "incitement against the state", deprived of his deputy mandate and sentenced to ten months in prison. Without waiting to be arrested, List fled the country and spent more than two years wandering around the neighbouring West European states.

He then returned to Württemberg hoping for a royal pardon, but was immediately seized and thrown into prison. The government preferred to get rid of this powerful political opponent who was by now known throughout the whole of Germany. After agreeing to emigrate to America List was released before his term was up. In June 1825 he and his wife and children disembarked in New York. At first List took up farming, then edited a German newspaper and finally became an industrial entrepreneur. He continued to be active in politics and drew up an economic programme based on protectionism for the USA. He thought the USA and Germany were in a similar position· both countries faced English competition in their industrial development.

In 1832 List arrived in Europe as an American citizen and became United States Consul in Leipzig. This was the period of feverish railway construction which embraced the whole of Western Europe. List had long been an enthusiastic supporter of this new enterprise which he regarded not only as a most important means of economic progress but also as a guarantee against war. He organised a joint-stock company for the construction of a railway from Leipzig to Dresden, one of the first in Germany. Enmeshed in political intrigues and financial affairs, he became disillusioned with the practical actions of Gründer and left for Paris in 1837. Incidentally, List retained his faith in the great future of railways to the end of his life.

THE *NATIONAL SYSTEM*. LIST'S LATER YEARS

List spent three years in Paris, in his third and last emigration. With his characteristic passion and energy he took up the study of political economy and began to expound his own fully developed views. The result of his labours was first a voluminous manuscript entitled *Das natürliche System der politischen Ökonomie*[1], an entry for a competition organised by the French Academy and then his main work, *Des nationale System der politischen Ökonomie* published in Augsburg in early 1841.

List conceived his book as the first volume of a large work which was to cover all the problems of political economy. Therefore it was subtitled *Der internationale Handel, die Handelspolitik und der deutsche Zollverein*. But his pretentious plan remained unfulfilled, and his role in the development of economic science rests mainly on this work. The *National System* was quite a success and another two editions followed in quick succession. It played an important role in the heated discussions on Germany's economic development and trading policy and had a considerable influence on German economic thought.

List developed his favourite idea: the way for Germany to become prosperous and united was through the growth of its industry, and German industry needed to be protected from strong foreign competition with the help of high import duties and other instruments of trading policy. Most of all this idea suited the growing industrial bourgeoisie of West and South Germany. His book also had a favourable reception among the democratic intelligentsia. In spite of List's monarchism and pandering to the nobility, the general spirit of the book was that of progressive bourgeois reforms. The reforms which he proposed were cautious and compromise ones, but in the

---

[1] It was not published until the 1920s.

stagnant air of Germany in the 1840s these ideas had an almost revolutionary ring.

The book unerringly found its enemies as well. List's ideas challenged the selfish interests of the Prussian Junkers, who exported corn to England and were only too willing to agree to the duty-free import of English industrial goods into Germany in exchange for the free import of German corn by England. The old caste of the commercial bourgeoisie in the North-German towns also had an interest in "free trade". In the latter years of List's life these circles organised a campaign of slander, insults and anonymous threats against him. In addition, List had made himself a fair number of enemies by his activities in railway construction and his biting publicistic writings in which he poked fun at landowners, university professors, the Church, and sometimes the authorities. Nor were the "sins" of his youth forgotten.

After his return to Germany List lived mainly in Augsburg, engaging in journalistic and research work. It was during this period that he wrote the works which later were used to argue that he was a great-power chauvinist and precursor of German imperialism. List maintained that overpopulated Germany should colonise the "free" lands of South-Eastern Europe (the present territory of Hungary, Yugoslavia, Rumania and Slovakia).[1] He wrote that the bulwark of the great German nation, the military bulwark, in particular, must be the middle independent peasantry.

In connection with these ideas List even changed his attitude towards England, which he had always regarded as the main opponent of German unification and industrial development. Now he thought England might support Germany against her powerful continental neighbours—France and Russia. In 1846 he even went to England to find out through talks with English politicians whether there was any ground for such a rapprochement. His visit was a total failure.

In the meantime List's health, which had always been good, was beginning to fail him. He was also finding it difficult to support his family financially. He no longer had the strength for the constant struggle which he was waging and the frantic activity to which he was accustomed. In the autumn of 1846

---

[1] At that time these territories were partly under the rule of Austria-Hungary and partly under Turkey.

List set off for Italy hoping for a rest and distraction from his various cares and disappointments. But he never arrived. In the small Tyrolean town of Kufstein Friedrich List shot himself in the head.

THE NATION'S INDUSTRIAL EDUCATION

In political economy List was a critic of the classical school which for him was embodied in Adam Smith. However, in fact his criticism did not touch the foundation of the classical doctrine — the theory of value and incomes. These spheres of economic theory did not interest List particularly. All his interest was concentrated on questions of economic policy, predominantly foreign trade policy.

In general List is not very impressive as a critic of Smith and his followers. His approach excludes the establishment and investigation of the general laws of capitalist production. The investigation of the latter and the analysis of the class structure of bourgeois society were the important achievements of the Smith-Ricardo school. List did not perceive this, however, and remained on the surface of phenomena. Nevertheless, by reflecting in his views different conditions and requirements of capitalist development from those expressed by the classics, he examined a number of problems in a new way and this was productive to a certain extent.

List called the Smith system of political economy cosmopolitan. He accused this system of ignoring the national features of economic development in individual countries and of dogmatically imposing on them general "natural" laws and rules of economic policy. "As the characteristic difference of the system proposed by me," he wrote, "I would mention *nationality*. My whole edifice is based on the nature of *nationality* as the intermediate link between the *individual* and mankind." [1]

The various nations, List said, were at different stages of development. Complete freedom of trade between them might entail some abstract advantage for the world economy as a whole from the point of view of exchange values, i. e., expenditure of labour, but it would impede the development of production forces in the backward countries. He called his

---

[1] Friedrich List, *Schriften. Reden. Briefe*, Bd. VI, Berlin, 1930, S. 34.

conception the theory of production forces as opposed to Smith's "theory of exchange values". It should be remembered that by production forces List meant something different from the meaning Marx later gave to the term. For List production forces were simply the whole aggregate of social conditions without which there could be no "wealth of the nation."

In order to bring unused resources into production and overcome backwardness it was permissible, even essential, to develop branches in which labour productivity was lower than it was abroad at a given moment. List wrote: "This loss of values is consequently to be regarded only as the *price of the industrial education of the nation.*"[1] Industrial development was the alpha and omega of List's views. He wrote that a nation which engaged in agriculture only was like a man who had only one arm. He suggested speeding up industrial growth with the help of "educational" protectionism—a system of state measures to defend national industry from foreign competition until it could stand on its own feet and compete with the foreigners "as equal". He relegated the introduction of free trade to the fairly remote future when all the main nations would be at roughly the same level of development.

The following statement by List, for example, is most interesting in the light of the present state of affairs and modern views: "One can regard it as a rule that the more manufactured produce a nation exports, the more raw materials it imports and the more it consumes products from the tropics, the richer and more powerful it is."[2] This statement is interesting with reference to Japan, which has exactly this type of foreign trade and which has recently become the second industrial power in the capitalist world after the USA as a result of rapid economic growth.

List's idea of the need to regard any economic decision, for example, about the creation of a new branch of production, not only from the point of view of immediate efficiency (which is usually equivalent to profitability), but also from the point of view of its long-term and indirect consequences, was to play an important role. Such situations are very familiar to the economist, and not to the economist alone. If a new factory is built in a certain neighbourhood, for example, important additional economic considerations may arise which were not

[1] Friedrich List, op. cit., p. 34.
[2] Ibid., p. 54.

directly taken into account in calculating the profitability of the production in question: improvement of working and living conditions for the population, an increase in the average qualification of the labour force in the neighbourhood, the drawing of natural resources which could not be used earlier, into economic turnover, etc.

Calculations showed that it was more profitable for India to ship foreign trade cargoes on chartered foreign vessels than to set up its own shipbuilding industry and merchant marine. Yet many important economic and political considerations made the Indian Government conclude that in the long term the creation of its own merchant marine was both profitable and essential for the country.

Naturally the implementation of measures of a dubious or excessively remote utility could lead to voluntarism in economics. It might involve, for example, the construction of obviously uneconomic enterprises for purely prestige or parochial considerations. On a nationwide scale abuse of the "List principle" leads to autarchy, that is, economically unjustified and basically unprofitable self-provision, to a rejection of the advantages of division of labour and production specialisation.

The indirect advantages of an economic and social nature which proceed from a given economic decision have been referred to as "external economies" since Marshall. The opposite effect, indirect losses connected with a concrete decision, also frequently take place and are called "external diseconomies". Lord Robbins in his authoritative work *The Theory of Economic Development in the History of Economic Thought* says that this kind of effects "... much earlier than Marshall, had been the focus of List's various disquisitions on the development of productive powers. List was a turbulent, tragic character, full of romantic prejudices and given to wild exaggeration, and his misrepresentation of his intellectual antagonists, particularly Adam Smith, is almost comic in its inaccuracy. But, divested of its sound and fury there remains surely a core of truth in his contention that the fostering of certain industries in certain historic context may carry with it an increase of productive potential, not to be measured merely in the value of particular outputs or the growth of capital values. In my judgement the influence of his exaggerations and misrepresentations did much harm, especially in so far as they contributed to the growth of economic nationalism in Europe. But that is no reason for denying some degree of analytical validity to his principal contention." [1]

List's theory was an attempt to answer a most important question: how to abolish within the capitalist framework the economic backwardness of countries which by virtue of their history and economy took a back seat in the "world community". Like many other economic ideas, it could be, and actually was, used for both reactionary and progressive ends. Today there is a revival of interest in List in the developing countries which are faced with developing their national industry in a situation where world markets are dominated by the monopolies of the developed capitalist countries.

The originality and scientific value of List is not that he developed economic theory, but that he carefully elaborated a single economico-political problem — the difficulties and factors of capitalist growth in underdeveloped countries.

PROTECTIONISM AND FREE TRADE

Capital is cosmopolitan by its very nature. But this feature operates in dialectical unity with militant nationalism which is also organically inherent in capital. "Zwei Seelen wohnen, ach, in meiner Brust!" as Goethe said. This unity and conflict accompany the whole development of capitalism. They also operate in modern conditions. Whereas the classics expressed the first tendency of capital with great force, List expressed the second one no less forcefully.

In the preface to *A Contribution to the Critique of Political Economy* Karl Marx describes how, as editor of the *Rheinische Zeitung* from 1842 to 1843, he was called upon to deal with economic problems. Among the events which first stimulated his study of economics he mentions the debates on free trade and protective tariffs. [2] There can be no doubt that these studies of the young Marx were linked with his reading of List's

---

[1] L. Robbins, *The Theory of Economic Development in the History of Economic Thought*, London, 1968, p. 116. Like Keynes Lionel Robbins was made a peer for his services in economics.

[2] Karl Marx, *A Contribution to the Critique of Political Economy*, London, 1971, p. 20.

333

book published in 1841, the author of which was right at the centre of the discussion on trade.

Subsequently Marx and Engels were compelled in their practical and literary activity to turn again and again to the problem of free trade and protectionism. In so doing they examined List's ideas. While they had a poor opinion of List as a theoretician and criticised the bourgeois apologetic essence of his teaching, the founders of Marxism nevertheless regarded him as the most outstanding German economist of his day.

The discussion on free trade reflects the struggle within the class of the bourgeoisie and also between the bourgeoisie of the various capitalist countries. Freedom of trade and protectionism are merely two forms of class policy, both equally aimed at increasing the capitalists' profit by exploiting the workers. But this does not mean that the proletariat and its parties can ignore this problem and leave it entirely to bourgeois economists and politicians. It is a matter of concern to the working class at what rate and in what forms their country's industry develops. And industrial development depends to a considerable extent on trade policy.

A policy of free trade is progressive from the point of view of the working class to the extent that it promotes the development of capitalism on a world scale, the growth of its production forces. First and foremost, this may in certain circumstances help to bring about an improvement in the material position of the working class. But in the final analysis the accelerated development of capitalism simultaneously develops its contradictions, raises the conflict between production forces and production relations to a higher level and thereby prepares the collapse of capitalism as a system. In 1847 Marx said: "...we are for Free Trade, because by Free Trade all economical laws, with their most astounding contradictions, will act upon a larger scale, upon a greater extent of territory, upon the territory of the whole earth; and because the uniting of all these contradictions into a single group, where they stand face to face, will result in the struggle which will itself eventuate in the emancipation of the proletariat." [1]

But the defence of free trade should on no account be regarded as universally applicable to any situation and any concrete circumstances. In the Germany of the mid-19th

---

[1] Karl Marx/Friedrich Engels, *Werke*, Bd. 4, Berlin, 1969, S. 308.

century free trade could only have perpetuated the country's backwardness and helped to conserve the relics of feudalism. In the final analysis protectionism was able to be of use to the working class as a means of accelerating capitalist development and overcoming feudal customs. Marx emphasised that List and his followers were demanding protection not for small-scale cottage production, but for large-scale capitalist industry in which manual labour was being ousted by machines and patriarchal production replaced by modern production. At the end of this road, however, Marx saw not the triumph of powerful German capital, but a socialist revolution. For similar reasons Engels at a somewhat later period regarded the protectionist trading policy of the United States as progressive in principle.

These principles are important for an assessment of the "liberal" and protectionist tendencies in modern capitalism and for working out the attitude of the working class and its parties in the period of GATT, the Common Market and the Kennedy and Nixon rounds.[1]

THE HISTORICAL SCHOOL

National features, national character, national destiny—these and similar concepts permeated the whole of German social thought in the late 18th and 19th centuries. What could be more national than *history*? The passion for history was also a kind of reaction to the rationalist philosophy of the preceding century, which regarded everything that had existed before it, i.e., feudalism and its institutions, as unnatural phenomena engendered by ignorance and lack of enlightenment.

List influenced the German historical school of political economy strongly in the three following ways: 1) like List the "historians" regarded political economy not as the science of the general laws of economic development, but as the science of the national economy, and stressed the decisive role of the

---

[1] GATT is the General Agreement on Tariffs and Trade concluded in 1947 and aimed at establishing international control and removing barriers to foreign trade. The rounds of talks within the framework of GATT on mutual reduction of customs duty, particularly in trade between the USA and the West European countries, bear the names of American presidents.

state; 2) they adopted a critical attitude towards the classical school and its followers, attacking, in particular, the cosmopolitan and abstract nature of their theories; 3) they proceeded from a country's given stage of economic development.

They went further than List, however, by creating a special *historical method* in political economy which played an important role in the subsequent development of the science, particularly in Germany and the United States. The ideas of the historical school are more easily understood if one takes into account the basic defects of the political economy expounded by the bourgeois Ricardians in England and the Say school in France. Their theories of value and incomes could appear either as hopelessly confused or as a meaningless oversimplification. They did not accept the view of social economic development as an historical, evolutionary process. Their abstract view of man, the calculator, the reasoned egoist, man void of all his real, inherent features, was unconvincing. The "cosmopolitanism" of these economists, particularly the English, reflected England's dominant role on the world market. The "historians" wanted to put concrete man with his complex psyche and morals, his national and historical features, at the centre of economic science.

But in feudal-bourgeois Germany of the first half of the 19th century and under the pen of Prussian professors the critique of the classical school (they did not distinguish between Smith, on the one hand, and Senior and Say, on the other) assumed a reactionary nature.

The historical school rejected the method of scientific abstraction as the basic method of investigation in political economy. It also rejected the cognition of the universal, objective laws of social development, elevating national features into an absolute principle. The methods of analysis inherent in economic science were replaced by vague and uncertain sphere which included history, ethics, law, psychology, politics and ethnography.

The history of economic science has its own clichés. The historical school is generally represented in the form of a trinity consisting of Roscher, Hildebrand and Knies. More serious studies show that one cannot speak of a "school" here, that there are considerable differences between these three writers, there was no personal and direct contact between them, and that apart from them there were many other economists working in the same trend. In other words, as usual, things are considerably more complicated than they are portrayed in textbooks. Knies, in particular, criticised Roscher and Hildebrand most strongly.

Nevertheless on the main questions of theory these three professors followed the same general line and were its most eminent representatives. Wilhelm Roscher in his early (1843) work *Ansichten der Volkswirtschaft aus dem geschichtlichen Standpunkt* expounded certain basic tenets of the future historical method. However, he accepted many theses of classical and French economists which suited his argument. The result was a hotchpotch lacking any real core. Roscher did the same in his subsequent works.

Marx regarded Roscher's writing as a model of eclectics and bourgeois apologetics: "The last form [apologetics — A. A.] is the *academic form*, which proceeds 'historically' and, with wise moderation, collects the 'best' from all sources, and in doing this contradictions do not matter; on the contrary, what matters is comprehensiveness. All systems are thus made insipid, their edge is taken off and they are peacefully gathered together in a miscellany. The heat of apologetics is moderated here by erudition, which looks down benignly on the exaggerations of economic thinkers, and merely allows them to float as oddities in the mediocre pap.... Professor *Roscher* is a master of this sort of thing and has modestly proclaimed himself to be the Thucydides of political economy."[1]

The books written by Roscher in his long life could fill a whole library, and include, in particular, two large works on the history of economic thought written with great academic precision. For almost fifty years he was a professor in Leipzig where he enjoyed respect in governmental and academic circles.

The life of Bruno Hildebrand was a turbulent one in the early years. He was compelled to flee from the persecution of the reactionary government of Hessen to Switzerland where he taught in the universities of Zurich and Bern. Hildebrand founded the first statistical service in Switzerland. He returned

---

[1] Karl Marx, *Theories of Surplus-Value*, Part III, p. 502.

A boastful reference to the famous Greek historian Thucydides is contained in Roscher's foreword to his book *Die Grundlagen der Nationalökonomie* (1854).

to Germany in 1861 and was a professor in Jena until his death. He is linked with the historical school mainly by his book *Die Nationalökonomie der Gegenwart und Zukunft* published in 1848. Hildebrand criticised the classical school more strongly and systematically than Roscher and introduced the historical method more aggressively. He had a great influence on the development of the historical school later.

The activity of Karl Knies extends considerably beyond the period under review, since he worked in the 1860s to 1890s. However, his main work in the spirit of the historical school, *Die politische Ökonomie vom Standpunkte der geschichtlichen Methode*, came out in 1853. Knies was a professor in Heidelberg for more than thirty years. In the 1870s a young generation of German scholars led by Gustav Schmoller formed the so-called new historical school. Knies and Schmoller attracted those who wanted a third path—not connected with the subjective school (the "neoclassicists") or socialism. They also had a considerable following in the Anglo-Saxon countries. The members of the historical school did a great deal in the sphere of concrete economic research. They made broad use of historical and statistical material in their works. They suffered from overdescriptiveness, however, extreme empiricism and super-ficiality. From the very beginning the historical school attacked all socialist doctrines. When it became the official trend in imperial Germany, it violently attacked Marxism which was rapidly spreading throughout the country.

RODBERTUS: A SPECIAL CASE

The following is a passage from a letter of Karl Rodbertus' to Zeller: "You will find that this" (the line of thought developed in it) "has been very nicely used ... by Marx, without, however, giving me credit for it."[1] In another letter Rodbertus states that he had explained the origin of surplus value earlier than Marx and done it more briefly and clearly. These letters were published in 1879 and 1881 respectively, i.e., after Rodbertus' death, but while Marx was still alive.

Thus, we are dealing with a man who accused Marx of plagiarism. What is more, Marx is alleged to have "borrowed"

---

[1] Karl Marx, *Capital*, Vol. II, p. 6.

from him not a trifle but nothing more or less than the theory of surplus value which forms the cornerstone to Marxist economic doctrine. When publishing the second volume of *Capital* in 1885, two years after Marx's death, Frederick Engels devoted his preface mainly to refuting the absurd fabrications of Rodbertus and—even more—of his followers, the German *Katheder Sozialisten*.[1] The answer was exhaustive and final.[2] (In particular, Engels proved convincingly that Marx had not been acquainted with Rodbertus' economic writings before 1859.)

Who was this Rodbertus?

He was born in 1805 in Greifswald in North Germany, studied law in the universities of Göttingen and Berlin, and worked as a civil servant. After retiring and travelling round Europe, he settled down in 1836 on the Jagetzow estate which he had purchased in Pomerania, and lived there almost uninterruptedly to the end of his days. Engels in a letter of 1883 writes of Rodbertus: "Once this man all but discovered surplus value. His Pomeranian estate prevented him from doing it."[3] Naturally a landowner is not bound to express the ideology of his class. But after he became one Rodbertus did in fact move to the right, and his social position affected his views.

In 1842 he published a book entitled *Zur Erkenntniss unser Staatswirtschaftlichen Zustände*. It was here that he "all but discovered" surplus value. He writes for example: "If the productivity of labour is so high that apart from the worker's means of subsistence it can also produce more consumer goods, this surplus becomes rent, i.e., it is appropriated without labour by others, if private ownership of land and capital obtains. In other words: the principle of obtaining rent is private ownership of land and capital."[4]

This is well said, to give Rodbertus his due. But at the very most it merely testifies to the fact that he had mastered Smith

---

[1] This term, first used in the 1870s and 1880s, was applied in Germany to bourgeois professors who reached "state socialism", i.e., the reconciliation and collaboration of the classes under the aegis of a firm monarchy.

[2] Schumpeter, an opponent of Marxism but a serious scholar, remarks in this connection: "I do not think that there is any cogent reason for challenging Engels' repudiation of the idea that Marx had 'borrowed' from Rodbertus" (J. Schumpeter, *History of Economic Analysis*, p. 506).

[3] *Marx and Engels Archives*, Vol. I, p. 338 (in Russian).

[4] Rodbertus-Jagetzow, *Zur Erkenntniss unser Staatswirtschaftlichen Zustände*, Berlin, 1842, S. 42.

and Ricardo and borrowed a number of scientific, profound tenets from them. In so doing he differed greatly from the representatives of the historical school, of course, and his other German economist contemporaries. But that is all.

Whereas in Rodbertus we see separate (albeit useful) bricks selected from the English classics, Marx proceeded from Smith and Ricardo to build the fundamentally new, harmonious edifice of proletarian political economy.

Considering profit and land rent the fruits of the unpaid labour of workers is not tantamount to creating the scientific theory of surplus-value. As we shall see in Chapter XIX, the English Ricardian socialists went further than Rodbertus in this question, but they did not create such a theory. Rodbertus did not treat "rent" as the universal form of the surplus product under capitalism. He did not explain the special nature of the buying and selling of working power. He was most cautious in treating "rent" as exploiter income. Finally, Rodbertus did not in fact go any further than Ricardo in examining average profit, a most important question which was solved by Marx's theory of the price of production.

The revolutionary events of 1848 brought Rodbertus to the fore. He became a member of the Landtag, the Prussian parliament, one of the organisers of the "Reform Party" and for a short time a minister in Hansemann's Prussian liberal government. The main aim behind Rodbertus' activity was to find reforms which would prevent the development of revolution, particularly a revolution of the working class. But he proved to be too liberal for the triumphant counterrevolution and retired to his Pomeranian estate. After this he ceased to play an active part in political life although he frequently felt the "ministerial itch", to quote Marx, and at one time sought to win the confidence of Bismarck. Rodbertus died in Jagetzow in 1875.

Apart from the above-mentioned works, Rodbertus' ideas are expounded mainly in four *Sociale Briefe an von Kirchmann* which form, as it were, one large volume. The first two letters were published in 1850, the third in 1851 and the fourth posthumously.

In his writings Rodbertus continued that which he failed to do in practical politics. He saw a number of negative aspects of capitalism, particularly its tendency to preserve the poverty of the mass of the people. As he himself wrote, it was essential to find a means of "saving capital ... from itself".[1] He urged capitalists to give the working class a share of the fruits yielded by increased labour productivity. It would then be possible to reach "a compromise between labour and ownership of land and capital". In Rodbertus one can see to a certain extent the precursor of views on the so-called incomes policy pursued today in the capitalist countries. It is rightly stated in the introductory article to the Soviet edition of the translation of Rodbertus' book *Zur Erkenntniss unser Staatswirtschaftlichen Zustände*: "Rodbertus' life cause was not to attack capitalism from the standpoint of proletarian socialism. It was to defend capitalism as its farsighted theoretician who sees the dangers contained in the system and draws attention to certain serious contradictions in capitalism...."[2]

[1] Dr Rodbertus-Jagetzow, *Briefe und Socialpolitische Aufsätze*, Berlin, Bd. I, S. III.

[2] K. Rodbertus, *Zur Erkenntniss...*, p. 25, Introduction by V. Serebryakov (in Russian).

CHAPTER XVIII

THE WONDERFUL WORLD OF THE UTOPISTS

SAINT-SIMON AND FOURIER

There have always been people in all ages who dreamt of a better life for mankind, a worthier social order. They were frequently compelled to fight the powers-that-be and became heroes and martyrs. In analysing and criticising the socio-economic system of their day, these people sought to outline and argue a more just and humane order. Their ideas exceed the bounds of political economy, but they also play an important part in the science.

Socialist and communist ideas developed in many works from the 16th to 18th centuries, of differing scientific and literary merit and different fates. But this was merely the prehistory of *utopian socialism*. Its classical period came in the first half of the 19th century.

By this time bourgeois relations were sufficiently developed to evoke thorough and profound criticism of capitalism. At the same time the class opposition of the bourgeoisie and the proletariat had not yet fully revealed itself and still appeared in the form of a more general conflict between riches and poverty, brute force and lack of rights. The conditions were not yet present for scientific socialism which substantiated the historical mission of the proletariat. But one of the sources of the doctrine of Marx and Engels was utopian socialism which reached its greatest heights in the works of the eminent thinkers Saint-Simon, Fourier and Robert Owen.

"I am descended from Charlemagne, my father was called Count de Saint-Simon, and I was the closest relative of the Duke of Saint-Simon."[1] These lines would simply sound like a piece of snobbish arrogance if we did not know that the person in question was Saint-Simon. He uses them to open his autobiographical essay written in 1808 when the former count, now a commoner, was being kept by his servant. The life of this extraordinary man is just as full of complexities and contradictions as his teaching. It contains great wealth and poverty, military honours and imprisonment, the ardour of a philanthropist and an attempted suicide, the betrayal of friends and the firm faith of disciples.

Claude Henri de Rouvroy was born in Paris in 1760 and grew up in the family castle in the north of France. He had a good home education. Love of freedom and strength of character soon revealed themselves in the young nobleman. At the age of thirteen he refused his first communion on the grounds that he did not believe in the sacraments and was not prepared to pretend. Another feature soon appeared in him to the considerable surprise of his family: a firm belief in his high social vocation. It is said that the 15-year-old Saint-Simon ordered his servant to wake him each day with the words: "Arise, my lord, great things await you."

But there was still a long way to go to these great things, and in the meantime Saint-Simon took up a military career, as was the custom in his family, and spent three years in tedious garrison life. Release from it came for the young officer when he went to America as a volunteer in the French expeditionary force sent to help the insurgent American colonies against England. He returned to France a hero and was soon put in charge of a regiment. The young count was faced with the prospects of a brilliant career. But the empty life soon bored him. A journey to Holland and then to Spain showed a new side of Saint-Simon—the adventure-seeker and deviser of crazy schemes. One has the impression that his indefatigable energy and inventive mind, not yet having found their true

---

[1] *Oeuvres de Saint-Simon*, publ. in 1832, by Olinde Rodrigues, Paris, 1848, p. XV. The quotation refers to the famous writer of memoirs, the Duke of Saint-Simon, to whom we referred in the biographies of Boisguillebert and Law (Chapters IV and V).

vocation, were seeking for an outlet in these wild schemes. In Holland he trained a naval expedition to conquer India from the English. In Spain he drew up a plan for a large waterway to link Madrid with the sea and organised a postal and passenger transport company which was a success.

Nurtured on the ideals of the encyclopaedists and the experience of the American revolution, Saint-Simon welcomed the events of 1789 most enthusiastically. For almost two years he took a fairly active part in the revolution, although "on a local level" only: he was living in the small town near his former family estate. He did not regret the loss of the estate and renounced his title and ancient family name officially, taking the name of citizen Bonhomme (ordinary person).

In 1791 the life of citizen Bonhomme took a sudden and at first glance most unexpected turn. He went to Paris and embarked on land speculation which assumed vast proportions in this period due to the sale of property confiscated by the state from the nobility and the church. As a partner he chose the German diplomat Baron Redern whose acquaintance he had made in Spain. Their success exceeded all expectations. By 1794 Saint-Simon was a very rich man, but then the chastising hand of the Jacobin revolution descended upon him. The counterrevolutionary Thermidore coup saved the prisoner from the guillotine. After about a year in prison he was released and again took up profiteering, which was no longer a dangerous business. In 1796 the joint fortune of Saint-Simon and Redern was valued at four million francs.

But at this point the successful profiteer's career was cut short. Baron Redern, who had sensibly sought refuge abroad during the reign of terror, returned to Paris and laid claim to the whole of their joint fortune since the operations had been carried out in his name. This strange mixture of diabolical cunning and childlike simplicity in Saint-Simon passes all understanding! After lengthy disputes he was forced to accept 150,000 francs as compensation from Redern.

Saint-Simon who had already been soldier and adventurist, patriot and gambler, turned into a devoted scholar. Fascinated by the great discoveries in the natural sciences, he began to study them with his customary passion and energy. The remains of his fortune went on the upkeep of a hospitable home where Paris' most distinguished scholars gathered. Saint-Simon then spent several years travelling about Europe.

By 1805 it became absolutely clear that his money had gone and he was almost penniless.

Later, looking back on his life, Saint-Simon was inclined to depict his rises and falls as a series of conscious experiments which he conducted in preparation for his true activity as a social reformer. This is an illusion, of course. His life was logical, a manifestation of Saint-Simon's personality determined by the age and its events, a personality which was original and talented but also extremely contradictory. Already at this time he had earned the reputation of being a strange and extravagant fellow. Mediocrity is often regarded by society as the norm, whereas talent seems extravagant and sometimes even suspect.

Saint Simon's first printed work, *Lettres d'un habitant de Genève à ses contemporains* (1803) also bears the stamp of great originality. Here we already have the utopian level of reorganising society, although it is expounded in vague, embryonic form. This small work contains two remarkable things. Firstly, Saint-Simon depicts the French revolution as a class struggle between three main classes—the nobility, the bourgeoisie and the poor (the proletariat). Engels called this "a most pregnant discovery"[1]. Secondly, he gave a penetrating outline of the role of science in the transformation of society.

Saint-Simon's literary style was energetic and passionate, sometimes exalted. From it emerges the picture of a man deeply concerned for the fate of mankind.

THE TEACHER

The last twenty years of Saint-Simon's life were full of hardship, struggle and intense creativity. Finding himself penniless, he began to look for any form of income and at one point worked as a copyist in a pawnshop. In 1805 he happened to meet his former manservant who had managed to amass a certain amount of money while working for Saint-Simon. Saint-Simon lived with him for two years and enjoyed his help. The story of Don Quixote and Sancho Panza was repeated in this strange pair! With his former servant's money Saint-Simon published his second work in 1808—the *Introduction aux*

---

[1] Frederick Engels, *Anti-Dühring*, p. 307.

travaux scientifiques du XIX-e siècle. This and several other works he printed in a small edition and dispatched to eminent scholars and politicians, requesting their criticism and assistance in continuing his work. There was no response.

In 1810-1812 Saint-Simon lived in dire poverty. He wrote that he sold all his possessions, including his clothing, that he was living on bread and water and did not have any fuel or candles. But the more difficult things became, the harder he worked. It was these years that saw the final crystallisation of the views on society which he expounded in a series of nature works published from 1814 onwards. The attention of the public was attracted to Saint-Simon by his brochure on the postwar structure of Europe. In this brochure Saint-Simon coined the popular and well-known phrase "The golden age of mankind is before us, not behind us". His subsequent activity consisted of arguing this thesis and seeking to elaborate ways to the "golden age".

As he approached sixty his affairs improved. He acquired pupils and followers. The preaching of the peaceful transformation of society, addressed to its natural, educated "leaders"—bankers, industrialists and merchants—attracted the attention of certain people in this class. Saint-Simon was given the opportunity of publishing his works, and they became known to a fairly wide public. His rich followers made it possible for him to live comfortably and work hard.

But in his life as in his works Saint-Simon remained the rebel, the enthusiast, the man of passion and fantasy. A group of bankers and wealthy men who had financed the publication of one of his works, publicly dissociated themselves from his ideas and announced that he had misled them and betrayed their trust. Shortly afterwards Saint-Simon was taken to court on a charge of *lèse-majesté*: he had published a *Parabole* in which he stated that France would lose nothing if the members of the royal family were to vanish miraculously without trace, together with the aristocracy, top-ranking officials, clergy, etc., but that it would lose a great deal if the finest scholars, artists, craftsmen and artisans were to disappear. The jury found him not guilty, seeing this as simply an amusing paradox.

Whereas this is a somewhat tragicomic episode in Saint-Simon's life, his attempted suicide in March 1823 was truly tragic. Saint-Simon shot himself in the head with a pistol, but remained alive, losing one eye. In a farewell letter to a close friend he wrote of his disillusionment with life caused by the general lack of interest in his ideas. No sooner had he recovered from the wound, however, than he proceeded to work hard and in 1823-1824 published his most complete and polished work—the *Catéchisme des industriels*. Throughout 1824 he worked feverishly on his last book *Le Nouveau Christianisme* striving to give the future "society of industrialists" a new religion and borrowing from Christianity only its initial humanism. In May 1825, a few weeks after the publication of *Le Nouveau Christianisme*, Claude Henri Saint-Simon died.

SAINT-SIMONISM

One might say that Saint-Simonism has gone through four stages of development. The *first* is represented by Saint-Simon's works up to 1814-1815. During this period its main features were a cult of science and scholars, and a fairly abstract humanism. The socio-economic ideas of Saint-Simonism existed in embryonic form only.

The *second* stage is embodied in the mature works of the last ten years of his life. In them Saint-Simon firmly refuses to acknowledge capitalism as a natural and permanent order and advances the thesis of its logical replacement by a new social order in which collaboration between people will take the place of antagonism and competition. This will be effected by the peaceful development of a "society of industrialists" in which the economic and political power of the feudal lords and parasitic bourgeois proprietors will be abolished, although private ownership will remain. Saint-Simon increasingly inclined to the defence of the interests of the largest and most oppressed class. Marx wrote that "in his last work, *Le Nouveau Christianisme*, Saint-Simon speaks directly for the working class and declares their emancipation to be the goal of his efforts"[1].

Saint-Simon believed that the society of his day consisted of two main classes—the idle proprietors and the working industrialists. This idea is a strange combination of the class contradictions of feudal and bourgeois society. Saint-Simon's first class included the large landowners and capitalist rentiers who did not take part in the economic process, and also the

---

[1] Karl Marx, *Capital*, Vol. III, p. 605.

strata of military and judicial bureaucracy which obtained advancement during the revolution and the Empire. The industrialists were everyone else who, together with their families, constituted in Saint-Simon's opinion up to 96 per cent of the total population of French society of that day. Here we find everyone engaged in any type of socially useful activity: peasants and hired workers, artisans and factory owners, merchants and bankers, scholars and artists. He considered the incomes of proprietors to be parasitic and the incomes of the industrialists to be legitimate. Expressed in economic categories, he amalgamated land rent and loan interest in the incomes of the former and entrepreneurial revenue (or all profit) and wages in the incomes of the latter. Thus Saint-Simon did not see the class opposition between the bourgeoisie and the proletariat or, at least, did not consider it significant. This is explained partly by the underdeveloped nature of the classes at the beginning of the 19th century and partly by his desire to subject his theory to a single aim: the uniting of the overwhelming majority of the nation for the peaceful and gradual transformation of society. Saint-Simon did not oppose private ownership on principle, simply its misabuse, so to say, and did not foresee its abolition in a future society, but thought a certain control could be established over it by society. His view of capitalist entrepreneurs as the natural organisers of production, essential for the well-being of society, is reminiscent of Say.

The writings, propaganda and practical activity of his disciples in the period from Saint-Simon's death to 1831 forms the *third* stage of Saint-Simonism and, in fact, its flowering. Saint-Simonism became a truly socialist doctrine, to the extent that it demanded the abolition of private ownership of the means of production, the distribution of goods according to labour and ability, and the social organisation and planning of production. These ideas are expressed most fully and systematically in the public lectures given in Paris in 1828-1829 by Saint-Simon's closest pupils, Saint-Armand Bazard and Barthélemy Prosper Enfantin. They were subsequently published under the title of *Doctrine de Saint-Simon: Exposition.*

His pupils gave Saint-Simon's views on classes and property a more obviously socialist bias. They no longer saw the industrialists as a single, homogeneous social class, but maintained that the exploitation to which it was subjected by the proprietors fell fair and square upon the worker. The worker, they wrote, "is exploited materially, intellectually and morally, as the slave once was". Here the capitalist entrepreneurs "participate in the privileges of exploitation".

Saint-Simonism linked exploitation with the institution of private ownership. It saw the defects of a social system based on private ownership as the main cause of the crises and production anarchy inherent in capitalism. True, this profound idea was not substantiated by an analysis of the mechanism of crises, but it formed one of the bases of their most important demand for a radical restriction of private ownership by abolishing the right of inheritance. The only heir should be the state which would then, as it were, hire out production resources to entrepreneurs. The directors of enterprises would then turn into the agents of society. Thus private ownership would gradually become public ownership.

Another new contribution of the Saint-Simonists was that they sought the material basis of the future society within the old society. Socialism, to their mind, should arise as the logical result of the development of production forces. They regarded the capitalist credit banking system as the embryo of the future planned organisation of production. True, these profound ideas of the Saint-Simonists turned later into "credit fantasies" of a petty-bourgeois or openly bourgeois nature. But the classics of Marxism-Leninism regarded the actual idea that socialist society could use the mechanism of large banks created by capitalism for public accounting, control and management of the economy as a brilliant piece of perception.

Like Saint-Simon, his pupils devoted a great deal of attention to the role of science in the development and transformation of society. Scientists and the most talented entrepreneurs were to take over the political and economic management of society. Political management would gradually die out, since in the future society the need for the "management of people" will disappear and only the "management of things" will remain, i.e., production. The Saint-Simonists also sharply criticised the position of science and scientists in the society of their day.

In the works of Saint-Simon and his disciples we do not find a special study of the main categories of political economy. They did not analyse the creation and distribution of value, or the laws of wages, profit and land rent. To a certain extent they were happy with the accepted ideas of bourgeois economy of that period. The main point, however, was that their thought developed in a fundamentally different direction and posed different tasks. Their merit in economic science is that they attacked the basic tenet of the bourgeois classics and the "Say school", namely, that the capitalist system was natural and permanent. Hence the question of the economic laws of this system was put on a completely different plane. Political economy was confronted with a new task: to show how the capitalist mode of production had arisen and developed historically, what were its contradictions, and why and how it was bound to give way to socialism. The Saint-Simonists could not solve this tasks, but the fact that they posed it was a great achievement.

Saint-Simon praised Say for having outlined the subject of political economy as a special science and separated it from politics. Without touching upon this question, his disciples subjected Say and his followers to searching criticism and revealed the apologetic nature of their doctrine clearly. Pointing out that these economists did not try to show how the present property relations had arisen, they said: "True, they claim to show how wealth is formed, distributed and consumed; but they are not concerned to discover whether this wealth, formed by labour, will always be distributed according to birth and consumed to a large extent by the idle." [1]

The period beginning in 1831 is the *fourth* stage and decline of Saint-Simonism. Lacking any firm support within the working class, Saint-Simonism was completely taken aback by the first revolutionary actions of the French proletariat. The religious, sectarian overtones which it acquired in this period divorced it even more from the working class and even from the democratic students. Enfantin became "le Pere" of the Saint-Simonist sect, a strange religious community was founded and special dress introduced, with waistcoats that buttoned down the back. Bitter discord arose within the movement between the various groups of Saint-Simon's followers. The disputes centred on the question of the relations between the sexes and the position of women in the community. In November 1831 Bazard left the sect with a

_____

[1] *Doctrine de Saint-Simon: Exposition*, Bruxelles, 1831, p. 235.

group of supporters. Shortly afterwards the Orleans Government, which came to power after the July Revolution of 1830, instituted legal proceedings against Enfantin and his group, charging them of immoral behaviour and the propagation of dangerous ideas. Enfantin was sentenced to a year in prison. The movement collapsed organisationally, some of its members continuing to preach Saint-Simonism independently and unsuccessfully, some joining other socialist trends, and others turning into respectable bourgeois citizens.

Nevertheless the influence of Saint-Simonism on the future development of socialist ideas in France and, to a certain extent, other countries was extremely great. For all the defects of their religion, the strength of the Saint-Simonists lay in the fact that they had a bold and consistent programme of struggle against bourgeois society.

THE HARD LIFE OF CHARLES FOURIER

"If in Saint-Simon we find a comprehensive breadth of view, by virtue of which almost all the ideas of later Socialists that are not strictly economic are found in him in embryo," wrote Engels, "we find in Fourier a criticism of the existing conditions of society, genuinely French and witty, but not upon that account any the less thorough.... Fourier is not only a critic; his imperturbably serene nature makes him a satirist, and assuredly one of the greatest satirists of all time." [1] Fourier was also the author of many excellent ideas on the organisation of a future socialist society. In one of his early articles Engels said that the value of the Fourier school was its "scientific investigation, sober, unprejudiced, systematic thinking, in short — *social philosophy*".[2] This social philosophy, which was the forerunner of the historical materialism of Marx and Engels, represents Fourier's main contribution to the science of political economy.

Fourier's writings are unique in their way in the social sciences. They are not only scholarly treatises, but also lively pamphlets and incredibly inventive fantasies. Brilliant satire is

---

[1] Karl Marx and Frederick Engles, *Selected Works*, in three volumes, Vol. 3, Moscow, 1973, pp. 121-22.

[2] Karl Marx/Friedrich Engels, *Werke*, Bd. I, Berlin, 1969, S. 483.

combined with strange mysticism, prophetic foresight with almost nonsensical fabrications, broad wise generalisations with tedious regulation of life in the future society. A century and a half has passed since the appearance of Fourier's main works. Life itself has separated the mysticism and groundless fantasy in Fourier's work from his truly brilliant ideas on the transformation of human society.

Charles Fourier was born in 1772 in Besancon. His father, a wealthy merchant, died when the boy was nine. The only son in the family, he would have inherited a considerable portion of his father's wealth and business. But very early Charles Fourier clashed with his environment and family. The cheating and swindling involved in commerce aroused his indignation even as a child.

Fourier was educated at the Besançon Jesuit College. He showed great talent for the sciences, literature and music. On leaving the college he tried to gain admittance to the military engineering school, but was unsuccessful. From then onwards Fourier could extend his knowledge only by reading. There were some serious gaps in his education which made themselves felt in his writing. In particular, he had never made a special study of English and French economists. He became acquainted with their ideas fairly late and from secondhand sources—journalistic articles and conversations. Nor did he ever attempt to analyse economic theories in any detail, but simply rejected their very spirit, regarding them as sheer apologetics of the foul "order of civilisation", i.e., capitalism.

After lengthy disputes and attempts at rebellion the eighteen-year-old Fourier was forced to bow to family pressure and start work as an apprentice in a large trading house in Lyon. He was to spend a considerable part of his life in this industrial town and his socio-economic ideas arose largely from his observations of social relations in Lyon. In 1792, after receiving part of his father's legacy, Fourier opened his own trading business.

Fourier's youth coincided with the revolution. Before this great historical events appear to have had little interest for him, but the fateful year of 1793 wrought a great upheaval in the young merchant's life. During the Lyon uprising against the Jacobin Convent Fourier was in the ranks of the insurgents, and after their surrender—in prison. All his possessions were confiscated. He managed to get out of prison and returned to his native Besançon. The young Fourier was evidently drawn into the counterrevolution not by convictions but by circumstances. Possibly he was made to join the insurgent forces. He soon joined the revolutionary army and served the Republic for eighteen months. Discharged for reasons of health (it was poor all his life), he found employment as a commercial traveller for a trading firm and then became a small trading broker in Lyon. During this period he travelled extensively around France and was able to observe the economic and political life of the age of the Directory and Consulate. He saw that the place of the nobility at the head of the social ladder had been taken by the *nouveau riche*—army suppliers, speculators, stockbrokers and bankers. The new phase which the "order of civilisation" had entered merely engendered new hardship and deprivation for the vast mass of the population.

By the time he was thirty Fourier had reached the firm conclusion that his vocation in life was that of a social reformer. As he relates, this conviction was prompted directly by his reflections on the economic absurdities which he had witnessed. In December 1803 Fourier published in a Lyon newspaper a small article entitled "Harmonie universelle" in which he announced his "remarkable discovery". He wrote that he would reveal (or had already revealed) on the basis of the methods of the natural sciences "the laws of social motion", as other scientists had discovered the "laws of material motion". Fourier's ideas were expounded more fully in a book which was published anonymously in 1808 in Lyon under the title of *Théories des quatre mouvements et des destinées générales.*[1]

For all the strangeness of the form of this work, it contains the bases of Fourier's "societary plan", i.e., his plan for transforming bourgeois society into the future "order of harmony". Unlike philosophers and economists who regarded capitalism as the natural and permanent state of mankind, Fourier announced: "Meanwhile what could be more imperfect than this civilisation which brings with it all the hardships? What more doubtful than its necessity and its future permanence? Is it not probable that it is merely a stage in social

---

[1] Fourier believed that in order to explain the laws of nature and mankind it was essential to study four types of motion, namely: material, organic, animal and social. Similar examples of dubious systematisation and classification, in which Fourier liked to indulge, abound in his writings.

development?"[1] "The Societary Order ... will succeed civilised incoherence ..."[2]

Fourier's book was barely noticed, but this did not dampen his enthusiasm. He continued to develop his ideas. His circumstances improved somewhat when he obtained a governmental post in 1811 and received a small pension from his mother's will in 1812. In 1816-1822 he lived in the provinces, not far from Lyon. He began to have followers. For the first time in his life he was able to study in a comparatively peaceful atmosphere. The fruit of this study was an extensive work published in Paris in 1822 under the title *Traité de l'association domestique et agricole*. In the posthumous collections of Fourier's works this book is published as the *Théorie de l'unité universelle*.

Fourier attempted to elaborate and substantiate in detail the organisation of working associations, which he called "phalanxes". The building in which the phalanxes were to live, work and enjoy their leisure was called a *phalanstere*. Fourier hoped that experimental phalanxes would be established immediately, without any change in the existing social order. When he lived in Paris he used to wait at home naively at a stated hour to receive rich donators on whose money a phalanstere could be built. Naturally no such rich donators appeared.

Fourier was again compelled to earn his living by office work in Paris and Lyon. Only in 1828 did he succeed in freeing himself from this repellent dependence thanks to the material assistance of friends and followers. He retired to Besançon and completed a book on which he had been working for several years. This book, the *Neouveau Monde industriel et sociétaire* (1829), is his finest work. By then a quarter of a century had passed since his first literary essays. The development of capitalism had provided a vast amount of new material for his criticism. At the same time Fourier had developed his views on the future society and expounded them in a more popular form, without his earlier mysticism.

The latter years of his life were spent in Paris. He continued to work hard, pedantically fulfilling his daily quota. The result of his labours was yet another large book, a series of articles in the various Fourierist journals and a large number of

[1]
[2] *Oeuvres complètes de Charles Fourier*, t. I, Paris, 1846, p. 4.
[2] Ibid., p. 9.

354

manuscripts published after his death. In these works he examines a broad range of social, economic, moral, ethical, pedagogical and other problems. His mind worked incessantly and with great creative energy, although his health had greatly deteriorated. Charles Fourier died in Paris in October 1837.

By 1830 there already existed a fairly considerable Fourierist movement, but Fourier himself was a very solitary person in his latter years. He became increasingly estranged from many of his pupils who sought to dilute his bold doctrine into a tame, reformist one. Many found it difficult to tolerate his character in which old age and illness had intensified his tendency to be suspicious, mistrustful and stubborn.

From the point of view of bourgeois commonsense Fourier, like Saint-Simon, was, of course, almost a madman. Wits even punned with the surnames of the great Utopians (saint, fou—madman). But he was one of the madmen of whom Béranger said:

> Messieurs, lorsqu'en vain natre sphère
> Du bonheur chercher le chemin,
> Honneur au fou qui ferait faire
> Un rêve heureux au genre humain.[1]

From Charles Fourier's point of view the world in which he lived and worked was a mad one.

THIS MAD WORLD

Fourier made a brilliant attempt to represent the historical logic of the development of human society. He depicts the history of mankind from its appearance on earth up to the future society of harmony as follows[2]:

Periods preceding industry	1. Primitive, called Eden.
	2. Savagery or inertia
Fragmented, fraudulent, repugnant industry	3. Patriarchate, small-scale industry
	4. Barbarism, medium-scale industry
	5. Civilisation, large-scale industry

---

[1] P.-J. Béranger, *Oeuvres choisies*, Moscou, 1956, p. 136.

[2] *Oeuvres complètes de Charles Fourier*, t. 6, Paris, 1848, p. XI.

| *Societary,* | *true,* | *attractive* | 6. Guarantism, semi-associa- |
| *industry* | | | tion |

6. Guarantism, semi-association
7. Sociantism, simple association
8. Harmonism, composite association

Fourier divides the period of civilisation into four phases. The first two are, basically, the slave-owning and feudal orders, and the third is the free-competition capitalism of Fourier's day.

As we see, Fourier not only defined the main stages of the development of human society, but linked them with the state of production at each of these stages. In so doing he paved the way for the concept of socio-economic formations introduced by Marx. Engels wrote that Fourier's greatness showed itself most clearly in his understanding of the history of society.

With regard to the fourth phase of civilisation, its treatment is one of Fourier's finest predictions: he foresaw in somewhat strange form the transition of capitalism to the monopoly stage, which he called trading feudalism. Showing a remarkable talent for dialectic thought, Fourier proved that free competition turns logically into its own opposite and leads to monopoly, which he pictured primarily in the form of the monopolisation of trade and banking by the "new feudal lords".

Fourier presented capitalism, which he called "the world inside out", with a bill of indictment which was unparalleled at that time in its boldness and depth and partially retains its significance even in our day. But this was Fourier's strength and weakness. In depicting capitalism's crimes, he could not discover their basic cause for he did not have a clear understanding of production relations and the class structure of bourgeois society. Like Saint-Simon, Fourier thought that entrepreneurs and hired workers were the only working class.[1] Hence his naive idealistic belief in the possibility of the peaceful transformation of society thanks to reason and, in particular, the acceptance of his doctrine by the powers-that-be.

---

[1] True, he included factory owners in the group of "social parasites", but only to the extent that "a good half" of them produced articles of poor quality and cheated society and the state.

Forced to engage in commerce in order to earn a living, Fourier had a pathological hatred of capitalist trade. Hundreds of pages in his works are devoted to exposing the vices, tricks and meanness of trade and traders. Trading and monetary capital were regarded by him as the main cause of exploitation and parasitism in bourgeois society. Fourier did not see that trading capital was only another form of industrial capital which invariably plays a subordinate role under capitalism, for all its independence and importance.

Fourier describes capitalist production as antisocial, disconnected and fragmented. In what sense? The sole aim of bourgeois production is the entrepreneur's profit and not the satisfaction of society's requirements. Therefore antagonism of interests between individual producers of commodities and society is a constant feature of capitalism. Competition between entrepreneurs does not serve the interests of society, as economists maintain, but rather destroys it by creating production anarchy, chaos and an atmosphere of each man for himself. The pursuit of profit and competition give rise to monstrous exploitation of hired workers. The example of England with its huge factories in which adults and children work for a miserable pittance shows where capitalism is heading.

Fourier saw the growing gulf between wealth and poverty, the indigence amid plenty, as important proof of the eventual collapse of bourgeois political economy with its principle of free competition. Sismondi, he writes, at least recognised these facts and in so doing took "the first step towards a frank analysis", but went no further than "semirecognition". Say, however, in arguing with him, sought to save the authority of political economy, but did not manage to do so. The following is one of Fourier's many caustic remarks about economists: "How many other parasites there are among sophists, beginning with economists, the rant against the body of parasites whose banner they bear." [1]

Labour, its organisation and productivity, this is what determines the structure and well-being of society in the final analysis. Realising this, Fourier paints a remarkable picture of the way in which labour is misappropriated and enslaved under capitalism. The "order of civilisation" has turned labour

---

[1] Charles Fourier, *Oeuvres choisis*, Paris, 1890, pp. 64-65.

from the normal activity of man, a source of joy, into a curse and a bane. In this society everyone who is able to do so gets out of working by fair means or foul. The labour of the small-scale proprietor—the peasant, craftsman, or even entrepreneur—is a constant struggle with competitors, insecurity and dependence. But incomparably more difficult is the labour of the hired worker, labour that is forced and incapable of yielding any satisfaction. With the growth of production, with its concentration and subordination to large capital, this type of labour becomes increasingly predominant.

In a number of his early works Marx developed the concept of alienation. This is the alienation of man in a capitalist society from the results of his labour and the destiny of society, his transformation into a wretched appendage of industrial Moloch. Here we undoubtedly find traces of Fourier's idea, and Marx directly links the problem of alienation with Fourier's name in one passage.[1]

Fourier by no means castigates only the economic defects of capitalism, but also its politics, morals, culture and educational system. He wrote particularly profusely and bitterly about the way in which capitalism corrupts the natural, human relations between the sexes and puts women in an inferior, oppressed position.

Let us now return to the table showing the periods of social development as Fourier saw them. Between civilisation and harmonism he has put two transitional periods which he called *guarantism* and *sociantism*. He frequently stated that his aim was not a few partial reforms of the order of civilisation but the destruction of this order and the creation of a fundamentally different society. Yet since Fourier excluded the revolutionary path of transition and realised the enormous difficulties involved, he was willing to compromise and granted that the people of civilisation would need a more or less prolonged period for the creation of harmonism.

The basic features of the first transition period—guarantism—he outlined as follows. Private ownership would not change substantially, but would be subordinated to collective interests and control. There would arise separate associations of groups of families for communal labour, and also meals, leisure, etc. In these associations labour would gradually lose

---

[1] Karl Marx and Frederick Engels, *Collected Works*, Vol. III, pp. 293-94.

the features of capitalist hired labour. Economic inequality would remain. Competition is controlled by society and becomes fair and simple. Great social projects are undertaken, in particular, the abolition of slums, and towns are replanned. Like all Fourier's utopias, guarantism does not require extensive changes in the political structure. It can begin under an absolute or constitutional monarchy, a republic or any other order.

Fourier believed that within the actual order of civilisation certain prerequisites of guarantism were already developing, that the "genius of the order of civilisation" was moving in this direction. Only people's delusions, and particularly the influence of the bourgeois social sciences, prevented the transition to guarantism. On the other hand, once guarantism was established it would soon convince mankind of the advantages of the new social system and prepare it for the order of full association.

But Fourier's guarantism can be seen in a different way: as system of reforms to improve capitalism and make it "tolerable" and not as the preparation for its abolition. Then Fourier's doctrine turns into commonplace reformism and takes its place, as it were, with the ideas that engendered the modern conceptions and practice of the bourgeois "welfare state". Fourier himself would have protested against such an interpretation of his ideas. However many of his followers have done precisely this.

In the 1830s and, to a lesser extent, the 1840s Fourierism was the main socialist trend in France. It proved to be more vital than Saint-Simonism for it was free from the latter's religious, sectarian character and advanced more immediate and realistic ideals, particularly the producer-consumer cooperatives in the form of phalanxes. Fourier's doctrine had little support among the French working class, however, and was widespread mainly among the young intellectuals.

The revolution of 1848 drove the Fourierists onto the arena of political action, where they adopted a position close to petty-bourgeois democracy. They did not support the popular June rising and a year later sought to challenge the government of Louis Bonaparte, but were easily repressed. The few Fourierists who remained in France later engaged in cooperative activity. The historical role of Fourierism was exhausted. Whereas Fourier, albeit unconsciously, had mainly expressed the interests of the working class, his followers adopted the standpoint of the petty and middle bourgeoisie.

The Manifesto of the Communist Party, which announced the appearance on the historical arena of scientific communism, a new revolutionary world outlook and a proletarian party, simultaneously sounded the death knell for utopian socialism and, in particular, Fourierism. Marx and Engels wrote: "The significance of Critical-Utopian Socialism and Communism bears an inverse relation to historical development. In proportion as the modern class struggle develops and takes definite shape, this fantastic standing apart from the contest, these fantastic attacks on it, lose all practical value and all theoretical justification. Therefore, although the originators of these systems were, in many respects, revolutionary, their disciples have, in every case, formed mere reactionary sects. They hold fast by the original views of their masters, in opposition to the progressive historical development of the proletariat. They, therefore, endeavour, and that consistently, to deaden the class struggle and to reconcile the class antagonisms. They still dream of experimental realisation of their social Utopias, of founding isolated 'phalansteres', and to realise all these castles in the air, they are compelled to appeal to the feelings and purses of the bourgeois." [1]

THE SHAPE OF THINGS TO COME

Saint-Simon left a brilliant general outline of the future social order, and Fourier worked out its details with great perception. The two utopias differed from each other in many respects, but had one most important feature in common: they depicted a socialist society in which private ownership and unearned income still existed. In both systems private ownership was to change its nature radically, however, and be subordinated to the interests of the collective, and unearned income was gradually to acquire the features of earned income.

Today the utopias of Saint-Simon and Fourier are both valuable in their own way. In Saint-Simon and his disciples the

---

[1] Karl Marx and Frederick Engels, *Selected Works*, in three volumes, Vol. I, pp. 135-36.

idea of a centrally planned national economy and system of managing it on collective principles is particularly interesting. In Fourier — the analysis of the organisation of labour and life in the separate cells of a socialist society.

Let us examine the economic aspect of Fourier's utopia. His phalanx is a producer-consumer association combining the features of the commune with those of the ordinary joint-stock company. Fourier envisaged that the number of members of the phalanx engaged in various work would total, together with their children, from 1,500 to 2,000. He believed that such a collective would possess the necessary variety of human character for optimal distribution of labour in terms of people's inclinations and useful results. The phalanx would combine agricultural and industrial production with a predominance of the former. Fourier pictured industry as a group of comparatively small but highly productive workshops. He firmly rejected the factory system as the product of the order of civilisation.

The phalanx would get its initial reserve of means of production from contributions by shareholders. Therefore it had to include capitalists. Poor people could also be members of the phalanx and need not be shareholders initially, in which case they would make their contribution in the form of labour. Ownership of shares would be private. There would be inequality of property in the phalanx. When a capitalist became a member of it, however, he would cease to be a capitalist in the old sense. The general atmosphere of creative labour would draw him into the process of direct production. If he possessed the talent of an administrator, engineer, or scientist, society would use his labour in this capacity. If not, he would work in a "series" (brigade) of his choice. But since the children of rich and poor would be educated in the same healthy environment, these differences would be erased in subsequent generations. Large shareholders would have certain privileges in the administration of the phalanx. But they could not have a majority in the governing body, and in any case the role of this body was to be extremely limited.

Fourier paid particular attention to the organisation of social labour. He hoped to abolish the negative aspects of capitalist distribution of labour by means of frequent switching from one type of labour to another. Each person would be guaranteed a certain minimum means of subsistence as a result of which his labour would cease to be compulsory and become the expression of free activity. Entirely new stimuli to labour would appear: emulation, social vocation, the joy of creativity.

The wealth and income of the society would grow rapidly, due mainly to an increase in labour productivity. Moreover, parasitism would disappear and everyone would work. Finally, the phalanx would avoid the numerous losses and unproductive expenditure inevitable in the old system. According to Fourier, the society of the future would be a real society of plenty, and also a healthy, natural and joyful one. Asceticism, which is frequently associated with ideas of future societies, was entirely alien to Fourier.

There would be no hired labour and no wages in the phalanx. The distribution of the product of labour (in monetary form) would be effected by giving phalanx members a special type of dividend according to labour, capital and talent. The whole net income would be divided into three parts: 5/12 to "active participants in labour"; 4/12 to the owners of shares, 3/12 to people with "theoretical and practical knowledge". Since each member of the phalanx would generally belong to two of these categories, sometimes all three, his income would be made up of different forms. Payment for the labour of each phalanx member would vary depending on its social value, pleasant or unpleasant nature. However the payment of ordinary (mainly physical) labour would be more or less equal thanks to the participation of members in various "labour series": if, for example, a person received slightly less than average as a gardener, he would get more than average as a groom or pig-tender.

Fourier hoped to increase the actual portion of labour in distribution at the expense of capital, in particular its tendency, by means of introducing a differentiated dividend for shares of various types. He proposed paying a high dividend for "workers' shares", which would be purchased in a limited quantity out of small savings, and a far lower one for the ordinary shares of the capitalists. By such methods Fourier sought to reconcile his principle of inequality, which he thought would stimulate the rapid development and flourishing of society, with the ideals of universal prosperity and priority of earned income equally dear to his heart. What he wanted was not to abolish private ownership, but to turn all the members of society into proprietors and thereby deprive private ownership of its exploitatory character and disastrous social consequences. He hoped that in this way class antagonisms would soon disappear and the classes would draw together and merge.

The monetary incomes of phalanx members would be realised in goods and services through trade which, however, would be entirely in the hands of the associations. The organisation, acting on behalf of the phalanx, would also trade with other phalanxes. Social arbitrators would fix the prices at which commodities were to be sold retail.

Fourier regarded the rational organisation of consumption as a most important task of the future society. Here, too, he was faced with the difficult task of combining inequality with collectivism. He sought to solve this by recommending the abolition of private housekeeping and its replacement by public catering and services organised in various categories depending on a person's means. Personal luxury would become pointless and ridiculous. It would be replaced by the luxury of public buildings, entertainments and festivals. This would greatly mitigate inequality in personal consumption. Incidentally, the latter would become healthy, sensible, economic and also more egalitarian. For example, even the richest members would not have more than three rooms.

Considerable attention in Fourier's utopia is devoted to the question of the development of man in the future society, his psychology, behaviour and morals. Hundreds of pages in the great utopist's writings deal with relations between the sexes, the upbringing of children, the organisation of leisure, and the role of science and the arts.

Fourier examined society in far less detail as the association of a number of phalanxes. He ignored the state almost completely, which later enabled the anarchists to take over some of his ideas. At least there was intensive economic contact and exchange between Fourier's phalanxes: an extensive division of labour exists between them.

Fourier's system is full of contradictions and obvious gaps. From the purely economic point of view a great deal in the phalanx remains unclear and dubious, despite his attempts to foresee and regulate everything. What is the nature and scale of the commodity-money relations within the phalanx? How do its subdivisions exchange the products of their labour, in particular, how are raw materials and semifinished products transferred to the subsequent stages? If there is no buying and selling, and only centralised accounting (as Fourier gives us to believe), why does the phalanx need the trading commodity-exchange which he describes in detail?

It is unclear how the public consumption funds are formed which are to play a great role in the phalanx (schools, theatres, libraries, expenditure on public festivities, etc.). There appear to be no allocations from the total income for these things and no taxation of private incomes. There is just a hint that the rich will donate generously towards public projects.

Even more important is the question of accumulation and its social aspects. Since no allocations are provided from the total income for capital investment, accumulation fund can evidently only be formed from the individual savings of phalanx members, a form of which could be the purchase of shares. But capitalists can save far more from their high incomes (and with the same level of consumption) than other phalanx members.

Therefore the tendency towards concentration of capital and income is bound to operate. Possibly Fourier proposed the differentiation of shares mentioned above because he feared this. But at the same time, concerned that the phalanx should be attractive to capitalists, he envisaged the possibility of owning the shares of "other" phalanxes. Most likely, this system would have engendered capitalism and real capitalists.

These and many other defects of Fourier's system compel one to draw the following two main conclusions.

Firstly, utopian socialism, by virtue of the historical conditions in which it emerged, could not rid itself of petty-bourgeois illusions and be consistent in its plans for the socialist transformation of society.

Secondly, all attempts to prescribe a certain method of action and behaviour for the people of the future and to regulate their life in detail are doomed to failure.

Yet it is not the illusions and blunders that we see primarily in Fourier's works. His genius consists in the fact that, basing his argument on his analysis of capitalism, he showed a number of true laws of socialist society. His views on the organisation of labour, the transformation of labour into a natural reguirement of man, and emulation are particularly remarkable. Fourier raised the problem of abolishing the distinction between physical and mental labour. His ideas on the rationalisation of consumption, the extension of the sphere of public services, the liberation of women from household drudgery, the freedom and beauty of love in the socialist age, and the inculcation of a proper attitude towards work in the younger generation still retain their significance today.

CHAPTER XIX

ROBERT OWEN
AND EARLY ENGLISH SOCIALISM

"In the drawing room was a small, frail old man, with hair as white as snow, a remarkably kind face and a clear, bright gentle eyes — those blue, childlike eyes that people keep into old age as the reflection of great kindness.

"The daughters of the house rushed up to the white haired old man; they were obviously acquainted.

"I stopped at the doors into the garden.

"'You couldn't have come at a better time,' their mother said, holding out her hand to the old man, 'today I have something to entertain you. Allow me to introduce you to our Russian friend. I think,' she added addressing me, 'you will enjoy meeting one of *your patriarchs*.'

"'Robert Owen,' said the old man, smiling genially. 'Very pleased to meet you.'

"I took his hand with a feeling of filial respect; if I had been younger, I might have got down on my knees and asked the old man to place his hands on me ....

"'I expect great things of your country,' Owen said to me 'the way is clear there, your priests are not so powerful prejudices not so strong ... and the strength there ... the strength!'"[1]

---

[1] A. I. Herzen, *Collected Works*, Vol. XI, Moscow, 1957, pp. 206-07 (Russian).

This is how Herzen describes his meeting with Owen in 1852, when the latter was over eighty years old. It is characteristic that Marx, in speaking of Saint-Simon, Fourier and Owen, uses the same word "patriarchs" which we find in Herzen.

Naturally the view of Herzen, who himself preached utopian peasant socialism, was substantially different. But for both Marx and Herzen Owen was one of the patriarchs of socialism.

THE MAN WITH THE BIG HEART

Robert Owen was born in 1771 in the small town of New-town (Wales), the son of a shopkeeper and later postmaster. At the age of seven he was already being used by the local schoolmaster as his assistant, but two years later his schooling ceased. With forty shillings in his pocket Owen set off to seek his fortune in the big towns. He served as an apprentice and shop assistant in textile shops in Stamford, London and Manchester. His only reading was done at spare moments. Like Fourier, Owen did not receive a systematic education, but was free of many of the prejudices and dogmas of orthodox scholarship.

At that time Manchester was the centre of the industrial revolution. The cotton industry developed here particularly intensively. An energetic and businesslike young man like Owen soon had the opportunity to make his way in the world. At first he borrowed money from his brother and with a partner opened up a small workshop for making spinning machines which were being rapidly introduced into the industry at that time. Then he set up his own small spinning shop where he worked with two or three other men. At twenty he became manager and then co-owner of a large textile factory.

When in Scotland on the firm's business, Owen made the acquaintance of the daughter of a large factory owner David Dale, the owner of a textile works in the settlement of New Lanark near Glasgow. His marriage to Miss Dale led to Owen moving to New Lanark in 1799 where he became co-owner (with several Manchester capitalists) and manager of his father-in-law's former factory. As Owen writes in his autobiography, he had already thought out his industrial and social experiment and arrived in New Lanark with a definite plan. Engels says: "At this juncture there came forward as a reformer a manufacturer 29 years old—a man of almost sublime, childlike simplicity of character, and at the same time one of the few born leaders of men."[1]

Owen did not at that time challenge either private ownership or the capitalist factory system. But he made it his task to prove, and did in fact do so, that the monstrous hired slavery and oppression of workers was by no means a necessary condition of efficient production and high profits. He simply created for workers reasonable working and living conditions and the result, both in terms of increased labour productivity and improved social health, was quite amazing.

Simply! But one must realise how much work, persistence, conviction and courage this required from Owen and his few helpers. The working day in New Lanark was reduced to ten and a half hours (as opposed to thirteen or fourteen in other factories), wages were also paid during periods when crises forced the factory to close down. Pensions were introduced for the aged and mutual benefit was organised. Owen built reasonable homes for the workers at low rents. Workers were able to purchase goods retail at reduced but profitable prices.

In particular, Owen did a great deal for children, giving them lighter work in the factory, and setting up a school which took infants from the age of two. The school served as a prototype for subsequent kindergartens. This concern for children corresponded to the main principle which Owen borrowed from the 18th-century philosophers: man is what his environment makes him; to make him better one must change the environment in which he grows up.

Owen was forced to wage a constant struggle with his partners who were annoyed by these ideas which they regarded as absurd, and by the even more absurd expenditure and demanded that all the profits should go to the shareholders. In 1813 he managed to find new partners who agreed to receive a fixed income of 5 per cent of the capital and gave Owen complete freedom of action in everything else. By then Owen's name was widely known and New Lanark had begun to attract crowds of visitors. Owen found patrons in the highest

---

[1] Karl Marx and Frederick Engels, *Selected Works*, in three volumes, Vol. p. 123.

London circles: his peaceful philanthropic activity hardly worried anyone yet and seemed to many a good way of solving acute social problems. Owen's first book *A New View of Society, or Essay on the Principles of the Formation of the Human Character* (1813) was given a cordial reception since its ideas did not go far beyond cautious reformism, particularly in the sphere of education.

But Owen became increasingly less satisfied with philanthropy. He realised that although it achieved something it was incapable of solving the basic economic and social questions of the capitalist factory system. He subsequently wrote: "In a few years I had accomplished for this population as much as such a manufacturing system would admit of, and although the poor work-people were content, and, by contrast with other manufacturing establishments and all other work-people under this old system, deemed themselves much better treated and cared for, and were highly satisfied, yet I knew it was a miserable existence, compared with that which, with the immense means at the control of all governments, might now be created for every population over the world."[1]

The direct stimulus which turned Owen from a philanthropic capitalist into a preacher of communism was the discussions of 1815-1817 connected with the deterioration of England's economic position and the growth of unemployment and poverty. Owen presented a government committee with his plan to ease these difficulties by setting up cooperative settlements for the poor where they would work communally without capitalist entrepreneurs. His ideas met with misunderstanding and indignation. Owen turned to the public at large. In several speeches given in London in August 1817 to considerable gatherings of people he expounded his plan for the first time. He subsequently continued to develop and extend it. Gradually the modest project connected with a concrete problem grew into a comprehensive system for the reorganisation of society on communist principles. Owen planned this reorganisation through labour cooperative communities, somewhat reminiscent of Fourier's phalanxes, but based on consistently communist principles. He strongly attacked the three pillars of the old society, which stood in the

---

[1] R. Owen, *The Revolution in the Mind and Practice of the Human Race*, London, 1850, pp. 16-17.

way of this peaceful revolution: private ownership, religion, and the existing form of the family. Owen expressed his views most fully in his *Report to the County of Lanark* published in 1821.

To attack the foundations of bourgeois society demanded great civic courage from Owen. He knew that he would arouse the anger of powerful forces and interests, but this did not stop him. With whole-hearted faith in his cause he embarked on the path which he was to follow to the end of his days. From 1817 to 1824 Owen travelled all over Great Britain, went abroad, gave many speeches and wrote a large number of articles and pamphlets, constantly preaching his cause. He believed that the powers-that-be and the rich would soon realise the beneficial nature of his plan for society. In these and subsequent years Owen constantly offered it to the English Government and the American presidents, Paris bankers and the Russian tsar Alexander I. All his efforts were in vain, although there were influential people who supported his plans to varying degrees.

Disillusioned with English "educated society", lacking any links with the working-class movement of those years and having lost even his influence in New Lanark, Owen and his sons left for America. He bought a plot of land and founded in 1825 the community of New Harmony, the charter of which was based on the principles of egalitarian communism. His practical cast of mind and experience helped him to avoid many of the mistakes made by organisers of other similar communities. Nevertheless this enterprise, which devoured almost all Owen's fortune, ended in failure. In 1829 he returned to Britain. Setting aside money for his children (seven in all), Owen proceeded to lead a very frugal existence.

By now he was about sixty. For many this would have been the end of an active life, a peaceful retirement. Owen, however, accomplished in the 1830s that which the other utopian socialists had never been able to do: he found his place in the broad working-class movement.

These years witnessed a rapid growth of producer and consumer cooperatives uniting craftsmen and also, to a lesser extent, factory workers. Owen soon found himself at the head of the cooperative movement in England. In 1832 he organised the Equitable Labour Exchange. This exchange accepted goods (from both cooperatives and other sellers) according to an estimate based on expenditure of labour and sold other goods for "labour money". Eventually the exchange went bankrupt and Owen was forced to pay its debts from his own money. He was also one of the pioneers of another working-class movement which was destined to play a great role — the trade union movement. In 1833-1834 he organised an attempt to create the first consolidated national trade union with half a million members. Poor organisation, lack of funds and the opposition of factory owners who had the support of the government led to the collapse of the union. Owen's splendid schemes were doomed to failure, but none of them was in vain.

Owen was not an easy person to get on with. His absolute conviction that he was right often made him stubborn and intolerant. His thirty years in New Lanark and New Harmony made him accustomed to manage, not to collaborate. He became unresponsive to new ideas. The charm of ardent humanism combined with efficiency, which so distinguished Owen in his youth and middle age and attracted people to him, gave way somewhat to an obtrusive monotony of speech and thought. Retaining great mental clarity to the very end, he did not avoid certain eccentricities of old age. In the latter years of his life Owen took up spiritualism and showed an interest in mysticism. But he retained the charm of kindness which Herzen noted.

After 1834 Owen ceased to play an important role in society, although he continued to write a great deal, published journals, took part in the organisation of yet another community and tirelessly preached his views. His followers formed a narrow sect and frequently supported fairly reactionary attitudes.

In the autumn of 1858 Owen, now 87 years of age, travelled to Liverpool and felt ill on the rostrum at a meeting there. He spent several days in bed and suddenly decided to go to his native town of Newtown where he had not been since childhood. It was there that he died in November 1858.

OWEN AND POLITICAL ECONOMY

Owen's attitude to political economy was different from that of Saint-Simon and particularly Fourier. He did not reject the science but, on the contrary, asserted that his plan was based on its principles, having in mind the works of Smith and Ricardo. Engels writes: "The entire communism of Owen, so far as it engages in polemics on economic questions, is based on Ricardo." [1] Owen was the first to draw anticapitalist conclusions from the principles of the classical school.

Incidentally, Owen borrowed from bourgeois classical political economy only that which he needed for his system, ignoring and even openly rejecting a great deal more. He touches upon economic questions in his works, but does not deal with them specifically. His main economic ideas are contained in *The Report to the County of Lanark.* Owen was a practical man and tried to put his economic ideas into practice: at first in New Lanark, then in America, and, finally, in the cooperative movement and the Equitable Labour Exchange.

At the base of Owen's views lies Ricardo's labour theory of value: labour is the creator and measure of value; the exchange of commodities should take place according to labour. But unlike Ricardo he believes that under capitalism exchange does not take place according to labour. In his opinion, exchange according to labour presupposes that the worker receives the full value of the commodity produced by him. In fact he receives nothing of the sort.

Yet in order to explain the violation of the "just" law of value Owen turns to ideas which are somewhat reminiscent of Boisguillebert: everything is the fault of money, that artificial measure which has ousted the natural measure — labour.

Owen's political economy is normative in the extreme: he uses all these ideas only to argue the measure which he is proposing: the introduction of the labour unit as the measure of value, the exchange of commodities on the basis of this measure, and the abolition of the use of money. This, to his mind, would solve society's most difficult problems. The worker would receive a just reward for his labour. Since the reward received by workers would correspond to the true value of commodities, overproduction and crises would become impossible. Such a reform would benefit not only the workers, but also the landowners and capitalists: it is "...only

---

[1] Karl Marx, *Capital,* Vol. II, pp. 13-14.

from labour liberally remunerated, that high profits can be paid for agricultural and manufactured products".[1]

Precisely how does money turn "fair" exchange into sheer deception? What determines prices in the final analysis, if commodities are not exchanged according to the amount of labour contained in each of them? Where will the incomes of the capitalist and landowner come from, if the worker receives the whole value of the product created by his labour? One could put such questions to Owen endlessly and he would not have anything like an answer to them.

Owen's economic views would not be in any way superior to petty-bourgeois illusions about abolishing capitalist defects by reforms in the sphere of circulation alone, particularly the abolition of money, were it not for the fact that are indissolubly linked with his plan for the radical transformation of society, including production relations. It transpires that fair exchange according to labour value requires the abolition of the capitalist system! Only in a future society without private ownership of the instruments and means of production will the worker give his labour "for its real value". In such a case the question of capitalists and landowners does not arise. They gain from the reorganisation of society not as capitalists and landowners but as *people*.

Naturally, the historical nature of commodity production and the law of value were quite unclear to Owen. For him they were just as permanent and natural as for Ricardo. But Ricardo proceeded from this to conclude that capitalism was permanent and natural, whereas Owen draws the opposite conclusion: that it is "temporary" and "unnatural". For Owen could not accept Ricardo's historical pessimism either, which he connected, not without justification, with the influence of Malthus and his population theory. Owen attacked this theory. Quoting statistics about the real and potential growth of production, agriculture in particular, he maintained that human poverty was the fault of the social order, not of nature.

OWEN'S COMMUNISM

Marx and Engels distinguished Owen's utopia from other utopias of the period, emphasising its *communist* character. In

---

[1] R. C. Owen, *The New Existence of Man upon the Earth*, Part III, London, 1854, p. XV.

Marx we read: "During the Ricardian period of political economy its antithesis, communism (Owen) and socialism (Fourier, St. Simon ...) [comes] also [into being]."[1] And in Engels: "His advance in the direction of communism was the turning-point in Owen's life."[2]

As we have seen, the systems of Saint-Simon and Fourier were not fully socialist. Their future society retained private ownership with this or that limitation, and also capitalists who disposed in some way or other of the means of production and received an income on capital. Owen's system is not only consistently socialist in character, but also depicts the second, higher phase of communism, in which private ownership and all class distinctions, are totally abolished, everybody should work and, on the basis of the growth of production forces, distribution is according to need. Owen's utopia is completely free from any religious or mystical overtones. It is remarkable for its realism, sometimes even its businesslike practical nature. This does not make Owen's system any the less utopian of course. Like Saint-Simon and Fourier, he did not see the real paths leading to communist society.

The important point is this, however. Owen's example shows that communist ideals have grown out of the real conditions of the more developed society which England was at the beginning of the 19th century. Owen is free of many of the petty-bourgeois illusions of the French socialists. He does not doubt the exploitatory nature of the capitalist class and the need for the total abolition of capitalist private ownership. Basing himself on the factory system, he saw far more clearly the concrete ways of achieving a growth in labour productivity which would make possible real abundance and distribution in accordance with need. Owen's communism is very different from and superior to the projects for crude, ascetically egalitarian "barracks" communism which appear periodically — unfortunately even in the present day. He dreamt of a society in which, together with the tremendous growth of production and wealth, man himself would develop harmoniously, in which the value of the human individual would grow immeasurably. Owen was one of the first to show that, in spite

---

[1] Karl Marx, *Theories of Surplus-Value*, Part III, p. 238.
[2] Karl Marx and Frederick Engles, *Selected Works*, in three volumes, Vol. 3, p. 125.

of the slander of bourgeois hirelings, *communism and humanism are not mutually exclusive concepts. On the contrary, true humanism flourishes in a truly communist society.*

The basic unit of communist society in Owen's scheme is a small cooperative community, preferably with 800 to 1,200 members. There is no private ownership or classes whatsoever in the communities. The only distinction which could create a certain inequality in labour and distribution is "that of age or experience". Owen hardly describes at all the mechanism of distribution, making (again like Fourier) a few vague remarks about the exchange of products according to labour within the community and limiting himself to the instruction that given a large surplus "each may be freely permitted to receive from the general store of the community whatever they may require".

Owen pays considerable attention to the development of the new man, linking a change in psychology primarily with two material factors — the growth of wealth and the satisfaction of requirements. As a result of these "every desire for individual accumulation will be extinguished. To them individual accumulation of wealth will appear as irrational as to bottle up or store water in situations where there is more of this invaluable fluid than all can consume".[1]

Going beyond the limits of the community, Owen sought to depict a society consisting of a large number of such units. There is a considerable division of labour between them and mutual exchange is carried out on the basis of labour value. For the purpose of this exchange a union of communities issues special paper labour money[2] against goods at stores. Owen imagined that this new society would coexist for a certain time with the "old society" and its state, pay the latter taxes and sell the old society commodities for ordinary money.

Owen ignored the most important question of how and from whom the communities would receive the initial means of production, including land. He seems to have thought naively that the means of production would be handed over to the communities gratuitously by the state or some enlightened capitalists. But in another passage he says more realistically that the members of the community will have to "pay the interest of the capital requisite to put their labour in activity".

---

[1] R. Owen, *The New Existence of Man upon the Earth*, Part III, p. XXXIV.

[2] Owen's Equitable Labour Exchange did, in fact, issue such money.

So the communities will not be able to do without capitalists after all. At best they could retain entrepreneurial income since they would be in charge of production, but they would have to give up loan interest.

Owen's system is utopian and hence full of contradictions and inconsistencies. We are aware of the main reason for this: the immaturity of class relations made it impossible for the utopists to work out a real way of reorganising society. This could not be done without an understanding of the historic mission of the working class, of the need for and inevitability of socialist revolution. It was objectively impossible for Owen and the other utopists to understand this.

Yet without their mistakes, just as without their achievements, the progress in the social sciences which led to the emergence of Marxism in Owen's lifetime would also have been impossible.

WORKING-CLASS THINKERS

England's economic difficulties after the Napoleonic Wars, the first Factory Acts and trade unions, the establishment of Ricardianism, Owen's agitation—this was the socio-economic and ideological background for the people who first gave conscious expression in political economy to the interests of the working class. They were not consistent and to a great extent fell back on petty-bourgeois reformist socialism. Nevertheless their services are great. These English socialists of the 1820s and 1830s are a most important link between classical political economy and utopian socialism, on the one hand, and the scientific socialism of Marx and Engels, on the other.

In the history of political economy their role is determined by the fact that, unlike the bourgeois "heirs" of Smith and Ricardo, they tried to use their doctrines for progressive, antibourgeois ends.

They were sometimes economists to a greater extent than Owen and sought to develop the Ricardian system in more strictly scientific forms, although their writings were often directly devoted to the concrete tasks of the working-class movement of those years. The most distinguished of this group of Ricardian socialists (as they are sometimes called) were

William Thompson, John Gray and John Francis Bray. A particularly important role was played by Thomas Hodgskin who produced some excellent ideas on the nature of capital, the relations between capital and labour, and the tendencies of the rate of profit under capitalism.

When Thomas Hodgskin died not a single London newspaper mentioned his name. Nor did he find a place in the *Dictionary of National Biography*, that monumental work of the Victorian age, among thousands of eminent Britishers. Hodgskin's works were not republished, and by the end of the century he had sunk into obscurity. He was "rediscovered" largely thanks to Marx who pointed out the importance of his writings for the development of socialist ideas, particularly political economy. It was only after this that Labour theoreticians and historians began to mention him. The Webbs even referred to Marx as "Hodgskin's illustrious disciple". In the same way Marx might be called the "disciple" of Hegel, Ricardo, Owen and many other thinkers. But precisely because of this such a statement is meaningless.

Hodgskin was born in 1787 and came from the family of a military servant. He was educated at a naval college and served in the navy during the Napoleonic Wars. His independent character brought the young officer into conflict with the authorities, and at the age of twenty-five he was discharged. In 1813 Hodgskin published a book in which he denounced the harsh customs in the British navy. The book attracted the attention of the liberals grouped around Bentham and James Mill and drew Hodgskin into their circle. In 1818 he read McCulloch's article about Ricardo's recently published book and later studied the book itself. Judging by his writings and correspondence by 1820 he was already well-acquainted with the main political and economic ideas of his day and had his own views on many questions. One of his letters contains the important statement: "I have therefore no hesitation in saying that I dislike Mr. Ricardo's opinions because they go to justify the present political situation of society, and to set bounds to our hopes of future improvement." [1]

Hodgskin retained this approach to Ricardo's doctrine: while recognising the correctness of many of its tenets, he criticised Ricardo for his inconsistency which meant that his ideas could be used against the working class. As for Mill and

[1] Elie Halévy, *Thomas Hodgskin*, London, 1956, p. 67.

McCulloch, Hodgskin's first important economic work, entitled *Labour Defended Against the Claims of Capital* with a subtitle that began *or the Unproductiveness of capital proved* ... , was aimed largely at them. This small pamphlet came out in London in 1825 and was linked directly with the struggle around the law to make trade unions legal. The author concealed himself behind a common pseudonym "By a labourer". By this time Hodgskin, after spending a few years in Edinburgh, had moved with his family to London. Earning a living by journalism, he took an active part in the growing working-class movement. His socialist convictions were already fully developed. Hodgskin as he has gone down in the history of political economy, socialism and the working-class movement is the Hodgskin of 1823-32.

Hodgskin regarded the education of the workers as a most important task and was one of the founders of the Mechanics' Institute for workers in London. It soon became obvious that the workers themselves would not be able to collect sufficient funds for the school and Hodgskin was removed from the management of his "brainchild" by bourgeois liberals and capitalist philanthropists who paid the piper and, naturally, wanted to call the tune. Nevertheless Hodgskin's main economic writings are connected with his activity in the workers' school. He wanted to use the school for the direct propagation of his ideas and gave the workers a series of lectures which were published in 1827 under the title of *Popular Political Economy*.

Hodgskin's books attracted considerable attention in England and were taken seriously, in particular, by the opponents of socialism, who mobilised the best liberal bourgeois publicists against him. In 1832 he published another book *The Natural and Artificial Rights of Property Contrasted*. Hodgskin regarded workers' ownership as natural, and all forms of ownership based on the exploitation of man by man as artificial, based on force and traditions supported by the state. In fact, he denied that capitalism was an economically logical stage in the development of society.

After 1832 Hodgskin disappeared from the arena of political and scientific activity and sank into the mire of obscure hack journalism. By this time he was the father of seven children. He was dogged by failure. His hopes of getting work in the University of London, recently founded under the aegis of the liberals, came to nought. There was no other way of ensuring a steady income. The journalist's pen was the only means of supporting his family. There were evidently other reasons as well. By this time Hodgskin had begun to disagree with the leaders of the working-class movement who were in favour of direct political action which he rejected on principle. Unlike the Owenites he saw no future in the cooperative movement. He also rejected Owen's community communism. It became clear that in fact he had no positive programme whatsoever. Hodgskin died at a ripe old age in 1869.

The socialists accepted the labour theory of value in the form which Ricardo had given it. They also developed its main tenet to its logical conclusion. The value of commodities is created by labour alone. Consequently, the capitalist's profit and the landlord's rent are a direct deduction from this value, which naturally belongs to the worker. Having drawn this conclusion, they saw the contradiction in classical political economy: how could it, based on such principles, regard the system of capitalism, the exploitation of labour by capital, as natural and permanent?

Marx puts the following tirade into the mouths of the proletarian opponents of bourgeois political economists: "Labour is the sole source of exchange value and the only active creator of use value. This is what you say. On the other hand, you say that *capital* is everything, and the worker is nothing or a mere production cost of capital. You have refuted yourselves. Capital is *nothing* but defrauding of the worker. *Labour is everything.*" [1]

---

[1] Karl Marx, *Theories of Surplus-Value*, Part III, p. 260. Note the word "active" in the definition of labour as the creator of use value (wealth). Means of production which are either an element of nature in its natural form (uncultivated land, mineral deposits, the energy of falling water, etc.), or elements of nature which have been subjected to the action of earlier labour (raw materials, fuel, implements of labour, etc.) take part in the production process as passive factors. In his *Critique of the Gotha Programme* Marx says: "Labour is *not the source* of all wealth. *Nature* is just as much the source of use values (and it is surely of such that material wealth consists!) as labour, which itself is only manifestation of a force of nature, human labour power" (Karl Marx and Frederick Engels, *Selected Works*, in three volumes, Vol. 3, p. 13). Labour and the means of production are to a certain extent interchangeable in production processes. The idea that capital (as usable means of production) is absolutely unproductive, is wrong and belonged to economists who gave Ricardo's doctrine "a left-wing slant", so to say. As Marx said: "In his investigations into the productivity of capital, Hodgskin is remiss in that he

This "speech" could be continued roughly as follows. You maintain, say the socialists to bourgeois political economists, that without capital labour cannot produce. But in your argument capital is a thing: machines, raw materials, stocks. In this case capital is dead without new, live labour. How can capital claim profit, a share of the value created by labour, if it is just a thing? That means it is making its claim not as a thing, but as a social force. What force? Private capitalist ownership. Only in the capacity of private ownership, which expresses a certain structure of society, does capital acquire power over the workers. The worker must eat and drink, and in order to do this he has to work. But he can work only with the permission of the capitalist, with the help of his capital.

And Hodgskin uses almost exactly the same words in the passage about which Marx said: "Here at last, the nature of capital is understood correctly." [1] Which means: here capital is seen as a social relation which boils down to the exploitation of hired labour.

The English socialist economists have rendered other important services too. They came closer than Ricardo to an understanding of surplus-value as the universal form of income on capital. They were the first to challenge the bourgeois apologetic theory of the wages fund. However, their criticism of bourgeois political economy contained some substantial weaknesses, which reflect the historical limitations and utopism of their views. Whereas Smith and Ricardo saw capitalism as the fulfilment of natural and permanent laws, the socialists saw it as the violation of those very same laws. They, like the bourgeois classics, based themselves on ideas of natural law inherited from the 18th century, and simply interpreted this law in a different way. This sort of socialism could only be utopian.

Like Owen, these economists thought that the exchange between labour and capital violates the law of labour value.

---

does not distinguish between how far it is a question of producing use-values or exchange-values" (Karl Marx, *Theories of Surplus- Value*, Part III, p. 267). These statements are important in connection with the above-mentioned idea that in studying production from the technical-economic point of view — as the process of the creation and transformation of use values — it is necessary to study the forms, conditions and proportions in which labour is combined with means of production.

[1] Karl Marx, *Theories of Surplus-Value*, Part III, p. 297.

They rightly rejected the economic justification of profit by the bourgeois science, but could not put a truly scientific analysis in its place. Since profit from capital did not fit into their system within the framework of "natural" economic laws, they were forced to turn for an explanation of profit to force, deception and other noneconomic factors. As a result the argument for the replacement of capitalism by the socialist order acquired an ethical nature in many respects: justice must prevail. The essence of justice was that the worker should receive the full product of his labour.

This "full (unreduced) product of labour" was destined to have a long life. This demand was utopian from the very beginning: even in a developed socialist society the workers cannot receive the "full product" for their personal consumption, for there would not be any funds left for accumulation, for public requirements, the upkeep of the administrative machine, the elderly, adolescents, etc. The point is that under capitalism there exists a special class of exploiters who appropriate the surplus product, not that the workers do not receive the full product of their labour. Nevertheless in the 1820s and 1830s this rallying cry was a progressive one, for it promoted the struggle of the working class, which had only just begun.

FROM A UTOPIA TO A SCIENCE

By the time Marx came to England (1849) three decades of British socialist literature existed in numerous volumes. He continued with the detailed study of it which he had begun in Brussels. The works of these English socialists, like the ideas of Saint-Simon, Fourier and Owen, form the heritage of earlier thinkers used by Marx in creating his revolutionary doctrine of society.

"Early socialism ... was *utopian* socialism," wrote V. I. Lenin in his article "Three Sources and Three Component Parts of Marxism". "It criticised capitalist society, it condemned and damned it, it dreamed of its destruction, it had visions of a better order and endeavoured to convince the rich of the immorality of exploitation.

"But utopian socialism could not indicate the real solution. It could not explain the real nature of wage slavery under capitalism, it could not reveal the laws of capitalist development, or show what *social force* is capable of becoming the creator of a new society." [1]

These great tasks were solved by Marxism. Marx and Engels transformed socialism from a utopia into a science. To do this it was necessary to create a fundamentally new theoretical system, a fundamentally new world outlook, on the basis of a critical revision of all the ideas developed in the social sciences by the most progressive thinkers of the preceding age, the progressive, revolutionary ideas of utopian socialism, German classical philosophy and English classical bourgeois political economy. The doctrine of Marxism developed on the basis of critical perception.

The cornerstone of Marx's economic teaching is the theory of surplus-value. It explains the very essence of the capitalist mode of production—the exploitation of hired labour by capital. As the classics of Marxism-Leninism showed, the early 19th-century thinkers, particularly Ricardo and his socialist commentators, came near to an understanding of surplus-value. However, although they described surplus-value more or less correctly as a deduction by the owners of capital and land from the value of a product created by labour, they went no further than this. The political economists of the classical school regarded this tenet as natural and permanent and tried merely to find out the quantitative proportions in which the distribution of value between labour and capital takes place. The socialists, however, found this distribution injust and elaborated utopian projects for removing the injustices.

What was for them the final point became merely the point of departure for Marx. Having described how surplus-value arises on the basis of the objective laws of the capitalist mode of production, he constructed an integrated and profound economic doctrine. Marx discovered the law of the development of capitalism and scientifically substantiated the main tendency of this development—the tendency towards the revolutionary replacement of the capitalist mode of production by socialism and communism. Marx showed that the working class is the social force which will accomplish this revolution and become the creator of the new society.

---

[1] V. I. Lenin, *Collected Works*, Vol. 19, Moscow, 1968, p. 27.

NAME INDEX

A

Adam, Robert (1728-1792) — 183
Aftalion, A. (1874-1956) — 296
Alexander I (1777-1825) — 370
Alexander of Macedon (356-323 b. c.) — 22-23
Alter, L. B. (1907-1968) — 150, 322
Anne (Queen Anne) (1665-1714) — 119
Aristotle (384-322 b. c.) — 21-30, 32, 40, 48, 90, 285
Aubrey, John (1626-1697) — 74

B

Bacon, Francis (1561-1626) — 45
Balzac, Honoré de (1799-1850) — 301
Barbon, Nickolas (1640-1698) — 126
Barone, Enrico (1859-1924) — 317
Bastiat, Claude-Frederic (1801-1850) — 162, 306, 311, 312
Bazard, Saint-Armand (1791-1832) — 348, 350
Beccaria, Cesare Bonesana (1738-1794) — 126
Bagehot, Walter (1826-1877) — 180, 200
Bell, John Fred (b. 1898) — 21, 25. 28, 205
Bentham, Jeremy (1748-1832) — 258, 259, 377

Béranger, P.-J. (1780-1857) — 355

Bismarck, Otto (1815-1898) — 340
Black, Joseph (1728-1799) — 183

Blanc, Louis (1811-1882) — 108, 113
Blanqui, Jérôme-Adolphe (1798-1854) — 311
Blanqui, Louis Auguste (1805-1881) — 311
Blyumin, I. G. (1898-1959) — 318
Böhm-Bawerk, Eugen (1851-1914) — 121
Boisguillebert, Pierre Le Peasant de (1646-1714) — 82-95, 108, 112, 126, 153, 343, 372
Bonaparte, Louis, Napoleon III (1808-1873) — 110, 297, 359
Bonaparte, Napoleon (1769-1821) — 16, 221, 283, 284, 301-04, 324
Boyle, Robert (1627-1691) — 54, 78
Bray, John Francis (1809-1897) — 377
Buccleuch (1746-1812) — 188, 191, 215
Buffon, J. L. (1707-1788) — 158
Byron, George Gordon (1788-1824) — 181, 222

C

Cabet, Etienne (1788-1856) — 150
Cannan, Edwin (1861-1935) — 188
Cantillon, Richard (1680-1734) — 15, 54, 126, 129

383